Table for Eight

Judith Huxley's

Table for Eight

Recipes and Menus for Entertaining with the Seasons

by Judith Huxley

INTRODUCTION BY WILLIAM RICE
WINES SELECTED BY ROBERT SHOFFNER

William Morrow and Company, Inc. • New York

Most of the content of this book first appeared in *The Washington Post*.

Grateful acknowledgment is made for permission to use the following recipes, which are reprinted or derived from the sources listed below.

"Kohlrabi in Cream with Dill Sauce," from *When French Women Cook* by Madeleine Kamman. Copyright © 1976 by Madeleine Kamman. Reprinted with permission of Atheneum Publishers.

"Tomato Aspic Squares": "Chili Tomato Cubes," from *Cool Entertaining* by Irma Rhode. Copyright © 1976 by Irma Rhode. Reprinted with permission of Atheneum Publishers.

"Bûche de Noël": "Coffee-Flavored Yule Log," from *Lenôtre's Desserts and Pastries* by Gaston Lenôtre. © 1977, Barron's Educational Series, Inc. solely with respect to the English language edition; © 1975, Flammarion solely with respect to the French language edition.

"Cold Roast Beef with Stroganoff Sauce": "Chilled Fillet of Beef with Sour Cream," from *The California Heritage Cookbook* by the Junior League of Pasadena. Copyright © 1976 by the Junior League of Pasadena. Reprinted by permission of Doubleday & Company, Inc.

"Consommé Belleview," from *Michael Field's Cooking School* by Michael Field. Copyright © 1965 by Michael Field. Reprinted by permission of Holt, Rinehart and Winston, Publishers.

"Onion Rolls," from *Bagels, Bagels, Bagels* by Sue Anderson Gross, published by Kitchen Harvest Press.

"Cold Braised Pork with Prunes": "Pork Braised with Bourbon," from *Simca's Cuisine* by Simone Beck in collaboration with Patricia Simon. Copyright © 1972 by Simone Beck and Patricia Simon. Reprinted by permission of Alfred A. Knopf, Inc.

"Palm Beach Brownies," from *Maida Heatter's Book of Great Chocolate Desserts* by Maida Heatter. Copyright © 1980 by Maida Heatter. Reprinted by permission of Alfred A. Knopf, Inc.

"Gâteau Milanese," from *The Dione Lucas Book of French Cooking* by Dione Lucas and Marion Gorman. Copyright 1947 by Dione Lucas; copyright © 1973 by Mark Lucas and Marion F. Gorman. Reprinted by permission of Little, Brown and Company.

"Italian Prune Plum Torte on a Short Dough *(Mürbeteig)*": "Plum Torte," reprinted with permission of Macmillan Publishing Company from *The Viennese Pastry Cookbook* by Lilly Joss Reich. Copyright © 1970 by Lilly Joss Reich.

"Escoffier's Red Pepper Conserve for Cold Meats": "Pimentos for Serving with Cold Meat," from *Le Guide Culinaire* by Auguste Escoffier. Copyright Flammarion by Flammarion. Published by Mayflower Books.

"Onion-Grenadine Jam" and "Puréed Celery Root," from *Michel Guérard's Cuisine Gourmande* by Michel Guérard. English translation copyright © 1979 by William Morrow and Company, Inc. By permission of William Morrow and Company, Inc.

Library of Congress Catalog Card Number: 83-63023

ISBN: 0-688-02639-7

Printed in the United States of America

First Edition

1 2 3 4 5 6 7 8 9 10

BOOK DESIGN BY LINEY LI

To Matthew
for whom I cook with love

•

ACKNOWLEDGMENTS

All my adult life I have been a writer and a cook. The two came together in *The Washington Post*, in which most of the contents of this book first appeared. Of the many members of the editorial and administrative staff to whom I am vastly indebted, I single out a few.

William McPherson, when he was editor of "Book World," bears responsibility for my having become a *Post* writer by making me his cookbook reviewer. William Rice, now editor in chief of *Food & Wine* magazine, when he was executive food editor of the *Post*, made me a full-fledged food writer and a regular contributor to the food section. He honors me by writing the introduction to this book. Phyllis Richman, who succeeded Bill Rice as the *Post*'s executive food editor, dreamed up the concept of "Table for Eight," asked me to write it and has been consistently generous with encouragement and support. I could always count on the good sense and professionalism of the food section staff, particularly Carole Sugarman and Shelley Davis, as well as Marian Burros when she worked with Bill Rice at the *Post*.

My debt to Robert Shoffner, wine and food editor of *The Washingtonian* magazine, is great. His thoughtful contribution of the wine suggestions which embellish these menus reflects his vast knowledge of food and what to drink with it.

I am grateful to Mary Henderson, a writer and cook of talent and taste, as is evident to those who know her splendid *Mary Henderson's Paris Embassy Cookbook*. While she was establishing the British Embassy as the best table in Washington during her husband's tenure as ambassador, she found more time than anyone could have deserved to become a friend and champion.

I wish also to thank friends and family for their generosity with ideas and expertise in cooking and otherwise, especially Joseph Alsop, Rita Belot, Veronica Björling, Edith Bralove, David Ginsburg, Leslie Hagan, Carole Huxley, Tessa Huxley, Elaine Kurtz, Dorothy Lagemann, Sheela

ACKNOWLEDGMENTS

Lampietti, Jeanne Neveux, Suzanne Nicolas, Françoise Norrish, Sylvia Nicolas O'Neill, Heather Perram, Nancy Purves Pollard, Carroll Purves, Andrew Reicher, Miriam Mednick Rothman, Corinne Wallet and June and Kenneth Wilson.

Finally, I salute Tessa, Trevenen and Matthew Huxley, whose selective taste buds were the making of this cook.

JUDITH HUXLEY
August 11, 1983

Contents

INTRODUCTION

"Her kitchen is dominated by a Vulcan stove with an elevated broiler and a hanging display of copperware. Elsewhere are various showpieces of modern technology, such as a food processor, pots and pans, spices, a large clock and an equally large timer originally intended for use in a photography studio darkroom.

"It's very impressive, but Judy Huxley, a woman who smokes, drinks, swears for emphasis and keeps an outspoken vigilance against pretense, is careful to keep the setting in perspective.

"'Let's say it's an extravagance, an indulgence,' she says. 'It's nice to have, it's beautiful, but it will not make me a better or worse cook. We won't eat much differently. I don't think the food will be better. What it does is provide the capacity to do more. There is space to put things down. The pasta machine is right here; it's a lot easier to pull it out. The KitchenAid is always on the counter. There are molds on the shelf, not buried in cupboards. You see them and immediately think of doing things with them.'

"The Huxleys entertain as they planned their dream kitchen, together. Matthew (yes, he is one of the celebrated Huxley family — the son of Aldous) is an expert at martinis and wine, at carving and at clearing tables. He makes breakfast daily and is, according to his wife, 'my biggest critic. He cares, he knows the difference. If Matthew thinks it's good food, I've succeeded. He's never lied to me. Sometimes I wish he would. I don't do anything, we do it. The style here is as much Matthew's as mine.'

"As a cook, Judy Huxley has two simple maxims: 'I use anything that works,' she says, 'and I'm not afraid to make mistakes.

"'If I want to eat a particular thing, I'll make it. I'm not competing. I hate all that tension. You're not what you cook. You're not even what you eat. You are what you are. I've tried the most outrageous things on guests. If the group is wonderful together, the food is an extra. What it is really doesn't matter.'"

•

Every editor dreams of discovering a writer or columnist who becomes a magnet for readers and enhances the reputation of his publication. That moment came for me when I "found" Judith Huxley several years ago and brought her to the attention of readers of *The Washington Post* by writing the article that is quoted above. I was delighted at the response to the article, which had been inspired by the completion of a "dream kitchen" at a time when a good many Americans were updating and expanding their home kitchens. I knew the quality of her writing through incisive cookbook reviews she had done for the newspaper's book review section. All that remained was to convince her to contribute articles. She did and they soon became regular columns on entertaining with the menus and recipes that form the basis for this book.

I didn't "find" Judith Huxley, of course. She and Matthew conduct what, in another time, would have been called a salon. Washington's brightest lights — in literature, the arts, diplomacy, medicine, even the stray politician — were, and are, regulars at the dinner table over which the Huxleys preside with intelligence, gusto and rare good humor. To use another word currently out of fashion, they are a truly civilized couple. Conversation counts greatly with them. So does creativity. So does loyalty. They love companionship and entertain constantly. Nevertheless, they rarely employ even a bartender, and never a cook.

I tell you this because nothing should send you more eagerly toward the remarkable array of recipes that lies ahead than the knowledge that, unlike too many other cookery writers, Judith Huxley does not create in solitude or cook in a laboratory. The food she makes is real, intended to be eaten by real people in an environment where company and conversation have equal rank.

As cook, Judy is both thrifty and quality conscious. She is steeped in culinary integrity, but refuses to equate her standards with rigidity. Economy of effort, as well as of cost, attracts her greatly, and she rejects convenience only when the results fail to live up to what she (or Matthew) considers valid taste or texture. For this volume, she has enlisted Robert Shoffner, food and wine editor of *The Washingtonian* magazine, to provide wine recommendations for her menus. This is entirely appropriate. Robert has shared many memorable meals with the Huxleys, and it has always been evident that his keen palate is as intrigued and stimulated by the flavors and tastes of food as by wine.

As individuals, and as a couple, Judy and Matthew are about as brave, and funny, and fine as individuals and couples come. There is nowhere I more keenly anticipate being a guest than at their table. Now, thanks to this book, we can all come into the kitchen and share Judith Huxley's creative but practical menus and remarkable food.

As for the table, like the Huxleys, we'll have to set it ourselves.

WILLIAM RICE
June 22, 1983

FOREWORD

This book consists of menus for entertaining at home, tips to defuse a cook's anxieties and clear, simple recipes using seasonal foods. It represents my approach to planning meals, shopping for ingredients, cooking and eating as relaxed and enjoyable pursuits. It will, I hope, help people who work or those whose time is filled with such other honorable pursuits as raising a family or training for the Olympics to entertain with style.

Menus for dinners, lunches, brunches, suppers and cocktail parties are organized by seasons starting with Spring, the true beginning of the year, and, within seasons, by months. In this way, ingredients are used as they reach the height of their availability and, not so incidentally, when they are freshest, most flavorful and least expensive.

The menus are made up of delicious, attractive but uncomplicated dishes, which I have developed so that they can be prepared mostly or entirely in advance. In the recipes you will find this symbol, ❀, at least once, or twice or even three times. It represents the stages in the preparation that can be completed (sometimes *must* be completed) in advance, and the recipes indicate how far in advance when that is important. The ❀ at the end of a recipe means that it may be prepared entirely in advance. At the beginning of each month is a page called "Provisioning the Pantry" containing recipes for relishes, condiments, flavorings and other foods that can be made at your leisure and are most satisfactory to have on hand.

None of the menus will deprive the cook of enjoying the guests for more than a few minutes before sitting down or while the table is cleared between courses. Although things don't always work out quite so neatly, on the day of a party, I believe the cook shouldn't have to do much more than set the table, arrange some flowers, finish a few fast, simpleminded preparations in the kitchen and put pots in the oven or on the stove.

Most of the menus call for three courses because, in our house, we place a bowl of salted almonds on the cocktail table but the real eating only starts when we sit down. In my experience, bits and pieces with drinks fill the gap should a first course be dropped, but finger-food hors d'oeuvre are less satisfying and more time-consuming to prepare than a first course served at table.

While the menus are for eight people or, in the case of buffet dinners and cocktail parties, for numbers in multiples of eight, almost all the recipes can be increased by one half for twelve, doubled for sixteen or halved for four. Eight is such a comfortable number for dinner—small enough for intimacy and large enough for variety.

Some of the menus contain show-off dishes, but not always and certainly not more than one per menu. Pretentious cooking forces the conversation to food while distracting from real talk, the reason, after all, for the party in the first place. There are casual meals for close friends and meals to impress, but none will make guests feel uncomfortable about the amount of effort that went into their care and feeding. Our own experiences with these meals have been a revelation of how competent planning and execution can make a party warm and intimate. And that is what entertaining is all about.

J.H.

SOME THOUGHTS ON CHOOSING WINE FOR THE MENU

One of the few negative results of the American gastronomic revolution is that it has generally divided its partisans — both professional and amateur — into two, often mutually exclusive, factions: the food people and the wine people. Those whose main interest is cooking know little, if anything, about wines, and those who proclaim a passion for wine don't really know very much about food. And whether it is a wine lover who serves indifferent food with a favorite vintage or an accomplished cook who accompanies a five-course dinner with red and white jug wines, both unwittingly deprive themselves and their guests of enjoying that consonance between food and wine which is the highest pleasure of dining. The serious student of wine, familiar with the general characteristics of regions and individual vineyards, is less likely to take a misstep than the good cook, whose knowledge of wine often begins and ends with the dictum "Red wine with red meat and white wine with the rest."

For the wine fraternity, the suggested wines appended to the menus in this book are superfluous. For every wine, many alternatives will readily come to mind. A cheese course can be added to enjoy another bottle of red, and many desserts will be complemented by serving a sweet white wine from France, Germany, or California. For the wine connoisseur, however, there is everything to admire about Judith Huxley's menus: They comprise a logical progression of dishes whose conscious lack of pretentiousness and avoidance of violent flavors are complementary to wines great and small. These are meals that have an affinity with the finest bottles in a collector's cellar as much as they do for the wines that have been suggested. Those who may find the choice of wines to be overly facile should understand that, ultimately, it is Judith Huxley's philosophy of entertaining at table that guided those choices: that just as pretentious menus force attention onto the food and away from the guests' enjoyment of each other, prestigious wines of great complexity demand a mixture of introspective contemplation, sensory evaluation, and discussion, which imposes an unnecessary burden of seriousness on guests who do not count the synergy between wine and food as one of life's major considerations.

For the dedicated cook who has forsaken the pursuit of knowledge of wine for the pursuit of perfect puff pastry and is intimidated at the prospect of having to learn what lies beyond matching the color of the meat to the color of the wine, there is no sure rule that can be imparted to achieve the perfect partnership of food and wine. As a start, however, it is important to respect the inherent qualities of a wine — its simplicity or complexity, its lightness or strength of scent, flavor, and body — because the food won't suffer as much as the wine from an ill-begotten marriage. In other words, while a full-flavored California Chardonnay or a complex Puligny-Montrachet can be just as successfully served with either a simply grilled sea bass or with a seafood preparation with a rich cream sauce, a lighter, less expensive California Chardonnay or a simple Macon-Villages is suited only to the grilled fish, because the rich sauce will make it seem thin and acid by contrast.

But wine and food affinities are better experienced than described. The beginner should find inexpensive wines that he really enjoys, analyze their suitablility when drunk with everyday foods, and experiment with new wines from time to time. The wines suggested with particular courses in each of Judith Huxley's menus are good examples of complementary partnership between wine and food, but it is pleasurably earned experience, rather than arbitrary rules, that best teaches one which wines and foods deserve to be served together. The wines are selected for their suitability to the individual dishes, their wide distribution, and their affordability. But just as it is not advisable to serve an untried dish for the first time to company, one is ill-advised to pour an unfamiliar wine without having previously tasted it. Both guests and hosts may enjoy a familiar Beaujolais-Villages from the previous year's vintage much more than an untried Châteauneuf-du-Pape of a dubious vintage, purchased because its higher price implied a better wine and served because this book suggested Châteauneuf-du-Pape for a particular dish.

Finally, as much as the menus inspire considered selection from among the various wines that can provide a harmonious accompaniment, for many these meals will be just as enjoyable if one serves honest jug wines decanted into carafes. During a number of the many evenings that went into testing these menus, Judith Huxley did just that and any guest who, at the time, may have wished for a less casual choice of wine, remembered only that he had been fed and entertained equally well at the Huxleys' table.

ROBERT SHOFFNER

Spring

March

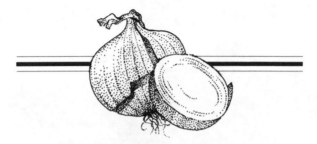

Michel Guérard's Onion-Grenadine Jam

MAKES 3 CUPS

•

¼	pound (1 stick) butter
1½	pounds onions, thinly sliced
1	teaspoon salt
1½	teaspoons pepper
⅓	cup sugar
6	tablespoons sherry vinegar
2	tablespoons grenadine syrup
1	cup red wine

Heat the butter until it is light brown in a stainless-steel, enamel-on-iron or other nonreactive frying pan. Add the sliced onions, salt, pepper and sugar. Stir well, cover, and simmer on low heat, stirring occasionally, for 30 minutes. Add the sherry vinegar, grenadine and wine. Uncover the pan and cook for 40 minutes more over low heat. Cool, decant into half-pint jars, and refrigerate. This jam will keep for months under refrigeration.

Serve with pâtés and other cold meats.

NOTE: This version of Guérard's jam has half the sugar of the original.

Endives with Goat Cheese and Savory

Rock Cornish Hens Cooked in the Manner of Quail

Individual Potato Puddings

Sautéed Cabbage and Bean Sprouts

Hot Vanilla Soufflés

•

FIRST COURSE:
Robert Mondavi Fumé Blanc
or Pouilly-Fumé La Doucette
MAIN COURSE:
Clos du Val Zinfandel
or Volnay "Santenots"

*T*his meal was inspired by remembrances of things past, specifically the quail my husband's French aunt Jeanne once prepared for us in Paris. It occurred to me that Rock Cornish hens, which are more available and less expensive than quail, could be cooked according to her recipe. The result was so felicitous that for once my husband didn't react to a chicken dish with a wrinkled nose.

The meal starts with a bed of tender Belgian endive slices topped with fresh, mild goat cheese impregnated with a fruity olive oil and gently touched with savory. Olive Oil Flavored with Provençal Herbs (see July, Provisioning the Pantry) would make a happy substitute. This is served with warm French bread. Next come the little birds, which are first browned, then cooked with two kinds of Cognac-saturated raisins plus juniper berries and finally sauced with their delicious braising liquids enriched with some cream. The masquerading hens are served, appropriately, with quail accompaniments: individual potato puddings, baked to a golden brown, and shredded cabbage quickly sautéed with bean sprouts. The meal ends with the glitziest of desserts, a pair of hot vanilla soufflés.

The first course offers immeasurable returns for the minimal effort involved in finding the ingredients. Endives, which are generally available in supermarkets, should be tightly headed, pale yellow or white. Those with green tips will be bitter and are not acceptable. Of the fresh goat cheeses, Montrachet Buche is my preference for this recipe because its small cylindrical form can be cut into neat slices that are most attractive on the endive leaves. However, Boucheron or any other goat cheese can be used as long as it is fresh. A fresh goat cheese has the slightest bite but no hint of rancidity. It is stark white, creamy in texture and light in density, all the better to absorb the oil in which it is soaked. Some of the Montrachets come with a gray-black sprinkling of ashes on the outside that some claim keeps the cheese fresh. I think of the ash coating as a frame on a picture, particularly when the cheese is cut into slices. The best extra-virgin fruity olive oil is not too good for this dish.

Very small (less than one pound) Rock Cornish hens make lovely individual servings and are my choice, but I also have used larger hens split in two with equally delicious, if less elegant, results. The method and cooking times are the same, whichever is used. Plain raisins can be substituted if seedless muscats cannot be found, but the inclusion of yellow or golden raisins, with their distinctive flavor and color, is essential. Juniper berries can be found in many supermarkets as well as in specialty food stores. The necks, wing tips, backbones and gizzards should be saved for stock and can be frozen. This dish deserves the best homemade stock.

The grating disk of the food processor is marvelous for grating potatoes, especially for those of us with a predisposition to bloodying knuckles on the hand grater. Rendered chicken, duck or goose fat is perfect in these little puddings, but butter is also good. The unbaked potato mixture can be refrigerated for an hour or so in the prepared muffin tins. Covering the tins tightly with plastic wrap will help keep the potatoes from darkening. When the hens and puddings are done, raise the oven heat to 400 degrees for the soufflés.

The cabbage can be shredded early in the day. The cabbage and sprouts are best when sautéed just before they are eaten, but for the convenience of preparing the dish earlier in the day and then reheating it quickly, the price is very small in terms of taste or texture.

I prefer the time-tested, foolproof, worry-free method when it comes to hot soufflés. The classic recipe I use is prepared with a safe base consisting of flour, milk, egg yolks, butter and flavoring. The base can be made in the morning and the molds can be buttered and sugared well in advance. Despite rumors to the contrary, the egg whites can be beaten and the entire soufflé assembled a good hour before it goes into the oven if the soufflé is kept in a cool part of the kitchen and is completely covered with a large mixing bowl or pot. The two critical steps are beating the egg whites and folding them into the base. The whites must be beaten just until they hold stiff peaks when the beaters are removed; the test should be applied early and often to avoid overbeating. After a large dollop of the beaten whites is stirred into the base to lighten it, the remaining whites are quickly folded, never stirred, in. A rubber spatula is held vertically to the bowl and cut through the whites until it reaches the bottom, where it is angled slightly, brought to the edge of the bowl nearest you and lifted up and out of the mixture. Each time the motion is completed, the bowl is rotated slightly. Not every last particle of foam need be incorporated. This is a case where it is better to be quick and not deflate the whites than it is to be thorough.

There is also the matter of timing. Six-cup dessert soufflés require a total of 35 minutes in the oven, so to be safe I place them in the oven 5 minutes into the main course. Five minutes later the oven is turned down and the soufflés finish cooking. This timing may mean that guests will have to wait for the soufflés, which is as it should be, since soufflés wait for nothing.

In my experience, two 1½-quart soufflés are not too much for eight people. A charlotte mold works as well as the traditional soufflé dish, so if you have one of each with a 6-cup capacity, as I do, there is no need to buy additional equipment.

I start a soufflé at each end of the table. The top crust is broken with a serving spoon and then two serving spoons are used to pull apart the portions.

Endives with Goat Cheese
and Savory

•

½   *pound fresh mild goat cheese,*
       preferably in cylinder form
½   *cup olive oil*
1   *teaspoon dried savory*
1   *pound Belgian endive*
½   *teaspoon red wine vinegar*

Up to a day before it is to be served, cut the cheese into 8 slices and place in a fairly deep, flat-bottomed dish. Pour the oil over the cheese and sprinkle with savory. If the kitchen is warm, refrigerate the cheese; otherwise leave it out. Whenever you think of it, baste the cheese with the oil and savory.

A few hours before serving, remove the leaves from the heads of endive and discard the cores. Pile several leaves on top of one another and cut them into ½-inch slices. Repeat until all the endives are cut.❁ Divide them among 8 salad plates, place a piece of cheese on each center, spoon the oil and savory over the cheese, and drizzle a few drops of vinegar on each slice.

Rock Cornish Hens Cooked in
the Manner of Quail

•

⅓   *cup seedless muscat raisins*
⅓   *cup seedless golden raisins*
½   *cup Cognac*
8   *Rock Cornish hens, each weighing less*
       than 1 pound, or 4 hens, each
       weighing about 1¾ pounds
3   *tablespoons butter*

> 1   tablespoon oil
> 16   juniper berries
> 1½   cups homemade brown chicken stock
>   (see Index) or beef stock or canned
>   beef bouillon
>   Salt and pepper
> ½   cup heavy cream

Place the raisins in a bowl, pour the Cognac over them, cover with plastic wrap, and set aside for 3 or 4 hours.

Leave small hens whole, reserving wing tips, gizzards, hearts and livers for stock and other purposes. Split large birds in two by cutting them up the backs and removing their tails and backbones, which can also be reserved. Clean the cavities of loose organs and pat the birds dry.

Melt butter and oil in a heavy casserole, preferably enamel on cast iron and large enough to hold the birds in one layer. It may be necessary to use two pots, with all ingredients divided between them. Brown the birds on all sides, one or two at a time, and remove as they are done. Return them to the casserole and add the raisins with their Cognac, juniper berries, stock and salt and pepper to taste. ❁   The dish can be prepared to this point an hour or two in advance.

To complete the cooking, bring the contents of the casserole to a simmer, cover, and place in a preheated 350-degree oven for 40 minutes. Remove the cooked birds to a warm serving platter, add the cream to the juices in the casserole, and cook over high heat, stirring, for a few minutes. Spoon the sauce, the raisins and the juniper berries over the birds.

Individual Potato Puddings

•

Softened butter or rendered chicken,
    duck or goose fat to grease the
    muffin tins

4   eggs
2¼ pounds russet potatoes
½ cup flour
1   teaspoon baking powder
1   teaspoon salt
    Pepper to taste
4   tablespoons melted butter or rendered
    chicken, duck or goose fat

Beat the eggs thoroughly and set aside. Grate the potatoes in a food processor fitted with a grating disk. Strain out the excess liquid. Stir the
potatoes into the beaten eggs along with the remaining ingredients. Spoon
into greased muffin tins, about two-thirds full, ❀ and bake in a preheated
350-degree oven for 45 to 50 minutes, or until the puddings are golden
brown. There will be from 14 to 16 puddings.

Sautéed Cabbage
and Bean Sprouts

•

2½ pounds green cabbage
¼ pound fresh bean sprouts
2   tablespoons peanut oil
1   medium onion, minced
2   cloves garlic, minced
    Salt and pepper

Quarter the cabbage, discard the core, and shred finely. Wash the bean sprouts and discard the little roots if you wish. Heat the oil in a large sauté pan, add the onions and garlic, and cook over low heat until soft but not brown. Add the cabbage and cook, stirring, for about 4 minutes until the cabbage is wilted but still crisp. Add the bean sprouts and salt and pepper to taste. Cook, stirring, for another 2 minutes. ❁ This dish can be prepared in advance and reheated quickly over high heat, stirring constantly.

Hot Vanilla Soufflés

•

*Softened butter to grease two 6-cup
soufflé dishes or charlotte molds and
sugar to line them*

FOR THE BASE	*1½*	*cups milk*
	6	*tablespoons flour*
	9	*tablespoons sugar*
	8	*egg yolks*
	4	*tablespoons butter, softened*
	4½	*tablespoons vanilla extract*
TO COMPLETE	*10*	*egg whites*
THE SOUFFLÉ		*Pinch of salt*
	¼	*teaspoon cream of tartar*
	2	*tablespoons sugar*
FOR THE SAUCE	*1½*	*cups heavy cream*
	2	*tablespoons sugar*
	1½	*teaspoons Vanilla Cognac (see April, Provisioning the Pantry) or 1¼ teaspoons Cognac plus ⅛ teaspoon vanilla extract*

Prepare the soufflé dishes or charlotte molds by buttering them generously and swirling sugar around the bottoms and sides to coat the butter. Set aside. The molds can be prepared several hours or even a day ahead and refrigerated.

To make the base, gradually whisk the milk into the flour to make a smooth paste. Stir in the sugar and cook over moderate heat, whisking constantly, until the mixture comes to a boil and is very thick. Remove from heat and whisk in the egg yolks one at a time. Beat in all but 1 tablespoon of the softened butter and the vanilla. Rub the remaining tablespoon of butter over the top of the mixture to coat it and prevent a film from forming. Cover tightly with plastic wrap and set aside.✿   The base can be made several hours or even a day ahead and refrigerated.

•

To complete the soufflé, beat the egg whites with the salt and cream of tartar in a large bowl until soft peaks are formed when the beaters are removed. Add the 2 tablespoons of sugar and beat only until the whites make stiff peaks. Do not overbeat. Stir the base to incorporate the butter coating and add to it about 1 cup of the beaten whites to lighten the base. Turn the base into a large bowl and then turn the whites onto the base. Carefully and quickly fold the two together. Divide the mixture between the prepared pans and rap each pan on the counter to settle the mixture and get rid of any air pockets.✿   The unbaked soufflés can be held for an hour before baking if they are placed in a cool place and covered with large, clean, empty bowls.

Just before baking, use your finger or the handle end of a dinner knife to make a ½-inch-deep circular indentation in the soufflé mixture 1 inch from the edges of the molds. This will make the soufflé rise higher and more evenly.

Place the soufflés in a preheated 400-degree oven for 5 minutes. Then turn the oven down to 375 degrees and bake an additional 30 minutes. Serve immediately with the whipped cream sauce.

•

Prepare the whipped cream sauce a couple of hours in advance. Whip the cream until it holds some shape, add the sugar and Vanilla Cognac or Cognac and vanilla and whip a bit more. The cream should be thickened but not stiff.✿   Store, covered, in the refrigerator.

*Chicken Soup with Quenelles Under
a Puff-Pastry Dome*

Roast Filet of Beef with Béarnaise Sauce

Watercress

Duchesse Potatoes

Prunes in Red Wine with Cream

•

APÉRITIF:
*Schramsberg Blanc de Blancs (California)
or Moët & Chandon Brut Imperial N.V.*
FIRST COURSE:
Amontillado
MAIN COURSE:
*Robert Mondavi Cabernet Sauvignon
or Château Figeac (St. Emilion)*

This is a noble meal of consistent deliciousness and descending complexity. It begins with luxurious abandon, moves on to understated exorbitance and ends with modest understatement. The execution is within the reach of all while the rewards are imposing.

Diners sit down to a regal presentation of perfect domes of browned puff pastry clinging to ovenproof soup bowls. When the crusty spheres are pierced, rich aromas are released at the same time that tiny, feathery veal *quenelles* are revealed floating in a well-endowed chicken broth.

Such a hard act deserves to be followed by a filet of beef. Here it is roasted quickly to a luscious rareness while the first course is being consumed. With the beef are mounds of gold-flecked duchesse potatoes, fresh watercress and a béarnaise sauce heady with tarragon.

The ending is an unobtrusive sigh, a dessert of dried prunes plumped in tea, then cooked in an infusion of red wine and sugar spiked with cinammon stick and orange rind. The prunes are served icy cold with cream.

The soup is a homespun variation of the truffle- and fresh *foie gras*-stuffed extravaganza produced by Paul Bocuse for the celebratory Elysée Palace luncheon in 1975 when the great chef was made a member of the Legion of Honor. The hot contents of the bowl force the puff pastry to balloon up as it bakes. I prepared this dish three times in one week. The first time confirmed that my low-cost version was more than worth eating. The soup was made the second time because I couldn't believe it was so easy to do. We had it the third time because it really was. Do not be daunted by the length of the recipe. Several steps are involved, but all the components can be prepared in advance and with great facility, what with the availability of good frozen puff pastry and the processor for making the *quenelles*. I am quite happy with the supermarket puff pastry, but if you have a source for pastry made with all butter, so much the better.

I use onion soup bowls brought out of retirement from the depths of a cupboard, but any ovenproof earthenware or ceramic bowls 4 to 5 inches in diameter and with a 1½-cup capacity are fine. Cooks with a yen for the genuine article can even find charming copies of Bocuse's white tureen-shaped bowl at Williams-Sonoma (see Mail-Order Sources).

There is no shortcut to making the stock. It must have a rich, concentrated, full-bodied flavor, meaning it does not come from a can. I use inexpensive chicken backs and necks that yield an added bonus of fat. The fat can be frozen and rendered whenever it suits. The stock should be made at least two days before the party (or weeks earlier and frozen). The bulk of the time is spent in cleaning the chicken parts of organs and thoroughly skimming the stock before the vegetables and herbs are added. Any leftover stock can be frozen. The vegetable garnish for the soup can be made anywhere from hours to a day in advance.

The *panade*, in reality a choux paste that binds the *quenelles*, is made the day before so it can be thoroughly chilled before it is added to the veal. Only half the *panade* is used for the recipe, but the other half can be frozen.

I have had perfect results using veal stew meat. However, every bit of fat, membrane and gristle must be trimmed away before the meat is reduced to a paste. The actual *quenelle* mixture is made the morning of the party and chilled for a few hours, since the balls are formed more easily when the paste is cold. The formed *quenelles* are held in the refrigerator until the dish is assembled. The *quenelles* are placed raw in the soup. By the time the pastry lids are baked, the little dumplings are poached to perfection.

The puff pastry is also rolled out and cut into rounds several hours in advance, stacked with pieces of waxed paper between them and refrigerated. The beaten egg yolk that is painted onto the edges of the rounds seals the pastry to the bowls. Placing the bowls on jelly-roll pans makes it easy to move the soup into and out of the oven.

Considering the cost, it is easy to be depressed by the amount that must be trimmed off a filet to prepare it for roasting. The good news is that everything can be used. The fat can be rendered and added to the oil for making French fried potatoes. The gristle and membranes go into the stockpot, as can the sinewy cord called the "chain," which becomes detached from the filet when the fat is removed. The chain can also be ground. The tail can either be tucked under itself and tied in order to make the roast of equal thickness or removed, as I prefer, and used to make a nice Stroganoff for two or three people. The oven must be raised to 500 degrees (or 475 degrees if yours smokes at 500 degrees) the minute the soup is removed. The filet, which is browned in advance, is placed in it and cooks, along with the duchesse potatoes, while the soup is being eaten. There may be a ten-minute hiatus between the time the first course is cleared and the roast appears, but this is not a disadvantage, since guests need the opportunity to recover from the glories of the soup.

The béarnaise sauce can be made a day in advance without loss of quality. Simply refrigerate the cooked sauce in a tightly covered bowl and bring to room temperature an hour or so before serving. Whisk the sauce vigorously before pouring it into a sauceboat.

The duchesse potatoes are prepared several hours in advance. The eggs and flavorings are beaten into the whipped potatoes and then the warm (not hot, otherwise you'll burn your hands) mixture is inserted into a pastry bag with a large star tube and piped into pretty mounds. These are covered loosely with plastic wrap and refrigerated until half an hour before baking. The potatoes go into the oven ten minutes after the filet and continue to cook while the filet rests before it is carved.

When buying watercress, examine the bunches upside down. Those with the thinnest stems will have the best flavor.

The prunes can be precooked in any kind of tea except for lapsang soochong or other smoky tea. The cinammon stick is removed immediately after the final cooking so as not to overpower the syrup.

Chicken Soup with Quenelles
Under a Puff-Pastry Dome
•

FOR THE **CHICKEN STOCK** (MAKES ABOUT 12 CUPS)	10	*pounds chicken backs and necks, fat removed and reserved for another purpose, loose organs discarded*
	6	*large carrots, peeled and cut into chunks*
	3	*large onions, peeled*
	3	*stalks celery, cleaned and cut into chunks*
	6	*sprigs parsley*
	1	*tablespoon salt*
		Pepper to taste
	1	*teaspoon thyme leaves*
	1½	*bay leaves*
FOR THE *PANADE* *FOR QUENELLES* (MAKES 1 CUP)	½	*cup water*
	3	*tablespoons butter*
	¼	*teaspoon salt*
	1	*cup sifted flour*
	1	*egg*
		About 1 teaspoon softened butter
FOR THE ***QUENELLES*** (MAKES ABOUT 56 HALF-INCH *QUENELLES*)	½	*pound veal*
	½	*teaspoon salt*
		Freshly ground white pepper
	¼	*teaspoon nutmeg*
	2½	*tablespoons butter, softened*
	1	*egg white*
	½	*cup chilled* panade *(above)*
	3	*tablespoons very cold heavy cream*
		Flour for shaking the quenelles

FOR THE	1	*medium carrot, peeled and trimmed*
VEGETABLE	2	*inner stalks celery, cleaned*
GARNISH	1	*small onion, peeled*
	1/4	*pound mushrooms, cleaned*
	2	*tablespoons butter*

FOR THE PUFF-PASTRY LIDS	*17¼-ounce package frozen puff-pastry dough, defrosted*
	Flour for the pastry board

TO ASSEMBLE	8	*onion-soup or other ovenproof bowls*
THE DISH	10	*cups chicken stock*
		Salt and freshly ground white pepper to taste
		The cooked vegetable garnish
	8	*teaspoons minced parsley*
		The uncooked quenelles
	8	*rounds of puff pastry, cut 1½ inches greater in diameter than the tops of the soup bowls*
	1	*egg yolk, beaten*

Make the stock 2 days or more in advance. Place the chicken parts in a large stockpot, cover with cold water, and bring to the boil. Skim off the scum as it rises. When the stock is clear, add the vegetables and skim until clear. Then add the remaining ingredients and enough more cold water to cover. Cook at the lowest simmer, with the cover slightly askew, for 5 hours. Ladle the stock through a strainer into bowls, cool, and refrigerate for several hours or overnight. Discard the congealed fat. If the stock has jelled, heat until it becomes liquid. Ladle the stock through a strainer lined with wrung-out cheesecloth and then cook the stock, uncovered, to reduce it until 12 cups remain. Cool ✿ and refrigerate (or freeze) until needed.

•

Make the *panade* for the *quenelles* a day before it is to be used. Combine the water, butter and salt in a small saucepan and bring to the boil. Remove the pan from heat and add the flour all at once. Beat the mixture with a wooden spoon until it comes away from the sides and forms a ball, about 1 minute. Return to heat, mash the mixture down onto the bottom of the pan, and then with the wooden spoon bring it up and fold it over, much as if you were kneading bread. This dries out the paste. Continue for about 3 minutes, or until a sandy-looking film of paste forms on the bottom of the pan. Remove from heat and let the paste stand for about 15 minutes, beating it occasionally as it cools. Then beat in the egg by hand or, if you wish, in the processor. (Turn the paste into the work bowl and, with the motor running, add the egg and process for about 15 seconds.) There will be 1 cup of *panade*. Measure off one half and freeze for later use or discard. Spread the remaining half onto a saucer smeared with some of the softened butter, spread the top with remaining butter, cover with plastic wrap, and refrigerate until very cold. ✿

•

The mixture for the *quenelles* can be made the morning of the dinner. Refrigerate the processor work bowl, lid and blade before using. Trim the meat of all fat and fibers. Process the veal, with the salt, pepper and nutmeg, until the mixture is reduced to a paste. With the motor running, add the following, processing for 15 seconds after each addition: first the softened butter, then the egg white, then the chilled *panade* and finally the cream. Turn the mixture into a bowl, cover, ✿ and refrigerate for 2 hours or longer.

The *quenelles* can be shaped several hours before cooking. Place a 12-inch piece of waxed paper on a counter and flour it lightly. Using a demitasse spoon, scoop up enough of the mixture to make a ball ½ inch in diameter. With a second demitasse spoon, push the mixture onto the waxed paper. Using fingers, not the palm of the hand, roll the *quenelles* into balls. It may be necessary to add more flour. Make 56 *quenelles* and place them on a platter or tray lined with waxed paper. Cover ✿ and refrigerate until the dish is to be assembled.

•

The vegetable garnish can be made up to a day in advance. Cut the vegetables into the smallest dice possible. Melt the butter in a small sauté pan and cook the vegetables without letting them color until they are soft. ✿ Refrigerate until needed.

•

Make the puff pastry lids a few hours before using. Lightly flour a board and roll out the defrosted puff pastry, one sheet at a time, each to measure 12 by 12 inches. Use a plate or, even better, a pot lid of the correct size or a *vol-au-vent* cutter, to cut circles 1½ inches greater in diameter than the tops of the soup bowls (¾ inch extra all around), cutting 4 rounds from each sheet of the pastry. Brush off excess flour and stack the circles on a plate with pieces of waxed paper between them. Cover ❁   and refrigerate until needed.

•

Assemble the soup bowls just before they are to go into the oven (this will take less than 10 minutes). Bring the stock to the boil and adjust seasonings. Ladle the soup into the bowls, filling them to within an inch of the lip. Divide the cooked vegetable garnish and the parsley among the bowls. Place 7 *quenelles* in each bowl. One at a time, brush the edges of the puff pastry rounds with the beaten egg yolk, making a ½-inch band. As each round is prepared, place it, painted side down, on top of a bowl and press carefully all around the outside edge to make a good seal. Place the bowls on two jelly-roll pans, making sure the bowls do not touch, and bake in a preheated 425-degree oven for 15 to 20 minutes, or until the pastry lids are dome-shaped and browned.

To serve, place each bowl on a salad plate and provide a fork, to pierce the dome, plus a spoon.

Roast Filet of Beef

•

> 5- to 6-pound filet of beef
> 2   tablespoons butter
> 1½   cups beef stock or bouillon
> 1 or 2   bunches watercress, washed, dried and
>   coarse stems discarded
> Béarnaise Sauce (following recipe)

The filet can be prepared for roasting as much as a day in advance. Trim the filet down to the meat, removing all membranes, sinews and fat. In the process of removing the fat, a cord 1½ inches or so thick of sinewy meat will become detached from along the side of the filet. This "chain" can be saved for stock or ground and added to hamburger meat.

Cut off the tail of the filet where the meat narrows considerably. (Reserve for beef Stroganoff or some other sautéed beef dish for two or three people.) Alternatively, the tail can be tucked under itself to make a longer piece of meat of more or less equal thickness. The tail must be tied every ¾ inch with soft butcher's twine. Should there be a cut in the roast, the meat should be tied at that place, too. ✿

The roast can be browned 2 hours before its final cooking. On the top of the stove, melt the butter in a long oval frying pan, in a roasting pan or in the bottom part of an oven broiler pan. Over high heat, brown the filet quickly on all sides. Remove the meat, add the beef stock or bouillon to the pan, bring to the boil, and scrape up all the brown bits from the pan. Turn these deglazed juices into a bowl and reserve. ✿ Wash the pan if it is to be used later.

If the browned meat has been refrigerated, bring it to room temperature before roasting. Place the meat on a rack over the roasting pan or oven broiler pan and roast in a preheated 500-degree oven for 20 minutes. If the meat is to be cooked in the same oven in which the soup was baked, when you remove the soup, turn up the oven to 500 degrees and immediately place the filet in the oven. Roast for about 24 minutes, the extra few minutes compensating for the time needed to bring the oven up from 425 to 500 degrees.

Remove the meat to a carving board and let it settle for 10 minutes. Meanwhile, return the reserved deglazing juices to the bottom of the roasting pan, bring to the boil, and scrape up any brown bits. Pour into a sauceboat.

To serve the meat, remove any strings, slice the meat, and arrange down the length of a warm serving platter. Surround the meat with a border of the duchesse potato mounds and then of the watercress. Serve with the pan juices and béarnaise sauce.

Béarnaise Sauce

MAKES ABOUT 1½ CUPS

•

¼   *cup white-wine tarragon vinegar*
¼   *cup dry white wine*

> 1   tablespoon minced shallots
> 1   tablespoon minced fresh tarragon or 1
>   teaspoon dried tarragon
>   Salt and pepper to taste
> ½   pound (2 sticks) unsalted butter
> 3   egg yolks
> 1½ teaspoons minced fresh tarragon or parsley

Combine the tarragon vinegar, white wine, shallots, tarragon and salt and pepper in a small saucepan and cook until the liquid is reduced to 2 table-spoons. Set aside and allow to cool. Cut one stick of the butter into 8 pieces and melt to foaming in a small saucepan over moderate heat, then lower the heat. Place the egg yolks in the container of an electric blender and blend at highest speed for about 15 seconds, or until the yolks are very thick. Add the vinegar-wine reduction, including the cooked tarragon and shallots, and blend at highest speed for another 15 seconds.

With the motor running still at highest speed, feed the hot butter into the container, preferably through the small opening in the cover, in a very thin but steady stream. Continue blending at high speed until the sauce thickens. Should it remain thin, pour it into a measuring cup and feed it into the blender once more in a thin, steady stream with the motor running at high speed. Pour the sauce into a bowl and heat the second stick of butter until it foams. In a thin, steady stream beat the butter into the sauce with a wire whisk. Then beat in the additional fresh tarragon or parsley. ❀   The sauce can be made a day in advance. Scrape it into a bowl, cover tightly with plastic wrap, and refrigerate. About an hour before it is to be served, remove from refrigerator and bring to room temperature. Beat the sauce with a wire whisk when it has softened and pour into a warmed sauceboat.

Duchesse Potatoes

•

> 2   pounds russet potatoes
> 2   whole eggs plus 2 egg yolks, well
>   beaten

 1/4 teaspoon ground nutmeg
     Salt and pepper to taste
     Softened butter

Peel the potatoes, cut them into 2-inch chunks, and cook in boiling water until tender. Drain, return to the saucepan, and shake over low heat to dry them out. Beat the potatoes until fluffy with an electric hand mixer. Then beat in the beaten eggs, nutmeg, salt and pepper. Adjust seasonings and let the potatoes cool to lukewarm.

Line a jelly-roll pan with foil and grease the foil lightly with the softened butter. Put the warm potatoes into a large pastry bag fitted with a number 7 open-star tube and squeeze 2½-inch-high mounds of potato onto the foil. The potatoes can be prepared to this point a few hours in advance.

Bake the potato mounds at 500 degrees for 25 to 30 minutes, or until they are lightly browned. Lift the mounds off the foil with a spatula and arrange around the carved meat.

Prunes in Red Wine
with Cream

•

 1½ pounds extra-large prunes
  6 cups strong tea
 1½ cups sugar
 2½ cups red wine
     The peel of 1 large orange, removed in
        one or two large pieces with a potato
        peeler
     3-inch piece stick cinammon
 1½ cups chilled heavy cream

Combine the prunes and the tea in a saucepan, bring to the simmer, and cook, covered, over low heat for 15 minutes. Drain the prunes, discarding the tea. Combine the sugar, red wine, orange peel and cinammon in a saucepan and bring to the boil. Add the prunes, bring to the simmer, and cook, covered, over low heat for 30 minutes. Discard the cinammon stick. Cool and refrigerate overnight.✿ Before serving, discard the orange peel. Serve cold with cream.

*Sole or Flounder and Smoked Salmon
Pinwheels*

Marinated Leg of Lamb

Braised Carrots

Roasted Potatoes

Kohlrabi in Cream and Dill Sauce

Strawberries with Rum Cream

•

FIRST COURSE:
*Pedroncelli Chardonnay
or St. Véran*
MAIN COURSE:
*Ridge Vineyards "San Luis" Zinfandel
or Fleurie*

What is wanted in March is a light,
pretty, easy meal that says spring but has enough substance should the
weather regress yet again to January. This dinner starts with lovely white,
pale pink and green pinwheels, made of sole or flounder fillets layered with
smoked-salmon butter and blanched spinach, then rolled, poached, cooled

and sliced. The pinwheels are served on a puddle of dilled cream and lemon sauce and can be topped with crushed pink peppercorns (which the FDA, in its wisdom, has removed from its list of dangerous foods). This dish and a bowl of tulips on the table will do much to sweep away remnants of winter depression.

Next is a leg of lamb cooked in an aromatic marinade heavy with onion, garlic and herbs.

The lamb is accompanied by thyme-flavored sliced or julienned carrots cooked to a succulence without benefit of a drop of water, potatoes roasted in flavored olive oil, and kohlrabi, a mystery vegetable unmasked and discovered to be different, delicious and well worth eating.

Dessert consists of strawberries, now finally down in price and up in fragrance, left whole and unsugared. They are embellished with a simple rum cream that smooths and highlights their fruity tartness.

The entire meals costs very little per person, despite the comparative priciness of the ingredients for the first course, where a little is made to go a long way.

Sole and flounder are both acceptable for the pinwheels. I make the choice on the basis of which is fresher, less expensive or available. I will not buy prepackaged fish because I don't know what it will smell like when I unwrap its plastic covering. Make sure the fillets, especially flounder fillets, have been completely skinned on both sides.

In experimenting with this dish I rolled some of the fillets with a layer of sliced smoked salmon and others with a layer of salmon butter. The salmon butter was superior both in texture and in flavor. Happily the recipe takes a quarter of a pound of smoked salmon very far indeed (which, considering its cost, is a blessing) and can be made in seconds in a food processor. It is easier to cut the coarse ribs out of the spinach leaves after parboiling. I fastened one batch of the fish rolls with toothpicks and poached them bare in a court bouillon. An easier way, which also resulted in neater rolls, was to wrap each in its own buttered foil package. These are placed in simmering water for only four minutes. The cooking is completed as the rolls cool in the foil. The sauce is an uncomplicated combination of heavy cream and lemon juice with dill, although any combination of fresh herbs would be pleasant. Dried dill weed is a disaster here that must be avoided. (Fresh dill freezes well. It should be washed and spun in a salad dryer. The coarse stalks are then discarded and the branches placed in a plastic bag. The frozen dill is brittle, so it crumbles nicely when spooned out of the bag.)

The pink peppercorns, which are available in specialty food and cookware stores, come only from the Ile de Réunion off the coast of Madagascar and are imported via France. While the berries that are produced from a related bush grown in Florida seemed to cause unpleasant reactions, the ones in commerce were found not to be the same. Those who are nervous about the safety of pink peppercorns should make sure the label identifies them as imports from France or Madagascar. Pink peppercorns are a matter of taste. I happen to like them and find their color attractive.

The lamb is simple to prepare once the fat and fell (the transparent tissue that surrounds the meat) have been removed, a necessary step if you dislike the flavor they impart. I have left a trimmed leg in its marinade for as long as five or six days — refrigerated, naturally. Do, however, cover the pan tightly with plastic wrap, to keep the aromas where they belong. It is important to remove the meat from the refrigerator a few hours before it is put into the oven; otherwise the cooking time will be off.

My husband, who is such an excellent carver that he can get enough meat out of a five-pound leg to feed twelve people and still have some left over, is of the parallel-carving, or French, school. That is, rather than cutting slices vertically down to the bone, as both we and the English tend to do, which only creates a gristly slice of meat, he slices thinly horizontally across the meat. You need a good sharp knife to carve anything properly.

The carrots can be julienned by hand if there is time, or sliced in a food processor. This works most efficiently when the carrots are packed tightly in the smaller opening of the wide-mouthed feed tube. Roasted potatoes do not hold well, so it's a good idea to time their cooking according to when the lamb is to be served. The potatoes won't suffer too much if kept in a turned-down oven for five or ten minutes, but are best eaten as soon as they are done.

My experience with kohlrabi has until recently been limited to curiosity, from a distance. Descriptions of it as a cabbagey turnip or a turnipy cabbage were not encouraging. However, I succumbed to a bunch because it was wonderful to look at. I vaguely considered using it as part of a vegetable centerpiece. Instead I cooked the kohlrabi according to Madeleine Kamman's recipe in her marvelous book, *When French Women Cook*, and a great success it was — delicate, interesting, a good change.

Use your nose when you buy strawberries; there must be detectable perfume. Strawberries should never be dumped into water, which is the enemy. They should be hulled only after they are rinsed quickly under cold running water, to keep the flavor from dging down the drain. The tip of a potato peeler is the perfect instrument for hulling strawberries.

Sole or Flounder and Smoked
Salmon Pinwheels

•

6   *fillets of sole or flounder, skin removed,*
     weighing a little more than a pound
     Milk to cover the fish
¾   *pound fresh spinach leaves*
¼   *pound smoked salmon*
6   *tablespoons butter*
1½ *teaspoons lemon juice*
     Salt and pepper to taste
     Melted butter to coat the foil
1½ *cups water*

FOR THE SAUCE

1   *cup heavy cream*
3   *tablespoons lemon juice*
2   *tablespoons minced fresh dill, or 1*
     tablespoon minced parsley mixed
     with 1 tablespoon minced fresh
     chives, or fresh tarragon to taste, or
     ¼ teaspoon dried tarragon mixed
     with 1 tablespoon minced parsley
1   *teaspoon pink peppercorns, crushed*
     (optional)
     Salt and pepper

Wash the fish fillets, pat them dry, and slit each in two, following the line of the backbone. Check with fingers and cut out any bones that might remain. Place in a gratin dish, barely cover with milk, and refrigerate.

Wash the spinach and drain it. Bring a large (6-quart) pot of water to a boil, add the spinach, and blanch it for 1½ minutes. Turn out into a colander and refresh under cold water. Open the spinach leaves flat and spread them between layers of paper towels to dry them.

Combine the smoked salmon, butter and lemon juice in a food processor and reduce to a purée with the steel blade. Season the mixture highly with pepper and then discreetly with salt. The amount of salt will vary according to the saltiness of the salmon.

Prepare twelve 6-by-8-inch pieces of aluminum foil and brush each with melted butter.

To assemble, remove the fillets from the refrigerator and pat them dry with paper towels. Spread the fillets with the salmon butter. Remove the coarse ribs from the spinach leaves and cover each fillet with a layer of spinach. Starting at the narrow end, roll each fillet as tightly as possible. Place each roll on a piece of buttered foil, fold over, and seal lengthwise and at the ends.

Bring the water to a simmer in a frying pan or sauté pan just large enough to hold the fish rolls in one layer. Add the rolls, cover, and steam for 2 minutes. Turn them over with tongs, cover the pan again, and steam for another 2 minutes. Remove the rolls, the smaller ones first, to a plate and set aside.

When the rolls are completely cool, remove and discard the foil. Using a very sharp knife, even off the ends of each roll (these are the cook's reward) and slice into thin pinwheels. Place on a platter in one layer, cover tightly with plastic wrap, and refrigerate unless the dish is to be served within the hour. ❀ The pinwheels can be made to this point one day in advance. They should be removed from the refrigerator one hour before they are served.

To prepare the sauce, pour the cream into a bowl and whisk in the lemon juice, the dill or whatever herbs you wish, plus salt and pepper to taste.

To serve, ladle the sauce onto eight salad plates and place an equal number of pinwheels on each. Sprinkle with crushed pink peppercorns.

Marinated Leg of Lamb

•

	5½- to 6-pound leg of lamb
⅔	cup olive oil
3	tablespoons lemon juice
1	teaspoon salt
½	teaspoon coarsely ground black pepper
2	teaspoons chopped fresh rosemary or 1 teaspoon dried

1   *teaspoon dried oregano*
3   *bay leaves, coarsely crumbled*
1   *cup thinly sliced onions*
4   *cloves garlic, thinly sliced*

Peel the leg of lamb of all its fell and as much fat as possible. Mix the remaining ingredients in a roasting pan, put the lamb in, and turn it over. Rub the lamb with the marinade, cover it with some of the onions, wrap the pan tightly with plastic wrap, and refrigerate for a day or two.❁   Turn the lamb occasionally.

Preheat the oven to 450 degrees. Scrape the onions from the lamb but do not remove them from the roasting pan. Sear the meat for 20 minutes, then reduce heat to 350 degrees. Cook the lamb for 1½ hours. Remove the lamb and let it sit for 10 minutes to settle its juices.❁   Then carve, cutting parallel to the bone. Arrange some of the browned onions from the marinade around the lamb.

Braised Carrots

•

2   *pounds carrots*
¼   *pound (1 stick) butter*
½   *teaspoon sugar (optional)*
1   *teaspoon dried thyme leaves*
     Salt and pepper to taste

Scrape the carrots, cut off the ends, and slice or cut into a ⅛-inch by 3-inch julienne. If you use a food processor, use the thick slicing blade. Put the carrots, along with the remaining ingredients, in a heavy pot, preferably enamel on cast iron. Stir over medium heat to coat the carrots with the butter as it melts. Reduce the heat to very low, cover, and cook for 20 minutes, stirring occasionally. If the carrots are old, they may need an additional 10 minutes of cooking.❁   These carrots can be made well in advance and reheated over a low flame.

Roasted Potatoes

•

2½ *pounds boiling potatoes*
2 *tablespoons flavored (see July,*
    Provisioning the Pantry) or plain
    olive oil
2 *unpeeled cloves garlic*
    Salt and pepper to taste

Peel the potatoes and trim them into approximately 1½-inch small potatoes, or cut them into chunks. Bring a large pot of water to a boil, add the potatoes, and boil for 5 minutes. Drain. Place the oil in a roasting pan and add the garlic and the potatoes. Turn the potatoes around to coat them with oil. Roast for 40 minutes in a preheated 350-degree oven (along with the lamb), shaking the pan periodically to brown the potatoes evenly. When the lamb is removed from the oven, turn the heat up to 425 degrees and continue to roast the potatoes for another 15 minutes or so, while the lamb is resting and being carved.

Kohlrabi in Cream
and Dill Sauce

•

2 *bunches (8 heads) kohlrabi*
1 *quart water*
    Salt
2 *tablespoons butter*
½ *cup heavy cream*
    Pepper
1 *tablespoon chopped dill*
½ *teaspoon lemon juice*

Peel the kohlrabi and cut them into a ¼-inch julienne. Bring the water to a boil. Add salt and the kohlrabi and blanch for 4 minutes. Drain.

Heat the butter in a saucepan, add the kohlrabi, and toss. Add the cream and pepper and cook until the cream coats the kohlrabi. Add the dill and lemon juice, taste for salt, and serve. ❀ Can be made in advance and reheated.

Strawberries
with Rum Cream

•

3   pints strawberries
1   pint sour cream
2   tablespoons sugar
2   tablespoons dark rum

Wash the strawberries, one at a time, under cold running water and hull with the tip of a potato peeler. Place in a perforated strawberry bowl or other serving bowl. In a small mixing bowl whisk together the sour cream and the sugar, then add the rum. Whisk well and transfer to a serving bowl. ❀

Kipper Pâté

*Portuguese Pork Medallions with Sausage
and Clams*

Fluffy Rice

Steamed Zucchini

Grapefruit Cake and Grapefruit Ice

•

*Pedroncelli Zinfandel Rosé
or Valdepeñas*

This meal consists of familiar foods in combinations peculiar enough to nudge winter-benumbed palates and good enough to satisfy. It starts with a smooth, delicately smoky kipper pâté that shines as an example of how good simple English food can be. Next is an intriguing Portuguese dish that astonishingly combines pork and sausages with fresh clams in a sturdy, savory sauce. The serving platter, with the meat sitting on the sauce and its border of parsley-sprinkled clams and lemon wedges, is very handsome. Accompanying the pork is plain, fluffy white rice, a perfect foil for the sauce, plus a docile dish of peeled, steamed and lightly buttered zucchini chunks. Dessert is an old standby, the 1 (cup butter), 2 (cups sugar), 3 (cups flour), 4 (eggs) cake, updated and made fragrant with grapefruit juice, rind and essence. A grapefruit ice served with the cake reinforces the freshness.

The kipper pâté, which is made in minutes with a food processor, can be served with drinks or as a proper first course at the table. The pâté will keep under refrigeration for a good three weeks if it is sealed, as the recipe directs, with clarified butter. It should be brought to room temperature before serving. Packed in an attractive terrine, it is passed with toast or bread. The pâté is super-rich, so small portions are appropriate.

The pork medallions are cut from as narrow a boneless loin roast as can be found. The slices of meat are first marinated, then browned and finally cooked with the sausages, tomatoes, onions, garlic and the marinade. The reduced juices from the clams are added only at the very end. (The pork roast can also be stuffed with the chorizos and cooked whole, according to directions in the July Menu 4 for Cold Stuffed Roast Pork.) Chorizos, which can be found in specialty food stores and, of course, Spanish stores, are authentic — but hot Italian sausages are a more than adequate substitution, a blessing considering their widespread availability. The entire dish can be prepared hours in advance or even the day before, but care should be taken to submerge the pork slices in the sauce so they won't dry out. The clams can be washed a few hours in advance, held in the refrigerator and cooked at the last minute and only just until they open. Any clams that refuse to open should be discarded. The sand that inevitably is found in clam cooking liquid can be trapped easily by a strainer lined with wrung-out cheesecloth. The smaller the clams, the better. Two clams are ample for each portion, but for those who prefer to err on the side of generosity, three are better.

The rice is cooked to a feathery lightness by treating it as though it were pasta. The grains are fed slowly into a large pot of salted boiling water, cooked for about 17 minutes until it is just done and drained in a colander.

It is odd to find small, tender zucchini on the market as this time of year, but they are there and this meal takes good advantage of them. The zucchini are peeled to a pale nakedness, cut into large chunks on the diagonal, lightly steamed and served with butter only. (The optional addition of Parmesan cheese would, I believe, be overwhelming for this particular meal but is quite wonderful with, say, a simply cooked fish, a steak or chops.)

The idea of a grapefruit cake was proffered by a friend in response to my moans about the paucity of edible fruits at this time of year and what if anything of interest could be done with members of the citrus family. The grapefruit rind contributes texture as well as taste, and the citrus zester makes short, happy work of grating the rinds. Freshly squeezed grapefruit juice provides the liquid for the cake, with the imported grapefruit essence (see Mail-Order Sources) intensifying flavor and perfume. As with all cake-baking, the pan should be prepared and all ingredients measured out before you begin. However, the sugar and grapefruit juice for the final glaze should be mixed only before the glaze is to be applied to the warm cake. For a darker cake, use the juice of pink grapefruit. The cake can be made at least a day in advance.

Fruit ices in general should be eaten the day they are made, ideally just after they have ripened in the freezer for four hours to bring up the flavor. A reasonable ice can be produced without special equipment, but the home ice cream machine with a dasher not only produces a better product, it takes far less effort and time than the freezer, which requires that the ice be beaten at least twice during the freezing. Most ice cream machines need about four or five pounds of ice cubes per batch plus enough salt to bring the temperature of the water surrounding the container down to at least 20 degrees. If the mixture is sluggish in freezing, take the temperature of the bath and, if necessary, add more salt to bring it to the proper coldness.

Fruit essences heighten flavor but must be used sparingly because too much can result in an artificial taste. Grapefruit essence has the additional happy effect of eliminating the slightly metallic backtaste inherent even in freshly squeezed grapefruit juice. All water ices are best stored at 20 degrees, but since home freezers are set at from 0 to 10 degrees, ices need to be softened by placing them in the refrigerator half an hour before serving.

Kipper Pâté

•

Two	*3¼-ounce cans kipper snacks, drained and skin removed*
½	*pound (2 sticks) unsalted butter, melted*
1	*tablespoon or more lemon juice, to taste*
¼	*teaspoon cayenne pepper*
	Salt to taste
3	*tablespoons butter to make about 2 tablespoons clarified butter*
2	*tablespoons minced parsley*

Reduce the kipper snacks to a smooth paste in a food processor. With the motor running, add the melted butter and process until amalgamated, stopping the motor once or twice to scrape down the bowl. Add the lemon juice, cayenne and salt and process, stopping the motor once or twice to scrape down the bowl. Adjust seasonings and pack into a 1½-cup terrine.

Melt 3 tablespoons of butter over low heat and let stand off heat for about 3 or 4 minutes. Skim the foam, which will have formed on the surface, and discard it. Pour the remaining butter through a strainer lined with wrung-out cheesecloth. There will be 2 tablespoons plus a bit more of clarified butter. Spoon it over the surface of the pâté and refrigerate. ❁ To serve, bring to room temperature and sprinkle with parsley. Crustless white toast triangles or warm, thinly sliced French bread are excellent with the pâté.

Portuguese Pork Medallions
with Sausage and Clams

•

FOR MARINATING THE PORK		*2½-pound boneless pork loin roast*
	1	*cup dry white wine*
	2	*teaspoons paprika, preferably imported from Hungary*
	1	*bay leaf*
	3	*cloves garlic, crushed*
FOR THE SAUSAGES	*½*	*pound chorizos or hot Italian sausages*
FOR COOKING THE PORK		*The marinated pork medallions*
	3	*tablespoons butter*
	1	*tablespoon peanut oil*
	2	*large onions, thinly sliced*
	2	*large cloves garlic, crushed*
		14-ounce can imported plum tomatoes, drained
		The reserved marinade from the pork
		The reduced cooking liquid from the clams

FOR THE CLAMS	*16 to 24*	*small clams, either littleneck or cherrystone*
FOR THE GARNISH	*2* *1/4*	*lemons, quartered* *cup chopped parsley*

Marinate the pork, starting several hours or the day before it is to be cooked. Cut the strings off the pork roast if it is tied and cut the roast into 16 equal slices, or medallions. Combine the white wine, paprika, bay leaf and 3 crushed garlic cloves, place the pork medallions in the marinade, cover, and refrigerate for several hours or ❀ overnight, turning the slices occasionally.

Cut the chorizos into ½-inch slices. Or, if Italian sausages are used, cook them whole in an inch of water for 5 minutes, turning them as they cook. Drain and cool. Slip off the casings and discard them. Cut the sausages into ½-inch slices. ❀ Refrigerate until needed.

To cook the pork, remove the medallions from the marinade, discard the bay leaf, and reserve the marinade. Dry the pork well on paper towels. Melt the butter and oil in a large frying pan and brown the medallions, a few at a time, quickly on both sides. As the pork is browned, remove it to a heavy, flameproof casserole. Then brown the sausage slices and add to the pork.

Add the sliced onions and garlic to frying pan and cook over low heat until onions are soft. Turn up heat and brown onions lightly. Add drained tomatoes and cook for 5 minutes. Then add reserved marinade and cook over high heat, stirring frequently, for 5 minutes. Add sauce to pork and sausage slices, cover, and cook over low heat for 25 minutes, stirring occasionally. ❀ The pork can be prepared in advance to this point and reheated.

•

Wash the clams under cold running water an hour or two before using. Refrigerate until needed. ❀ Ten minutes before pork is to be served, place half an inch of cold water in a large pot, add clams, cover, and place over high heat. Shake pan from time to time, for 5 or 6 minutes, or until the clams open. Remove them with a slotted spoon, place in a shallow bowl, and cover with a cloth towel to keep them warm. Continue to cook clam juices over high heat for 5 minutes. Pour reduced juices through a strainer lined with wrung-out cheesecloth and add to the pork. Raise heat and cook pork for a few minutes, stirring.

To assemble, spoon the sauce onto a large, warm serving platter and arrange the pork medallions and sausages on the sauce. Surround with clams and lemon wedges and sprinkle the parsley around the border.

Fluffy Rice

•

1   *tablespoon salt*
2   *cups long-grain rice*

Fill a 6-quart pot three-quarters full with *cold* water, add the salt, and bring the water to the boil. ❀   Slowly feed in the rice and start testing for doneness after 15 minutes. When the rice is just cooked, drain it well in a colander. If desired, the rice can be arranged in a ring on a serving platter and the center filled with the zucchini chunks.

Steamed Zucchini

•

8   *small, thin zucchini, about 2 pounds*
2   *tablespoons butter*
3   *tablespoons freshly grated Parmesan*
     cheese (optional)

Trim ends of zucchini and peel them with a potato peeler. Cut each zucchini into three pieces on the diagonal and steam pieces in a vegetable steamer over hot water for about 8 minutes, or until they can be pierced easily with a thin, pointed knife. Place in a serving dish and coat with butter. If Parmesan cheese is used, place zucchini in one layer in an oven-proof serving dish and sprinkle with the cheese. ❀ Place in a preheated 400-degree oven for about 10 minutes, or until cheese has browned.

Grapefruit Cake

•

FOR PREPARING THE PAN	*Softened butter to grease a 10-inch Bundt pan or tube pan* *Bread crumbs to coat the pan*
FOR THE CAKE	*3 cups sifted cake flour* *1 tablespoon baking powder* *½ teaspoon salt* *1 cup (2 sticks) unsalted butter* *2 cups sugar* *Grated rind of 1 medium grapefruit* *¼ teaspoon imported grapefruit essence (optional)* *4 eggs* *¾ cup fresh grapefruit juice*
FOR THE GLAZE	*⅓ cup fresh grapefruit juice* *⅓ cup sugar*

Prepare the pan by greasing it liberally with the softened butter. Add the bread crumbs and swirl them around the bottom and sides of the pan to coat it. Turn the pan upside down and discard excess crumbs. Set aside.

Sift the flour with the baking powder and salt and set aside. Beat the butter with an electric mixer until light. Add the sugar gradually and beat until fluffy, about 5 minutes. Add the grapefruit rind and grapefruit essence and beat thoroughly. Add the eggs, one at a time, beating well after each addition. Add a third of the flour mixture and beat until just incorporated. Repeat with another third of the flour, the remaining juice and finally the last of the flour. Do not overbeat. Turn the batter into the prepared pan. Rap the pan on the counter to get rid of any air pockets and swirl the pan to level the batter. Bake in a preheated 350-degree oven for 1 hour, or until a cake tester, straw or toothpick comes out clean.

Remove from oven and set the cake in its pan on a rack for 5 minutes. Then turn the cake out onto the rack. Place a piece of waxed paper under the rack and glaze the cake. Make the glaze just before it is used. Combine the grapefruit juice and sugar and spoon the mixture over the warm cake until all the glaze has been absorbed. Let the cake cool before transferring it to a serving plate.✿   The cake can now be refrigerated overnight, which will make it even better. It will hold a few days under refrigeration.

Grapefruit Ice

MAKES ABOUT 1 QUART

•

1¼   cups sugar.
1   cup plus 1 tablespoon cold water
2½   cups fresh, strained grapefruit juice
Up to ¼ teaspoon or to taste
grapefruit essence (optional)

Make the syrup a day or more in advance. Combine the sugar and water in a saucepan, place over high heat, and stir with a wooden spoon until the sugar is dissolved. Bring to a boil without further stirring, immediately remove from heat, and pour into a bowl. Cool and refrigerate.✿

If using an ice cream freezer, make the ice about 6 hours before it is to be served. If using the refrigerator freezer, start 8 hours in advance. Measure out 1½ cups of cold syrup (there will be a few tablespoons left over) and combine with the grapefruit juice. Add the grapefruit essence two drops at a time and taste. Do not use too much essence. Freeze in an electric ice cream freezer according to manufacturer's instructions. Turn the frozen ice into a covered container and cure in the refrigerator freezer for 4 hours or more.✿   Serve the same day.

If using a refrigerator freezer, pour the mixture into a wide-bottomed bowl and place in freezer for 3 hours, or until it becomes mushy. Remove and beat with an electric mixer or, in several batches, in the processor. Work quickly to prevent the ice crystals from liquefying. Return the bowl to the freezer for 3 more hours. Beat again until fluffy, pack into a covered container, and freeze for another 2 hours. ❁

Half an hour before serving, remove the ice from the freezer and place in the refrigerator to soften.

April

PROVISIONING·THE·PANTRY

Vanilla Cognac

MAKES ABOUT 3½ CUPS

•

6   *vanilla beans*
1   *bottle (about 3½ cups) Cognac or*
       brandy

Slit the vanilla beans in half lengthwise, add them to the bottle of Cognac or brandy, cap tightly, and let ripen for 6 weeks. Use to flavor whipped cream and in lieu of vanilla extract.

Eggs in Eggs in Aspic with Herb Sauce

Beef Birds in Fried Potato Bird's Nests

Asparagus Tips in Sheaves

April Fool

•

FIRST COURSE:
Chandon Blanc de Noirs
MAIN COURSE:
Beringer Cabernet Sauvignon
or Vieux-Château Certan

*T*his April Fool's Day dinner consists of delicious foods in the guise of feeble jokes. It starts with seemingly whole eggs in aspic sitting innocently in a ring of egg yolk-parsley grass. But when the eggs are cut, red salmon caviar spills out from the cavities. A pale-green herb sauce adds sparkle.

The main course is a quasi-sylvan still life: Braised beef birds perch in crispy brown nests of grated potatoes fried in a special tool, with the scene completed by little thickets of lightly buttered asparagus tips tied into sheaves with blanched strands of scallion. The meal ends fittingly with a frivolous (English) April fool. The height of frivolity, indeed, is the fresh raspberry garnish at this season. It is optional.

The aspic is made by cooking a turgid mixture of chicken broth, tomato juice, gelatin, seasonings and lightly beaten egg whites and then passing it through a strainer lined with wrung-out cheesecloth. The miracle occurs when the crystal-clear amber aspic drips through the strainer, leaving behind a miserable-looking mass of particles. Aspic can be made at least a day in advance, refrigerated, reliquefied over heat and cooled to room temperature before it is used.

The eggs are hard-cooked rather than poached, as they are traditionally for eggs in aspic, which simplifies matters considerably. The addition of a little aspic thickens the red caviar and makes it easier to put the halves together without losing the filling. The eggs are placed in the molds uncut sides uppermost and thus appear to be intact when they are unmolded. Little oval metal molds made especially for eggs in aspic can be found in good kitchenware stores, but ordinary custard cups work perfectly well. The eggs can be assembled the day before or the morning of the dinner.

If thinly sliced boneless round steaks, which are needed for the beef birds, are not to be found already packaged in supermarket cases, ring the service bell and ask for them. I use the food processor to grind the pork for the filling. The beef birds consist of 4-by-5-inch pieces of thin round steaks spread with the ground pork mixture. Should the steaks not cut into perfect rectangles, begin rolling the uneven end first so that the final roll nevertheless measures 4 inches long.

The potato nest maker, which comes in three sizes, is sold by most kitchenware stores, although prices vary, so it pays to shop by telephone. The tool consists of two tinned steel wire baskets attached to handles. The larger basket appropriate for main courses measures 4¾ inches in diameter at the top. This basket is packed with a layer of grated potatoes. The smaller basket, whose diameter is 4 inches, fits into the larger one and molds the potatoes into shape. The two baskets are fastened with clips that attach to the handles. The handles are 17 inches long so the cook can stand back when the baskets are lowered into the hot oil, which at first boils up with fury no matter how well the potatoes have been dried. Fortunately, the cauldron subsides quickly.

These nests are made one at a time. They are more easily released from the baskets after they are half-cooked to a pale brown rather than when they are completely done. The nest maker is removed from the oil and set on a jelly-roll pan lined with paper towels. A dinner knife is run over the wires to loosen the nest. Then the freed nest is returned to the oil with tongs and cooked to a deep brown. The nests can be made earlier in the day and left to drain on the paper towels, or they can be made a day or two in advance and stored in a tightly covered container. In the unlikely case they lose their crispness, they can be placed in a moderate oven for a few minutes before they are filled.

The asparagus tips are cooked for a few minutes just before they are served. I blanch a few extra scallion strands in case some of them break when the sheaves are tied. This can be done in advance or in the asparagus water just before the tips go in. (Asparagus stalks can be used for soup. Discard the white, woody ends, cut the stalks into ½-inch pieces, and cook in water until they are very soft. Drain well and purée in the processor. Then sauté some minced onion in butter until soft, add chicken broth, the puréed asparagus, a little cream, a bit of milk, salt and pepper. The soup is good hot or cold.)

The dinner plates are composed in the kitchen. Place a nest on each plate. Then remove the strings from the beef birds and cut each bird in half. Arrange three of the halves cut-side down in each nest and spoon some of the sauce with its vegetables over them. Tie the asparagus tips and stand one sheaf upright on each plate.

The April fool is an uncomplicated concoction of frozen raspberry purée, beaten egg whites, whipped cream and some of the raspberry juice. The purée can be made the day before, but the fool, which is put together in no time, should not be assembled more than four hours before serving. It can be refrigerated and then brought to room temperature. The fool also can be made with fresh strawberries, but rather than puréeing the fruit, mash it with a fork, since the flavor is better when the berries retain a little body.

Eggs in Eggs in Aspic

•

FOR THE ASPIC	3	*cups condensed canned chicken broth*
	1	*cup tomato juice*
	4	*tablespoons (4 envelopes) unflavored gelatin*
	1	*teaspoon sugar*
		Salt and pepper to taste
	2	*egg whites, lightly beaten*
	2	*tablespoons Cognac*

FOR THE FILLING		*4-ounce jar red salmon caviar*
	2	*tablespoons of the aspic*
FOR ASSEMBLING	*8*	*hard-cooked eggs*
THE EGGS		*The remaining aspic*
		The reserved yolks of the eggs
	1	*cup minced parsley*

To make the aspic, combine the chicken broth, tomato juice, gelatin, sugar, salt, pepper and lightly beaten egg whites in a saucepan. Place over low heat and, stirring constantly, bring to the boil. Ladle the mixture through a strainer lined with wrung-out cheesecloth. Discard residue remaining in the cheesecloth and wash the cheesecloth, which can be reused. Stir the Cognac into the clear aspic and set aside.

When the aspic is cool but still liquid, spoon a thin layer into 8 egg molds or custard cups and refrigerate. Empty the red salmon caviar into a bowl, stir in 2 tablespoons of the aspic to thicken the caviar, and refrigerate.

To assemble the eggs, slice them in half lengthwise. Remove the yolks and reserve them. Place the halves on a plate side by side, marking the beginning with, for example, a plastic bag tie, so that each half can be matched later with its mate.

Fill each hollow of the whites with the caviar mixture and paint a bit of aspic on the cut surfaces of the eggs. Fit each pair of filled whites together. Spoon a little liquid aspic into the molds. Then place the eggs in the molds or custard cups with the uncut sides facing bottom and top. Spoon the remaining aspic into the molds and refrigerate until set. ❀   The eggs can be made the day before.

To unmold, run the tip of a thin, pointed knife around the edges of the molds or custard cups. Dip each mold in a bowl of hot water for 5 or 6 seconds if the molds are made of metal. Porcelain or glass custard cups need to be dipped for from 12 to 15 seconds. Invert the molds onto individual serving plates and rap sharply to release the eggs.

Drop the hard-cooked yolks one at a time through the processor tube with the motor running. Then feed in the minced parsley and process for a second. Spoon the egg yolk-parsley mixture around each egg to make a "bed" and pass the herb sauce separately.

Herb Sauce

MAKES ABOUT 2 CUPS

•

1   egg yolk
½   teaspoon Dijon mustard
2   tablespoons red wine vinegar
    Salt and pepper to taste
½   cup peanut oil
½   cup olive oil
4   tablespoons minced parsley
2   tablespoons minced shallots

Place the egg yolk, mustard, vinegar, salt and pepper in the bowl of a food processor and process for 30 seconds. With the motor running, slowly feed in the peanut oil and the olive oil. Stop the motor, add the minced parsley and shallots, and process for another second or two. Turn out into a sauceboat and refrigerate, covered, until needed. ❁   The sauce can be made a day in advance.

Braised Stuffed Beef Birds

•

1¾   pounds top round steaks, thinly sliced
      (¼ inch)

FOR THE   3   tablespoons butter
STUFFING   1   large onion, minced
             1   large clove garlic, minced
             ½   teaspoon thyme
                 Salt and pepper to taste
             1½ pounds lean pork loin, trimmed of
                 sinews and ground in the food
                 processor
             3   tablespoons medium-sweet or dry Madeira

FOR COOKING	2	*tablespoons vegetable oil*
THE BEEF BIRDS	2	*tablespoons butter*
	1	*large onion, thinly sliced*
	1	*large carrot, thinly sliced*
	1	*tablespoon flour*
	1	*cup dry white wine*
	1	*cup beef bouillon*
	4	*tablespoons minced parsley*

Cut the steaks into 12 rectangles measuring 4 by 5 inches each. Place the pieces between sheets of waxed paper and flatten with a meat pounder or the side of a large can.

To make the stuffing, melt the butter in a small frying pan, add the minced onions and garlic, and sauté over low heat until transparent but not browned. Add the thyme, salt and pepper and cook, stirring, for another minute. Combine with the ground pork, add the Madeira, and mix well. Spread each piece of beef with the stuffing and roll so that the finished rolls measure 4 inches long. Use soft butcher's twine and tie the rolls in three places — 1 inch from each end and at the middle.❁

To cook the beef birds, heat the oil and butter in a frying pan and brown the rolls, one or two at a time. Transfer to a heavy casserole as they are browned. Add the carrots and onions to the frying pan and cook slowly until soft and browned. Blend in the flour and cook, stirring, until browned. Add the wine and bouillon to the frying pan and bring to the boil, stirring and scraping up all the browned bits from the bottom of the pan. Transfer the contents of the pan to the casserole, cover, and bake in a preheated 325-degree oven for 1¼ hours, or until the rolls are tender. Remove the rolls from the casserole, cut off the strings with scissors, and discard. Cut each roll in half, using the indentation made by the middle tie as a guide. Stand three halves, cut side down, in each potato nest and ladle the sauce over the meat. Garnish each nest with minced parsley.

Fried Potato Nests

•

4   *pounds russet potatoes*
2   *quarts vegetable oil*
    Salt to taste

Peel the potatoes, grate them with the coarse-grate blade of a food processor, and turn the shreds into a large bowl of cold water. Soak for about
10 minutes, place in a colander, and rinse under cold water. Drain well,
squeeze out as much water as possible, spread on a cloth dish towel, and pat
dry. Roll the grated potato in a dry towel and set aside.

   Heat the oil over medium heat in a deep-fat fryer to 375 degrees. Dip
the potato nest maker in the oil for a minute and remove. Remove the
clamps from the potato nest maker and pack the entire bottom basket with
a ½-inch layer of potatoes. Be sure the potatoes come all the way to the top
edge of the basket. Then fit the smaller top basket into the potato-filled
bottom basket and replace the clamps. Lower the basket slowly into the hot
fat. The oil will bubble up as the basket meets it, so be sure to hold the
basket at arm's length and stand back. Fry the potatoes until golden brown.
Then remove the basket from the oil, remove the clamps, and loosen the
potato nest, with the help of a knife, from the top and bottom baskets.
Using tongs, return the nest to the fat and fry on both sides until deep
brown. Set the nest, right side up, on a jelly-roll pan lined with paper
towels to drain. Skim off any loose potato shreds in the pot, using a slotted
spoon. Check the temperature and fry the next basket when the oil is at 375
degrees. Continue until all the nests are made, and sprinkle with a little
salt. ❀   The nests can be made several hours in advance and recrisped, if
necessary, in a 325-degree oven for a few minutes before filling.

Asparagus Sheaves

•

40   medium-thin spears asparagus (about
     3½ pounds)
8 to 10   long green strands from scallions
4   tablespoons butter, melted

From each asparagus spear, cut a 5-inch piece from the tip and remove the scales below the head. Reserve the bottom end of the stalk for soup or other uses. Bring water to the boil in a large frying pan and blanch the scallion strands for about 2 seconds. Remove to a paper towel. ✿

Cook the asparagus tips in the water for about 5 minutes, or until they are just done. Remove to a cloth towel, pat dry, and tie them, using the scallion strands, into 8 sheaves of 5 tips each. Set a sheaf upright on each dinner plate and dribble with butter.

April Fool

•

Two   10-ounce packages frozen raspberries, defrosted
2   egg whites
1   cup heavy cream
     Fresh raspberries for garnish (optional)

Place the raspberries in a strainer over a bowl and let them drain. Reserve about 5 tablespoons of the juice for the fool. Place the raspberries in the food processor with 2 tablespoons of juice and reduce to a purée. Push the purée through a strainer and discard the seeds. The purée can be made a day in advance. ✿

To assemble the fool, beat the egg whites until they are stiff but not dry and fold into the purée. Whip the cream and fold into the raspberry mixture. Divide among 8 champagne or wine glasses and spoon about 1 teaspoon of the remaining juice into each glass. Garnish, if possible, with whole fresh raspberries. ❁   The fool will hold in the refrigerator for a few hours. Bring to room temperature before serving.

Savoy Soup

Salmon Steaks Broiled in Foil

Tarragon-Egg Sauce

French Peas

Nut Gâteau

•

Robert Mondavi Chardonnay
or Châteauneuf-du-Pape Blanc

*A*pril is the cruelest month for plan-
ning a dinner party. Presumably it's spring and almost time for salade
niçoise. In actuality, it's often closer to midwinter, so the menu needs some
stolidness. But this must be tempered and lightened; otherwise nobody will
believe the peonies will ever bloom again.

This meal takes a classical winter soup from the French mountains,
gussies it up by cutting the root vegetables into a nice julienne and trans-
forms it with the untraditional addition of mixed fresh herbs. Herbs may
not yet be up in home gardens, but pots of them are flourishing in nurseries
by now.

The rosemary and thyme, which winter indoors in our house but will
vacation outside in pots this summer, lighten and brighten the soup. The
tarragon, eventually to be planted outdoors (and, I suppose, to be killed off

again next winter), perfumes the salmon steaks and the simple, lovely sauce that accompanies them. Unherbed, the green peas, cooked as the French do with Boston lettuce and the white bulb parts of scallions, are, as usual, the perfect match for salmon. Had the meal not started with soup, we would have had a few new potatoes boiled and served in their skins absolutely plain, without butter. Some of the sauce for the fish would have been sneaked over to the potatoes' side of the plate.

The meal ends with an Americanized version of Mary Henderson's mysteriously delicious nut gâteau which was served at the British Embassy during her husband's tour of duty as ambassador. The original recipe calls for almonds or walnuts, but the pecans I used gave it a slightly southern decadence. Just what a dessert wants.

The soup is interesting, since it is made with root vegetables but manages to present a very fresh flavor, due clearly to the celery root, which happily is still to be found at local produce sellers although not usually at supermarkets. The vegetables, all of them whitish, are sautéed gently in butter until they become almost translucent before they are cooked in water and milk. This very white soup is topped with golden slices of French bread fried in butter and topped with a thick layer of melted Swiss cheese. The herbs, added at the last minute, provide color. The croutons are best made just before serving, but there is no reason why the frying pan or pans can't be ready to receive the bread slices, which cook very quickly. I buy the best imported Swiss cheese I can find by the chunk and slice it as thin as needed with a wire cheese slicer. The soup, which can be made a few days in advance if you wish, is filling, so it's wise to keep portions small.

To broil salmon steaks in the usual way, a cook needs highly developed motor skills, an impeccable sense of timing, intense powers of concentration and enough luck so that the phone doesn't ring while the fish is being turned. Otherwise, this most wonderful of fishes becomes a dry, tasteless thing. Broiling salmon steaks using the foil packet/cookie sheet method at least gives the cook some control and quite a bit of leeway against disaster. Here the salmon steaks are first sealed in individual buttered foil packets into which some fresh tarragon has been tucked. The fish is kept moist and fragrant while it cooks. Of course, other fresh herbs can be used, or none at all. The foil also allows the fish to be placed extremely close to the flame without burning, so that the steaks cook quickly and take on a nice smoky undertone. By placing the steaks on a cookie sheet, all of them can be removed simultaneously from the flame, which means the cook no longer has to be overwhelmed with the anxiety of overcooking the last piece because it is taking altogether too long to turn the others. It is also nice not to be in a position where the hand is very close to a flame.

The sauce, which is a lemony vinaigrette emulsified with soft-cooked egg yolks, incorporates the chopped whites along with some shallot and fresh herbs. This version, with fresh tarragon, is lovely with salmon. It can be made, and easily, at least a day in advance. As the French discovered probably centuries ago, cooking tiny peas with scallion bulbs and a chiffonade of Boston lettuce only underscores the flavor of the peas. Frozen peas are helped even more by this treatment.

The nut gâteau practically makes itself if you own an electric mixer on a stand. In addition to a simple custard, the filling consists of nuts, butter, confectioners' sugar and over an hour of beating and creaming. It is very agreeable to go about one's kitchen business while the machine makes such a glory of a dessert. The British Embassy often serves this nut gâteau with a chocolate nut sauce, but if you do, make sure the portions are small. It is not the sort of dish you'd find in the authorized column of a diet.

Savoy Soup

•

¼	pound (1 stick) butter (reserve half for frying the croutons)
3	large leeks
¼	pound young turnips
2	small celery roots (about ¾ pound in all)
	Salt and pepper to taste
3	cups water
3	medium potatoes
2½	cups milk
8 to 16	thin slices French bread
8 to 16	paper-thin slices imported Swiss cheese, trimmed to cover the bread
1	small sprig fresh rosemary
½	teaspoon fresh thyme leaves
1	tablespoon minced parsley

Melt half the butter in a 2½- or 3-quart saucepan and remove from heat. Slit the leeks through the center, remove root ends and outer leaves, and wash carefully under running water, making sure no sand remains. Cut the leeks into fine 2-inch-long shreds and place in the saucepan. Peel the turnips, cut them into a ⅛-by-2-inch julienne, and add to the saucepan. Peel the celery roots one at a time, cut them into a ⅛-by-2-inch julienne, and add to the pan as they are cut. Toss the slivers to coat them with the melted butter. Place the pan over medium heat and heat the butter and vegetables, swirling the pan so the vegetables will heat evenly. Then lower the heat, season with salt and pepper to taste, cover the pan, and braise the vegetables for 15 minutes, stirring them occasionally. They must not be allowed to brown.

Meanwhile, peel the potatoes, cut them into a ⅛-by-2-inch julienne, and place in a bowl of cold water to prevent them from becoming brown. When the vegetables have finished sautéing, drain the potatoes and add them to the saucepan along with 3 cups of fresh water. Bring to a boil, reduce heat, cover, and simmer for 15 minutes. Then add the milk, bring to the boil, reduce heat, cover, and simmer for another 10 minutes. The vegetables should be just tender, not falling apart.

Just before serving, melt the remaining 4 tablespoons of butter in one or two frying pans large enough to hold the bread in a single layer. When the butter is hot, add the bread and fry until one side is nicely browned. Do not let the bread burn. Turn the slices over, place a slice of Swiss cheese on each, and fry until the other sides are browned. The cheese will melt as the bread fries.

Strip about a dozen rosemary leaves from the stalk and finely cut them into a small bowl with scissors. Add the fresh thyme leaves and minced parsley and mix the herbs. To serve, ladle some hot soup into bowls, place a crouton or two on the soup, and sprinkle with the mixed fresh herbs. If you cannot find fresh herbs, omit herbs; do not used dried.

Salmon Steaks
Broiled in Foil

•

8   *salmon steaks, ⅜ to ½ inch thick*
2   *tablespoons melted butter*
1   *teaspoon minced fresh tarragon*
    Salt and pepper

Wash the salmon steaks and pat them dry. Cut 8 pieces of foil, each large enough to hold a steak, and brush the foil with the butter. Place a steak on each piece of foil and divide the tarragon among the steaks. Add salt and pepper to taste and close the packets, making a tight seal. Place these on a cookie sheet or jelly-roll pan that will fit under the broiler. ❋   The packets can be prepared at least an hour in advance up to this point and placed in the refrigerator.

   To cook the salmon, preheat the broiler. Place the cookie sheet with the salmon packets under the broiler, about an inch from the heat. Broil for 3 minutes. Remove the cookie sheet, turn the packets, using tongs, and return to the broiler for 2 more minutes. Remove the cookie sheet, cut the foil, and turn it back to expose the salmon steaks. Place the cookie sheet under the broiler for 1 more minute to brown the salmon a bit. Test for doneness by pulling some flesh from a center bone. If the fish looks raw, return to the broiler for 30 seconds or so. Remove the salmon steaks to a hot serving platter and pour any juices remaining in the foil over them. Serve with tarragon-egg sauce.

Tarragon-Egg Sauce

MAKES ABOUT 1¾ CUPS

•

3   *eggs*
4   *tablespoons lemon juice*
1   *cup peanut oil*

2 tablespoons minced shallots
2 teaspoons minced fresh tarragon
1 tablespoon minced parsley
1 tablespoon minced chives
Salt and pepper to taste

Bring a small saucepan of water to a boil, add the eggs, and cook them for 3½ minutes (or 3 minutes if they are at room temperature). Immediately plunge the saucepan under cold running water and cool the eggs. Crack the eggs, shell them, cut them in half, and scoop the yolks into the container of a food processor. Mince the whites and set aside.

Add the lemon juice to the egg yolks and process for 2 minutes, or until the mixture becomes very thick. Then, with the motor running, add the oil very slowly through the feed tube. The mixture will thicken and emulsify like a mayonnaise. Place the sauce in a small mixing bowl and beat into it the minced shallots, fresh herbs, salt and pepper. Stir in the minced egg whites. ❀ The sauce should hold in the refrigerator for at least a day. Should it begin to separate, whisk it just before serving. Serve at room temperature. Transfer to a serving bowl and pass with the salmon.

French Peas

•

Four 10-ounce packages frozen tiny green peas
16 scallions
1 large or 2 small heads Boston lettuce
4 tablespoons butter
Salt and pepper to taste
1 teaspoon sugar
10¾-ounce can condensed chicken broth

Remove the peas from the freezer an hour before cooking and empty the packages into a colander. Trim the root ends from the scallions, cut off the green parts, and reserve for another use. You will be left with little white bulbs.

Wash the lettuce, spin dry, and shred the leaves finely. Melt the butter in a saucepan and add the scallion bulbs. Reduce heat, cover, and cook for about 5 minutes, shaking the pan frequently to prevent the scallions from browning. Then add the peas, lettuce shreds, salt, pepper, sugar and chicken broth. Bring to a boil, reduce heat, cover, and cook for about 4 to 5 minutes. ❀ Remove the cover, raise the heat and, shaking the pan to keep the peas from sticking, boil off any remaining liquid.

Nut Gâteau

•

½	pound shelled pecans, walnuts or blanched almonds (2 cups whole nut meats)
½	pound (2 sticks) unsalted butter
½	pound (2 cups loosely spooned into a measure) confectioners' sugar
1	scant cup milk
½	teaspoon vanilla extract
3	egg yolks
	Pinch salt
24	ladyfingers

Chop the nuts coarsely and combine them with the butter and sugar in the large bowl of an electric mixer, on a stand. Cream the mixture for at least 30 minutes, longer if possible. Scrape down the sides occasionally. This creaming cannot be overdone.

Meanwhile, make a custard. Scald the milk by bringing it just to a boil and removing from heat. Add the vanilla. Place the egg yolks and the salt in the top of a double boiler and beat with a wire whisk. Slowly beat in the scalded milk-vanilla mixture. Place over hot water, but don't let the water touch the top pan of the double boiler. Cook, stirring constantly, until the custard thickens and coats a wooden spoon. Test by running a finger down the center of the spoon and holding the spoon vertically. If the custard does not fill in the channel, it has cooked enough. Immediately remove the top of the double boiler from the heat and set it in a few inches of cold water to stop the cooking. Stir the custard until it is cool. Only then add it to the creamed sugar-butter-nut mixture. Continue to cream for another 30 minutes, or longer, scraping down the sides of the bowl occasionally.

Line the bottom and sides of a 6-cup charlotte mold with ladyfingers. Turn out the nut cream into the mold, smooth the top, and place on it a layer of ladyfingers. ✤   Cover tightly with plastic wrap and refrigerate one or several days.

To serve, place a platter on the mold and flip both over together to turn the gâteau onto the platter. Slice as you would a cake.

Bagna Cauda with Crudités

Paella

Exotic Fruit Tray

Madeleines

•

FIRST COURSE:
Corvo Bianco
MAIN COURSE:
Beaujolais-Villages

*T*his meal consists of a series of "one-pots." It begins with a potpourri of raw vegetables served with drinks (or wine) rather than at the table. The vegetables are dipped into a bagna cauda, a warm, deep-brown Mediterranean bath of olive oil, butter, garlic and anchovies. Then guests sit down to that most refined of casseroles, a steaming paella redolent with saffron, studded with shellfish, harboring wonderful bits and pieces of shrimp, Spanish chorizos and chicken thighs within the rice, and garnished with lemon wedges and parsley. Finally, there is a tray of exotic fruits to clear the palate and the senses. The fruits are accompanied by madeleines, light and lovely little French cakes flavored, preferably, with raspberries in the form of an *eau de vie de framboise*.

The bagna cauda, a dish from the Italian Piedmont that deserves to be better known, is best kept warm over a candle, although it is eminently edible even at room temperature. The trick is to get your guests to swish the vegetables around and stir up the garlic and melted anchovies that sink to the bottom of the bowl. I make bagna cauda half an hour before guests arrive and leave it over the smallest flame possible, with a Flame Tamer in between the pot and the heat. A nice, easy way to mince the large amount of garlic needed for this recipe is to start the food processor motor going and drop the garlic buds through the tube one at a time. As the garlic is minced, it is thrown to the sides of the bowl; thus the mush that usually results when the motor is pulsed is avoided. Most of the vegetables can be prepared a day in advance, although cucumbers are best peeled and seeded as close to eating time as possible, since they seem to acquire a sliminess rather quickly. I can't think of a vegetable or green that isn't good with bagna cauda, so choices should be made by what looks fresh and good and by price.

Part of the paella can be cooked in advance, and all the ingredients can be prepared well in advance. The final cooking does require last-minute attention, which the cook can give without guilt, knowing her guests are occupied in the living room with dipping their vegetables. The paella recipe may seem intimidating because of its length and the number of ingredients, but the time-consuming part is all in the advance preparation.

I use a 15-inch-diameter aluminum paella pan made by Leyse and available in most kitchenware shops. It has the needed six-quart capacity and can also be used for a sauté pan. However, a wok or a large sauté pan will work, as will a six-quart casserole, especially if it is wide and shallow. It is important that the rice, once it is added, is never stirred, since it will become soggy and unpleasant. The ingredients are pushed into the rice with a spoon. I have excellent results with converted rice.

The one thing that mustn't be stinted in a paella is saffron; only saffron gives the distinctive flavor that is wanted. Saffron flowers are far preferable to powdered saffron, and once you accept the fact that you will need to spend around $3 for this wonderful flavoring agent, the results absolutely justify the investment.

Many paella recipes call for precooking the shrimp, but I find that sinking the marinated raw shrimp into the rice avoids the rubberiness that shrimp take on when they are overcooked. It is very easy to peel and devein raw shrimp if you cut through the back of the shell with a good pair of kitchen scissors. The shell comes off and the black line is exposed with one motion. The line is then easily rinsed out.

Chorizos are preferable to Italian sausages, not only because they are Spanish and thus authentic, but also because they add a nice color and flavor to the paella. Chorizos can be found at Latin and Spanish stores and sometimes in supermarkets. Should they not be available, hot Italian sausages can be substituted. Some recipes for paella list mussels and clams as optional ingredients, but to me they are essential. They are quite simple to cope with, especially if the mussels have been grown on strings, which keeps them mud- and barnacle-free. They cost a bit more, but the difference is well worth the trouble saved. The easiest way to trim the beard (and mussels must be trimmed of their beards) is to hold the mussel with one hand, then grab the beard with a paring knife with the other hand, and pull down hard. If you can't find clams, double the numbers of mussels, or vice versa.

In choosing fruits, use your nose as well as your thumb, because a ripe fruit without perfume is not worth much.

Madeleine molds are available in cookware stores, and while buying two may seem an indulgence, they pack compactly and are comparatively inexpensive. It is very nice to be able to bake the entire two dozen at one time, and this recipe, from the Paris Cordon Bleu, is so sure-fire that I think the molds will get a lot of use.

Bagna Cauda with Crudités

•

¼ pound (1 stick) unsalted butter
¾ cup olive oil
4 teaspoons finely minced garlic
1 can flat anchovy fillets, drained and
 chopped

RAW
VEGETABLES

Very thin, tight-headed asparagus, the
 stalks peeled with a vegetable peeler
Cucumbers, peeled, seeded and cut into
 sticks
Zucchini, soaked, then scrubbed but
 unpeeled, and cut into sticks
Whole red radishes or white radishes
 cut into sticks

*Tiny carrots, peeled, trimmed and cut
into sticks
Cauliflower, separated into florets
Whole green beans, trimmed and
strings removed with a vegetable
peeler
Scallions, trimmed, with a few inches
of green remaining*

Cut the butter into ¼-inch slices and combine with the olive oil in a small heavy saucepan. Place over low heat and stir until the butter is melted but not foaming. Add the garlic and stir for a few seconds. Then add the anchovies and cook over the lowest heat possible, stirring until the anchovies have dissolved. This will take from 10 to 15 minutes. Pour into a bowl and set over a warming candle if you have one. Serve with a variety of the above raw vegetables, arranged on a platter or a flat basket.

Paella

•

½ *pound fresh chorizos or Italian hot
        sausages*
1 *pound raw medium shrimp*
1 *tablespoon lemon juice*
7 *tablespoons olive oil
        10-ounce package frozen tiny peas*
18 *small mussels*
18 *small cherrystone clams*
½ *pound lean bacon*
8 *chicken thighs*
1 *large onion, sliced vertically*
1 *green pepper, sliced vertically and
        seeded*
4 *cloves garlic, minced*

TO FINISH THE	3	cups chicken broth
PAELLA	1	cup beef bouillon
	1	cup dry white wine
	1	teaspoon dried saffron flowers (two .2-gram vials)
	1	bay leaf, crumbled
	½	teaspoon ground coriander
	1	teaspoon dried oregano
		Salt and pepper to taste
	2½	cups converted or short-grain rice
	1	can artichoke hearts, drained, refreshed under cold water, gently squeezed to get rid of excess moisture and halved
	½	cup drained, seeded and chopped canned imported plum tomatoes
	1	roasted red pepper, seeded, or a 4- or 5-ounce jar pimientos, cut into strips
	2	lemons, quartered
	5	tablespoons minced parsley

Simmer the chorizos or Italian sausages in water for 10 minutes, drain, and slice. Set aside.

Peel and devein the shrimp, place them in a bowl, and stir in the lemon juice and 3 tablespoons of the olive oil. Cover and refrigerate.

Bring a large saucepan of water to a boil, drop in the peas, and cook for 3 minutes. Turn the peas into a colander, refresh under cold water and refrigerate.

Scrub and debeard the mussels and scrub the clams. Place the shellfish in a colander and set the colander in a large dishpan of cold water. After 10 minutes, change the water, repeating six times to rid the shellfish of sand. Drain the shellfish and refrigerate.

Cut the bacon into a small dice and place in a large frying pan. Add the remaining 4 tablespoons of olive oil and sauté the bacon for 5 minutes. Add the reserved sliced chorizos or Italian sausages and sauté for another 5 minutes. Remove the bacon and sausage with a slotted spoon to a paella pan, wok or casserole with a 6-quart capacity.

Dry the chicken thighs and brown them over high heat on all sides in the oil remaining in the frying pan. Remove the browned chicken to the paella pan.

Add the onions, green peppers and the garlic to the frying pan and cook, covered, over low heat until the onions are soft, about 10 minutes. Remove the vegetables to the paella pan, using a slotted spoon, and discard the fat remaining in the frying pan. ❀   The dish may be done in advance to this point, cooled and then refrigerated in the paella pan.

•

Add the chicken broth, beef bouillon, wine, herbs and flavorings to the chicken, vegetables and sausage in the paella pan. Bring to a simmer, cover, and cook over low heat for 10 minutes. Remove the lid, bring the liquid to a rapid boil, and add the rice, pushing it down into the liquid with a spoon. Do not stir. Then bury the reserved peas in the rice along with the halved artichoke hearts, the tomatoes and the roasted red pepper or pimiento strips, pushing them down also with a spoon. Again, do not stir. Finally, insert the shellfish into the rice, hinged side down, and the shrimp. Reduce heat, cover the pan, and cook for another 5 minutes. Remove the lid and cook for another few minutes, or until all the liquid has been absorbed by the rice and the clams and mussels have opened. (The paella takes 20 to 25 minutes in all to cook.)

Garnish with lemon wedges, sprinkle parsley over all, and serve immediately.

Exotic Fruit Tray

•

5   *kiwis, peeled and sliced into thin rounds*
1   *pineapple, peeled, cored and cut into*
      strips
1   *cantaloupe, peeled, seeded and sliced*
      into wedges
1/4   *watermelon, rind removed, seeded and*
      cut into chunks
1   *papaya, peeled, seeded and cut into wedges*
1   *pint strawberries, washed and drained*
      but not stemmed
2   *limes, quartered*

Arrange the fruits in a pretty pattern on a platter or tray, garnish with lime wedges, ❀ and serve with madeleines.

Madeleines

MAKES 2 DOZEN

•

2	tablespoons butter, melted
	Flour to coat the molds
1⅓	cups all-purpose flour
¾	teaspoon baking powder
¼	pound (1 stick) unsalted butter, softened to room temperature
½	cup sugar
2	whole eggs
2	egg yolks
2	tablespoons framboise *or other* eau de vie *or* Cognac
½	teaspoon vanilla extract
	Confectioners' sugar

Brush two madeleine molds (each making 12 madeleines 3 inches long by 1¾ inches at their widest point across) with the melted butter. If you have only one mold, use half the butter and reserve the rest for a second baking. Sprinkle some flour into each indentation, shake the pan to distribute the flour, turn upside down, and tap out excess flour.

Sift the flour and baking powder together and set aside. Cream the butter and sugar with an electric hand mixer until light and fluffy. Add the eggs, one at a time, and then the egg yolks, beating thoroughly after each addition. Beat in the flour and baking powder mixture and then the *eau de vie* or Cognac and the vanilla. Divide the batter among 24 indentations (or half the batter among 12 indentations) and bake in a preheated 425-degree oven for 10 to 12 minutes, or until the tops are lightly browned. Turn the madeleines out onto a cake rack, set them right side up, and cool. If a second batch is needed, wash the pan, prepare it as before and repeat. ❀ Just before serving, sprinkle the madeleines with confectioners' sugar.

Cold Asparagus with Egg Vinaigrette

*Roast Butterflied Rock Cornish Hens
Stuffed Under the Skin*

Glazed Carrots

Stir-Fried Escarole

*Caramel Custard Ring with Vanilla
Cognac Whipped Cream and Fruit*

•

FIRST COURSE:
Geyser Peak Chardonnay
MAIN COURSE:
Pedroncelli Carbernet Sauvignon

*T*his spring meal deserves a center-piece of azaleas in vulgar assortment. If the idea of such blowziness offends, several small nosegays can be made of whatever tiny things are blooming in the garden. These are charming when set in equally tiny containers at each person's place. Once such weighty decisions are made, very little can go wrong with this reassuring meal. No special equipment is needed, nor is any great skill required. Yet the results are out of the ordinary, well balanced and, as such things go, inexpensive.

Spears of cold asparagus dressed with a contrapuntal lemony sauce are a perfect beginning at this time of year. They say spring, and the price gets more right each day. Next are juicy Rock Cornish hens, butterflied, stuffed under the skin and roasted to a deep brown sheen. With the hens are glazed carrots cooked in beef bouillon to provide a mild sweetness and richness, plus stir-fried escarole, a green with a nice edge to it. Once cooked, escarole miraculously loses the coarseness of its raw state, an Italian discovery from which we all benefit. Dessert is a cool, smooth caramel custard ring filled with whipped cream and surrounded by strawberries or any other full-flavored fruit. One alternative would be peaches frozen the summer before, which should in any case be emptied from the freezer now in anticipation of things to come.

To me it is worth the effort to remove from the asparagus stalks the scales and knobbles, which tend to act as sand traps. However, I feel more benign about the asparagus if I have done this mindless job while we watch the news or something. The asparagus can be cooked the evening before they are served. They might get slightly crinkled, but the sauce, which is poured on a couple of hours before serving, masks this. The flavor is still good. I get bored with the inexorable vinaigrette sprinkled with mimosa (chopped hard-cooked egg whites and their sieved yolks), so for a change I make a sauce whose deliciousness I first discovered in slightly different form on a grilled salmon steak. This is a classic but uncommon lemony vinaigrette that is thickened and smoothed with the yolks of soft-cooked eggs.

When I think chicken, I usually turn to Rock Cornish hens, because my husband claims these have some flavor of their own. He consistently insults chicken by complimenting the sauce in which it has been cooked, but the meat itself is never worthy even of comment. For this dish I buy the larger Rock Cornish hens, which weigh around 1½ to 1¾ pounds. Half a hen is then ample for each person. By butterflying them — cutting through their backs and flattening them — they can be carved simply by being snipped through the middle before they are placed on a serving platter. And because I stuff them under the skin, the birds remain moist without needing to be basted or having any other attentions paid during their cooking. I prepare the birds and the stuffing the day before the dinner. The stuffing gets patted under the skin just before they go into the oven, a process that takes no more than 15 minutes.

Rock Cornish hens prepared in this way are also very good cold. I sometimes cook an extra one for the next day, and we eat it with a cucumber salad or, when they get to taste like real food, tomatoes.

The carrots can be cooked in advance and finished just before serving. The escarole is stir-fried in no time but at the last minute.

While caramel custard does not suggest great festivity, when it is made in a ring filled with whipped cream and surrounded by fruit, it looks impressive and tastes even better. Cognac plus vanilla can be used to flavor the whipped cream, although I reach for my Vanilla Cognac (see April, Provisioning the Pantry) for its deeper richness. The caramel custard ring can be made the day before the party but is completed just before serving.

Asparagus with Egg Vinaigrette

•

40	*spears of tight-headed, medium-plump asparagus*
4	*large eggs*
3	*shallots, finely minced*
1	*teaspoon Dijon mustard*
	Salt and coarsely ground pepper to taste
¹/₂	*cup olive oil*
¹/₂	*cup peanut oil*
2	*tablespoons finely minced parsley*
1	*tablespoon finely cut chives*
3	*tablespoons lemon juice*
1	*tablespoon good red wine vinegar*

Line the asparagus spears up at the heads and cut off the ends to fit either a steamer or a 12-inch frying pan. Trim off the scales with a small paring knife if such refinements are worth the effort to you, and rinse the asparagus. To cook in boiling water in a frying pan, tie the spears with soft kitchen twine into bundles of 10. They can be removed more quickly when they are cooked. Or stand the stalks in the upper portion of an asparagus steamer and set it over boiling water. Start testing the spears after 8 minutes with the tip of a sharp, thin knife. They are done when they are crisp-soft. Turn the asparagus onto a dish towel to drain and arrange them on a serving platter. (Cut the strings if you have made bundles.) Cool, cover with plastic wrap, and ❀ refrigerate until an hour or two before serving.

For the sauce, soft-boil the eggs for 3 minutes if they are at room temperature, or 3½ minutes if they have just come out of the refrigerator. Put them under cold water to stop the cooking and cool the shells so they can be handled. Crack the eggs in half and scoop the yolks into a warmed bowl. Discard the whites and the shells. Whisk in the shallots, mustard, salt and pepper. Add the oils slowly, whisking all the time, as though you were making a mayonnaise. Beat in the parsley, chives, lemon juice and vinegar. Taste. If the dressing is too acid, add a little more oil. If it is too flat, add a little more vinegar. Adjust the other seasonings. ❀ If the dish is not to be served immediately, the sauce can be refrigerated for at least a day. You may have to whisk it before pouring it over the asparagus.

About an hour before your guests arrive, remove the asparagus from the refrigerator, dress it with the sauce, and set aside. ❀

Butterflied Rock Cornish Hens
Stuffed Under the Skin

•

4	Rock Cornish hens, about 1¾ pounds each
12	ounces cream cheese
1½	cups fresh bread crumbs
	Livers, hearts and gizzards of the hens
4	tablespoons butter
2	tablespoons minced shallots
4	tablespoons minced parsley
½	teaspoon dried tarragon
½	teaspoon salt
½	teaspoon pepper
2	cups chicken stock
	Watercress or parsley (optional)

Defrost the hens if only the frozen were available and set aside the gizzards, hearts and livers for the stuffing. Cut off the wing tips and put these along with the necks into a plastic bag and freeze. (When you have accumulated enough you can cook them in water with some carrot, celery and onion and make a stock.) Put the birds, one at a time, on their breasts on a work surface. Take a good sharp pair of kitchen shears and start cutting around the tail and along the backbone, straight up through the back. Trim off the backbone and the tail and add these to your stock bag. Then turn the birds skin-side-up and give the breastbone a good whack to break it and flatten the hen. Next you separate the skin from the meat. The skin tends to adhere only at the center of the breast. Snip at these places with shears, but cut against the meat, not the skin. Work with your fingers gently and enlarge the pocket into the thighs. ❀   The hens can be refrigerated for a day.

To prepare the stuffing, bring the cream cheese to room temperature to soften it and beat it together with the bread crumbs. (These can be made in seconds in a food processor.) Peel the gizzards and mince them. Mince the hearts. Cut away any green or fat from the livers and mince them. Heat 2 tablespoons of the butter in an 8-inch frying pan and cook the shallots for about 2 minutes. Add the minced giblets and cook for another 3 minutes. Remove from heat and beat into the cheese-bread crumb mixture. Add the parsley, tarragon, salt and pepper. ❀   If the birds are not going to be cooked immediately, refrigerate the stuffing.

Before assembling and cooking the hens, preheat the oven to 425 degrees. Lightly grease a roasting pan large enough to hold all the birds, or use two pans. Take a quarter of the stuffing at a time and work it in between the flesh and the skin of the birds. Move it around into the thighs and pat the birds until the stuffing makes a relatively smooth layer. Place the hens in the pan and brush them with the remaining 2 tablespoons butter, melted. Cook for 1 hour and remove to a board to set for 15 minutes.

Deglaze the pan drippings with the chicken stock and reduce by half. Serve the sauce separately in a bowl. Snip the birds down the middle with kitchen shears and arrange on a serving platter. If the platter is large enough, alternate around the edge bundles of carrots, which will have been glazed while the birds were resting, and the escarole, which would have been stir-fried at the same time. Otherwise, serve the vegetables in separate dishes but decorate the hens with watercress or parsley.

Glazed Carrots

•

> 2   pounds carrots, scraped
> 4   tablespoons butter
> 1½   cups beef bouillon, plus water if
>   necessary
> 1   tablespoon sugar
>   Salt and pepper to taste

Cut each carrot into 3-inch pieces and round off each end to make little carrots. (Add the carrot trimmings to the stock bag and freeze them.) Put the carrots into a shallow sauté pan or a frying pan, cover them with cold water, bring them quickly to a boil over high heat, and cook for 2 minutes.

Put the carrots in a colander and drain them. Melt the butter in the pan, add the carrots, and pour in the bouillon. The carrots should be barely covered. Add water if necessary. Bring to a boil, lower the heat, and simmer, covered, for about 20 minutes. Shake the pan and check for doneness and amount of liquid remaining. There should be almost no liquid left by the time the carrots are tender. It may be necessary to add water to complete the cooking. ✿   The carrots can be set aside at this point.

Just before they are served, reheat the carrots, shaking the pan to make sure they don't burn. Add the sugar, cover the pan, and shake it for 2 or 3 minutes. Then uncover the pan and shake it for another minute, or until the carrots are shiny and lightly browned. Season lightly with salt and pepper.

Stir-Fried Escarole

•

> 4   pounds escarole
> 2   tablespoons butter
> 2   tablespoons peanut oil
>   Juice of ½ lemon
> ¼   cup chicken stock

Wash and dry the escarole, separate and trim the leaves, and roll into packets. Slice these crosswise into a chiffonade.✿   This can be done a few
hours in advance of cooking. Refrigerate until needed. Heat the butter and
oil in a wide-bottomed pan with about a 6-quart capacity. (The escarole will
be bulky, but it will cook down to less than a quarter of its raw volume.)

Toss the escarole to coat it with the butter and oil, add the lemon juice
and stock and, over high heat, cook, stirring continuously, until almost soft,
about 5 or 6 minutes. Drain the escarole in a strainer over a bowl (and
freeze the juices for stock).

Caramel Custard Ring
with Vanilla Cognac
Whipped Cream and Fruit

•

FOR THE CARAMEL	*1 cup sugar*
FOR THE CUSTARD	*6 eggs*
	½ cup sugar
	1 teaspoon vanilla extract
	Pinch of salt
	4 cups scalded milk
FOR THE TOPPING	*1 cup whipping cream*
	1 tablespoon sugar
	1 tablespoon Vanilla Cognac (see April, Provisioning the Pantry) or 1 tablespoon Cognac and ¼ teaspoon vanilla extract
	2 cups fresh strawberries or frozen blueberries, peaches or raspberries (not packed in syrup), defrosted

Place the cup of sugar in an 8-inch frying pan, put it over moderate heat, and cook it, without stirring, until it caramelizes. The syrup should be the color of walnut, not mahogany. Pour it into a 12-inch ring mold and, holding the mold with potholders, rotate it to coat the bottom. (You can use two 6- or 7-inch ring molds. The cooking time for the custard will be cut by about 10 minutes.)

Bring a large kettle of water to a boil and reduce the flame so the water simmers. Beat the eggs together with the ½ cup of sugar, vanilla and salt. Then beat in the scalded milk. Set the mold in a roasting pan, pour the mixture into the mold (some will be left over), and put the roasting pan on the center rack of the oven, preheated to 350 degrees. If some of the mixture spills into the roasting pan, replenish the mold with whatever has remained. With the door open, add enough hot water to the roasting pan to reach halfway up the sides of the mold. Try to do this quickly. Then shut the oven door and bake the custard for about 50 to 60 minutes, or until a knife comes out clean.

Lift the mold out of the water and cool it on a cake rack.❁   Refrigerate overnight. Before serving, loosen both edges with a knife and turn out by inverting a serving dish on top of the mold and then flipping both over to release the custard. Whip the cream together with the tablespoon of sugar, and the Vanilla Cognac or Cognac and vanilla until it just holds its shape. It shouldn't be too stiff. Spoon the cream into the center, and arrange the fruit around the outside edge of the custard.

May

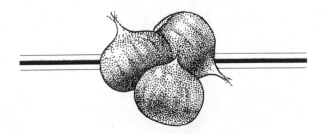

Chestnuts
in Cognac Syrup

MAKES ABOUT 3 CUPS

•

16⅓-ounce jar roasted whole chestnuts
    (imported from France)
2   cups sugar
1½   cups water
½   vanilla bean (split in half lengthwise),
    cut into 3-inch pieces
⅔   cup Cognac

Place the chestnuts in a colander, rinse under cold running water, drain well, and set aside. Combine the sugar and water in a saucepan and bring to the boil, stirring. Lower heat, add the pieces of vanilla bean, and simmer for 10 minutes without stirring. Add the drained chestnuts and cook for 1 minute after the syrup comes back to the boil. Remove from heat, cool, and stir in the Cognac. Serve over ice cream, with puddings or on plain cakes. The chestnuts will keep under refrigeration indefinitely.

Seviche

Whole Loins of Lamb

Minted New Potatoes

Cherry Tomatoes with Chives

Asparagus with Orange Butter

Parslied Carrots

Mandarin Mousse

•

FIRST COURSE:
Louis M. Martini Gewürztraminer or Hugel Gewürztraminer
MAIN COURSE:
Château Léoville-Las-Cases

This festive meal starts with a refreshing seviche made with bay scallops or any firm, white-fleshed fish "cooked" overnight in fresh lime juice and seasoned with avocado, tomato, scallion, a bit of jalapeño pepper, fresh cilantro and other spices. The seviche is a fine palate-jogger for the simple but very special main course. Whole loins of lamb are first roasted, then broiled and carved into elegant chops and served surrounded with bouquets of fresh vegetables. Dessert is a mandarin chocolate mousse, made from a recipe I abandoned years ago when chocolate mousses began to be called "wicked" and became *de rigueur* at every dinner party. It is an anachronism whose time has come once again.

Only the freshest scallops or fish will do for the seviche. If fish is used, the fillets must be thoroughly skinned and checked over for bones before they are cut up. I use small scallops, especially when they are plentiful and reasonable. Cilantro (also sold as Chinese parsley or fresh coriander) is sometimes available at supermarkets. It is always, or almost always, to be found at Hispanic stores — and at every kind of Asian store, since it is an essential ingredient for all cuisines from the Indian subcontinent through Southeast Asia to Korea and Japan. Tomatoes remain tasteless and will until the local crop comes in, so this recipe calls for the more flavorful cherry tomatoes, borrowing from one of the pints used as an accompaniment to the lamb.

As impressive a main course as whole loins of lamb are, I would never serve them for dinner parties until I figured out a way to cook them that didn't keep me in the kitchen for a half hour before they came to the table. I now preroast the loins in a very hot oven and then let them rest while the first course is being eaten. Just before the lamb is to be served, the loins are seared under a hot broiler and carved into charming little chops whose insides are perfection-pink, not red, and whose outsides are beautifully browned.

A loin of lamb weighs around 1¾ pounds and yields eight decent chops. Two loins are ample for eight people, especially when served with several vegetables. Whole loins can be found at fancy butcher shops, but I buy mine at a supermarket with a reputation for good meat. They must be ordered a day or two before they are wanted, to salvage them before they are cut up into chops. Butchers are obliging about cracking through the chine bone so that the loins can be carved easily. New Zealand loins are sometimes available in frozen food cases and are somewhat less expensive, but I do not buy them because the chine bone is intact, which makes the loins difficult to carve, and because New Zealand lamb often has a strong taste that I have never become accustomed to. A simple lemon juice and oil marinade seasoned only with a couple of branches of fresh rosemary gives the lamb a delicate lift.

If the potatoes are put on to boil when you sit down for the first course, they will be cooked by the time the lamb is carved. The fresh mint makes the potatoes even fresher and, of course, is superior with the lamb. The cherry tomatoes, which are critical for color, must be only heated through very quickly, no more than perhaps three minutes, for any real cooking will result in shriveled, collapsed balloons. The chives are elegant with tomatoes.

The asparagus can be deknobbed or peeled (a bore, but it pays dividends in tenderness and elimination of sand) and tied into bundles a good day in advance. They are put on to cook while the first-course dishes are being cleared and will be ready when the lamb is carved. Nobody wants soggy asparagus, but I think it is a mistake to undercook them so that their flavor is pale and imprisoned. The grated orange rind in the butter is delicious with asparagus.

The mandarin mousse is a heady combination of chocolate and orange. The recipe does not use sugar, nor is whipped cream folded through the mixture, as is called for in many mousses. But it would be foolish to call this anything but rich. The mixture seems quite liquid when it is poured into little pots or the serving dish. However, it becomes much more substantial, although it still remains airy, after sitting in the refrigerator for a few hours. The mousse can easily be made a day in advance. The little bit of whipped cream garnish softens the flavor, and the grated orange rind is pleasant to the eye and the palate.

Seviche

•

1 pound fresh bay scallops or 1 pound skinless, completely boneless, firm-fleshed, white fish fillets, cut into ¼-inch dice

½ cup fresh lime juice

1 ripe avocado

10 cherry tomatoes

7 to 8 scallions with half their green tops, thinly sliced

2 canned jalapeño peppers, chopped

1 teaspoon ground coriander

3 tablespoons olive oil

1 tablespoon wine vinegar

4 tablespoons chopped fresh cilantro
Salt and pepper to taste
Lettuce (optional)

The day before the seviche is to be served, remove the tendons from the scallops, wash, and drain. Or wash and drain the diced fish. Place in a bowl, add the lime juice, cover with plastic wrap, ❀ and refrigerate overnight. A few hours before the seviche is to be eaten, use a slotted spoon to remove the scallops or fish to another bowl. Reserve the lime juice. Peel and stone the avocado, cut it into ¼-inch dice, and add to the lime juice. Swirl the avocado pieces around in the juice to coat them well, and then remove the avocado with a slotted spoon and add to the scallops or fish. Add a tablespoon or two of the lime juice if desired and discard the remaining juice.

Cut the stem ends out of the cherry tomatoes and squeeze the seeds and juices out into the sink. Chop the tomatoes and add to the scallops. Then add the scallions, jalapeño peppers, ground coriander, oil and vinegar. Cover the bowl with plastic wrap and refrigerate. ❀ Just before serving, drain off most of the excess liquid and stir in the chopped cilantro. Taste for salt and pepper. Serve the seviche on lettuce leaf cups or in medium-size scallop shells.

Whole Loins of Lamb

•

2 *whole loins of lamb, about 1¾ pounds each*
Juice of half a lemon
4 *tablespoons peanut oil*
2 *tablespoons olive oil*
2 *sprigs fresh tarragon*

Ask the butcher to crack the chine bone on each loin so that the loins can be carved into 16 chops, or 8 chops from each loin. Trim off as much fat as possible. In the process of removing the fat from the inside curved portion of the loins, end strips of meat will be left with only a flimsy attachment. Don't worry about this.

The day before the lamb is to be cooked, place the loins in a dish or pan large enough to hold them, along with the lemon juice, the oils and the tarragon. Cover and refrigerate, turning the loins in the marinade whenever you remember to. ✿   Bring the meat in this marinade to room temperature before cooking.

Remove the loins from the marinade and reserve the marinade. Place the loins curved side down on a rack in a roasting pan and leave as much space as possible between them. Tuck the strips of end meat in toward the bone. Half an hour before you are to sit down to the first course, place the loins in a preheated 450-degree oven and cook them for 25 minutes. Do not bother to turn them. Remove from the oven and set aside. The internal temperature should be just below 140 degrees. Turn off the oven and turn on the broiler to preheat it. ✿

To finish off the loins, paint them with the marinade and place them under the broiler, directly on the grids, about 4 inches from the source of heat. Broil for 3 minutes on one side and 2 minutes on the other. Remove to a carving board.

To carve, remove the thin end strips of meat and slice them into bite-size morsels. Then carve the loins into 16 chops. Arrange the chops down the center of a large serving platter and end with the morsels. Arrange the vegetables around the meat and serve.

Minted New Potatoes

•

16 *small new potatoes, of uniform size,*
     unpeeled and scrubbed
1 *teaspoon salt*
2 *tablespoons melted butter*
1 *tablespoon minced fresh mint*

Place the potatoes in a pan containing an inch of boiling water and 1 teaspoon salt. Cover and cook the potatoes until tender, about 15 minutes. Drain. Place on a section of the lamb loin platter, drizzle with butter, and sprinkle with mint.

Cherry Tomatoes with Chives

•

2 tablespoons butter
2 pints less 10 cherry tomatoes (for the
    Seviche), washed and stemmed
2 large cloves garlic, crushed
2 tablespoons chopped chives

Combine the butter, tomatoes and garlic in a sauté pan large enough to hold the tomatoes in one layer. 🏵 About 5 minutes before serving, place the pan over medium heat and cook, shaking the pan occasionally, until the tomatoes are heated through, but remove from heat before the skins burst. Turn out onto a section of the lamb loin platter and sprinkle with chives.

Asparagus
with Orange Butter

•

24 medium-thin asparagus (about 2
    pounds)
2 tablespoons butter
1 tablespoon grated orange rind
    Salt and pepper to taste

Peel the asparagus with a potato peeler, working from just below the head to the base, or nip off each knob on the stalk below the head, using a small, sharp paring knife. Trim the bottoms to make even-size spears. Tie the spears into three bundles of eight, using soft butcher's twine.

Bring about 2 inches of water to a boil in a large frying pan, add the asparagus bundles, and cook for 4 minutes. Turn the bundles over and cook for another 3 minutes, or until the asparagus are tender but retain some crispness. Remove to a dry dish towel, cut the strings holding the bundles, and drain on the towel.

Melt the butter in a small pan with the orange rind, salt and pepper. Place the asparagus on a section of the lamb loin platter and pour the orange butter over the spears.

Parslied Carrots

•

2 *pounds young carrots, scraped and trimmed*
1½ *tablespoons sugar*
Pinch of salt
4 *tablespoons butter*
1 *tablespoon chopped parsley*

If the carrots are small, leave them whole. If they are large, cut them into 3-inch pieces and shape the ends so that they look like whole, small, plump carrots. Combine the carrots, sugar, salt and butter in a saucepan and add enough water barely to cover them. Bring to a boil and cook, uncovered, until the carrots are tender but still crisp and the liquid has a syrupy consistency. This can take 15 minutes or longer, and must be watched at the end. ✤ These carrots can be prepared in advance and reheated before serving. However, take care to shake the pan constantly to keep them from burning. Place on a section of the lamb loin platter and sprinkle with minced parsley.

Mandarin Mousse

•

6   ounces bittersweet chocolate, preferably
     Belgian or Swiss
6   tablespoons orange juice
2   tablespoons Cointreau, Triple Sec or
     Grand Marnier
6   eggs, separated
½   cup heavy cream
     Grated rind of 1 brightly colored
     orange

Place the chocolate and the orange juice in the top of a double boiler and set over hot water until melted. Remove from heat, stir a few times, add the orange liqueur, and stir again. Set aside.

Beat the egg yolks with an electric beater for about 5 minutes, or until they are very thick and pale yellow. Beat the chocolate mixture into the yolks. With clean beaters, beat the egg whites until they are stiff but not dry. Fold the whites into the chocolate mixture. Spoon the mousse into a 6-cup serving dish, or into 8 to 10 individual *pots de crème* or custard cups, and refrigerate for at least 6 hours.❀   Just before serving, beat the cream until quite stiff. Place a dollop of whipped cream on top of each individual mousse and sprinkle some of the orange rind over it. Or serve the cream in a bowl, sprinkle with the orange rind, and pass separately.

Ham and Asparagus Rolls with Sherry Vinegar-Hazelnut Oil Sauce

Spiced Fish and Shrimp Stew

American Strawberry Shortcake

•

FIRST COURSE:
Fino Sherry (Tío Pepe or Averys Fino)
MAIN COURSE:
Simi Rosé of Cabernet Sauvignon
or Pedroncelli Zinfandel Rosé

*T*his meal includes plentiful, reasonably priced spring foods that have already begun to pall, so they are prepared in ways to whet and jog the senses.

The first course has asparagus — yet again, so cheap, so available, so, dare it be said, boring. But here it is made into a mystery with a lovely mayonnaise flavored with sherry vinegar from Spain and hazelnut oil from France. The cooked asparagus, rolled in a thin slice of baked or Smithfield ham or prosciutto, is good to look at and to eat.

Next is a spicy fish and shrimp stew that, despite the quantity of its Indian flavorings, owes allegiance to no one country or even continent. A heady amalgam of tastes, the stew is a soupy dish in which the amounts of fish and shrimp go a long way. It is served over rice in a soup plate and eaten with a spoon. Dessert is the uncomplicated deliciousness of real

American strawberry shortcake, with the berries piled on and between flaky halves of buttered, special baking powder biscuits topped with lightly whipped, barely sweetened, flavored whipped cream. This is a far cry from the ignominious so-called strawberry shortcake based on pale, commercial, packaged sponge cake and makes a clean ending to the mélange of tastes that precede it.

The first course can be prepared in advance — the sauce the day before, the asparagus perhaps cooked in the morning — and assembled just before you sit down. An affinity among asparagus, sherry vinegar and hazelnut oil, two exotica of the *nouvelle cuisine* available in specialty food and cookware stores, results in a nuttiness with a tiny overlay of muskiness that I find very agreeable. (Hazelnut oil should always be kept in the refrigerator after the tin or bottle has been opened; no other oil I know will turn rancid as quickly.) The basis of the sauce is the thick processor mayonnaise that is so adaptable to many variations. Those who are not ready for experimentation can make a delicious sauce by substituting lemon juice for the sherry vinegar in the recipe, by using all peanut oil and no hazelnut oil and by thinning the result with a well-flavored sherry such as Dry Sack.

Supermarket delicatessens are usually willing to cut thin slices of baked ham or Smithfield ham on request. Prosciutto should be bought only at Italian groceries or specialty food stores that do a brisk business, to assure buying it at its best. A small bit of the sauce smeared over the slice of ham holds the asparagus nicely in place. The sauce can also be used to "glue" two small pieces of ham together if large enough slices cannot be found. The asparagus should be peeled or deknobbed before being cooked and cut to even lengths. The heads are placed on the ham so that they stick out on one side; thus, when the ham is rolled, nobody has to wonder just what is in there.

The stock for the fish stew can be made two days or more in advance, but the fish and shrimp should not even be bought until the day they are to be eaten. While frames and heads of nonoily fish make the best stock, the clam juice–white wine reduction is acceptable and an easy substitute for the real thing, especially in this stew whose spices tend to obliterate subtleties. If fish frames and heads are to be had, these should be either made into a stock and frozen or frozen as is and used when such refinements make a difference.

The base for the stew — the actual soup in which the fish is cooked — should be made at least a day in advance and allowed to sit in the refrigerator overnight to blend its flavors. Red pepper in quantities up to a tablespoon can be used, depending on the cook's preferences. The only thing left for the night of the party is to cook the fish and shrimp in the soup, check the seasonings and put the rice on. Any leftover stew is delicious reheated the next day.

Pound cake and sponge-cake bases for strawberry shortcake may be acceptable for some, but as any New Englander or Southerner knows, the genuine article is made with baking powder biscuits, split and slathered with sweet butter the minute they are removed from the oven. The shortcake recipe here, with its sugar and extra shortening, and the tips for successful biscuit-making, came from Dorothy Lagemann, who learned all from her North Carolinian mother. Foremost, biscuit dough must not be worked any more than absolutely necessary. Although the shortening can be cut in with a pastry blender, my friend has a mystical feeling about the fork, which she feels belongs to biscuit-making. She mixes the dry ingredients, cuts the shortening in and stirs in the milk to make a dough, all with this homely utensil. Bleached flour will result in a whiter biscuit, but those with no objections to a slightly tan color can make a delicious biscuit with unbleached flour. The amount of milk listed is meant to vary with the flour, but I have never used more than the minimum. The mixture is stirred just until a dough forms and comes away from the sides of the bowl. It is then turned out onto a lightly floured board, where it is kneaded only three times and then patted, never rolled out, to the desired thickness. The large cutter makes a generous single portion. The extra biscuit or two from the recipe can be offered as seconds. If the baked biscuits contain brown flecks, the shortening wasn't cut in finely enough. Even a desultory cook can prepare these biscuits from start to oven-readiness in less than 20 minutes.

Ham and Asparagus Rolls
with Sherry Vinegar-Hazelnut
Oil Sauce

•

FOR THE SAUCE		
	1	*egg yolk*
	2	*teaspoons sherry vinegar*
	1/2	*cup peanut oil*
	3	*tablespoons hazelnut oil*
		Salt and pepper to taste

| FOR THE ROLLS | 8 | thin slices baked ham, prosciutto or Smithfield ham, each slice about 5 inches wide and 5 to 6 inches long, or 16 smaller slices that can be pieced to make the needed size |
| | 32 | medium or 40 thin stalks asparagus, cleaned and peeled, cut into equal lengths, cooked and cooled |

Place the egg yolk and sherry vinegar in a food processor bowl and process for about a minute. With the motor running, slowly add the peanut oil through the feed tube, then the hazelnut oil. Add salt and pepper to taste. ✿

To assemble the rolls, spread each ham slice with a bit of the sauce. If two slices are needed to construct one of the size needed, overlap them slightly and paint on some sauce to hold the pieces together. Then place little packets of 4 or 5 asparagus spears on the edge of the ham, allowing the spears to protrude. Roll and place seam side down on individual plates. Garnish with a dollop of the remaining sauce.

Spiced Fish and Shrimp Stew

•

FOR THE STOCK	Four	8-ounce bottles clam juice
	3	cups water
	2	cups dry white wine
	1	onion, sliced
	1	stalk celery, cut into 1-inch pieces
FOR THE STEW	5	tablespoons olive oil
	1½	cups minced onions
	2½	tablespoons curry powder, preferably Madras

2	tablespoons powdered cumin
Two	1-pound, 12-ounce cans imported plum tomatoes, drained well and processed briefly to a coarse purée
6	cups fish stock (from above)
2	teaspoons dried thyme leaves
½	teaspoon to 1 tablespoon crushed red pepper (optional)
3	large garlic cloves, crushed
2	cups dry white wine
2	pounds fresh cod or haddock, or other firm white fish, cut into large chunks
¾	pound medium shrimp, shelled and deveined
	Salt and pepper to taste
1½	cups converted rice
4	tablespoons minced parsley

To make the stock, use a stainless steel, enameled or other nonreactive pan. Combine all stock ingredients and cook uncovered for 30 minutes over medium heat. Strain the liquid and measure. If necessary, return to pan and reduce to 6 cups. If there is less than 6 cups, make up the difference with white wine. Cool, cover and ❀ refrigerate until needed.

To make the stew, heat the oil in a 6-quart stainless steel, enameled or other nonreactive pan, add the onions, and cook for about 7 minutes, or until soft and transparent. Do not let brown. Add the curry powder and cumin and cook, stirring constantly, another 3 minutes. Add tomatoes, stock, thyme, optional red pepper, crushed garlic and wine. Bring to a simmer and cook, uncovered, over medium-low heat for 20 minutes. This makes the soup that constitutes the base for the stew and is best made a day or two before. Cool, cover, and ❀ refrigerate until needed.

About 45 minutes before the stew is to be served, bring the base to a simmer and add the fish. Cook only until it begins to lose its transparency and do not be concerned that it breaks into smaller pieces or flakes. Turn off heat, cover, and let "ripen" on the stove for about 30 minutes. Just before serving, bring to a simmer, add the shrimp, and cook over low heat for 3 to 5 minutes to cook the shrimp. Taste for salt and pepper.

About 20 to 25 minutes before the stew is to be served, cook the rice according to directions on the package.

To serve, place some hot rice on the bottom of a shallow soup plate, ladle fish and shrimp stew over it, and garnish with minced parsley.

American
Strawberry Shortcake

•

FOR THE	2	*pints ripe strawberries*
STRAWBERRIES	2	*tablespoons sugar*
	1	*tablespoon Kirsch*
FOR THE	2	*cups bleached all-purpose flour*
BISCUITS	1	*tablespoon baking powder*
	2	*tablespoons sugar*
	1	*tablespoon salt*
	6	*tablespoons vegetable shortening*
⅔ to 1	*cup milk*	
		Unsalted butter to butter the biscuits
FOR THE	½	*pint heavy cream*
TOPPING	1	*tablespoon sugar*
	½	*tablespoon or more Kirsch or ½ teaspoon vanilla extract*

Prepare the strawberries a few hours before serving by rinsing, stemming and slicing them. Place in a bowl, stir in the sugar and the Kirsch, cover, and ❋ refrigerate until needed.

Up to an hour before sitting down to dinner, prepare the biscuits. Combine the dry ingredients in a bowl and mix together with a fork. Cut in the shortening with either a fork or a pastry blender until the mixture resembles coarse cornmeal. Make a well in the center and add the milk, beginning with the minimum amount. Using a fork, gather the dry ingredients into the milk until a dough forms and pulls away from the sides of the bowl. Add more milk if necessary. Work lightly and do not mix more than necessary. Turn the dough onto a lightly floured board and knead three times. Then pat the dough out until it is ½ inch thick. Cut out biscuits with a 3-inch cutter and work scraps lightly together to make a last biscuit. Place on an ungreased baking sheet or jelly-roll pan and bake in a preheated 400-degree oven for 10 minutes, or until the biscuits are lightly browned. Remove from oven, split the biscuits in half, and slather the insides with butter. Replace the tops and set aside on a plate until needed. ❁

Just before assembling the shortcakes, make the topping. Whip the cream with the sugar until it is lightly whipped. It should not be stiff. Beat in the Kirsch or vanilla.

To assemble the shortcakes, place the bottoms of the biscuits on individual dessert plates, pile each with sliced strawberries and a bit of the juices that will have accumulated, top with the lids, pile with more strawberries, and drizzle the cream over them.

Fresh peaches, when they come into season, are a wonderful substitution for the strawberries.

Shrimp in Wine Sauce

Duck with Pears in Aspic

Salad with Duck Livers, Hearts and Crispy Skins

Strawberry-Almond Cup

•

FIRST COURSE:
Pouilly-Fuissé
MAIN COURSE:
Juliénas

*T*his most stylish meal satisfies yearn-
ings for balanced elegance. It starts with a stellar first course of warm
herbed shrimp and finely julienned vegetables in a sauce worth eating by
itself. Next comes a cold main course of succulent duck and pears in aspic
whose flavor is underscored with a fragrant pear vinegar. With the aspic is
a fashionable salad that combines the fresh sweetness of Boston lettuce with
slices of broiled livers and hearts of the ducks and bits of their crispy skins.
The salad presents delicious contrasts in taste and texture and looks very
handsome. For the end, there is an unusual and wonderful concoction of
strawberries and almonds baked in a sabayonlike cream and served warm
in champagne glasses.

Nothing is wasted in this meal. Even the shells of the shrimp are used to deepen the flavor of the sauce. The dish's component parts are prepared quickly before guests arrive, with the final assembly taking about three minutes just before diners sit down. Dry white wine (and there is nothing wrong with using a decent jug wine here) is cooked down with the shrimp shells and some minced shallots; the strained reduction is simmered with cream and finished with an egg-yolk enrichment. The sauce is poured over the lightly sautéed vegetables and shrimp, which have been flavored with fresh herbs. The dish is served with fork and spoon so that not a drop of the sauce need be left behind.

One of the joys of May is to see fresh tarragon pushing up in the garden or to find tarragon and young basil plants at herb specialists and nurseries. Basil, if it is used for flavoring, can be gathered by pinching back the top shoots, which will benefit the young plants later and the dish now. Should neither fresh tarragon nor basil be available, do not used dried. Simply stick to parsley.

The main course is equally frugal in its use of every bit of each ingredient. The preparation is done in two stages, starting two days before the dinner. First, the ducks are roasted in a hot oven. They need no attention during this process, not even to be pronged with a fork to drain off fat, since the cooked skins will be peeled and crisped later for the salad. After the meat is removed from the birds, the carcasses are crushed and used with wing, thigh and leg bones as the basis for the aspic. Those willing to sacrifice the satisfaction derived from such commendable thrift can use canned chicken broth for the aspic's liquid, but the end product, while acceptable, is not as good. Some of the stock is also used to deglaze the roasting pan juices so that none of the goodness is lost.

The inspiration for this dish came from a wonderful pear vinegar I found at a specialty store. The vinegar combines the quintessence of pears with a mild acidity that benefits both the pears and the aspic. The pears, which should be hard but have perfume, are cooked with a little sugar and some of the vinegar. All the tendons and membranes that make duck tough are carefully removed from the meat along with all fat, and the meat is cut into a coarse julienne. By placing the pieces of duck and pear wedges so that they radiate in a sun shape from the center to the edges of the mold or bowl, wedges of the aspic can be cut without resistance for serving. The aspic can be unmolded an hour or two before guests arrive and held in the refrigerator. When the meal begins, it is brought out and allowed to sit at room temperature to rid it of its chill.

Since they keep better cooked than raw, the livers and hearts are broiled in advance, preferably the day the ducks are cooked. An hour or two before serving, they are sliced thinly and added to the salad, which then remains at room temperature. The skins from the cooked ducks are snipped into quarter-inch pieces and sautéed, also an hour or two before serving, to crisp them and render any remaining fat. They drain on paper towels and are added at the last minute, just before the mildly mustardy vinaigrette is poured over the salad.

The strawberry-almond cup can be assembled in the afternoon, refrigerated and brought to room temperature before its final cooking. It is either placed in a hot oven when you sit down for the main course or put under the broiler for a few minutes just before serving. The dish consists of a *crème pâtissière* enriched with cream flavored with *framboise*, my preference, or Grand Marnier or whatever you think helps strawberries. A bottom layer of cream is poured into a gratin dish. This is topped with halved berries that have been macerated in the liqueur of choice along with toasted almond slivers and covered with the remainder of the cream. When the dish is baked, the result is creamy but still liquid. The broiled version has a firmer, and I think better, texture. The dessert is spooned into flat champagne glasses, sprinkled with more toasted almonds, and served warm.

Shrimp in Wine Sauce

•

FOR THE SHRIMP	1¾	*pounds medium shrimp (40 to 50 count)*
	1	*large carrot, peeled and trimmed*
	1	*large inner stalk celery, strings removed*
	4	*tablespoons butter*
	2	*tablespoons minced parsley*
	2	*tablespoons minced fresh tarragon or basil*
FOR THE SAUCE	4	*cups dry white wine*
	4	*tablespoons minced shallots*
		Reserved shells from the shrimp
	1½	*cups heavy cream*
	2	*egg yolks*

Shell the shrimp by cutting through the backs with kitchen shears. Place the shells in a colander, rinse under cold running water, and reserve for the sauce. Devein the shrimp and rinse under cold running water. Place the cleaned shrimp in a bowl, cover, and refrigerate.

Cut the carrot and celery into a very fine 2-inch-long julienne. Cook the vegetables in the butter in a medium-large sauté pan or frying pan for about 5 minutes, or until they are cooked but retain a bit of crispness. Leave in the pan and set aside.

Combine the wine, shallots and shrimp shells in a nonreactive saucepan and cook over medium heat for about 15 to 20 minutes, or until the liquid has reduced to 1 cup. Strain the liquid into another nonreactive saucepan, pushing down on the shells to extract all the fluid. If more than 1 cup remains, reduce further over medium heat. Add 1 cup of the cream and simmer for 5 minutes. Set aside. ✿

To finish the shrimp and the sauce, add the shrimp to the pan with the vegetables, and sauté over medium heat, turning the shrimp, for about 3 minutes, or until the shrimp take on a pink color and stiffen. Beat the remaining ½ cup of cream with the egg yolks. Bring the wine-cream reduction to the simmer and whisk in the egg-yolk-cream mixture. Cook, stirring, over low heat until the sauce thickens, but do not let it boil. Meanwhile, heat the shrimp and julienned vegetables and stir in the minced parsley and tarragon or basil. Pour the sauce over the shrimp and stir to mix thoroughly. Serve immediately in gratin dishes, in small soufflé dishes or on first-course plates, apportioning the shrimp evenly and spooning the sauce over them. Serve with forks and spoons for the sauce.

Duck with Pears
in Aspic

•

FOR THE DUCKS   *Two*   *4-pound ducks, defrosted if frozen; wing tips, necks and gizzards reserved, if desired, for stock; hearts and livers reserved for the salad (see following recipe)*

FOR THE STOCK (OPTIONAL BUT DESIRABLE)		*Wing tips, necks and gizzards of the ducks, chopped, if possible, into 1-inch pieces*
		Carcasses of the cooked ducks, broken up, plus wing, thigh and leg bones without meat
	3	*carrots, peeled, trimmed and cut into 2-inch chunks*
	3	*onions, peeled*
	2	*stalks celery, cleaned and cut into 2-inch chunks*
	6	*sprigs parsley*
	½	*teaspoon thyme*
		Salt and pepper
FOR THE PEARS	8	*small, hard pears with some perfume*
	4	*cups water*
	1	*cup sugar*
	4	*tablespoons pear vinegar*
FOR THE ASPIC		*Degreased duck stock plus enough chicken broth to make 12 cups, or 12 cups chicken broth*
	5½	*tablespoons (5½ envelopes) plain gelatin*
	4	*tablespoons pear vinegar*
	4	*egg whites, lightly beaten*
	½	*cup medium-sweet Madeira*

Two days before the dinner, roast the ducks on racks in roasting pans in a 450-degree oven for 1 hour. Allow the ducks to cool. Discard the fat in the roasting pans and reserve the pans.

Remove all the skin from the ducks, place in a bowl, and refrigerate for use in the salad. Remove all the meat in large pieces from the ducks, including the wing and leg meat, cover, and refrigerate. ❁

•

Reserve the wing, thigh and leg bones and the carcasses for the stock if you elect to make it. Make it two days before the dinner. Combine the raw

wing tips, necks and gizzards, the wing, thigh and leg bones and the carcasses, broken up, in a large pot. Cover with cold water and bring to the
boil. Skim the scum and, when the liquid is clear, add the carrots, onions
and celery. Skim again until clear. Then add the parsley, thyme, salt and
pepper plus more cold water, if needed, to cover. Simmer, with lid slightly
askew, for 2 hours. Strain the stock into a large bowl.

Add 1 cup of the stock (or chicken broth) to each roasting pan and
cook, stirring with a wooden spoon, until all the brown bits have loosened
from the bottoms. Add the deglazing mixture to the stock. ❋   Refrigerate
overnight and remove fat that will have congealed on the surface.

•

The pears can also be cooked two days before the dinner. Peel the
pears, core them, and cut each into 6 wedges. Bring the water, sugar and
pear vinegar to the boil, stirring. Add the pear wedges, reduce heat, and
simmer, without stirring, 10 to 15 minutes, or until the pears test just tender
when pierced with a thin, pointed knife. Cool the pears in their cooking
liquid and refrigerate. ❋

•

The day before the dinner, make the aspic and assemble the dish. Combine the duck stock, with enough chicken broth to make 12 cups, or use all
chicken broth, in a large saucepan with the gelatin, pear vinegar and lightly
beaten egg whites. Bring to the boil over medium-low heat, stirring constantly.

Line a large strainer with several layers of wrung-out cheesecloth, set
the strainer over a bowl, and ladle in the aspic. If the debris clogs the
cheesecloth, lift the strainer, bring it to the sink, turn it over, and wash the
cheesecloth under hot water. Reline the strainer and continue until all
the aspic has clarified. Stir in the Madeira. Cool the aspic and refrigerate
until it is slightly syrupy. If it jells, it must be melted and recooled.

While the aspic is cooling, finish preparing the duck meat and pears for
the final assembly. Drain the pears well in a strainer placed over a bowl.
(The pear cooking syrup can be refrigerated and reused.) Trim the duck
meat carefully of all gristle and membranes, then cut it into strips 2 inches
long by ¼ inch wide.

Ladle a cup of aspic into a 2½-quart metal mold or wide-bottomed bowl
and arrange pear wedges in a sunburst pattern, rounded sides down, radiating from the center of the bottom of the bowl. Arrange a layer of duck, also
radiating from the center of the bowl out to the sides, and ladle on aspic to

cover the duck. Then add a layer of pears, a layer of duck, with aspic poured over each layer, until all ingredients are used. Cover the contents with aspic, cover with plastic wrap, and refrigerate. Pour any leftover aspic into a cake pan and refrigerate. ✿

•

An hour or two before guests arrive, unmold the aspic by running a knife around the inside of the bowl and dipping the bowl in a dishpan of hot water for about 10 seconds if the bowl is metal, longer if it is not. Place a platter over the bowl and invert. Chop any extra aspic and use to decorate the platter. ✿ Refrigerate until 20 to 30 minutes before serving.

Salad with Duck Livers, Hearts and Crispy Skins

•

2 *duck livers, reserved from the ducks*
2 *duck hearts, reserved from the ducks*
3 *tight, firm heads Boston lettuce*
 The cooked skins reserved from the 2 ducks
½ *teaspoon Dijon mustard*
2 *tablespoons red wine vinegar*
½ *cup olive oil*
 Salt and pepper to taste

The day the ducks are cooked, place their livers and hearts on a foil-lined pie plate and broil close to the source of heat under a preheated broiler for 2½ minutes per side. Test for doneness — they should be pink when cut but not bloody. Return to the broiler for another minute if necessary. Bring to room temperature and then refrigerate, tightly covered. ✿

In the morning, separate the lettuce leaves, wash and spin-dry them, and tear into bite-size pieces. Refrigerate in a plastic bag until needed. ✿

The salad can be assembled an hour or two in advance. Place the lettuce in a salad bowl or, preferably, in a large, shallow bowl such as a pasta serving dish. Thinly slice the cooked livers and hearts and strew the slices over the lettuce. Cut the cooked duck skins into ¼-inch pieces and sauté over medium heat in a frying pan, stirring frequently, until all the fat is rendered and the skins are crisp. Remove with a slotted spoon to paper towels and allow to drain well. ✽ Sprinkle over the salad just before serving.

Whisk together the mustard, vinegar, olive oil, salt and pepper and set aside. Just before serving, pour the dressing over the salad, and toss lightly.

Strawberry-Almond Cup

•

Softened butter to grease a 13½-inch gratin dish

FOR THE CREAM		
	2	cups milk
	6	egg yolks
	⅔	cup sugar
	¼	cup flour
	1	tablespoon butter
	2	teaspoons vanilla extract
	3	tablespoons framboise, Grand Marnier or other liqueur of choice
	1½	cups heavy cream

FOR THE FILLING		
	1½	pints strawberries
	1	tablespoon sugar
	1	tablespoon liqueur of choice
	½	cup slivered toasted almonds

FOR THE ASSEMBLY		
	6	tablespoons confectioners' sugar
	3	tablespoons slivered toasted almonds

Butter the baking dish and set aside. Make the cream. Bring the milk to a boil and lower heat to keep the milk at a simmer. Combine the egg yolks and sugar in a bowl and beat with a hand electric mixer until the egg mixture becomes very light and forms a ribbon when the mixer whisks are lifted. Stir in the flour with a wire whisk. Then, whisking constantly, add the hot milk in a thin stream. Pour the mixture back into the saucepan and, whisking constantly, bring to a boil and boil for 1 minute. Remove from heat and beat in the butter, vanilla and *framboise* or other liqueur. Pour into a cold mixing bowl and let cool for 10 minutes. Then whisk in the cream. ❀ Cover with plastic wrap and set aside.

Wash and hull the strawberries, cut them into halves, or thirds if they are large, and place in a bowl with 1 tablespoon of sugar and 1 tablespoon of the liqueur of choice. Mix, cover, and let the berries macerate for about an hour.

Toast the slivered almonds (½ cup for the filling plus 3 tablespoons for the topping) in a preheated 425-degree oven (or toaster oven) for 10 minutes, or until they are golden brown. Stir the nuts occasionally so they will toast evenly.

To assemble, pour half the cream into the buttered baking dish. Drain the strawberries and distribute them on the cream. Sprinkle ½ cup of the almonds on the berries and pour the remaining cream over the filling. Sprinkle the confectioners' sugar over the top. ❀   The dish can be refrigerated for a few hours at this point and brought to room temperature before baking or broiling.

Bake in a preheated 400-degree oven for 25 minutes, or until the berries and cream are warmed and the top is lightly browned. Or place the gratin dish 4 inches from the source of heat of a preheated broiler and broil for about 5 minutes, or until the top is lightly browned and the berries and cream are heated through. Watch closely and do not let the top burn. Spoon the berries and the cream into flat champagne glasses and sprinkle each serving with about 1 teaspoon of toasted almonds.

Wilted Cucumbers Vinaigrette

Poached or Steam-Baked Whole Salmon

Hollandaise or Mousseline Sauce

Green Beans and Jerusalem Artichokes

Steamed New Potatoes

Chocolate Roll

(For Leftovers: Puffed Salmon Pie)

•

*Château St. Jean "Robert Young Vineyard" Chardonnay
or Grand Cru Chablis*

*I*t is one of life's satisfactions that a whole cooked salmon is pleasing to the eye, delicious to the taste buds and simple to prepare. This most wonderful fish comes on the market on schedule, along with peonies, foxglove and clematis, for Memorial Day.

This almost-summer menu begins lightly with dilled cucumbers, whose flavor is brought up by being wilted. The salmon is served warm with a hollandaise or a mousseline sauce (a hollandaise lightened with whipped cream), steamed rather than boiled new potatoes and, for color, crunch and a bit of variety, cut green beans parboiled and stir-fried in butter with thinly sliced Jerusalem artichokes. Peas are traditional, but I am tired of them. Snow peas, which I did a test run on, have too strong a flavor for the salmon.

Dessert is a feathery chocolate roll, which mercifully has nothing in common with the fashionable chocolate glops that eradicate all memory of the rest of the meal.

Most of this meal can be prepared in advance. The cooking liquid for the salmon can be made at least a day before and refrigerated until needed. The cucumbers can be wilted and seasoned the morning of the party. The green beans can be cleaned, cut and parboiled the day before. The potatoes can be scrubbed anytime and put on to steam 35 minutes before the salmon is to be served. (Steaming the potatoes takes longer than boiling them.) The Jerusalem artichokes can be peeled and sliced in the morning and set in a bowl of water with lemon or vinegar until they are rinsed, dried and cooked. The cooking, which takes 2 minutes, can be done just before the salmon is served. The chocolate roll can be made the morning of the party.

The wilted cucumbers would have accompanied the salmon had the fish been served cold with mayonnaise. Here this cool vegetable prepares the palate for wonderful things to come. The cucumbers can be sliced in the processor, with the thin-slice disk, on a mandoline or by hand. They need a little French bread and good unsalted butter.

I either poach salmon in a court bouillon or steam-bake it with an aromatic mixture in foil. One advantage of the second method, besides the moist and flavorful fish it produces, is that it can be done without having to invest in a pricey fish poacher (the cheap ones are too thin and not good). The salmon can be fitted into a large shallow roasting pan or even put on a jelly-roll pan, if necessary, on the diagonal.

In order to poach a whole salmon, an old-fashioned covered turkey roaster will do. But the best is a heavy aluminum or tinned steel fish poacher, equipped with a rack that conveniently lifts the fish out of its cooking liquid. It is a good idea to wrap the fish in cheesecloth, leaving enough of the cloth at both ends to use as handles. This makes it easier to manipulate the cooked fish, whose skin needs peeling and which must be placed on a platter. The cheesecloth can be washed, rinsed thoroughly and reused. The foil can be made to serve the same function for the steam-baked recipe.

For the salmon's cooking, count backward from the time you plan to sit down. Skin the salmon just before you start the first course, arrange it on a platter, cover with a tent of foil, and place it in a 250-degree oven to keep warm. Then decorate the platter before the salmon is served.

A headless salmon that weighs 4½ to 5 pounds (this is considered small for a salmon) is ample for eight, plus some leftovers. It is, however, often easier to find a larger fish, and this has its advantages. Served cold the next day, it would make a lovely informal meal for family and a few friends. A couple of cups of salmon will make a cold mousse. One cup, along with a pound of shrimp, will make a terrific puffed salmon pie, which I adapted from Henri-Paul Pelleprat's *The Great Book of French Cuisine*. This serves six and is good for another party.

Salmon is not an inexpensive item, but to me it is a justifiable if occasional indulgence because it goes far and it does tell guests they are special. A fine salmon can be had for less than the price of a handful of truffles if you shop selectively.

While the hollandaise sauce can be made in a processor, I find the old-fashioned blender more satisfactory. The addition of the whipped cream, to make a mousseline sauce, lightens the hollandaise and stretches it further. (The egg whites can be frozen in individual ice-cube cups and used for meringues, soufflés or whatever. I freeze whites whenever any are left over from a recipe and decant the frozen cubes into heavy plastic bags for storage in the freezer.)

The chocolate roll is actually a soufflé baked flat in a jelly-roll pan to make a sheet cake. The pan is greased with butter and lined with waxed paper, which is then also buttered. The chocolate mixture is spread over the pan, baked quickly, cooled, and turned out onto fresh waxed paper and sprinkled liberally with cocoa. The cocoa coats the roll and masks any cracks that might develop during the rolling, a kind of disaster insurance. More cocoa can be sprinkled over any cracks that might develop when the filled roll is transferred to a board or plate for serving. A good Dutch cocoa makes the roll taste even better.

Wilted Cucumbers
Vinaigrette

•

8	*thin firm medium-sized cucumbers*
2	*tablespoons salt*
1	*bunch dill, stripped and chopped*
1/4	*teaspoon Dijon mustard*
2	*tablespoons red wine vinegar*
1	*tablespoon lemon juice*
9	*tablespoons olive oil*
	Pepper to taste
8	*Boston lettuce leaves*
	4- or 5-ounce jar pimientos, cut into
	long narrow strips (optional)

Peel the cucumbers, cut them into 3-inch chunks, and scoop out the seeds (use the parer or a demitasse spoon). Slice the cucumbers as thin as possible into a bowl and sprinkle with about 2 tablespoons salt. Weight them with a dish and let them stand for 1 hour or more.

The cucumbers will shrink, and a large amount of water will be in the bowl. Place the cucumbers in a colander, rinse quickly with cold water, and drain off as much water as possible. Then dry them in a dish towel, which is easier and more efficient than paper towels. Put the cucumbers in a bowl and add the dill.

In a second bowl, place the mustard and whisk in the vinegar, lemon juice, oil and pepper. Pour over the cucumbers, mix, and taste. You may need to add more vinegar, or oil or salt. ✽   This dish can be completed several hours in advance and refrigerated. Just before serving, arrange the lettuce cups on individual plates and divide the cucumbers among them. Use a slotted spoon if the cucumbers seem to be floating in the vinaigrette. Garnish, if desired, with strips of pimiento.

Poached Whole Salmon

•

FOR THE COURT BOUILLON	4	*quarts water*
	3	*cups dry white wine*
	3	*carrots, peeled and chopped*
	4	*onions, peeled and chopped*
		Bouquet garni consisting of 6 parsley sprigs, 2 bay leaves, 1 teaspoon thyme
	1	*teaspoon peppercorns*
	2½	*tablespoons salt*
		4½- to 5-pound whole salmon
FOR THE GARNISH		*Paper-thin lemon slices*
		Sprigs of dill
		Blender Hollandaise or Mousseline Sauce (recipe follows)

Combine the ingredients for the court bouillon and bring slowly to a boil. Simmer for 40 minutes, remove from heat, strain, and let cool. ✿

Pour the court bouillon into a fish poacher or other pot large enough to hold the fish. Wrap the salmon in cheesecloth and lower it into the liquid. Slowly bring the liquid to boil, reduce immediately to a bare simmer, cover the pot, and poach, counting 8 minutes for each pound. Turn off the heat and let the salmon sit in the liquid for about 20 minutes.

Remove from liquid, drain, and place on a platter. Strain the liquid, reserving 2 tablespoons for the hollandaise. (Freeze the court bouillon for future use, augmenting with ½ cup of water to each quart when it is to be reused.) Peel the skin from the salmon and remove the fins and the little side bones. Surround with lemon slices and sprigs of dill.

Whole Salmon
Steam-Baked in Foil

•

4½- to 5-pound salmon

FOR THE	*1*	*cup dry white wine*
AROMATIC	*½*	*teaspoon thyme*
LIQUID	*½*	*teaspoon rosemary*
	2	*tablespoons minced shallots*
	1	*teaspoon lemon juice*

FOR THE	*Paper-thin lemon slices*
GARNISH	*Sprigs of dill*
	Blender Hollandaise or Mousseline
	Sauce (recipe follows)

Combine the aromatic liquid ingredients and simmer, covered, for 35 minutes. ✹

Place a sheet of heavy-duty foil large enough to enclose the fish on a large baking pan or jelly-roll pan, put the fish on the foil, bring up the sides, and pour in the aromatic liquid. Crimp the foil over the fish and seal it completely. Place it in a preheated 375-degree oven and cook for 12 minutes to the pound, or until the fish flakes.

Let the salmon sit in the sealed foil for 15 minutes. Then turn it over onto a platter, peel the skin, and remove the fins and the little side bones. Surround with lemon slices and sprigs of dill. Strain the steaming liquid and use 2 tablespoons for the hollandaise. Freeze the rest of the liquid for future use in sauces.

Blender Hollandaise or
Mousseline Sauce

•

This sauce must be made in two increments to serve eight. For each recipe:

  3   egg yolks
 1/4 teaspoon salt
1 1/2 tablespoons lemon juice
  1   tablespoon hot water or poaching stock
          or aromatic liquid
 3/8 pound (1 1/2 sticks) unsalted butter
      Dash of white pepper

 1/2 cup heavy cream (if preparing
          mousseline for double the above
          recipe)

Blend the egg yolks, salt and lemon juice with the hot water, poaching stock or steaming liquid until the eggs become thick and sticky. Cut the butter into pieces, heat it until it bubbles, and let cool for a minute. Turn the blender back on and add the butter in a thin, steady stream. Add the pepper and blend for 15 more seconds.

Pour the sauce into a bowl, scrape out the blender container, and wash it. Repeat the recipe and add to the first batch.❀   The sauce can be made to this point up to a day in advance. Cover tightly with plastic wrap, refrigerate, and bring to room temperature 2 hours before serving in a warmed sauceboat. To make a mousseline sauce, beat 1/2 cup heavy cream until it barely mounds and fold into the softened hollandaise about an hour before serving.

Green Beans and Jerusalem Artichokes

•

¾	*pound fresh young green beans*
¾	*pound Jerusalem artichokes*
	Lemon juice
4	*tablespoons butter*
1	*tablespoon peanut oil*
	Salt and pepper to taste

Cut the beans into 2-inch pieces and boil in a large pot of salted water for 6 minutes. Drain in a colander and cool quickly under cold running water. Drain and dry on a dish towel or paper towels and set them aside. ✿ The beans can be refrigerated for a day.

Peel the Jerusalem artichokes, trim off the knobs, and slice as thin as possible. Drop the slices into a bowl of water with a little lemon juice to keep them from turning black. Rinse and dry them well in a dish towel before cooking. ✿

Heat the butter and oil in a wok or any pot large enough for the vegetables. When the foam has subsided, add the green beans and the artichoke slices and cook over a high flame, stirring constantly, for 2 minutes.

Steamed New Potatoes

•

24	*small new potatoes of uniform size,*
	unpeeled and scrubbed
2	*tablespoons chopped fresh dill*
2	*tablespoons chopped parsley*

Use a vegetable steamer or improvise one by setting a colander in a pot. Pour boiling water into the bottom of the pot, set the steamer or colander in the pot, and add the potatoes. Make sure the water level is below the potatoes. Put a lid on the pot and steam for about 35 minutes. Test with a sharp pointed knife after 25 minutes.

Place potatoes in a dry pot as soon as they are done and shake over heat for a minute or two. Serve in a bowl and garnish with the chopped dill and parsley.

Chocolate Roll

•

FOR PREPARING THE PAN		*Softened butter to grease a 10-by-15-inch jelly-roll pan and the waxed paper lining*
FOR THE SHEET CAKE	6	*ounces semisweet chocolate, broken into bits*
	3	*tablespoons strong espresso coffee*
	5	*egg yolks*
	½	*cup superfine sugar*
	5	*egg whites*
		Pinch of salt
FOR FILLING THE SHEET CAKE		*About ¾ cup sifted Dutch cocoa*
	1½	*cups heavy cream*
	2	*tablespoons confectioners' sugar*
	1½	*teaspoons Vanilla Cognac (see April, Provisioning the Pantry) or 1¼ teaspoons Cognac plus ⅛ teaspoon vanilla extract*

Prepare the pan. Butter a 10-by-15-inch jelly-roll pan, cover the pan with waxed paper, leaving about a 3-inch overhang at each end, and butter the paper. Set aside.

To prepare the sheet cake, combine the chocolate and coffee in the top of a double boiler and melt over hot but not boiling water. Stir and set aside, leaving the chocolate over the water. With an electric hand beater beat the egg yolks until they are light. Slowly beat in the sugar and continue beating until the mixture is fluffy. Stir in the melted chocolate.

In a large bowl, combine the egg whites with the salt and beat with clean beaters just until stiff peaks are formed when the beaters are lifted out of the whites. Do not overbeat, which dries the whites. Stir about ½ cup of the beaten whites into the chocolate-egg yolk mixture, then turn the mixture into the bowl with the beaten whites. Carefully fold the whites in. Pour into the prepared pan and spread with a spatula to cover the pan evenly and into the corners. Bake in a preheated 350-degree oven for 15 minutes. It is done when it puffs and when a knife inserted in the center comes out clean. Remove from the oven immediately.

Rinse a cloth towel in cold water, wring it out, and place it over the cake. Let stand at room temperature for 15 minutes. Remove the towel and slide a small knife around the edges of the pan to loosen the cake. Sprinkle ½ cup of the cocoa evenly over the top of the cake and cover it with two pieces of waxed paper both longer than the pan. Hold the paper firmly with the ends of the pan and carefully but quickly flip the pan over. The long side of the cake will be parallel to the edge of the work surface. The cake will be lying on the fresh waxed paper, with the lining paper and the jelly-roll pan on top. Lift off the jelly-roll pan and carefully peel off the lining.

Beat the cream in a cold metal bowl. When it begins to hold shape, add the confectioners' sugar and Vanilla Cognac or Cognac and vanilla extract. Beat until the cream is stiff.

Spoon the cream on top of the cake and spread it evenly with a spatula. Using the waxed paper, roll the cake. Still using the waxed paper, roll it onto a long wooden board or serving platter. Camouflage any cracks with more cocoa.

The chocolate roll will keep for several hours in the refrigerator✿ but should be covered with foil or waxed paper.

To serve, cut on the diagonal into 1¾-inch slices.

Puffed Salmon Pie

MAKES 6 SERVINGS

•

This is a recipe for leftover salmon.

    1   *pound shrimp, cooked, peeled and*
        deveined
    ¾   *cup heavy cream*
    ¾   *cup Medium-Thick White Sauce*
        (recipe follows)
        Salt and ground white pepper
    1   *cup cooked salmon*
    2   *tablespoons butter*
        Lemon juice
    4   *egg yolks*
    2   *egg whites*
        9-inch unbaked pie shell made of
        Unsweetened Pie Pastry,
        refrigerated (see Index)

Combine the shrimp, ⅓ cup of the cream, ¼ cup of the white sauce and salt and pepper to taste. Set aside.

Purée the salmon in a food processor or blender. Add the butter, remaining cream and remaining white sauce. Process until smooth.

Heat the salmon in a saucepan, stirring constantly, until a paste is formed. Season with salt, pepper and lemon juice to taste. Beat in the egg yolks. Beat the whites until they stand in soft peaks and fold into the salmon mixture.

Remove the pastry shell from the refrigerator, cover the bottom with the shrimp mixture, and fill the shell with the salmon mixture. Bake in a preheated 425-degree oven for 10 minutes, reduce heat to 375 degrees, and bake 30 minutes more or until the pastry is browned and the filling is puffed.

Medium-Thick White Sauce

MAKES 1 CUP

•

2   tablespoons butter
2   tablespoons flour
3/4 cup milk
1/4 cup heavy cream

Melt the butter in a small saucepan, stir in the flour, and, stirring constantly, cook over medium heat for a minute or two. Remove from heat and whisk in the milk. Stirring, bring to a boil. Add cream and cook another 30 seconds.

• COCKTAIL PARTY FOR TWENTY-FOUR •

Herbed Scallops

Marinated Shrimp

Eggs with Curry, Sardine, Smoked Oyster and Anchovy Stuffings

Filled Bread Ring

Chicken Liver Pâté

Comforting End-of-Party Soup

•

*H*aving friends for cocktails, which I think of as a six to eight o'clock happening, is gratifying at this time of year; since it stays light late, the garden can be used or at least admired through a window.

We move our round table into a corner of the dining room to leave space for people to congregate. The table is covered with a cloth, a raucous display of cut azaleas and a variety of finger foods, all of which have been made in advance. There is nothing to do before the party other than set up the bar, place bowls of olives and nuts in the living room and set the food out. I usually avoid hot hors d'oeuvre because they keep me in the kitchen when I want to be with guests. Nor do I allow anything that requires plates, however small, because juggling a drink and a plate inhibits conversation and movement.

The herbed bay scallops can be made a day in advance. The scallops are speared with toothpicks or spooned onto crackers by the greedy. This hors d'oeuvre couldn't be simpler to make.

Another platter contains marinated shrimp, which must be made a day or two in advance. They are marinated in bottled lime juice, dressed and left in the refrigerator for a day or two.

Four kinds of stuffed eggs, each of them different, sit on a bed of alfalfa sprouts, mildly reminiscent of an Easter basket. The sprouts keep the eggs from tilting on their sides. I use "small" eggs for stuffing because guests don't feel as piggish as they might when bolting half a large or even medium egg. Small eggs are not available everywhere, but are worth the hunt. I usually begin by serving half the eggs and replenish the platter midway through the party.

The cottage-cheese, herb-filled bread ring is satisfying to make, especially for those who have a dough hook on a mixer. However, only ten minutes of kneading is required, so the bread is not all that great an imposition for the machineless. I bake this filled bread in a 12-inch savarin (ring) mold, and the result is a lovely wreath whose center can be filled with radishes, well-drained olives, cherry tomatoes, tiny broccoli florets or whatever. The bread can be made a day in advance, refrigerated overnight and brought to room temperature before it is sliced and served.

The wonderful rich, creamy-with-butter chicken liver pâté is from that excellent book *Michael Field's Cooking School*. I have adapted it for the food processor and halved it. I sometimes put it in individual tiny pots for a first course with hot toast and, say, *céleri rémoulade* or plain watercress.

Always in the kitchen is an unadvertised pot of something or the makings of supper for friends who can't bear to leave or who are persuaded to stay because we don't want the party to end. By nine, it is time for real food, and I have used various dishes to fend off starvation — leftover *cassoulet* taken from the freezer earlier in the day and reheated in a slow oven, or frozen ravioli or tortellini, which can be cooked in a few minutes. The best of all is a vegetable-filled, end-of-party soup that can be made a day or two in advance and that comforts the soul.

Herbed Scallops

24 HORS D'OEUVRE SERVINGS

•

1½	*pounds bay scallops*
1½	*cups Thick Processor Mayonnaise (recipe follows)*
1	*teaspoon capers, washed in cold water, drained and minced*
1½	*tablespoons minced fresh herbs (dill, thyme or tarragon)*
1½	*tablespoons minced parsley*
2	*large cloves garlic, minced*
1	*hard-cooked egg, chopped*
	Salt and pepper to taste
2	*tablespoons minced chives*

Wash and drain the scallops and place them in a large frying pan. Barely cover with cold water, place over high heat, and bring to a boil. Reduce heat and simmer for 1 minute. Remove from heat, drain the scallops in a colander, and cool. Set aside.

Mix mayonnaise in a bowl with capers, herbs, parsley, garlic, egg, salt and pepper. Add the scallops and combine. ❀ Refrigerate until needed.

To serve, place the scallops on a flat platter and sprinkle with chives. Serve with toothpicks or on crackers.

Thick Processor Mayonnaise

MAKES 2¼ CUPS

•

3	*eggs yolks*
1½	*teaspoons Dijon mustard*
2	*tablespoons lemon juice, or more, to taste*

³/₄   teaspoon salt
     White pepper to taste
1   cup peanut oil
1   cup olive oil

Place the egg yolks, mustard, lemon juice, salt and pepper in the processor bowl fitted with the steel blade. Process for a minute or two, or until the yolks are thick. With the motor running, slowly pour both oils through the tube. Reserve 1½ cups of mayonnaise for the scallops, ¼ cup for the filled bread and the remainder for the stuffed eggs. Or use a good brand of commercial mayonnaise if necessary for the eggs.

Marinated Shrimp

24 HORS D'OEUVRE SERVINGS

•

2   pounds medium to large shrimp (21 to
      25 per pound)
    8-ounce bottle lime juice
6   tablespoons minced red onion
6   tablespoons minced parsley
½   cup olive oil
½   teaspoon dried oregano, or more to taste
1   teaspoon salt
     Pepper to taste

Rinse the shrimp under cold running water, place them in a large pot, and cover with cold water. Bring to a boil and set aside, off heat, for 5 minutes. Place in a colander and shell the shrimp when they are cool enough to handle. Place them in a bowl, add the lime juice, and let marinate for 2 hours. Stir the shrimp frequently. Then drain the shrimp in a colander, discarding the juice. Add the remaining ingredients to the shrimp, stir, cover, and refrigerate overnight. ❀ To serve, arrange on a tray or platter and have toothpicks available.

Stuffed Eggs

MAKES 56 TO 60 HALVES

•

30 *small eggs*
2 *packages alfalfa sprouts*

To hard-cook eggs, place them in a large pan, cover them with cold water, bring to a boil, and cook for 10 minutes. Immediately drain the hot water off and run cold water over the eggs. Crack the shells, then peel the eggs. Cool and refrigerate until needed. ✿

   When the eggs have been stuffed (see recipes below), cover them loosely with plastic wrap but seal the wrap to the edges of the plate. ✿   To serve, arrange them on a large platter or tray lined with alfalfa sprouts. The sprouts will help keep the eggs upright.

Curry Stuffing

ENOUGH FOR 7 EGGS

•

 7 *small hard-cooked eggs, halved and*
   yolks removed
 4 *tablespoons butter, at room*
   temperature
 4 *teaspoons mayonnaise*
 1 *tablespoon minced onion*
1½ *teaspoons Madras curry powder*
   Salt and pepper to taste
14 *small pieces mango chutney*

Combine the egg yolks, butter, mayonnaise, minced onion, curry powder, salt and pepper in a food processor container fitted with the steel blade.

Process until the mixture is smooth. Scoop into a pastry bag fitted with a number 4 star tip and pipe the mixture into the egg whites. Garnish each half with a piece of chutney.

Sardine Stuffing

ENOUGH FOR 7 EGGS

•

7   *small hard-cooked eggs, halved and
      yolks removed
      3³⁄₄-ounce can skinless and boneless
      sardines, drained*
1   *tablespoon Dijon mustard*
2   *teaspoons minced onion*
2   *teaspoons mayonnaise*
1   *teaspoon grated lemon rind*
¹⁄₂ *teaspoon lemon juice, or more to taste
      Salt and pepper*
7   *paper-thin slices lemon, cut in half*
14 *tiny parsley sprigs*

Combine the egg yolks, sardines, mustard, onion, mayonnaise, lemon rind, lemon juice, salt and pepper in a food processor bowl fitted with the steel blade. Process until smooth. Taste for lemon and add more juice if needed. Turn into a pastry bag fitted with a number 4 star tip and pipe mixture into the egg whites. Garnish each egg half with half a lemon slice and a parsley sprig.

Smoked Oyster Stuffing

ENOUGH FOR 7 EGGS

•

7   *small hard-cooked eggs, halved and*
     yolks removed
1   *teaspoon Dijon mustard*
4   *tablespoons mayonnaise, or more if*
     needed to bind the mixture
¼   *teaspoon Worcestershire sauce*
1   *teaspoon chopped dill*
     Salt and pepper to taste
14   *smoked oysters, drained*

Combine the egg yolks, mustard, mayonnaise, Worcestershire sauce, dill, salt and pepper in a food processor bowl fitted with the steel blade. Process until smooth. Add more mayonnaise if the mixture seems dry. Scoop into a pastry bag fitted with a number 4 star tip and pipe the mixture into the egg whites. Garnish each egg half with a smoked oyster.

Anchovy Stuffing

ENOUGH FOR 7 EGGS

•

7   *small hard-cooked eggs, halved and*
     yolks removed
2½   *tablespoons anchovy paste*
1   *garlic clove, minced*
2   *tablespoons mayonnaise*
1   *tablespoon butter, at room temperature*
1½   *tablespoons sour cream*
2   *tablespoons chopped cashew nuts*

Combine the egg yolks, anchovy paste, minced garlic, mayonnaise, butter and sour cream in a food processor bowl fitted with the steel blade. Process until smooth. Scoop into a pastry bag fitted with a number 4 star tip and pipe the mixture into the egg whites. Garnish the egg halves with the chopped nuts.

Filled Bread Ring

24 SERVINGS HORS D'OEUVRE

•

FOR THE BREAD	2	*packages active dry yeast*
	1	*cup lukewarm water*
	3	*cups bread flour*
	2	*teaspoons salt*
	1	*tablespoon sugar*
	1½	*tablespoons butter, at room temperature*
	1	*egg, lightly beaten*
		Poppy seeds
FOR THE FILLING	1	*cup small-curd cottage cheese, placed in a strainer, set over a bowl and left to drain in the refrigerator for 2 hours or more*
	4	*tablespoons mayonnaise*
	1	*medium onion, minced*
	4	*tablespoons chopped scallions*
	3	*tablespoons butter*
	3	*tablespoons minced chives*
	3	*tablespoons minced parsley*
	1	*teaspoon cracked black pepper*
		Salt to taste
FOR THE GARNISH		*Radishes, olives, cherry tomatoes and tiny broccoli florets*

Combine the yeast with the water in a large mixing bowl and let sit for 10 minutes, or until the yeast begins to bubble. Then add the flour, salt and sugar and stir into a dough. Knead in the softened butter. Then knead the dough until it is smooth and elastic, about 10 minutes. Place the dough in a clean bowl, dust it lightly with flour, cover with plastic wrap, and let it rise in a warm place until it has doubled in bulk. Punch down the dough, knead it briefly, and let it rest, under a bowl, for 10 minutes.

•

While the dough is rising, prepare the filling. Combine the drained cottage cheese with the mayonnaise. Soften the onion and scallions in the butter over low heat for about 6 or 7 minutes and add to the cottage cheese mixture. Then add the remaining filling ingredients and combine well.

•

To assemble the bread, roll out the dough on a floured board into a rectangle about 27 inches long, 6 inches wide and about ¼ inch thick. Brush the dough with beaten egg and spread the filling over it, leaving ¼ inch on one long side without filling. Roll the dough like a jelly roll toward the plain edge. Brush on a little more of the beaten egg if necessary to seal the edge of the dough and place the bread, seam side down, in a well-buttered 12-inch savarin (ring) mold. Pull the ends together and again, using beaten egg, seal them to make an unbroken circle. Brush the top with beaten egg and sprinkle with poppy seeds. Bake in a preheated 400-degree oven for 45 minutes, or until the bread is nicely browned. Remove to a rack and allow to cool. ❁ Place on a large tray and fill the center with radishes, well-drained olives, cherry tomatoes and tiny broccoli florets. To serve, cut the bread into thin slices.

Chicken Liver Pâté

MAKES 1½ CUPS

•

¼ *pound (1 stick) butter, at room*
temperature
¼ *cup minced onions*
1 *tablespoon minced shallots*

2   tablespoons minced tart apple
½   pound chicken livers, trimmed and
      halved
2   tablespoons warmed Calvados
1   tablespoon heavy cream
½   teaspoon lemon juice
¾   teaspoon salt
¼   teaspoon freshly ground white pepper
3   tablespoons clarified butter
2   tablespoons minced parsley

Cut two 1½-tablespoon chunks off the stick of butter and set the rest aside, at room temperature. Melt 1½ tablespoons butter in a frying pan, add the minced onions and shallots, and cook over low heat for about 6 minutes, or until the onions are soft. Add the minced apple and cook for another 3 minutes. Transfer the mixture to the bowl of a food processor fitted with the steel blade.

Melt the second 1½ tablespoons of butter in the same frying pan, this time over high heat. Add the livers and, still over high heat, cook them for about 4 or 5 minutes, turning them. The livers should be brown on the outside and pink but not raw in the inside. Remove the pan from heat. Warm the Calvados in a small butter warmer, tilt the pan over the livers, and touch it with a lighted match. Pour the flaming Calvados over the livers and allow the alcohol to burn itself out. Add the liver mixture to the processor along with the cream, and process until the mixture is completely smooth. It will be slightly liquid. Transfer the mixture to a bowl and allow to cool. Stir occasionally.

When the liver mixture is completely cool, and only then, beat in the remaining butter, about a teaspoon at a time. When the butter has been incorporated, add the lemon juice and salt and pepper. Taste for seasonings, remembering that the pâté will be served cold, so the flavor will be somewhat deadened.

Pack the pâté into a 1½-cup terrine, smooth the top, and pour the clarified butter over it to cover the liver mixture completely. (For 3 tablespoons of clarified butter, cut 4 tablespoons of butter into small pieces and melt the butter in a small pan over low heat. Remove the pan from heat and skim off the foam from the top. Next spoon off the clear butter onto the pâté, leaving behind the milky solids that have settled to the bottom. Or pour the butter through a strainer lined with wrung-out cheesecloth.)

Refrigerate the terrine.✿   Just before serving, sprinkle a narrow ring of minced parsley around the edge of the clarified butter. Serve with plain crackers, Melba toast or thinly sliced French bread. This pâté should keep for a week under its butter seal.

Comforting
End-of-Party Soup

10 TO 12 SERVINGS

•

	15-ounce can red kidney beans
	15-ounce can Great Northern beans
1	*bay leaf*
½	*teaspoon dried basil*
½	*teaspoon dried oregano*
2	*whole cloves*
¼	*cup olive oil*
2	*medium onions, minced*
2	*cloves garlic, minced*
10	*cups chicken broth*
2	*cups Italian plum tomatoes with their juice*
2	*stalks celery, cleaned and sliced thin horizontally*
2	*large carrots, peeled and cut into a 3-by-¼-inch julienne*
2	*tablespoons salt*
1½	*teaspoons freshly ground white pepper*
⅓	*cup rice*
6	*large inside leaves of a cabbage, rolled and sliced into a chiffonade*
½	*cup cauliflower florets*
2	*small white turnips, peeled and coarsely chopped*

1   medium zucchini, washed and scrubbed
    but unpeeled, and cut into ⅛-inch
    slices
1   medium boiling potato, peeled and
    coarsely chopped
½   cup ditalini or elbow macaroni
½   cup frozen peas
3   tablespoons chopped parsley
    Grated Parmesan cheese (optional)

Place the beans from both cans in a colander and rinse well with cold running water. Drain and set aside. Combine the bay leaf, basil, oregano and cloves on a small piece of cheesecloth and tie the cloth with a string to make a bag. Set aside.

Heat the oil in a large pan and cook the onions and garlic over low heat for about 7 minutes, or until they are soft and transparent. Do not let them color. Add the broth, the tomatoes with their juices, the celery, the carrots, the cheesecloth spice bag, the salt and the pepper. Bring the mixture to a boil over low heat, cover the pan, and simmer for 30 minutes. Add the rice and cook for 10 minutes more. Then add the cabbage leaves, cauliflower and turnip. Bring to a boil and add the zucchini and potato. Cook for 10 minutes more and add the *ditalini* or elbow macaroni and the peas. Cook for another 8 minutes and add the reserved beans. Bring to a simmer, remove the spice bag, and add the parsley. ❁ Reheat before serving. Serve grated Parmesan separately, if desired.

Summer

June

Marinated Olives with Citrus and Fennel

MAKES 2 CUPS

•

These are lovely with drinks or as part of *hors d'oeuvre variés*.

> 1-pound jar (11 ounces drained
>   weight) calamata olives in olive oil
>   and vinegar, drained and rinsed
>   under water
> 2 garlic cloves, peeled and lightly crushed
>   Rinds of 1 orange and 1 lemon, peeled
>   with a citrus stripper into long, thin
>   strips
> 2 tablespoons fennel seed
>   Juice of 1 lemon
>   Juice of 1 orange

Pack the olives, garlic, strips of rind and fennel seed in layers in a pint jar. Add juices and fill jar to the brim with olive oil. Cover, refrigerate, and shake the jar when you think of it. Use after a day or two and bring to room temperature before serving.

Scallop-Stuffed Artichokes with Green Processor Mayonnaise

Navarin Printanier (Lamb Stew with Spring Vegetables)

Gâteau Milanaise with Strawberries

•

FIRST COURSE:
Principe Palavincini
MAIN COURSE:
Clos du Val Merlot
or *Château Prieuré-Lichine*

N *avarin printanier*, a fancy way of saying lamb stew with spring vegetables, is full-bodied but light, pretty and perfect for an early June evening. Presented on a large, shallow serving platter, the meat and its fragrant sauce are surrounded by a lovely bouquet of carrots, potatoes, turnips, onions, peas and green beans that has been brightened by a sprinkling of mixed fresh minced herbs. Such a dish would be soothing even if the temperature were 90 degrees and the air conditioning had broken down.

The meal starts with scallop-stuffed artichokes, an uncomplicated dish as elegant as the lamb. Dessert involves strawberries again, and why not, since local berries are coming onto the market in most parts of the country and the California imports finally have developed some flavor. They are served in Dione Lucas's *gâteau milanaise*, a sponge cake with the flavor and lightness of a *génoise* but which doesn't require the more precarious *génoise* techniques.

Bay scallops, in all their sweetness, are plentiful in June and, if you shop around, they can be surprisingly inexpensive. They combine beautifully with young artichokes, which are also in season and reasonably priced. Stuffing the artichoke gives an added bonus for the family, since the center tuft of tender leaves, which is removed, can be eaten the next day with leftover green sauce. The prickly tips should be cut off with scissors before cooking, since they are very disagreeable to the touch. After the artichoke has been cooked, the choke is scooped out with a teaspoon.

The presentation is very attractive: The bottom two rows of artichoke leaves are pressed down to suggest a flower. The scallop-filled artichoke itself is then topped with a flowerlike slice of lemon, an effect achieved with a stripper (a gadget used to remove strips of peel from citrus while leaving behind the white pith of the fruit). I make my strips (or stripes) from the top of the lemon to the bottom and then slice it. The stripper is also useful for making stripes down unpeeled cucumbers (when unwaxed ones can be found) and on zucchini. The lemon slice is then sprinkled with a bit of finely minced parsley. Additional green mayonnaise is served on the side as a dip for the artichoke leaves.

The thick processor mayonnaise is the same basic one I use in other recipes and is as simple to make as unscrewing the lid from a jar and much better than what you can buy in any jar. The recipe produces a dense mayonnaise that can be thinned and simultaneously made more delicious with some of the reserved liquid in which the scallops have cooked. I mince the greenery (rinsed and very thoroughly dried) in the processor, set the herbs aside and then make the mayonnaise. This way I avoid having to wash the bowl and blade an extra time.

All the elements of this first course can be prepared the day before the dinner and put together just before you sit down.

As with other stews, the *navarin printanier* is underrated, undervalued and largely ignored, the victim of pretensions about "company" as opposed to family food. Being a stew, it benefits from being made in advance and sitting overnight in its own juices, to be finished off a few minutes before it is served.

Moreover, since the cheaper cuts — shoulder, short ribs, neck and breast — are best (they don't dry out and become stringy with braising the way fancier chops or the leg do), this stew is also an economical dish. Try to include some of all (or as many as possible) of the four cuts, since each contributes something different in texture and flavor. If you aren't sure you're mad about lamb, try it after you've trimmed off all the fat and the fell (the papery tissue that surrounds much of the meat). The fat, not the lamb, is responsible for the heavy unpleasant flavor that I think of as "muttony." This is also the reason that the sauce must be degreased. The fell tends to toughen with cooking and imparts an undesirable texture.

Fresh herbs are especially good for the *navarin* and indispensable for the green mayonnaise that accompanies the artichokes. Fresh herbs are more and more available in specialty food stores and even at some supermarkets, but the best way to ensure a good supply is to grow your own. Early June is not too late to buy herb plants, which can be found now in many nurseries and even at hardware stores, and are also available by mail order (see Mail-Order Sources).

Making a *milanaise* could not be simpler, particularly if you have an electric mixer on a stand. The strawberries (or raspberries, blueberries or sliced peaches) are combined with melted red currant jelly and a little Madeira and lemon juice The fruit becomes the filling and the topping, and the sides of the cake are frosted with whipped cream. The *milanaise* is also delicious as is, dusted only with confectioners' sugar.

Scallop-Stuffed Artichokes
with Green Processor
Mayonnaise

•

	8	*artichokes*
FOR THE	*3/4*	*cup dry vermouth*
SCALLOPS	*1*	*finely minced small onion*
		Sprig of parsley
		Bay leaf
	1	*pound bay scallops or 1 pound sea scallops, quartered*
	1	*lemon*

FOR THE
MAYONNAISE

2   *cups, lightly packed, parsley leaves*
    stripped from stems, washed and
    dried
    About 25 medium-size spinach leaves,
    coarse spines removed, washed and
    dried
¼   *cup minced green onion, white and*
    green parts
¼   *cup minced chives*
1   *tablespoon minced fresh tarragon or* ¼
    to ½ *teaspoon dried*
1   *tablespoon minced fresh dill*
2½ *cups mayonnaise (recipe follows)*

Cut off the stems and tops of the artichokes and trim the prickly points off
the leaves with scissors. Boil in salted water for 18 minutes, or until bottoms test tender with a thin pointed knife. Turn out into a colander and
drain them, stem ends up. When they are cool, squeeze them gently to
remove remaining water, place them on their bottoms, and make a hollow
by removing the tender inside leaves. (Save these for the next day.) The
choke should now be exposed. Remove it with a spoon and refrigerate the
artichokes, standing them upright on a dish. ❀

Bring the vermouth, onion, sprig of parsley and bay leaf to a boil, add
the scallops, and simmer for 2 minutes, shaking the pan as they cook. Turn
off the heat, cover the scallops, and leave in pan for another 2 minutes.
Drain them and reserve the cooking liquid. (The minced onion will remain
with the scallops. Discard the bay leaf and parsley.) Cool the liquid and the
scallops. ❀

•

In a processor fitted with the metal blade, mince the parsley and spinach. Add the minced green onions and herbs and give the motor one more
quick buzz. Add the mixture to the mayonnaise. The sauce will be very
thick. Thin it a bit with the reserved scallop liquid—it should have the
consistency of a thinnish commercial mayonnaise. ❀

Add about 1 cup of the mayonnaise to the scallops and mix. The scallops should be well coated, so you may need to add more. Place the remaining mayonnaise in a small bowl. Fill each artichoke cavity with scallops.

Use a stripper, if you have one, to cut narrow strips of peel from the lemon, working from top to bottom. Slice the lemon thin — the slices will be scalloped. Top each filled artichoke with a thin lemon slice and sprinkle a little finely minced parsley on it. Place artichokes on individual plates. Press down the bottom two rows of leaves to make a "flower." Pass the extra green mayonnaise for the artichoke leaves.

Any leftover sauce can be used with the tender leaves the next day or mixed with some cooked minced chicken and celery for a lovely salad.

Thick Processor Mayonnaise

MAKES 2¼ CUPS

•

3	*egg yolks*
1½	*teaspoons Dijon mustard*
2	*tablespoons lemon juice, or more, to taste*
½	*teaspoon each salt and white pepper, or to taste*
1	*cup peanut oil*
1	*cup olive oil*

Process the yolks and seasonings for 2 minutes. Then, in a thin stream pour the peanut oil slowly through the processor tube. Then pour in the olive oil.

Navarin Printanier

(LAMB STEW WITH SPRING VEGETABLES)

•

FOR THE LAMB	3½	*pounds lamb stew meat (a good combination would be 1½ pounds shoulder, 1 pound short ribs, ½ pound breast meat, ½ pound neck meat), boned, trimmed of fat and fell, and cut into 2-inch cubes*
		Salt and pepper to taste
	1	*tablespoon sugar*
	3	*tablespoons butter*
	2	*tablespoons peanut oil*
	1	*large onion, studded with a clove*
	2	*tablespoons flour*
		About 6 cups warm beef bouillon (homemade if possible)
	2	*tablespoons tomato paste*
	2	*cloves garlic, crushed*
		Bouquet garni made up of a sprig each of fresh thyme, rosemary and parsley and a bay leaf
FOR THE VEGETABLES	24	*very small new potatoes, peeled and covered with cold water to keep them from turning dark*
	24	*small white onions, about 1 inch in diameter, scalded and peeled*
	8	*turnips, quartered lengthwise and ends rounded*
	8	*carrots, quartered and ends rounded*
	4 or 5	*medium-size tomatoes, scalded in hot water, cored, peeled and seeded*
	¾	*pound fresh green peas in the pod, shelled, or 10-ounce package frozen tiny peas*
	½	*pound fresh green beans, trimmed and cut into 1½-inch pieces*

*2   tablespoons mixed fresh herbs —
      parsley, thyme, rosemary or whatever
      you are growing*

Salt and pepper the meat lightly and sprinkle the pieces with the sugar.
(This helps the meat to brown evenly.) Heat the butter and oil in a large
heavy-bottomed casserole that is large enough to hold the meat and all the
vegetables. Add the onion and then the pieces of meat and brown them
slowly and evenly. Do not add all the meat at once, and remove pieces to a
bowl as they are browned. Return all the browned meat to the casserole,
sprinkle it with flour, and place it in a preheated 450-degree oven for about
6 minutes until the flour is golden brown. Remove the casserole from the
oven and lower the oven temperature to 325 degrees.

Place the casserole over medium heat on top of the stove and stir in the
warm bouillon. The meat should be just barely covered. Bring the liquid to
a boil and add the tomato paste, garlic and the bouquet garni. Cover, return
to the oven, and cook for 1 hour.

Remove the casserole from the oven, discard the bouquet garni and,
using a slotted spoon, transfer the pieces of meat to a bowl. Pick out and
discard any bones. Let the sauce stand for a few minutes so that the fat rises
to the surface. Tilt the casserole and degrease the sauce with a spoon. Blot
off any remaining fat with a paper towel, passing it rapidly over the surface.
Strain the sauce into another bowl.

•

Wash and dry the casserole and return the meat to it. Pour in the
strained sauce. Drain the water from the potatoes. Add them, the onions,
turnips, carrots and tomatoes to the casserole and baste them with sauce.
Push the vegetables between the pieces of meat. Bring to the simmer on top
of the stove, cover, and return to the 325-degree oven for 1 hour, or until
the lamb and the vegetables are tender when pierced with a sharp, pointed
knife. Test the meat and vegetables after 30 minutes. Remove the casserole
from the oven, tilt it, and degrease once more, using a spoon. Set aside with
the lid askew if serving in a hour or two.❀   Otherwise, let the stew cool
and refrigerate.

Drop the peas and beans into a large pot of boiling salted water and boil
uncovered for 5 minutes. Immediately drain in a colander and run cold
water over them for several minutes to stop the cooking.❀   Put aside (or
refrigerate) until the stew is to be finished.

Just before serving, bring the casserole to the simmer, add the peas and beans, and baste with the sauce. Cover and simmer about 5 minutes, or until the vegetables are tender.

Place the pieces of meat in the center of a large, heated platter, surround with the vegetables, alternating colors, and pour the sauce over all. Sprinkle the vegetables with the minced fresh herbs and serve with warm French bread.

Gâteau Milanaise

•

2	whole eggs
2	eggs, separated
1	cup superfine sugar
⅜	cup (¼ cup plus 2 tablespoons) all-purpose flour
⅜	cup (¼ cup plus 2 tablespoons) potato starch (also called potato flour)
	Grated rind of 1 lemon
	Pinch of salt

FOR THE
FRUIT FILLING
AND TOPPING

	10-ounce jar red currant jelly
2	tablespoons Madeira or sherry
1	teaspoon lemon juice
2	pints strawberries, blueberries, or raspberries, or 4 cups sliced peaches or other similar fruit

¾	cup whipping cream
1	tablespoon sugar
	Few drops of vanilla extract

Butter and flour an 8- or 9-inch springform pan. Preheat oven to 350 degrees. Combine 2 eggs, 2 egg yolks, sugar, flour and potato starch in a mixing bowl and beat on high speed continuously for 15 minutes. Then beat in the grated lemon rind. Using clean, dry beaters and bowl, beat 2 egg whites together with pinch of salt to soft peaks. Fold the whites into the yolk-and-flour mixture — the batter should be smooth, with no egg-white lumps showing. Turn it into pan and bake for 45 to 50 minutes. Place a cake rack on top of the cake in its pan and flip over. When the cake is cool, unsnap the sides of the pan and remove the sides and bottom.

•

To prepare the fruit filling and topping, melt the jelly along with the Madeira or sherry and lemon juice in a small saucepan. Mix 2 cups of the fruit with ⅓ cup of the melted jelly mixture.

Slice the cake into two horizontal layers and place the bottom layer, cut side up, on a plate. Spread this with the fruit and jelly filling and then place the top layer over it. Brush the top and sides of the cake with some of the melted jelly mixture. Then dip the remaining fruit in the mixture and arrange it on top of the cake in a pretty pattern. Spoon whatever melted jelly mixture remains over the fruit. ❀

Three to four hours before the cake is to be eaten, whip the cream, flavor it with the sugar and vanilla and use it to frost the sides of the cake. ❀ Refrigerate until served.

Cold Herbed Crabmeat

Veal Chops in Papers

String Beans in Cream

Sautéed Mushrooms with Fresh Coriander

Buttered Noodles

Fresh Peach Tart

•

FIRST COURSE:
Robert Mondavi Chenin Blanc
or Vouvray
MAIN COURSE:
Château Ducru-Beaucaillou

This quintessential June meal is in perfect harmony with the old roses, clematis and Japanese iris blooming in the garden. It begins with fresh crabmeat, in full, succulent season and more affordable every day, prepared according to the precept that the less done to this lovely crustacean, the better. The crab is dressed with fresh herbs and a lemony vinaigrette, then barely touched with mayonnaise to bind it lightly. The slivers of red pepper which brighten the mounds of crab in their lettuce cups have a sweetness that accords with the shellfish.

Next are veal chops *en papillotes*. The chops, which are first browned and then cooked with herbs and a few drops of lemon juice in envelopes of parchment paper, are served in their packets. Crosses are cut in the puffed papers and the corners folded back to release the intoxicating aromas of meat and herbs. With the veal are string beans tenderized in cream, whole sautéed mushrooms freshened with coriander and lightly buttered thin noodles to mop up the sauce. The meal ends with the first peaches of the season in a luscious tart that announces the real advent of summer.

The beauty of backfin crabmeat is its white, sweet chunkiness, but even the best quality crab must be picked over for bits of cartilage and shell that manage to elude skillful packers. In my experience, commensal cats become giddy with joy when fed the discards. The trick in cleaning crab is to employ a gossamer touch with the tips of the fingers so as not to shred the meat more than necessary or reduce it to a stringy mush. The crab and its seasonings are tossed lightly with two forks, again to preserve the integrity of the pieces. The crab is prepared in three quick stages. In the morning, it is cleaned and seasoned with lemon, oil and herbs. It sits in the refrigerator absorbing the flavors until the mayonnaise is added, just before guests arrive. The final assembly takes only minutes.

The greaseproof parchment paper for the veal chops can be found in rolls at most kitchenware stores and is useful also for lining pans for baking meringues and tortes. Foil can be substituted, but the presentation is less striking than paper, which puffs up gloriously. Good bond stationery will also do in a pinch, although the 8½-by-11-inch pieces are a bit small for comfort. Whatever is used, the paper must be buttered or oiled. The packets can be prepared for baking several hours in advance and held in the refrigerator. The chops are dried thoroughly with paper towels, browned quickly in butter and sandwiched between two layers of minced herbs in the papers. As they bake, the juices of the meat blend with the herbs. I serve the chops in the papers and have no difficulty in eating the meat, but my husband declares this to be barbarous and empties chop and juices onto his plate. For the likes of him, a dish should be provided for discards.

It is probably an unkindness to share this discovery, but removing the strings from each side of green bean pods with a potato peeler makes the most enormous difference, particularly in helping the beans to absorb the cream. If you don't try it, you won't have to learn that this tedious little job, which is best done when absorbed in a fascinating conversation, is, in fact, worth the doing.

The mushrooms can be cooked a few hours in advance and reheated before serving, although they cook so quickly that it seems a pity not to do the whole operation at the last minute. The fresh coriander (also sold as cilantro and Chinese parsley) is a surprising and very good addition. Someone I know flutes mushrooms by removing strips of skin from the caps with a lemon stripper. For anyone with a penchant and the time for dumb but satisfying tasks, the technique is to start at the center of the cap and pull the stripper down to the edge of the mushroom. The mushrooms don't taste any better, but the result of these labors is very pretty.

The water for the noodles can be put on to boil when you sit down for the first course. They cook in minutes while the vegetables are heating.

The peaches for the tart should be bought a few days in advance so they can ripen in a plastic bag. Peaches must be checked each day, and those that have begun to feel like edible fruit removed to the refrigerator lest they develop brown spots and infect the less ripe fruits. Peaches that have even a tinge of green, in my experience, will not ripen . . . ever. Even very hard peaches (and these seem to be the only kind that can be found) should have a hint of peach aroma, which, one hopes, will intensify as the fruit ripens. Poaching them lightly in syrup brings up flavor. It also helps to add a couple of drops of a pure peach essence imported from France to the pastry cream (see Mail-Order Sources).

The pastry shell is delicious and so indestructible that the tart can be assembled hours in advance. I discovered the first time I made this and a leftover slice spent the night in the refrigerator that it was as good the next evening as it had been when it was first cut, without even a hint of sog in the crust. This tart can also be made with uncooked blueberries, or a combination of peaches and blueberries, or fresh strawberries, or raspberries, or any summer fruit, as long as it's ripe.

Cold Herbed Crabmeat

•

1   *pound cooked fresh backfin crabmeat,
      picked over and all cartilage and
      bits of shell discarded*
1   *tablespoon lemon juice*
2   *tablespoons olive oil*
2   *tablespoons peanut oil*

2	tablespoons minced shallots
4	tablespoons minced parsley
1	tablespoon minced chives
1½	teaspoons minced fresh tarragon or ¼ teaspoon dried
	Pinch of cayenne pepper
	Salt to taste
4 to 6	tablespoons homemade (see Index) or unsweetened commercial mayonnaise
8	Boston lettuce leaf cups
Sixteen	¼-by-2-inch strips roasted skinned red bell pepper or drained canned pimiento
	Additional minced parsley for garnish

Combine the crabmeat with the lemon juice, oils, shallot, parsley, chives, tarragon, cayenne and salt. Toss carefully with two forks so as not to break up the crabmeat. Cover tightly with plastic wrap and refrigerate anywhere from one to several hours. ❀ Half an hour before serving, add the mayonnaise, starting with 4 tablespoons, and mix carefully. If necessary, add remaining mayonnaise to bind the crabmeat lightly. Just before serving, divide the crabmeat among the lettuce cups placed on scallop shells or salad plates. Arrange 2 red pepper or pimiento strips in the shape of an X on each mound of crabmeat and sprinkle with a little parsley. Serve with crustless toast points or thinly sliced French bread.

Veal Chops in Papers

•

Eight	4- to 6-ounce veal loin or rib chops
2	tablespoons butter
4	tablespoons minced shallots
6	tablespoons minced parsley
2	teaspoons minced chives

> *Melted butter or olive oil for the*
> *parchment paper*
> About 1   *teaspoon lemon juice*
> *Salt and pepper to taste*

Dry the chops thoroughly with paper towels. Heat the butter in a frying pan and brown the chops, one or two at a time, and remove to a dish as they are browned. Combine the shallots, parsley and chives. Cut 8 pieces of parchment paper (or foil) measuring 12 by 15 inches each. Brush the papers with melted butter or oil and make a bed of 2 teaspoons of the mixed herbs on the center of each piece. Place a chop on the herbs and spread 2 more teaspoons of the herbs on each chop. Add the veal juices from the dish to the frying pan and spoon the combined juices over the chops. Sprinkle each with a few drops of lemon juice. Season with salt and pepper to taste.

Make a tight package of each paper by bringing the two long ends together and pleating the paper twice over itself to make a "butcher's" fold. Turn the ends back to the side of the paper with the fold and secure with transparent tape. Place the chops, fold side down, on a jelly-roll pan. The chops can be prepared to this point several hours in advance and refrigerated. Bring to room temperature before the final cooking.

To bake the chops, place the pan in a preheated 375-degree oven for 15 to 20 minutes, depending on the size of the chops. To serve, place each packet on a dinner plate, fold side down, cut a cross in the papers and turn back the corners. If desired, the papers can be discarded and the sauces in them spooned over the chops.

String Beans in Cream

•

> 2   *pounds string beans*
> ½   *cup heavy cream*
> 1   *tablespoon butter*
> *Salt and pepper to taste*

Cut off ends of the beans and, using a potato peeler, remove the strings from each side of the pods. Bring a large pot of water to a boil, add the beans, and cook for 4 minutes after the water returns to the boil. Turn into a colander, refresh under cold water to stop the cooking, drain well and pat dry on a clean towel. Wrap the beans in a paper towel and refrigerate for up to a day. ❀ Just before serving, place the cream and butter in a saucepan and boil for several minutes to reduce the cream and thicken it. Then add the beans and cook, shaking the pan, for another 3 minutes, or until the beans have absorbed most of the cream. Season with salt and pepper and turn out onto half of a serving platter; the mushrooms will go on the other half.

Sautéed Mushrooms with Fresh Coriander

•

24   *large mushrooms, about 2 inches in*
  diameter
2   *tablespoons butter*
1   *tablespoon peanut oil*
  Salt and pepper to taste
  Few drops lemon juice
2   *tablespoons minced fresh coriander*
  (also called cilantro and Chinese
  parsley)

Trim off the mushroom stems even with the caps and freeze the stems for later use for stock or *duxelles.* Clean the mushrooms by wiping them with a damp paper towel. Flute them with a citrus stripper if you wish. Heat the butter and oil in a sauté pan or frying pan large enough to hold the mushrooms in one layer and place them in the pan, cut side down. Season with salt and pepper and sauté over medium heat for 4 minutes. Turn them over and sauté for another minute. ❀ The mushrooms can be cooked a few hours in advance to this point. Just before serving, turn over the mushrooms so that the cut side is down once again. Sprinkle a little lemon juice over them and cook for another minute or two over medium-high heat, or until they are hot. Place the mushrooms, cut side down, on the platter with the beans, pour any butter and juices remaining in the pan over them, and sprinkle with the chopped coriander.

Buttered Noodles

•

1   *pound very fine noodles*
2   *tablespoons butter*
    Salt and pepper to taste

Cook the noodles in a large quantity of boiling, salted water according to package directions and immediately drain in a colander. Place the noodles in a warm serving dish, toss with the butter, and season with salt and pepper.

Fresh Peach Tart

•

   10-inch baked Sweet Tart Shell (recipe
    follows)
1   *cup Pastry Cream (recipe follows)*
2   *pounds ripe peaches (about 10 medium*
    peaches)
   Lemon juice or powdered ascorbic acid
    for acidulated water
1   *cup sugar*
1   *cup water*
½   *teaspoon vanilla extract*
½   *cup Apricot Glaze (recipe follows)*

Make the pastry shell and the pastry cream enough in advance so both will be completely cool when the tart is assembled.

To prepare the peaches, drop them, a few at a time, into a pot of boiling water. Let them remain for about 15 seconds, remove with a slotted spoon, and peel. Place in a bowl of cold acidulated water to keep the peaches from discoloring and set aside.

Combine the sugar and water in a wide-bottomed pan just large enough to hold the peaches in one layer. Bring to a boil, simmer until the syrup is clear, and add the vanilla. Add the peaches to the syrup, bring back to a simmer, and cook for 3 minutes. Then turn the peaches over and cook them for another 3 minutes, or until the peaches test just done when pierced with a sharp pointed knife. Remove from heat and allow the peaches to cool in syrup. When they are cool, choose one with a pretty blush and reserve the better half for the center of the tart. Slice and pit the remaining peaches and return them to the syrup.

To assemble the tart, heat the glaze for a few minutes so that it is spreadable, and, using a pastry brush, paint the baked shell with a thin layer of glaze. Let the glaze set for a few minutes. Then pour the pastry cream over the glaze and spread it evenly over the shell. Drain the peaches. (Strain the syrup into a jar, if desired, for the next batch of peaches. It will keep refrigerated for at least 2 weeks.) Place the reserved peach half in the center of the shell and arrange the slices around it. Then paint the peaches with the remaining apricot glaze. ✿

Sweet Tart Shell

•

1½ cups sifted all-purpose flour
⅓   cup sifted confectioners' sugar
     Pinch of salt
1   stick cold unsalted butter, cut into 16 pieces
3   tablespoons ice water

Combine the flour, sugar and salt in the container of a food processor fitted with the steel knife and process for a few seconds. Place the butter in the container and process, rapidly turning the machine on and off until the mixture resembles coarse cornmeal. With the motor running, add the ice water through the tube and process only until the dough seems to be coming together. Turn the dough out onto a lightly floured board, knead it three times, form into a ball, and place in a plastic bag. ❀ Refrigerate for at least 2 hours before rolling out.

To roll out, lightly flour a board and roll into a circle about 12 inches in diameter. Place on a two-piece 10-inch tart pan, fold the overhanging dough back into itself, and crimp to make a rim of double thickness. Prick the bottom and sides with a fork, place a layer of parchment paper over the shell, and arrange pastry weights or dried beans over the paper to cover the shell. Bake in a preheated 350-degree oven for 15 minutes, remove the shell, and lift out the parchment paper and the weights. Prick the bottom and sides with a fork once again. Return the shell to the oven and bake for another 15 minutes, or until the shell is nicely browned. Remove and allow the shell to cool completely. Then remove it from the pan and place on a serving dish. ❀ The shell is now ready to be filled.

Pastry Cream

•

1 cup milk
3 egg yolks
1/3 cup sugar
2 tablespoons flour
1½ teaspoons butter
2 teaspoons vanilla extract
2 drops peach essence (optional)
  Dab of butter to rub on the surface of
    the completed pastry cream

Bring the milk to a boil and lower heat to keep the milk at a simmer. Combine the egg yolks and the sugar in a bowl and beat with an electric mixer until the mixture becomes very light and forms a ribbon when the mixer whisks are lifted. Beat in the flour with a wire whisk. Then, whisking constantly, add the hot milk to the mixture in a thin stream. Pour the mixture back into the saucepan and, whisking constantly, bring to a boil and boil for 1 minute. Remove from the heat and beat in the butter, vanilla and peach essence, if it is used. Rub the surface of the pastry cream with a little butter to keep a skin from forming and set aside to cool. ✿

Apricot Glaze

MAKES ABOUT ½ CUP

•

½   cup apricot jam
2   tablespoons Kirsch or dark rum

Combine the jam and the Kirsch or rum in a small saucepan, bring to a simmer, force through a strainer, and return to the saucepan. Set aside. ✿ Reheat to liquefy the glaze so that it can be painted onto the fruit.

*Tomato and Sorrel
(or Spinach) Soup*

*Farsumagru
(Hot or Cold
Sicilian Stuffed
Braised Beef Roll)*

*Hot or Cold Broccoli with
Olive Oil, Garlic and Lemon*

*Ekolsund Cream Waffles with
Softened Vanilla Ice Cream
and Hot Blueberry Sauce*

•

*Corvo Rosso
or Parducci Zinfandel*

When the weather behaves as it should, it is reasonable and even intelligent to plan a nice cold meal for a June evening, which, as we know, will be warm if not hot. But when the weather takes a turn, with temperatures hovering stubbornly in the fifties and the rain barely stopping long enough to allow a person to cut a few soggy blooms for the table, the cold meal is unfriendly and even ludicrous. The cold dinner I had planned was served on just such a wet and frigid evening and turned out to be deliciously convertible, as good hot as cold. Had the same meal been planned to be eaten hot, it could just as successfully have been turned around and served cold on a sultry evening.

This useful and adaptable menu starts with a fresh, light tomato and sorrel soup, or tomato and spinach soup if sorrel is not to be had. The soup takes off from an Elizabeth David recipe and is best eaten hot as soon as it is made or cold as soon as it cools off. This poses no problem, since the cooking is completed in less than 10 minutes. Next is a braised Sicilian beef roll stuffed with ground beef, hard-cooked egg and other morsels, all of which are very festive-looking when the meat is sliced and the mosaic of stuffing is revealed. Peas are added to the gravy only if the meat is served hot. Accompanying the beef is crisp-cooked broccoli, also equally good hot or cold, dressed with olive oil, a bit of garlic and a squeeze of lemon juice. The textures, colors and flavors of meat and vegetable are perfect together. Dessert consists of Scandinavian cream waffles made from a recipe given to me by the Danish cook who made them for us when we were guests at Ekolsund, a grand eighteenth-century manor house in the Swedish countryside between Stockholm and Uppsala. The waffles, which contain no egg at all, are light and crisp. They are served at room temperature, as at Ekolsund, with softened vanilla ice cream and hot blueberry sauce. This would make a fabulous ending to a meal any time of the year, especially if some blueberries were put into the freezer when they were at their least expensive.

Fresh sorrel, which my grandmother used to pick wild as "sour grass," is not always to be found but generally is on sale at specialty markets. The only way to assure the availability of this tangy leaf for soups or for sauces is to grow it, which is stunningly uncomplicated for anyone with a small patch of earth and some sun. Sorrel is a perennial that thrives and returns each year. I am profligate enough to keep a couple of plants in a barrel on my handy kitchen porch, but these do freeze in the winter and must be replenished each year. Two plants are ample for an occasional supply, but four are better for aficionados. Spinach is a passable but not totally satisfactory substitute and must be complemented with some but not too much lemon juice to provide a hint of the benign bite of sorrel. I use fresh tomatoes for this soup only when they are full of sunshine and flavor. Otherwise, imported canned Italian plum tomatoes are more desirable than fresh.

The Sicilian beef roll is called *farsumagru,* which translates literally as "false lean," although nobody seems to know why. Waverley Root in *The*

Food of Italy speculates vaguely on the "magru" part relating to Lent but then rejects the notion since it is made of meat. Whatever the reason for the name, this is an impressive dish, which must contain hard-cooked eggs and nutmeg, among other ingredients. It costs about a dollar a portion and can be made totally in advance. I dealt with a young, willing supermarket butcher who agreed to slice a ½-inch-thick round steak horizontally on the slicing machine, stopping before it was cut all the way through, so that it would open up to be ¼ inch thick by about 8 by 11 inches. It could then be pounded, stuffed and rolled. Most recipes suggest tying the roll at intervals, but I prefer to sew it closed, which keeps the stuffing from falling out the ends and makes a very neat-looking piece of cooked meat. Be sure to put the needle away the minute you have finished with it. It is too easy for it to become lodged and hidden in the roll. The threads should not be removed until the meat has cooled and settled into its shape. For slicing the roll, it is essential to have a very sharp knife. If the knife is dull or if it is pressed down too hard, the studded bits of stuffing get mashed together and lose their allure.

The broccoli can be parboiled in advance. It can also be dressed in advance if it is to be served cold. Otherwise it takes only a few minutes to heat it in the oil and seasonings.

The waffles can be made a couple of hours beforehand and held in a turned-off oven with a pilot light, especially if the weather is humid. If they are held any longer, they become hard to cut, although they still manage to taste good. I had great success using some leftover batter that had sat in the refrigerator for three days, so if all is not used at once, the remaining batter will keep. I have made these waffles with three kinds of irons: the Jøtul top-of-the-stove iron that produces charming but very thin heart-shaped waffles; the top-of-the-stove iron that produces a retangular waffle; and a large electric waffle iron. I found very little real difference in the results, although my husband thought the waffles produced by the top-of-the-stove rectangular waffle iron far superior to the others.

Tomato and Sorrel
(or Spinach) Soup

•

A large handful of sorrel leaves or ½
pound spinach leaves
4 *tablespoons butter*
28-ounce can imported peeled plum
tomatoes
Two *10¾-ounce cans condensed chicken broth*
½ *pint heavy cream*
Salt and pepper to taste
Lemon juice to taste (if using spinach
instead of sorrel)

Wash the sorrel or spinach in several waters, discard the coarse stems, and chop fine. Heat 2 tablespoons of the butter in a saucepan and add the chopped leaves. Cook until the sorrel or spinach is very soft and "melted." Set aside.

Heat the remaining 2 tablespoons of butter in a 3-quart saucepan and add the entire contents of the can of tomatoes, liquid and all. Break tomatoes up into smallish chunks, and stir over heat for about 5 minutes. Add the chicken broth, the sorrel or the spinach and the cream. Season to taste with salt and pepper and add a little lemon juice if spinach has been used. Heat through and serve immediately.❀ Or allow the soup to cool and serve cold.

Farsumagru (Hot or Cold
Sicilian Stuffed Braised Beef Roll)

•

1¼-pound piece round steak, ¼ inch thick and at
least 8 inches wide by 11 inches long.
2 *slices white bread (heels are fine),*
soaked in milk and squeezed dry

Scant ¾ pound lean ground beef
2 raw eggs
2 tablespoons freshly grated Parmesan
cheese
2 cloves garlic, crushed
¼ teaspoon marjoram
¼ teaspoon thyme
¼ teaspoon nutmeg, freshly ground if
possible
3 tablespoons minced parsley
Salt and pepper to taste
2 hard-cooked eggs, cut lengthwise into
slivers
⅛ pound corned tongue or Italian salami
or baked ham, cut into ¼-inch-thick
slivers
Scant ⅛ pound provolone cheese, cut
into ¼-inch-thick slivers
2 tablespoons vegetable oil

FOR THE SAUCE
2 onions, chopped
1 stalk celery with leaves, chopped
2 cloves garlic, minced
½ cup red wine
2 cups canned tomato sauce
Salt and pepper to taste
10-ounce package frozen peas (if the
dish is to be served hot)

Have the butcher "butterfly" a ½-inch-thick, 8-by-5½-inch piece of round
steak to open up to a ¼-inch-thick, 8-by-11-inch piece of meat (see text if
further instructions are wanted). Lay the meat flat and pound it, particularly at the joined seam. Lay it on a board, the long side parallel to the edge
of the counter.

Add the squeezed bread to a bowl along with the ground beef, raw eggs,
Parmesan cheese, 2 cloves crushed garlic, marjoram, thyme, nutmeg, parsley, salt and pepper. Mix well and fry a tiny bit to check flavor. The mixture should be highly seasoned, particularly if the dish is to be served cold.
Then spread the mixture over the round steak, to within an inch of the

edges. Place the slivers of hard-cooked egg, meat and cheese in rows on the hamburger mixture and roll the steak into a large "salami." Either tie the roll at short intervals with butcher's twine or sew it closed, using a darning needle and heavy thread.

Add the oil to a heavy oval pot just large enough to hold the meat, and heat until it smokes. Add the meat and brown it on all sides. Then add the sauce ingredients. First add the onions, celery and minced garlic and cook over low heat until soft. Add the wine and raise the heat. Cook until almost all the wine has evaporated. Add the tomato sauce, salt and pepper and bring to a simmer. Cover, reduce heat to very low, and braise for 1½ hours, turning the meat every half hour or so.

Remove the meat to a dish and when it is cool, cover tightly with plastic wrap and refrigerate. ❁   Remove the string or threads when the meat is cold. Cool the sauce and store it in the refrigerator in a jar. ❁   To serve the dish cold, arrange some of the cold sauce on a large serving platter, slice the meat, and arrange the slices down the platter on the sauce. Serve remaining sauce separately.

To serve the dish hot, return the sauce and the meat to the oval pot and place over low heat for an hour. When the meat is hot, add the frozen peas and cook for about 10 minutes, or until the peas are done. Arrange some of the hot sauce with the peas on a large serving platter, slice the meat, and arrange the slices down the platter on the sauce. Serve the remaining sauce separately.

Hot or Cold Broccoli with Olive Oil, Garlic and Lemon

•

1½   *pounds broccoli*
3   *tablespoons olive oil*
2   *cloves garlic, crushed*
   A few drops lemon juice
   Salt and pepper to taste

Wash the broccoli, cut off the tops, and separate into small florets. Reserve. Peel the stalks, removing all the tough parts, and cut into slivers ¼ inch thick by 3 inches long. Bring a large pot of salted water to a boil, add the slivers, and cook for 5 minutes. Then add the florets and cook for 5 minutes more. Drain and refresh under cold water. ✿

Heat the oil in a wok or a frying pan, add the garlic and the broccoli, and stir-fry for a few minutes until heated through. Season with lemon juice, salt and pepper. Serve immediately if the broccoli is to be eaten hot. Otherwise, let it cool, ✿ refrigerate until an hour before it is needed, and bring it to room temperature before serving.

Ekolsund Cream Waffles

•

1½ cups all-purpose flour
Pinch of salt
1 cup water
1 teaspoon vanilla extract
4 tablespoons melted butter
1⅓ cups heavy cream
Melted butter for the waffle iron
Confectioners' sugar, vanilla ice cream
and Hot Blueberry Sauce (recipe
below) for serving

Combine the flour, salt, water, vanilla and melted butter in a bowl and whisk until the batter is smooth. Whip the cream stiff and fold it into the batter. Cover the bowl with plastic wrap and refrigerate the batter for at least an hour. Heat the waffle iron and brush it lightly with melted butter. Pour batter in until it spreads to about an inch from the edges, bring the cover down gently, and bake at high until the iron stops steaming and the waffles are brown. ✿ The waffles will keep for a couple of hours in a turned-off oven with a pilot light. Sprinkle with confectioners' sugar and serve with softened vanilla ice cream and hot blueberry sauce.

Hot Blueberry Sauce

MAKES ABOUT 3 CUPS

•

3   *cups blueberries, rinsed and picked over*
⅔   *cup sugar*
4   *teaspoons lemon juice*
     Grated rind of ½ lemon

Combine the blueberries and the sugar in a saucepan, bring to a boil, reduce heat, and simmer for 3 minutes. Stir in the lemon juice and rind and serve hot. The sauce will keep under refrigeration and loses nothing on being reheated.

• LUNCH FOR EIGHT •

Cold Veal and Ham Pie

Molded String Bean Salad in the Russian Style

Secret Sensational Soft Ice Cream with Blueberries

•

Fetzer "Lake County" Zinfandel
or Beaune "Le Cent-Vignes"

While this meal is lovely as a summery Sunday lunch, with a bit of rearrangement it will do for dinner any evening of the week. Among the meal's blessings is that all the dishes are cold and made in advance, but it has enough substance to be satisfying.

The centerpiece is a veal and ham pie, a gorgeous show-off dish with a shiny crust and pastry decorations in the shape of flowers, leaves, little animals or whatever you like. The recipe, one I have made over the years, keeps evolving and, I think, getting better. The pie is a snap to put together, when you realize that in cooking, as anything else, things work best one step at a time.

The molded string bean salad in the Russian style (this means the presence of mayonnaise) is a ravishing accompaniment to the meat pie at lunch.

As a first course for dinner, it is best embellished by a ring of good sliced Italian salami or ice-cold shrimp. The pie would then be served without any accompaniment and be followed by a plain green salad and a selection of good cheeses. The recipe for the bean salad is Mary Henderson's and was served frequently at the British Embassy when her husband, Sir Nicholas Henderson, was ambassador.

Dessert, which can only be called "Secret Sensational Soft Ice Cream," is, I believe, making its public debut. Françoise Norrish gave me her recipe shortly after her husband, Frank, became ambassador from New Zealand, but with the proviso that I never serve it to her and that I not reveal it to anyone as long as she was in Washington. Now it can be told.

The ice cream is extraordinary for many reasons. It is nothing to make, it needs no churning or second whippings or any other attention once it is put in the freezer, it is versatile enough to accept any kind of flavoring, and the result is creamy, smooth and delicious.

When I made the veal and ham pie last, I substituted for one of the two pounds of veal a pound of less expensive turkey cutlets, which I found at the supermarket. The introduction of the turkey was thoroughly successful, but I would not use less veal or none at all; the texture and flavor would be adversely affected. The minced aromatics, which get sprinkled over the layers of the meats, add freshness and flavor. The black Chinese mushrooms are for texture and interest.

As for the choices for the crust, I love the traditional English Raised Pie Pastry, first because it is very good and second for old times' sake. I started to use this crust years ago, when pastry terrified me and I was convinced I would never be clever enough to roll out a piece of dough. I have long since faced up to Unsweetened Pie Pastry, for which the directions are also given. Puff pastry is another alternative. (However, I caution against using it when the humidity is high.) I buy puff pastry frozen at the supermarket and find it very good. Frozen puff pastry should be refrigerated after it is defrosted and kept cold at all times until it goes into the oven. The pan (springform pans are useful because unmolding is foolproof) should be filled with puff pastry according to the directions in the recipe for the Unsweetened Pie Pastry, which is what the French use for their *pâté en croûte*.

A sharp knife is essential because the meats for the pie must be sliced very thin. I found a packaged country ham that was sliced thin and well trimmed, exactly what is wanted. However, the smoked ham center slices needed to be slit horizontally, and so did the veal leg steaks. Thin slices of veal scalopinni would certainly do, but they are more expensive. The turkey cutlets come boned and are easily pounded thin.

For flattening the meats, I use a heavy meat pounder that we dragged back from Italy after a trip when every new acquisition seemed to weigh pounds and pounds. These meat pounders are now available in kitchenware stores. A rolling pin will also do, as will the side of a large can of, say, tomatoes. The meat is sandwiched between two pieces of waxed paper and the pounding, really a light tapping, should start from the center and be directed outward.

When you make the string bean salad, remember that the sides of the egg slices that face down will be facing up when the dish is unmolded; a good egg slicer is invaluable. Look for the best-tasting tomatoes you can find and the youngest string beans.

For this dish, I make thick processor mayonnaise in the following proportions: 2 egg yolks, 1 teaspoon Dijon mustard, 4 teaspoons lemon juice and ½ teaspoon salt processed until thick, and 1½ cups olive oil added in a slow, steady stream. I then thin the mayonnaise with a tablespoon of very hot water, beaten in, and a little cream if it is still too thick. A delicious variation is to use half hazelnut oil and half peanut oil instead of olive oil. The hazelnut oil, which can be found in good specialty stores, is not cheap, but you don't need much and it seems to be made for string beans.

The soft ice cream is glorious with any fruit and very economical if you have a cache of frozen egg whites (see Index). For this meal I coupled it with blueberries and flavored the ice cream very successfully with *mirabelle*, the liqueur the Alsatians make from a tiny yellow plum of the same name. The combination was right. *Mirabelle*, like other good liqueurs, represents a substantial cash outlay, but if you can prevent greedy people from drinking it, it lasts for a very long time. My stash of various liqueurs lives in the kitchen and is sequestered for cooking only, so I manage to stretch this investment for what seems forever. Cheap liqueurs or bad "cooking" sherry only muck up food.

Cold Veal and Ham Pie

•

8   *black Chinese dried mushrooms*
¼   *cup finely minced parsley*
½   *cup finely minced onion*
½   *cup finely minced celery*

½   cup finely minced green pepper
     Freshly ground black pepper to taste
2   tablespoons (2 envelopes) unflavored
        gelatin
2   cups beef bouillon
½   cup sherry, of a quality such as Dry
        Sack
1   tablespoon Worcestershire sauce
3   slices bacon, blanched for 10 minutes
        in a quart of boiling water, rinsed
        under cold water, drained and patted
        dry with paper towels
½   pound country ham, thinly sliced and
        pounded thinner
1   pound center slice smoked ham, boned,
        sliced horizontally through the
        middle and pounded thinner
1   pound leg of veal, sliced very thin and
        pounded thinner
1   pound turkey cutlets, pounded thin
     Raised Pie Pastry or Unsweetened Pie
        Pastry (recipes follow), or 1½
        pounds frozen puff pastry, defrosted,
        formed into 2 balls and refrigerated
1   egg, beaten

Rinse the mushrooms, pour boiling water over them to cover, and set aside to soften for about 20 minutes. Drain the mushrooms, squeeze them gently, cut out and discard the stems, mince the caps, and place in a bowl. Add the minced parsley, onion, celery, green pepper and black pepper and set aside.

Soak the gelatin in ½ cup of the beef bouillon for 5 minutes. Add the remaining bouillon and heat until the gelatin is dissolved. Add the sherry and Worcestershire sauce.

Place each of the meats in separate bowls and add enough of the gelatin-bouillon mixture to barely cover. Set the remaining mixture aside. Cover the bowls of meat with plastic wrap and set aside while you prepare the pan.❁

Line a 9-inch springform pan 3 inches deep with pastry. Pour off the gelatin-bouillon mixture from each of the bowls and add it to the pan of reserved gelatin-bouillon mixture. Cover the bottom of the pastry-lined pan with a layer of veal, then a sprinkling of the mixed minced vegetables, then a layer of smoked ham and a sprinkling of the vegetables, next a layer of turkey cutlets and a sprinkling of the vegetables, then a layer of the country ham and vegetables. Repeat until all the ingredients are used, pausing at the middle to put in one layer of bacon. Put the top crust onto the pie and cut a hole in the center of it. Make a funnel of foil (or use a metal pastry bag tube), butter the outside of the funnel, and place it in the hole.

Brush the crust with beaten egg, make decorations with the scraps of dough, place them on the crust, and brush these plus the entire surface with beaten egg. Cover the remaining egg with plastic wrap and refrigerate. It will be used later.

Bake the pie in a preheated 350-degree oven for 1½ hours. Remove and let it cool a bit, or until the sides sink in — this will take about 45 minutes. Then remove the side of the pan by releasing the springform mechanism. Brush the sides of the pie with the reserved beaten egg, place it, still on the base of the springform pan, on a baking sheet, and return to a 375-degree oven to brown the sides. Do not remove the funnel. If the top of the pie is browning too quickly, cover it with a tent of foil. Remove the pie when the crust is nicely browned and let it cool for 1½ hours. ✿

If the reserved gelatin-bouillon mixture has jelled, place it over a bowl of warm water to soften. Then, a tablespoon at a time, pour the mixture into the funnel. If the crust has developed a leak, let the gelatin mixture thicken a bit and add it to the pie slowly enough for the meats to absorb it before it has a chance to leach out. Pour any gelatin mixture that the pie won't absorb into a shallow tin and refrigerate. Remove the funnel and refrigerate the pie. ✿   When you are ready to serve, to remove pie from pan bottom, slide 2 long spatulas under the crust so that they cross each other and form an X between the crust and the bottom. Lift off onto a serving dish and slide spatulas out. Chop the remaining gelatin and place around the pie. Slice into wedges and serve.

Raised Pie Pastry

•

3½ cups (1 pound) all-purpose flour
1 teaspoon salt
1 scant tablespoon confectioners' sugar
      (optional)
¾ cup water
¾ cup lard

Sift together the flour, salt and optional sugar (this adds richness to the pastry) into a large bowl. Make a well in the middle. Bring the water and lard to a boil together and pour into the well immediately. Bring the flour into the well with a wooden spoon until the dough forms a smooth ball. You may need to add a little more flour or a little more water (very hot) to make the dough firm but pliable.

Reserve a quarter of the dough for the top crust. Flatten the remainder and place it on the bottom of a 9-inch springform pan 3 inches deep. Now, using your knuckles, press the dough from the center to the sides. Use light, firm movements. When the base is covered, press the dough up the sides of the pan and allow ½-inch overhang at the top rim. Take care there is no thick layer of dough at the joint of the base and sides of the pan but that the dough has not been pressed too thinly, especially on the sides. If the dough slips down the sides, it is too hot. Wait a few minutes and start again.

Fill the pastry case as directed in the pie recipe. Paint the top edge of the dough with beaten egg. Roll out the dough for the top crust and place it on the pie. Press down so that it adheres to the overlap, press together and make a decorative edge. Keep the edges inside the rim of the pan. Otherwise they will crack when you remove the pie. Proceed as directed to cut a hole in the center, insert a greased funnel, and glaze and decorate the crust.

Unsweetened Pie Pastry

·

3½   cups (1 pound) all-purpose flour
1   teaspoon salt
¼   pound (1 stick) unsalted butter, chilled
6   tablespoons lard, chilled
3   egg yolks, beaten, plus enough ice
      water to make ¾ cup liquid

Sift the flour and salt together into a large mixing bowl. Either cut the butter and lard into the flour with a pastry blender until the mixture resembles coarse cornmeal, or use a hand electric mixer to do this, but be careful not to overbeat. Stir or beat in the liquid and mix until the mixture masses into a dough. Add more ice water if necessary.

To make this pastry in a food processor, put half the flour and salt into the bowl and process for 2 seconds. Cut the butter and lard into ½-inch pieces and add half of each to the bowl. Process for 3 seconds. Then add half the liquid and process for a second or two, or until the dough barely begins to mass. Turn the dough out onto a work surface, and make a second batch the same way. Then, using the heel of your hand, blend the two batches together. Cut the dough in half, form into two balls, wrap with plastic, and refrigerate for at least 2 hours.❁

Line a 9-inch springform pan 3 inches deep: Remove one of the balls of pastry (or of puff pastry) from the refrigerator and cut it in half. Roll out each half into a long rectangle that is 1 inch wider than the side of the pan and to a thickness of ⅛ inch. Press the rectangles to the insides of the pan and pinch the ends together to make one continuing strip. Reserve any excess pastry. Allow ½ inch of extra dough on the bottom edge and press down around the base of the pan. Also allow an extra ½-inch overhang on the top. Trim to even off the edges and make a ball of all the excess dough. Refrigerate this until needed later for decorating the top crust.

Next remove the second ball of pastry from the refrigerator, cut it in half, rewrap one half, and return to the refrigerator. Roll out the half you are working with into a circle for the bottom crust. Paint the rim of dough on the bottom of the pan with the beaten egg, lay the rolled-out bottom crust on it, and press gently to make the doughs adhere to each other. Then fill the crust as directed.

Roll out the remaining pastry. Brush the top overhang with beaten egg and place the top crust on the pan. Roll the overhang over the top crust and pinch together to make a decorative edging, but be sure to keep the pastry inside the rim of the pan. Otherwise you will crack it when you remove the springform.

Proceed as directed to make a hole in the center, insert a funnel, decorate and bake.

Molded String Bean Salad
in the Russian Style

·

4	*eggs, hard-cooked, cooled and sliced*
1½	*cups mayonnaise, preferably homemade (see Index)*
4	*large ripe tomatoes, scalded for 30 seconds in boiling water, then peeled, cored and sliced thinly*
1½	*pounds string beans, boiled for 8 minutes in a large quantity of water and cooled under cold running water*
1	*tablespoon finely minced parsley or dill*

Cut a round of parchment or waxed paper to fit an 8-inch springform pan 2½ inches deep and line the bottom of the pan with it. Place one layer of the sliced hard-cooked eggs on the bottom of the pan. Use the best slices. Carefully spread a layer of mayonnaise over the eggs so that they will stick to the next layer, not to the pan. (A flexible spatula is efficient for this.)

Next add a layer of sliced tomatoes and spread a layer of mayonnaise over these. Mix about a cup of mayonnaise into the string beans and add a layer of these. Then add a layer of eggs, spread with mayonnaise, and then a layer of tomatoes. Repeat until the pan is full. Cover with a piece of waxed paper, place a plate that fits within the rim of the pan on top and press down well. ❀ Refrigerate for at least 4 hours, or overnight. When you are ready to serve the salad, remove the waxed paper, upturn the salad on a round serving dish and remove the rim and the base of the pan. Sprinkle the top with chopped parsley or dill.

If you are serving this dish as a first course, you can surround the salad with salami slices or shrimp. Slice the salad with a sharp knife in wedges, as you would a pie.

Secret Sensational Soft
Ice Cream

MAKES 2 QUARTS

•

6   egg whites
6   tablespoons liqueur or other flavoring
        (see NOTE)
2   cups heavy cream
1   scant cup superfine (not confectioners')
        sugar

Beat the egg whites until they are stiff but not dry. Fold in the liqueur or other flavoring. Beat the cream, and when it starts to thicken, add the sugar gradually. Beat until fairly stiff. Fold the cream mixture into the egg-white mixture and turn into a pretty serving bowl. Freeze for at least 4 hours. ❀ This ice cream remains relatively soft.

Serve with fresh berries or sliced peaches. The recipe can also be halved to make 1 quart.

NOTE: *Mirabelle* is a lovely flavoring if you serve the ice cream with blueberries. *Framboise*, of course, is good with raspberries. Grand Marnier, Cointreau or Kirsch is delicious with strawberries or peaches.

• SUMMER PICNIC •

Iced (or Hot) Spinach and Pea Soup

Cold Chicken Breast Chunks en Brochette

Marinated Potatoes and Artichoke Hearts

Chocolate-Coated Strawberries or Watermelon Chunks and Buttery Sugar Cookies

•

*Ruffino Chianti
or Beujolais-Villages*

*J*une is the time for picnicking, before the heat settles in and when even the ants are less pestiferous than they surely will be as summer takes over. Or so we hope. This transportable meal would make for a dashing open-air feast at lakeside, on the beach, in a park or at the table in your own garden.

To begin the picnic, there is an assertive chilled spinach and pea soup poured from Thermoses into mugs. Fresh mint can be snipped into tiny slivers at home and sprinkled on the soup when it is served. Slightly bitey and a lovely green, the soup can also be served hot in winter. The main course consists of chunks of chicken breast left on the small skewers on which the meat was broiled, the more comfortably to fit into a basket. Spiked with a tasty marinade of lime juice, white wine, olive oil, garlic and tarragon, the chicken is at its best at room temperature. With it is a handsome, subtly sauced salad of cold halved red potatoes with their skins left on, the better to contrast in color with the accompanying artichoke hearts and green onion speckles. The meal ends with festive chocolate-covered strawberries or, if the weather is so warm the chocolate is in peril, seeded watermelon chunks, or any other edible fresh fruit, accompanied by my daughter Tessa's buttery sugar cookies.

The soup, which balances the lightness of spinach with the density of peas, is quickly made one or even two days in advance, since it seems to improve with a little time. Onions are softened in butter, with some flour and a bit of curry cooked in the mixture for a minute or two to tone down the spice's rawness. Defrosted whole leaf spinach and its liquid plus frozen peas are then added along with some water and the vegetables are cooked for a few minutes. The whole batch is puréed in the processor and returned to the pan along with chicken broth and milk. After this is cooked up, the soup is cooled and then chilled, ready to pack. Thermoses can be chilled by filling them with ice cubes for half an hour. The ice is discarded and the soup poured into the cold containers just before setting out.

The boneless skinless chicken breasts must be trimmed of all gristle before they are cut into chunks. Once this is done, the rest of the preparation takes minutes. The pieces marinate overnight in the refrigerator, a process that "cooks" them to a certain extent, what with the lime juice content of the marinade. The morning of the picnic, the chicken chunks are strung onto small skewers (for portability) or large ones, if they are to be packed off the skewer, and grilled quickly.

The potato-artichoke salad is made the night before and held in the refrigerator. This salad is best eaten no later than the day after it is made, since oddly enough it loses flavor with time. I have used both frozen artichoke hearts, which are not always easy to find, and canned hearts and find very little difference in quality if the canned vegetable is washed thoroughly under cold running water to rid it of any metallic taste. The artichokes are then gently squeezed of excess liquid and quartered before they are added to the potatoes. Be careful not to overcook the potatoes. Frequent testing with a sharp, pointed knife is preferable to the soggy, crumbly mess that potatoes turn into with too much boiling. The combination of white wine with white wine vinegar and olive oil makes for a delicate and complementary dressing.

Chocolate-covered strawberries are easily made even with supermarket chocolate, although a little unflavored oil must be added to it to make up for the higher cocoa-butter content of more expensive "dipping" chocolate. The best dipping chocolate I have tried is Carma, a Swiss brand, in the semisweet bar called Bourbon-Vanilla. I have had no trouble holding the strawberry by the stem for dipping, but some find spearing the fruit with toothpicks facilitates the process. The coated berries will hold for a few hours in the refrigerator; they can be made the night before for a picnic lunch, or in the morning for a dinner. I count from four to five strawberries per serving, depending on the size of the berries. Be sure to follow the suggestions for melting chocolate. Overheating can be ruinous.

For adult picnics, watermelon should be cut into manageable chunks and seeded at home. However, children should be provided with whole slices of fruit and the opportunity to spit seeds, particularly if the ideal location of a back porch can be provided for this cherished occupation. The sugar cookies, which can be made a couple of days in advance and stored in a tightly covered container, are very good with any fruit. They are most satisfactory if you have a small child as a helper, since once the butter and sugar have been creamed, the rest is a matter of mushing flour into the butter mixture with the fingers and then rolling balls by hand. Very satisfactory for the mud-pie set. They take no time to make, even less to cook and are very good indeed.

Iced (or Hot) Spinach
and Pea Soup

•

1	*medium-large onion, minced*
2	*tablespoons butter*
2	*tablespoons flour*
1	*teaspoon Madras curry powder*
	10-ounce package frozen whole leaf spinach, defrosted with liquid reserved
	10-ounce package frozen green peas
2	*cups water*
Two	*13-3/4 ounce cans chicken broth*

2   *cups milk*
    Salt and pepper to taste
1½ *tablespoons minced fresh mint leaves*
    (optional)

Cook the minced onion in the butter in a saucepan until the onions are soft and transparent but not colored, about 10 minutes. Add the flour and curry powder and cook, stirring constantly, for 2 minutes. Then add the spinach, its juices, the peas and 2 cups of water. Bring to the boil, lower heat, and cook for 10 minutes, stirring occasionally. Turn the mixture into a processor bowl and process, stopping to scrape down the sides of the bowl at least once, until the vegetables are puréed. Return the purée to the saucepan, stir in the chicken broth, milk, salt and pepper, and bring to the boil, stirring. Pour the soup into a large bowl, cool to room temperature, and refrigerate overnight or longer. ✿   When the soup is thoroughly chilled, taste again and adjust seasonings. To serve, pour soup into mugs or bowls and garnish with minced mint leaves, if desired.

Cold Chicken Breast Chunks en Brochette

•

2¼ *pounds boneless, skinned chicken*
    breasts (about 3 whole breasts)
3 *tablespoons lime juice*
¼ *cup white wine*
¼ *cup olive oil*
1 *clove garlic, crushed*
1 *teaspoon dried tarragon*
   Salt and pepper
   Paprika

Dry the chicken breasts and cut them into 2-inch chunks, removing tendons and gristle, to make about 35 to 40 chunks. Combine the lime juice, white wine, olive oil, crushed garlic, tarragon and salt and pepper to taste. Add the chunks of chicken, stir, cover, and refrigerate for several hours or overnight. If the marinade does not cover the chicken, stir when you think of it.

To cook the chicken, remove the chunks from the marinade (reserve it) and string them onto 8 large or 16 small skewers, leaving ample room between the chunks so they will brown nicely. Sprinkle with paprika and arrange the skewers about an inch apart on a large roasting pan. Place the pan under a preheated broiler and broil for 3 minutes. Remove the pan, turn the skewers, baste with the marinade, and return to the broiler for another 3½ minutes. Remove the pan and cut through one of the chunks. If the juices run pink, cook the chicken for another minute. The chicken is done when the juices run yellow. Leave the chicken chunks on the skewers, if desired.✿ Cool and pack in the picnic hamper. Or refrigerate and bring to room temperature before serving.

Marinated Potatoes
and Artichoke Hearts

•

2 *pounds small or medium Red Bliss*
   potatoes, unpeeled
Two *14-ounce cans (8½ ounces drained*
     weight) artichoke hearts, rinsed well
     under cold running water, drained
     and squeezed to get rid of excess
     water and quartered, or two 9-ounce
     packages frozen artichoke hearts,
     cooked according to package
     directions, drained, cooled and
     quartered
3 *tablespoons dry white wine*
4½ *teaspoons white wine vinegar*
3 *tablespoons olive oil*
5 *green onions, cleaned with some green*
   parts remaining and sliced very thin
   Salt and pepper to taste

Wash the potatoes and cook them in boiling water until they test done when pierced with a sharp, pointed knife. Drain well. Do not remove the skins. Cut the potatoes in half if they are small or quarter them if they are medium-size. Place in a large bowl. Add the quartered artichoke hearts and the remaining ingredients to the warm potatoes. Toss to mix well, cool to room temperature, ✿ cover and refrigerate overnight. Serve at room temperature.

Chocolate-Coated Strawberries

•

35 to 40 *strawberries (about a pint and a half, depending on the size of the berries)*
6 *ounces semisweet "dipping" (high cocoa-butter content) chocolate or 6 ounces semisweet chocolate and 5 teaspoons peanut oil or other tasteless cooking oil*
8 *grape leaves or other pretty leaves (optional)*

Brush the strawberries with a pastry brush to clean them, but do not wash or hull them.

Place a few inches of water in the bottom of a double boiler and bring to the boil. Remove from heat. Put the chocolate, broken up into small pieces, and the oil (if you are not using dipping chocolate) into the top of the boiler and cover. Let it sit, away from heat, for 2 minutes. Stir with a wooden spoon. All the chocolate pieces should be melted. If they are not, cover and wait another minute. Do not let even a drop of water fall into the chocolate.

If you have a yogurt or cheese thermometer, check the temperature of the chocolate before dipping — it should be no hotter than 90 degrees, with the ideal temperature 86 degrees. Pick up a strawberry by its stem, dip it two-thirds of the way into the chocolate, and set it, stem end down, on a cake rack, using the grid spaces to hold the berries upright. Continue until all the berries are coated (you will need two racks for 40 berries) and refrigerate for 30 minutes to set the chocolate. For each person's portion, just before serving, arrange 4 or 5 strawberries on their sides, so that some of the red shows, on a grape leaf or other pretty leaf on a dessert dish.

The strawberries ideally should be dipped not too long before they are eaten. Three or 4 hours❀ is best, but they can be held overnight❀ in the refrigerator for a picnic lunch the next day.

NOTE: Any leftover chocolate can be kept in a jar, refrigerated. It can be melted over low heat and used again for dipping or it can be mixed into a bar with toasted almonds and eaten as a candy.

Buttery Sugar Cookies

MAKES ABOUT 60

•

½   *pound (2 sticks) butter*
5   *tablespoons sugar*
1   *teaspoon vanilla extract*
2   *cups all-purpose flour*
About ⅓   cup sugar for rolling the baked cookies

Cream the butter and sugar with an electric mixer until light and fluffy. Beat in the vanilla. Work in the flour with the fingers. Roll into balls about ¾ inch in diameter and place on a cookie sheet, about 1 inch apart. The cookies will swell by one-third as they bake. Place in a preheated 350-degree oven for about 5 minutes, or until the cookies are pale gold. Roll in additional granulated sugar, cool,❀ and store in a tightly covered container.

July

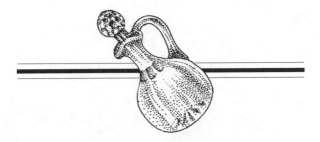

Olive Oil Flavored with Provençal Herbs

•

1	*small stalk or ½ teaspoon dried thyme*
1	*small stalk or ½ teaspoon dried rosemary*
1	*stalk or 1 teaspoon dried savory*
1	*dried wild fennel shoot*
8	*coriander seeds*
2	*unpeeled garlic cloves*
2	*cups olive oil*

Place the herbs and the garlic in a 1-pint or ½-liter bottle, pour in oil, cork or cap, and set aside in a dark place for one week. Use the oil within 6 weeks on tomatoes, in vinaigrettes, on pasta, on goat cheese, to baste broiled fish, to marinate lamb and for roasting potatoes.

NOTE: To dry fresh herbs, cut stalks just before herbs flower, tie into bundles, and hang upside down in a warm, dark place; or place stalks in paper-towel-lined jelly-roll pans and dry overnight in a turned-off gas oven with a pilot light. The sooner the dried herbs are used, the more flavor they will have.

Dried wild fennel shoots are available in specialty markets.

Consommé Belleview

Poached Salmon Filled with Leek Purée

Caper Mayonnaise

Cold Vegetable Platter of French Potato Salad, Wilted Cucumber Sticks and Asparagus Sticks in Cream Dressing

Glorious Fourth Blueberry Pie with Vanilla Ice Cream

•

*Corton-Charlemagne Louis Latour
or Sonoma Vineyards "Chalk Hill" Chardonnay*

W hen I was growing up in New England, we ate salmon, peas, potatoes and blueberry pie on the Fourth of July. Still a nice tradition at this time of year, particularly since excellent fresh salmon can be found now, whole or cut into steaks or fillets, at reasonable prices.

This celebratory meal starts with consommé Belleview embellished with full-bodied dry sherry. The salmon is a classic poached fish made contemporary by being boned, stuffed with a thin delicious green line of sautéed leeks and minced parsley and served cold with a caper mayonnaise. The cold vegetable platter accompanying the salmon consists of cooked potatoes cut into sticks, saturated with bouillon and finished off with a mild mustard vinaigrette and sprinkles of paper-thin scallion slices. With the potatoes are wilted cucumber sticks flavored with dill and a vinaigrette plus just-cooked asparagus sticks presented in a light tart dressing of heavy cream and lemon juice. Dessert is a Glorious Fourth blueberry pie; a super-short crust burnished to a stunning brown, fat with berries, more tart than sweet — the perfect vehicle for vanilla ice cream.

The consommé Belleview, which appeared in *Michael Field's Cooking School* as a modified classic, is a combination of clam and chicken broth simmered with minced garlic, then strained and garnished with lemon rind and parsley. The sherry is my husband's White Knight invention, which, I believe, gives the soup a bit of body and further smooths it. However, purists of my acquaintance shake their heads, so the addition is optional. What a joy it is to have such a refreshing first course in minutes. Even though the soup is served hot, its light tang makes it perfect for a warm summer night.

Salmon and leeks, both in full season in July, combine to make a beautiful and delicious dish. The salmon is boned but remains in one piece since the back is left intact rather than cut through. This operation can be performed at the fish store or by the cook at home. I find a long, thin, flexible filleting knife a most effective tool. The fish can then be flipped open and the leek and parsley stuffing spread in a thin layer on one side. When the fish is closed back on itself, it is lightly wrapped in cheesecloth to hold it together while it is cooked. When the salmon is cool, it is sliced to reveal a pretty green line of stuffing in the center.

The salmon is poached in a simple white court bouillon, which can then be reduced and made into a sparkling aspic, all in advance. It is always a wonder to clarify an aspic. In this case, the reduced court bouillon starts out as a cloudy mess full of globules of egg whites and pieces of egg shell, but then when it passes through cheesecloth it miraculously becomes a sparkling, clear liquid that sets into a jewellike jelly. When the chopped aspic is placed around the fish on its serving platter, the fish looks as though it is afloat in a pale amber sea. If an aspic is not wanted, the court bouillon can be decanted into jars, frozen and reused for the next fish.

The salmon is served with a caper mayonnaise made mild by washing and drying the capers before they are chopped and added to the sauce. A platter of cold, individually dressed vegetables cut into sticks of various widths makes a fine accompaniment to the fish. In addition to a superb, light-textured French potato salad, there are wilted cucumber sticks, without which cold salmon should not be eaten, and crunchy asparagus in a mild cream dressing. For some, French bread is a natural and necessary accompaniment to the main course.

My recent experiments with blueberry pie-making revealed that most recipes call for too much sugar in the blueberries and too ordinary a crust for the pie. The berries in this recipe are definitely not cloying. I find the addition of a few drops of imported French blueberry essence helpful, especially since wild blueberries with their dashing flavor are rarely to be found and because cultivated blueberries can be a bit bland.

The crust here is very short indeed; that is, it contains a maximum of butter and shortening. I make this crust, as I do most crusts, in the food processor. The butter and shortening must be very cold when they are incorporated into the flour. I measure these and cut the butter into pieces in advance so they can sit in the refrigerator for at least an hour before I make the dough. The dough must also be very cold before it is rolled out, so it is a good idea to make it the day before and leave it in the refrigerator until it is needed. It also helps to work quickly, particularly if the day and the kitchen are hot.

The worst thing about berry pies is their proclivity for leaking juices out of the crust and over the rim. A jelly-roll pan placed judiciously on the oven floor catches these juices and prevents the cook's having to clean out the caramelized mess that would otherwise spill onto the oven.

Consommé Belleview

•

Three	*10³/₄-ounce cans condensed chicken broth*
Two	*8-ounce bottles clam juice*
1	*teaspoon minced garlic*
	Pinch of cayenne
2 to 4	*tablespoons full-bodied dry sherry, such as Dry Sack (optional)*
1	*teaspoon grated lemon rind*
2	*tablespoons minced parsley*

Combine the chicken broth, clam juice, minced garlic and cayenne in a saucepan, bring to a simmer, cover the pan, and cook over very low heat for about 10 minutes. Add 2 tablespoons of the sherry, at the last minute, if you have decided to use it, stir and taste. Add more sherry if necessary. Strain the consommé into a bowl or tureen and garnish with the lemon rind and parsley. Ladle into bouillon cups or shallow soup bowls.

Poached Salmon Filled with Leek Purée

•

4-pound piece of salmon, preferably a center cut or from the tail end

FOR THE COURT	*8*	*cups cold water*
BOUILLON	*4*	*cups dry white wine*
	2	*large onions, coarsely chopped*
	3	*stalks celery with leaves, coarsely chopped*
	3	*medium carrots, cut in chunks*
	2	*bay leaves, crumbled*
	6	*sprigs parsley*
	1/2	*teaspoon dried thyme*
	1/2	*teaspoon cracked peppercorns*
	1	*tablespoon salt*
FOR THE	*3*	*leeks, white parts only*
STUFFING	*3*	*tablespoons butter*
		Salt and pepper to taste
	1/2	*cup minced parsley*
FOR THE	*4*	*cups reduced court bouillon*
(OPTIONAL)	*1/2*	*teaspoon lemon juice*
ASPIC	*2*	*tablespoons (2 envelopes) gelatin softened in 1/2 cup cold water*

2   *egg whites plus the shells of the eggs*
        (reserve yolks for the mayonnaise)
    Lemon slices
    Parsley sprigs
    Caper Mayonnaise (following recipe)

Have the salmon boned but left in a single piece so that the fish remains hinged along the back.

First, make the court bouillon. Combine all ingredients in a large pot, bring to a boil, reduce heat, and simmer, partially covered, for an hour. Let cool and strain into a fish poacher or a roasting pan.

Next, make the stuffing. Slit the leeks down the middle and wash carefully under cold running water. Be sure no sand remains. Drain the leeks and chop them fine. Melt the butter in a sauté pan, add the leeks along with salt and pepper to taste, and cook very slowly over low heat, stirring occasionally, for about 20 minutes or until the leeks are very soft. Do not allow them to color. Remove to a bowl and let them cool. Stir in the parsley.

•

Wash the salmon and pat it dry. Open the fish and place the stuffing in an even layer over the entire surface of one side. Close the fish and wrap it in a large piece of damp cheesecloth that has been rinsed and wrung out. Leave about 6 inches of cloth at each end of the fish and tie the ends to make handles so they can be used to maneuver the fish later. Do not wrap the fish too tightly, since it must have room to expand and not become too dense in texture.

Lower the salmon onto the rack of the poacher or into the roasting pan with the cooled court bouillon. Place the poacher or pan over two burners and bring the court bouillon to a boil over high heat. Watch carefully. The minute the liquid begins to boil, lower the heat to just below the simmer and start timing the cooking. Poach the salmon for 25 minutes, then turn off the heat and let it cool in the court bouillon. When the salmon is cool, remove it from the pan, place it on a board, and open the cheesecloth. Peel off the skin and the brown surface layer between the skin and the pink flesh, using the side of a fork. Turn the salmon over, using the cheesecloth to maneuver the fish, and remove skin and brown layer. Place the salmon on a serving platter, cover tightly with plastic wrap, and refrigerate. ❁

•

Strain the court bouillon into a saucepan if you wish to make an aspic. Otherwise, strain it into jars and freeze. It can be reused to poach the next fish.

To make the aspic, boil down the court bouillon over high heat so that 4 cups remain. Add the lemon juice. Then with a wire whisk beat in the softened gelatin and the egg whites and crushed shells. Keep beating until the mixture comes to a rolling boil. Turn off the heat and let it stand for about 15 minutes. Place a sieve over a bowl and line the sieve with a double layer of wrung-out cheesecloth. Ladle the mixture into the sieve. The impurities in the court bouillon will be held in suspension by the egg whites and shells, and the aspic that strains through will be crystal clear. However, do not disturb or stir the mixture as it goes through the sieve. Pour the aspic into a cake pan, cool, and refrigerate until it is set. ❁ Just before serving, turn the aspic out onto a board and chop it. It will look jewellike. Surround the salmon with the aspic and garnish with lemon slices and sprigs of parsley. Serve with caper mayonnaise.

Caper Mayonnaise

MAKES ABOUT 1½ CUPS

•

2	*egg yolks*
1	*teaspoon Dijon mustard*
1	*tablespoon lemon juice*
1	*teaspoon red wine vinegar, or more to taste*
	Salt and white pepper to taste
¾	*cup mild olive oil*
¾	*cup peanut oil*
2	*tablespoons capers, rinsed in a sieve under cold water, dried in paper towels and minced*
3	*tablespoons minced parsley*
1 to 2	*tablespoons, or more if needed, whipping cream*

Combine the egg yolks, mustard, lemon juice, vinegar, salt and pepper in a food processor bowl and process for a few minutes, or until the mixture thickens. With the motor running, slowly pour the olive oil and the peanut oil through the feed tube. Place the mayonnaise (it will be very thick) in a bowl and stir in the capers and parsley. Then thin the mayonnaise with cream to the desired consistency. ❀

French Potato Salad

•

2	*pounds medium-size new potatoes*
³/₄	*cup beef bouillon*
½	*teaspoon Dijon mustard*
2	*tablespoons red wine vinegar*
4	*tablespoons olive oil*
	Salt and pepper to taste
3	*scallions, with half the green parts*

Scrub the potatoes and boil them, in their skins, in salted water for from 15 to 20 minutes, or until they are just cooked. Remove the skins and slice the potatoes lengthwise into ½-inch-thick sticks. Place the potatoes in a bowl and while they are still warm pour the bouillon over them. Let them sit for an hour or two ❀ until they have absorbed as much of the bouillon as possible. Pour off any remaining bouillon. Beat the mustard, vinegar, oil, salt and pepper together and pour over the potatoes. Toss gently. Slice the scallions as thin as possible and add to the potatoes. ❀

Wilted Cucumber Sticks

•

4 cucumbers, peeled, sliced in half
   lengthwise and seeded
1 tablespoon salt
3 tablespoons olive oil
1½ tablespoons red wine vinegar
4 tablespoons minced fresh dill

Cut the cucumbers into thin 3-inch-long sticks, place in a bowl, and mix the salt through the cucumbers. Let the cucumbers sit for an hour or two and turn them out into a colander. Rinse with cold running water, pat dry on paper towels, and return to the bowl. Add the oil, vinegar and dill, mix thoroughly, and refrigerate until needed. ❀

Asparagus Sticks in Cream Dressing

•

1 pound asparagus, preferably thin
   stalks
5 tablespoons heavy cream
1 tablespoon lemon juice
   Salt and pepper to taste
2 tablespoons minced parsley

Peel the asparagus and halve each stalk vertically if they are thin; otherwise quarter them. Cut the asparagus into 3-inch pieces, setting the pieces with the heads aside. Bring some salted water to boil in a frying pan or sauté pan and add the stalk portions. Cook for 3 minutes. Then add the reserved heads and cook for another 3 minutes. Drain the asparagus and cool. ❀ Just before serving combine the cream, lemon juice, salt and pepper and add to the asparagus. Garnish with minced parsley.

Glorious Fourth
Blueberry Pie

•

FOR THE CRUST	2½	*cups all-purpose flour*
	½	*teaspoon salt*
	¼	*pound (1 stick) cold unsalted butter, cut into 16 pieces*
	7	*tablespoons cold vegetable shortening*
	5 to 7	*tablespoons ice water*
FOR THE FILLING	2	*pint boxes blueberries*
	1	*tablespoon lemon juice*
	3	*drops imported blueberry essence (optional)*
	½	*cup sugar*
	5	*tablespoons flour*
FOR THE EGG WASH	1	*egg*

To make the crust, combine in a food processor bowl the flour, salt, butter and shortening. Process in about 10 short bursts, or until the mixture resembles cornmeal. With the motor running, add the ice water through the feed tube, starting with 5 tablespoons and adding more only if necessary. Process until the mixture begins to form a ball. Turn the dough onto a lightly floured board, knead once or twice to bring the mass together, and divide into two equal pieces. Form both into balls, flatten them somewhat, wrap in plastic, and refrigerate for at least 8 hours or overnight. ❀

To make the filling, pick over the blueberries, rinse them quickly under cold water, and drain thoroughly. Set aside. Combine the lemon juice and blueberry essence, if used. Set aside. Combine the sugar and flour. Set aside. ❀

•

To assemble the pie, use a 10-inch pie plate, preferably ovenproof glass. Remove one ball of dough from the refrigerator and roll out on a lightly floured board to a circle 13 inches in diameter. Place this bottom crust on the pie plate, even off the edges if necessary with kitchen shears, leaving an inch and a half or so overhang, and refrigerate. Place the drained berries in a large bowl and sprinkle the lemon juice over them. Toss gently. Then add the sugar-and-flour mixture and toss again to distribute the dry ingredients. Remove the pie plate from the refrigerator and turn the berries out into the bottom crust, forming a mound in the center. Roll out the second ball of dough on a lightly floured board to a circle 13 inches in diameter. Moisten the edge of the bottom crust with a little cold water, using your finger or a pastry brush, and place the top crust over the berries. Turn the edge of the bottom crust over the edge of the top crust and with your fingers crimp the edges to stand up around the plate. Cut slashes in the top crust along the mound. Beat the egg well and brush it all over the top crust.

The oven should be preheated to 450 degrees. Place a jelly-roll pan on the bottom of the oven. Place the pie on a rack one-third up from the bottom of the oven. Bake at 450 degrees for 20 minutes, lower the temperature to 375 degrees, and bake for another 40 minutes. The crust should be very brown but not burned. Remove the pie from the oven and place it on a rack to cool for several hours. ❀ Serve at room temperature with vanilla ice cream.

Tomato Ice

Cold Braised Pork with Prunes

Cold Zucchini, Summer Squash and
String Beans Avgolemono

Dinner Biscuits

Fresh Blackberry-Currant Tart

•

*Georges duBoeuf California Gamay Beaujolais
or Juliénas*

*T*he dishes in this "cold" meal have a
range of temperatures that contribute almost as much contrast as do their
flavors and textures.

The tomato ice is a refreshing beginning. Tomatoey, slightly tart and
smoothed by cream cheese and egg whites, it is the best of all the recipes for
this dish that I have tried. I serve it in flat champagne glasses, either small
balls formed with the Italian scoops that appeared in kitchenware shops a
couple of years ago, or in one large ball made with an ice cream scoop. The
rounds of ice are garnished with fresh basil sprigs to suggest fresh tomatoes.

The coldness of this frozen soup nicely bounces off the warmth of the
biscuits, which add substance without heaviness to the icy first course. The
biscuits are equally successful with the main course, cold loin of pork slices

studded with the pink of prosciutto or smoked ham that lards the meat. The slices of pork marching down the center of a large serving platter, surrounded by a dark Madeira-rich jelly and plumped prunes, make a festive presentation.

The vegetable dish was totally serendipitous. I came home from a farmers' market with lovely string beans, tiny zucchini, young bright yellow summer squash and the problem of what to do with them. Dressing them with yet another vinaigrette sauce seemed heavy-handed. The solution was to parboil the vegetables and then to bathe them in an *avgolemono* sauce, that lovely Greek contribution to the table made of egg yolks, lemon juice and a bit of the vegetable cooking liquid. Served at room temperature, it turned out to be the find of the sticky season. On a cool day, it would be just as wonderful served hot.

The tart for dessert, which is best lukewarm, was inspired by magnificent baskets of blackberries and currants at a local farmer's market. Unlike raspberries, which for me are to be eaten with a smidgeon of sugar and lots of cream and no other fancying up, blackberries and currants ask to be cooked, although not too much. I fussed this creation into existence. The circles of purple-black blackberries surrounded by circles of bright red currants make a tart that is showier than it deserves to be, considering how easy it is to put together.

An ice cream maker produces a smoother ice with far less fuss than freezing in ice cube trays, beating and refreezing. I use an attachment to one of my machines, but so many ice cream makers are on the market that it would be hard not to find one within anyone's price range. And then if you have it, you tend to use it, or at least I do. If you use egg whites you have kept frozen (see Index), remember to put a couple of them into a bowl to defrost a few hours before you start the ice.

The boneless pork loins I look for are long, narrow, tightly rolled and tied. (I also look for them on sale and put them in the freezer for later.) It is amazing how much mileage you can get from a relatively small amount of meat by slicing it thin. Of course, this is much easier to do when the meat is chilled. The pork in this recipe is remarkably moist because it is braised, rather than roasted, after it is browned. The mustard and brown sugar coating on the pork gives it a deep rich glaze and a good underbody of flavor. The original recipe, from *Simca's Cuisine*, does not use the frying pan to brown the meat, but I find it easier to use it and then remove the meat to the braising pot. This gets rid of both the browning grease and the burned bits of sugar that for me are inevitable.

If you have never larded meat, this is a good time to start. Get the largest, simplest larding needle you can find (they exist in good kitchen-ware shops), fill the hollow of the needle with a strip of ham, poke it into the roast lengthwise, and retract. The ham stays inside, and the process is almost as satisfying as cutting out paper dolls. You could forgo this step, but don't. I sometimes use prunes that I have bottled at some point in cognac and Madeira, with the liquor also going into the sauce.

The vegetables *avgolemono* can be made a day or even two in advance and brought to room temperature before serving. Nothing more is required than parboiling the string beans and the zucchini and squash sticks and then making the sauce by whisking the ingredients over medium-low heat until the sauce becomes foamy and the yolks thicken slightly. However, the sauce must not be allowed to boil.

The biscuits take no time to do. I have made them less than an hour before guests were expected, and with no hassle, using Dorothy Lage-mann's recipe and method. (For more information on biscuit-making, see Index.)

For thickening the fruit for this tart, I prefer potato starch because, unlike cornstarch, it never makes food gummy, and it has no taste. For some mysterious reason, I find potato starch (also called potato flour) among the specialty foods in one of the supermarkets I patronize. It can also be found in Oriental food shops.

If you are uncomfortable about unmolding a tart from a pan with a removable bottom, use a dish that can be brought to the table. You can prepare all the elements of the tart the day before, but they should be put together a few hours before guests arrive. At least for me, no matter what I do, crusts baked with the filling in them get soggy if left too long.

Tomato Ice

•

½ tablespoon blue cheese
   3-ounce package plus 1½ tablespoons
   cream cheese
½ teaspoon dried minced onion
1   teaspoon Worcestershire sauce
2   tablespoons tomato paste

1   teaspoon salt
1/4   teaspoon cracked black pepper
2   tablespoons lemon juice
2   cups tomato juice
2   stiffly beaten egg whites
     Sprigs of basil (optional)

Cream together the two cheeses. Beat in the onion, Worcestershire sauce, tomato paste, salt, pepper and lemon juice. Add the tomato juice gradually. If you are using an ice cream machine, fold in the egg whites, freeze and let ripen in the freezer for a few hours. ✽

If not, pour mixture into ice cube trays and freeze until all but a portion of the center is frozen. Then remove from trays, break up the mixture in a bowl, and beat smooth with a chilled rotary beater. Then fold in the beaten egg whites and return to the freezer. ✽   Set in refrigerator 30 minutes before serving to soften.

Scoop into champagne glasses and garnish, if desired, with a sprig of basil. Pass biscuits and unsalted butter.

Cold Braised Pork with Prunes

•

24   large prunes
4   cups beef bouillon
1/4   pound smoked ham or prosciutto, cut
     in thick slices
     2½- to 3-pound boned loin of pork
6   tablespoons Dijon mustard
1/2   cup dark brown sugar
2   tablespoons peanut oil
2/3   cup Cognac
     Salt and pepper
     Bouquet garni of thyme, sage and parsley
1/2   cup Madeira
     Watercress (optional)

Put the prunes to steep in 1½ cups tepid bouillon, or to cover.

Cut the ham or prosciutto into strips to fit a larding needle and lard the pork along its length. Paint the meat with the mustard, then roll it in the brown sugar. (I do this in a long gratin dish to reduce the mess.)

Heat the oil in a large frying pan and brown the meat in it, turning it as each face is colored. The sugar will caramelize and this in turn may burn — keep turning so that the sugar in the pan burns, not the meat. Remove the meat to a large enamel-on-iron pot or Dutch oven and heat the pot. Then pour half the Cognac over the meat and set it aflame. When the flame goes out, pour in 1 cup bouillon, cover the pot, and set it in a preheated 375-degree oven for a total of 1¾ hours.

After 50 minutes of cooking, turn the meat, season with salt and pepper, add the bouquet garni, and lower the heat to 350 degrees. About 45 minutes later, add the prunes and their liquid. When the pork is cooked, remove it and the prunes from the pot, cool, and refrigerate. ❃

Add whatever bouillon remains to the juices in the pot plus the Madeira and the remaining ⅓ cup of Cognac. Bring to the boil and stir to dislodge the sediments and incorporate them into the sauce. Set aside to cool, and refrigerate. ❃ Then remove the fat that will have risen to the surface. What will remain is a lovely jellied stock.

To serve, remove the strings from the meat and slice with a sharp knife into thin slices. Arrange in one or two rows down the center of a long serving platter. Chop the jelly and arrange this around the meat. Then arrange the prunes around the jelly. The dish can be garnished with watercress.

Zucchini, Summer Squash
and String Beans Avgolemono

•

½ *pound string beans*
¾ *pound young thin zucchini*
¾ *pound young thin yellow summer squash*
¾ *cup cooking liquid from the vegetables*
2 *egg yolks*
2½ *tablespoons lemon juice*

Wash the string beans, trim the ends, and set aside. Soak the zucchini and summer squash in a large pan of cold water for 15 minutes, wash them under cold running water, rubbing the skins gently to loosen any grit, and drain. Trim the ends and cut the vegetables in half lengthwise. Cut each half lengthwise into thirds or quarters to make sticks more or less the same size and shape as the string beans.

Bring a large pot of salted water to the boil, drop in the string beans, and cook for 5 minutes. Add the zucchini and squash strips, rapidly bring the water back to the boil, and cook for another 2 minutes. Ladle off ¾ cup of the vegetable water and set aside. Turn the vegetables out into a colander and drain thoroughly.

Combine the egg yolks and lemon juice in a small saucepan and whisk. Slowly whisk in the hot vegetable liquid. Place over medium-low heat and cook, whisking constantly, until the mixture becomes foamy and thickens slightly. Do not let the sauce boil.

Put the hot, drained vegetables in a bowl and add the sauce. Toss the vegetables to coat them and let sit at room temperature, tossing them every 15 minutes or so, until they are cool. ❀　Cover tightly with plastic wrap and refrigerate. Bring to room temperature before serving, arranged on a serving platter.

Dinner Biscuits

MAKES 16 TO 20 BISCUITS

•

2	cups bleached or unbleached all-purpose flour
1	tablespoon baking powder
1	teaspoon salt
3	tablespoons vegetable shortening
⅔ to ¾	cup milk

Up to an hour before sitting down, combine the dry ingredients in a bowl and mix together with a fork. Cut in the shortening with either a fork or a pastry blender until the mixture resembles coarse cornmeal. Make a well in the center and add the milk, beginning with the minimum amount. Using a fork, gather the dry ingredients into the milk until a dough forms and pulls away from the sides of the bowl. Add the remaining milk if necessary. Work lightly and do not mix more than necessary. Turn the dough onto a lightly floured board and knead three times. Then pat the dough out until it is ½ inch thick. Cut out biscuits with a 2-inch cutter and work scraps lightly together to make a last biscuit or two. Place on an ungreased baking sheet or jelly-roll pan and bake in a preheated 400-degree oven for 10 minutes, or until the biscuits are lightly browned.

If desired, the pan of biscuits can be refrigerated and brought to room temperature before baking. ❊   The baked biscuits can be frozen❊   and reheated, and the recipe can be doubled or tripled.

Fresh Blackberry-Currant Tart

•

10-inch Unbaked Pie Shell (see following recipe)
1   *quart fresh blackberries*
4   *tablespoons plus ½ cup sugar*
1   *quart fresh red currants*
1   *tablespoon potato starch (or potato flour)*
5   *tablespoons red currant jelly
Whipped cream flavored with sugar and* cassis *liqueur, and confectioners' sugar for garnish (optional)*

Cover the bottom of the tart shell with foil or parchment paper, pour beans, rice, clean pebbles or pie weights over it to keep the pastry flat, and bake in a preheated 350-degree oven for 12 minutes. Set the shell (in its pan) on a rack to cool. ❊   Can be made up to this point the day before. Refrigerate the shell.

Rinse the blackberries in cold water, discard any that have mold or are spoiled, drain well, place them in a heavy enameled pan, and sprinkle with 2 tablespoons of sugar. Stem the currants, pick them over, rinse under cold water, drain well, put them into another enameled pan, and sprinkle with 2 tablespoons of sugar. Set each pan over low heat and cook, without stirring, for about 8 to 10 minutes, or until the berry juices are released.

Line two strainers with 3 thicknesses of paper towels and set them over separate bowls. Turn the berries into the strainers and let them drain until they are cool. Turn out the berries into separate bowls and add ½ tablespoon of potato starch to each bowl. Mix lightly. The berries can be refrigerated until the next day, if desired. ❀   Combine the juices of both berries in a saucepan and add the remaining ½ cup of sugar. Cook for 10 minutes or until the syrup falls in drops when poured from a spoon. Remove the syrup from heat and stir in the red currant jelly until it is dissolved. Set the syrup aside to cool and thicken. It can also be refrigerated until the next day. ❀

To assemble the tart, paint the bottom of the partially baked shell with some of the syrup. Arrange the berries on the shell, beginning in the middle with a small mound of blackberries. Then surround this with a circle of currants, then a circle of blackberries, until the shell is filled. Spoon 4 or 5 tablespoons of the syrup over the berries, but put most of it on the blackberries, since the syrup is dark and will kill the red color of the currants. Bake in a preheated 375-degree oven for 15 minutes, or until the pastry is lightly browned. Remove from oven and place on a rack to cool. Spoon the rest of the syrup over the top of the tart.

If you have used a pan with a removable rim, remove the rim when the tart is cool, but leave the tart on the base of the pan. ❀   Slide the tart onto a cookie sheet and warm it in a preheated 325-degree oven for about 10 minutes before serving. If the tart does not want to slide off the base, simply put it, base and all, on a flat round serving dish, preferably with a rim.

Serve if desired with stiffly beaten whipped cream flavored with a little sugar and a bit of *cassis*. If you wish, sprinkle some confectioners' sugar over the tart just before serving.

Unbaked Tart Shell

•

2   cups sifted all-purpose flour
1   tablespoon sugar
     Pinch of salt
⅜   pound (1½ sticks) cold unsalted butter
3 to 4   tablespoons ice water

Put the flour, sugar, salt and butter, cut into ½-inch pieces, in the bowl of a food processor fitted with the steel blade. Process on and off for a few seconds, or until the mixture takes on the texture of oatmeal. With the motor running, add 3 tablespoons of ice water. Turn the motor off the second the dough gives some sign of massing and do not wait for it to form a ball. Turn the dough out onto a board and, if necessary, add another table-spoon of ice water to hold it together. Form into a ball, flour lightly, place in a plastic bag, and refrigerate for at least 1 hour before rolling out. ❀

To roll out, place the dough on a floured surface and flatten it a bit with the heel of your hand. Flour the rolling pin and roll, always away from yourself, turning the dough a quarter-turn after each roll so that an even circle is formed. The final circle should measure about 13 inches in diameter and the dough should be about ⅛ inch thick.

Roll the dough onto the rolling pin and then unroll it onto the pan. Use either a 10-inch tart or quiche pan with a removable base or a 10-inch porcelain tart dish (from which the tart can be served). Pat the dough into the edges and against the sides of the pan. Roll back the top edge of the dough and crimp to make a lip. ❀   Refrigerate the shell for at least ½ hour before baking.

Orange, Black Olive and
Pink Peppercorn Salad

Pasta with Seafood

Peaches with Rum, Brown Sugar,
Cream and Pistachios

•

Corvo Bianco

*T*his mildly Mediterranean meal is very satisfactory on a summer night when you have tired of all-cold meals. The first course, a somewhat startling combination of orange slices, purple onion, black olives and pink peppercorns, is cheerful to look at and to eat. The seafood in a barely cooked, garlicky, fresh-herbed tomato sauce lightens the pasta, and pasta itself suits summertime casualness. Dessert is a heavenly agglomeration of peaches, brown sugar, dark rum, a pseudo *crème fraîche* and pistachios.

The capacity of oranges to live happily with such unlikely foods as ducks, pâtés, tomatoes and onions is a constant and pleasant surprise. The first course is an example of this versatility of the orange, whose tart sweetness is a lovely foil for the other ingredients. I peel the oranges first with a potato peeler, which leaves the white rind behind, and then dry the strips of peel for an hour or so on a cookie sheet in a turned-off oven with a pilot light. They are then put into jars, and very handy they are for the next bouillabaisse or Provençal stew. The white rind of the orange should be attacked with a sharp, nonrustable paring knife.

Canned olives are acceptable for this dish, but blah compared to good Greek *calamatas*. I have a fabulous heavy-duty olive pitter (which also does cherries) that stones olives neatly and in seconds.

The pink peppercorns, whose peppery sweetness is a perfect foil for the oranges and onions, I liberated from the back of a shelf where they have languished, a relic of the *nouvelle cuisine* that had them strewn on everything from poached eggs to ice cream. Do, however, be sure that the pink peppercorns are the Madagascar variety, imported via France, since these are the ones cleared for consumption by the FDA. A good fruity olive oil is wanted to bring these ingredients together.

The main course needs very little preparation and almost no cooking time. The sauce base is made in the morning and finished off just before you sit down. I also shell the shrimp early in the day, as well as scrub the clams, halve the scallops (if I couldn't find bay scallops) and slice the fish. The clams are opened in another pot, since they always throw off sand. The juices can then be filtered through cheesecloth and added to the sauce.

I make fresh linguine to accompany the seafood for three reasons: first, I love to use my electric pasta machine; second, homemade pasta is delicious; and, third, most people who make pasta think the dough must be rolled as thin as possible. This is true for fettucine and stuffed pasta, but other possibilities exist. By leaving the strips of dough comparatively thick and cutting them on the noodle cutter, the result is a flat, nicely square-cut linguine, with the substance needed for this dish.

The easiest way to prepare a large batch of dough is to roll each strip through the machine at one setting, lower the thickness a notch and roll the pieces through again at that setting. Repeat the process at each lower notch until the strips are as thin as needed.

There is nothing wrong with using a commercially made spaghetti or linguine for this dish, but the cooking time will be longer than for homemade. The pasta water can be put on to boil before guests sit down for the first course so that the pasta can be cooked while the table is being cleared. There is no way that pasta can be cooked in advance. Again, *al dente* does not mean raw. The pasta must not be mushy, nor should it bite back. The only way to tell is to keep testing as it cooks. The teeth know better than the timer when to turn the contents of the pot into the colander.

Dessert depends on the ability to amass a sufficient number of peaches that have no green and therefore have possibility of ripening, a feat that seems to get harder every year. The only thing to do is to stand at the bin and go through every peach, if necessary, to find ungreen albeit hard fruit. And if the produce manager doesn't like it, tell him why you are forced to pick over his wares. I buy several more peaches than I need since some inevitably go rotten in the ripening process, which takes several days in a closed brown paper or plastic bag. Remember to check the peaches every day because one can go bad very quickly and infect the others. As the peaches ripen, refrigerate them until you have enough for your dish.

If all this is too discouraging or the results fruitless (sorry), you can happily substitute three pints of strawberries, which at this time of year are full of perfume. They are delicious prepared this way, although I use white sugar for them instead of brown. I do stick with rum because it is wildly successful with strawberries.

We are told that buttermilk or sour cream added to heavy cream produces real *crème fraîche*. It doesn't. Buttermilk and sour cream are made with two cultures, only one of which is appropriate for *crème fraîche*. The second culture fights the desirable one and keeps the cream from acquiring the nutty, creamy, dairy taste of the real thing. Having said this, I find the combination of lightly whipped cream and sour cream is sensational. Unlike other mock *crème fraîche* recipes, where the buttermilk or sour cream and the cream must stand in a warm place to thicken for 24 hours, this can be refrigerated immediately. It is worth finding heavy cream that is not the ultrapasteurized abomination in supermarkets. I use Myers's rum, or, even better, Ron Negrita, which has a deep flavor, and unsalted pistachios.

Orange, Black Olive and Pink Peppercorn Salad

•

5	*medium to large navel oranges*
1	*large red onion, minced*
32	*calamata olives or pitted canned olives*
About 3	*tablespoons olive oil*
	Salt to taste
2	*teaspoons freeze-dried pink peppercorns*

Use a sharp paring knife that doesn't turn black when exposed to acid, and peel the oranges right down to the flesh. Remove every trace of the pith.

Slice the oranges thin and pick out the white rings in the centers. Divide the slices evenly on 8 salad plates, making a bed of them. Sprinkle the minced onion evenly over the orange slices. If you are using *calamata* olives, pit them with a cherry or olive pitter and arrange 4 on each plate. Drizzle each portion with a teaspoon or so of olive oil. Then sprinkle on each a little salt and about a quarter of a teaspoon of the pink peppercorns.✿   This can be prepared about an hour in advance and left out in a not-too-hot kitchen.

Pasta with Seafood

•

1½	cups olive oil
1½	cups chopped parsley
6	cloves garlic, finely minced
¾	cup chopped green pepper
¼	cup chopped serrano, poblano or any mildly hot peppers
Two	35-ounce cans Italian plum tomatoes
2	tablespoons chopped fresh basil, or 1 tablespoon dried
1	teaspoon chopped fresh mint (optional)
	Salt and pepper
3	dozen cherrystone clams
24	medium-size raw shrimp, peeled and deveined
1½	pounds fresh haddock, cut into 2-inch strips
1	pound whole bay scallops or sea scallops cut in half
1	cup dry white wine
2	pounds homemade linguine (see following recipe) or fettucine or 2 pounds packaged linguine (de Cecco, Conte di Luna or some other good brand)
6	tablespoons butter
½	cup Cognac

Early in the day, heat the oil in a large sauté pan or in a wide-bottomed 6-quart pot. Add the parsley, garlic and both peppers. Chop the tomatoes and add them with their liquid. Add the basil, optional mint and salt and pepper to taste. Simmer for 5 minutes and set aside.

Clean the clams by scrubbing them with a brush or plastic pot cleaner under running water and refrigerate. Prepare the shrimp, haddock and scallops and refrigerate. ✿

Half an hour before you sit down, bring a large pot of salted water to a boil for the pasta.

Twenty minutes before you sit down, heat the sauce to a simmer and add the shrimp, haddock and scallops. Cook for 15 minutes and set aside. ✿

Meanwhile, in another pot, add the clams to the cup of white wine and put over a high flame. Cover tightly. Toss the clams so that they cook evenly, holding the handles and the cover at the same time. The clams should open in 10 to 15 minutes at most. Remove the clams and add to the sauce. Then strain the clam liquid through a double layer of wrung-out cheesecloth and add to the sauce. Simmer the sauce for 5 minutes and set aside. ✿   Of course discard any clams that did not open.

Cook the pasta. This will take about 2 to 3 minutes if it is homemade — keep testing. Packaged pasta should be tested when it has cooked for the minimum recommended time. Drain and add the pasta to the sauce. Then add the butter and Cognac.

Put the pot over low heat, ✿   cover but leave the lid slightly ajar and leave until you are through with the first course.

Homemade Linguine

•

3   *cups unbleached flour or bread flour*
4   *eggs*

Process the flour in a food processor for 30 seconds. With the motor running, add the eggs, one at a time, and process until the dough forms a ball. Turn out onto a lightly floured board, knead two or three times, dust lightly with flour, wrap in plastic, ✿   and refrigerate for at least 2 hours.

Sometime in the afternoon, make the pasta. Break off a piece of dough the size of a small lemon and put through the widest opening of the pasta machine. Do this about 10 times, folding the dough in half each time you put it through, to knead the dough. Continue until all the dough is kneaded. Tighten the rollers by one notch and feed a strip of dough through the machine. Do not fold the dough from here on. Continue, reducing the notch until reaching opening number 3½, or whatever setting on your machine that still leaves a thickish strip of dough. Lay out to dry in single layers on dish towels or hang on a rack for 15 to 20 minutes. Then run the strips through the fine noodle cutter. Place the pasta on a jelly-roll pan and cover with a dish towel to keep it from drying out too much until you are ready to cook it. ❁   (For fettucine, roll the dough thinner, dry for 15 minutes, and cut on the wide cutter.)

Peaches with Rum, Brown Sugar, Cream and Pistachios

•

16 *ripe peaches, about 3 pounds, or*
        enough to make 6 cups, sliced
4 *tablespoons dark brown sugar*
4 *tablespoons dark rum*
1 *cup heavy cream*
½ *cup sour cream*
½ *cup chopped shelled and skinned*
        unsalted pistachio nuts

Scald the peaches for 30 seconds in boiling water, turn them into a colander, and slip off the skins. Slice the peaches, put them into a bowl, and sprinkle the sugar and rum over them. Mix lightly, cover tightly with plastic wrap, and ❁   refrigerate for 4 hours or more.

Whip the cream, but not too stiffly. Add the sour cream and blend well. ❁   Refrigerate. Before serving, place the peaches in a pretty bowl, glass if you have one. Pour the mock *crème fraîche* over the peaches and sprinkle on the chopped nuts.

Iced (or Hot) Leek and Potato Soup

Cold Stuffed Roast Pork

Composed Salad

Strawberry Bombe

•

Mill Creek Merlot
or Moulin-à-Vent

*T*his cold meal has advantages for a hot summer evening. For one, every dish can be prepared well enough in advance to assure a cool, calm, clean kitchen and cook. More important, the meal itself strikes a desirable balance between lightness and substance.

The first course is an unadulterated classic, an icy cold puréed leek and potato soup, thinned with a good quantity of milk to avoid thickness on the tongue yet rich with an underbody of clean leek flavor. The main course consists of boneless pork loin roast sliced to reveal an aromatic, pistachio-studded pâtélike stuffing, the sort of show-off dish that causes the cook to lower the eyelids modestly in response to assorted oohs and aahs. No mention need be made that the dish takes a tiny bit of courage, but no special talent, to prepare. A composed salad accompanies the pork. This is arranged with simplicity on a flat serving platter, the better to display subtle contrasts among the greeneries and rounds of heart of palm and dashes of red and black provided by pimiento strips and black olives from Nice. Dessert is a bombe — an outside layer of vanilla ice cream encompassing a strawberry mousse, the whole frozen within the confines of a decorative mold and served surrounded by whole fresh strawberries.

Making the soup is a worry-free operation with one exception. The leeks must not be allowed to color. When disaster strikes, as it did to me when I became overinvolved in a telephone conversation, it can only be viewed as irreversible. There is no point in trying to pick out the browned bits. The leeks must be discarded and the whole process begun anew with another bunch of leeks. If the soup is to be served hot — and it's perfect that way whenever the weather cools off — it can be puréed or not, as my father-in-law preferred it, in which case the potatoes should be diced rather than sliced. This makes a lovely peasanty soup, with the bits of potato taking on a deep chicken taste from the broth.

Despite their comparative priciness, boneless pork loin roasts are a good buy, since a 2½- to 3-pound roast is ample for eight people. I prefer tenderloin roasts, with the tails trimmed off, because they are neat and compact. Buy them on sale and stock them in the home freezer.

The pork roast is untied (with the string saved to use on the meat later) and cut lengthwise to within an inch and a half of the bottom. Then, starting at the base cut, the meat is sliced to within an inch and a half of both left and right sides. A good chef's knife is an invaluable instrument for this operation. The meat is opened up and the stuffing is placed inside. Then it is re-formed into a roll and sewn and tied to hold its shape during the roasting. I make the first cut through the fat side up because fat-reinforced meat is stronger and therefore easier to sew through.

Since cold food loses flavor, the stuffing should be highly seasoned. After it is mixed, it is a good idea to fry a bit of it and adjust the seasonings accordingly. This stuffing is a marvelous foil for fresh thyme. Fresh sausage meat — far preferable to prepackaged sausage — can be found at most local markets with meat counters. The pistachio nuts can be shelled and blanched well in advance and kept in the freezer until needed. I also keep a supply of fresh bread crumbs, made in the processor from the heels of white bread, in the freezer.

The composed salad shows off best on a platter. The kind used for pasta, with slightly raised edges, is most satisfactory. Greenery can be cut neatly to manageable size with scissors, which are also useful for removing the spines of leaves for those who think this is desirable. The hearts of palm should be drained and washed thoroughly under cold running water. They add a texture and taste to this salad as well as a feeling of great opulence. Only fresh herbs should be used to season this salad. If you do not have tarragon and savory, use parsley and chives, although variety adds a great deal. The salad can be assembled a few hours before your guests arrive and held, tightly wrapped with plastic, in the refrigerator. The dressing, however, should be drizzled on at the very last minute.

Bombes are best made in metal molds. The ever-useful six-cup charlotte mold with lid is a perfect receptacle for this dessert, as is any decorative mold that might be found in the kitchen. To avoid a horrible struggle at the table with trying to cut through a frozen-stiff mound, the bombe must be unmolded at least an hour and even more before it is to be eaten. It is then allowed to soften, but not melt, in the refrigerator. The pale pink core of strawberry mousse makes a pretty contrast with the vanilla shell and the whole strawberries.

Iced (or Hot) Leek and Potato Soup

•

1	*bunch leeks*
6	*tablespoons butter*
Three	*10³/4-ounce cans condensed chicken broth*
3	*medium-large potatoes (a little more than 1 pound)*
	Salt and pepper to taste
1	*quart milk, approximately*
½	*pint heavy cream*
3	*tablespoons minced chives*

Trim the leeks and remove the coarse green outer leaves as well as the top two-thirds of the green leaves. Slice each leek down the middle and wash well under cold running water. Drain and mince the leeks. Heat the butter in a saucepan, add the leeks, and cook them very slowly, stirring frequently. Watch carefully to be sure the leeks do not color. When the leeks are transparent and soft, add the chicken broth and bring to a simmer. Meanwhile, peel the potatoes and cut them into ¼-inch-thick slices. Add these to the pot, bring the broth to a boil, and cook over low heat for about 20 minutes, or until the potatoes are very soft. Season with salt and pepper.

In about 3 batches, purée the soup in a processor and pour the purée into a large bowl. Let cool to room temperature. Beat in enough milk to thin the purée to the desired consistency; it should not be thick. Taste once again for salt and pepper. ❀ Refrigerate. To serve, swirl in the cream and the chives and ladle into bowls. To serve hot, heat the soup after adding the cream and add the chives at the last minute.

Cold Stuffed Roast Pork

•

	2½- to 3-pound boneless pork tenderloin roast
5	*tablespoons peanut oil*
1	*tablespoon lemon juice*
48	*pistachio nuts*
	Scant ½ pound fresh sausage meat
1	*egg, lightly beaten*
½	*cup fresh bread crumbs*
1	*clove garlic, crushed*
2	*tablespoons medium-sweet Madeira, or more to taste*
1	*tablespoon Cognac*
2	*teaspoons fresh thyme leaves or 1 teaspoon dried*
3	*tablespoons minced parsley*
2	*cloves garlic, unpeeled*
½	*cup boiling water*
	Salt to taste
1	*cup beef bouillon*

Untie the pork roast and reserve the string. Place the pork, fat side up, on a board and cut through the roast lengthwise to within 1½ inches of the bottom of the meat. Then, starting at the cut, slice to within 1½ inches of both the left and right sides of the roast. Open up the meat and place it in a pan. Mix the peanut oil and lemon juice and rub this into all sides of the pork. Cover with plastic wrap and refrigerate while the stuffing is prepared. ✿

Shell the pistachio nuts, blanch them for 5 minutes in boiling water, drain, and rub off the skins. Dry the nuts on paper towels and combine them in a bowl with the sausage meat, egg, bread crumbs, crushed garlic, Madeira, Cognac, thyme and parsley. Mix well and fry a bit of the mixture. Taste and adjust seasoning and taste again. Remember, the meat will be served cold and will lose flavor.

Remove the pork from the refrigerator, pat it dry, and spread the stuffing on the meat. Re-form the roast into a roll and sew the meat closed through the fat. Wash the needle and put it away after you have finished with it. Re-tie the meat with the reserved string so that it will keep its shape while roasting.

Place the meat in a roasting pan and roast in a preheated 450-degree oven for 20 minutes. Reduce the oven heat to 350 degrees and add the unpeeled garlic cloves and ½ cup boiling water. Sprinkle the meat with a little salt. Roast for 1½ hours more, turning the meat every ½ hour. The roast is done when its internal temperature reads 170 to 180 degrees. Remove the meat to a dish and allow it to cool to room temperature. Then cover it tightly with plastic wrap and ✿ refrigerate it overnight. Deglaze the roasting pan with the beef bouillon and strain this sauce into a pitcher. Degrease when cold. ✿

About an hour before serving, remove the meat from the refrigerator and discard the string and the sewing thread. Slice the meat and arrange on a platter. Serve the sauce separately.

Composed Salad

•

½   *head romaine lettuce, leaves separated, washed and dried*

1   *full, tight head Boston lettuce, leaves separated, washed and dried*

2   *heads Belgian endive, leaves separated, washed and dried*

14-ounce can hearts of palm, rinsed
well under cold water, drained and
cut into rounds
1 cucumber, peeled, seeded and cut into
thin strips
4- or 5-ounce jar roasted pimientos,
drained and cut into strips
24 black Niçoise olives, drained
6 tablespoons minced fresh herbs, if
possible a combination of parsley,
chives, thyme, tarragon and savory
½ cup good-quality olive oil
½ cup red wine vinegar
Salt and pepper to taste

Use a pair of scissors to cut the romaine and Boston lettuce leaves through their spines to make attractive pieces of a manageable size. Cover a flat serving platter with alternating leaves of the romaine and Boston lettuce. Then arrange the Belgian endive leaves on the green romaine leaves. Arrange the hearts of palm rounds on the Boston lettuce. Place cucumber strips on each side of the hearts of palm rounds and decorate as desired with pimiento strips. Arrange the olives around the circumference of the platter and strew the fresh herbs over the entire platter. The salad can be prepared to this point a few hours in advance.❁   Cover tightly with plastic wrap and refrigerate. Just before serving, mix the oil, vinegar and salt and pepper, and drizzle evenly over the salad.

Strawberry Bombe

•

2 quarts vanilla ice cream
2 pints strawberries
¾ cup sugar
3 tablespoons eau de vie de framboise
or Kirsch
1 teaspoon vanilla extract
1 cup heavy cream

A 6-cup mold is needed for this dessert, preferably metal. A charlotte mold will do, as will a melon mold or any other decorative mold. It is nice if the mold has a tight-fitting cover, although this is not absolutely necessary.

Remove the ice cream from the freezer for about 10 minutes to soften it a bit. Line the entire mold with at least an inch of ice cream, leaving a hollow in the center for the strawberry mousse. Return the mold and left-over ice cream to the freezer while the mousse is being made.

Wash and stem one pint of strawberries and place the berries in the bowl of a food processor. Add the sugar, *framboise* or Kirsch and vanilla and reduce the strawberries to a purée. Whip the cream until it is stiff and fold the strawberry purée into it. Remove the mold from the freezer and pack the mousse into the hollow. Cover with plastic wrap and the lid, if there is one, or with foil if not. Return to the freezer for at least 6 hours, ❀ or until the mousse is frozen. Then fill in the mold with a top layer of the ice cream, using as much as necessary. Cover again with plastic wrap and replace the lid or rewrap tightly with foil. Return to freezer. ❀

Wash and stem the second pint of strawberries and leave the berries whole. Cover and refrigerate. An hour to 1½ hours before serving, remove the mold from the freezer and dip it quickly in a basin of hot water. Dry the mold, run a knife around the rim, and unmold the bombe onto a platter. Arrange the whole berries around it and place in the refrigerator ❀ (not the freezer) until serving time.

August

PROVISIONING · THE · PANTRY

Pistou

MAKES ABOUT 1¾ CUPS

•

   8   *fat cloves of garlic, peeled*
 32 *large basil leaves*
 ¼ *cup olive oil*
1½ *pounds ripe tomatoes, scalded for 10*
        seconds, peeled, seeded amd chopped
        Salt and freshly ground pepper

Put the garlic and basil in a food processor with the olive oil. (If you use a blender, you will have to do this in two batches.) Process them briefly and then add the tomatoes. Process until the tomatoes are puréed. Add pepper.

Decant into a jar, label, and freeze. Use for Soupe au Pistou (see Index) or on pasta. You can also process only the garlic, basil leaves and olive oil and serve poured over peeled, sliced tomatoes. Season to taste with salt and pepper.

Gravad Beef with Green Sauce and Red Caviar

Cold Rock Cornish Hens Stuffed with Toasted Rice and Herbs

Tomato Aspic Squares or "Chickens"

Blueberry Cream-Puff Ring

•

*Juliénas
or Fetzer "Lake County" Zinfandel*

*T*his is a cold meal to take the bark if not the bite out of dog days. Original, whimsical and good to eat, it can be made in advance, with just a few no-sweat, hassle-free final preparations left for the day of the party in a mercifully cool kitchen.

Dinner begins with a new discovery brought back from Sweden: steak that has been cured, rather than cooked, with the same salt and sugar mixture that turns salmon into *gravad lax,* but with the addition of thyme and sage, instead of dill. Paper-thin slices of the *gravad* beef are topped with wilted cucumber slices, a refreshing green sauce and red caviar for color and tang. The main course consists of Rock Cornish hens, roasted, cooled, halved and presented cut side down. The toasted rice and herb stuffing that has cooked in the birds is revealed only when the little hens are eaten. The serving platter is garnished with a shimmering accompaniment of intensely flavored tomato aspic cut in shapes, preferably of small chickens (with an appropriate cookie cutter), for a bit of amusement. Dessert is a luscious cream-puff ring filled with bourbon-flavored whipped cream and fresh blueberries and accompanied by a blueberry sauce.

The *gravad* beef combines mystery and elegance with the virtue of a great bargain. Unlike *carpaccio,* the Venetian raw beef dish that really requires top of the line steak, *gravad* beef is made with reasonably priced top round steak, one pound yielding eight ample servings. Five days before it is to be eaten, the round steak is rubbed with the *gravad* mixture, refrigerated in a plastic bag, and turned every day to ensure an even cure. The cured meat is cut diagonally on a wide angle against the grain into paper-thin slices, for which a long, sharp knife is essential. The meat is distributed among first-course plates and its deep brown color is brightened with wilted cucumbers (preferably pickling cucumbers or even the long hothouse kind whose wax-free skins can be left on), an uncomplicated green sauce consisting of sour cream, dill and chives, and a dollop of red lump-fish or salmon caviar. Thin slices of French bread and unsalted butter are the perfect accompaniment. The green sauce is also delicious with any fish pâté and an excellent change from tartar sauce with crab cakes, especially when half as much mayonnaise is beaten into the sauce along with some minced scallion and finely chopped *cornichons.*

The Rock Cornish hens can, of course, be made a day in advance since they are served at room temperature. They are stuffed, cooked, refrigerated and halved easily when they are cold. Toasting the rice in a hot oven imparts a nutty flavor that is particularly agreeable. The stuffing is also spiked with softened scallion, the minced livers, gizzards and hearts of the birds plus, if you can possibly manage it, fresh herbs.

Half of a larger hen with the rice stuffing is simply too much for one portion so I use only tiny birds that weigh about three-quarters of a pound. I do cook an additional small hen to calm my fears that a heavy eater might leave our table hungry. Such anxieties usually pay off in leftovers, which are wonderful the next day, either cold as is or with the meat cut into strips and heated with the stuffing. A trussing needle, which is usually about eight inches long and has an eye large enough for kitchen string, makes trussing a snap and even a joy.

The tomato aspic, a recipe I have changed only slightly from the one in Irma Rhode's excellent and unpretentious little book, *Cool Entertaining,* is also made a day in advance and is delicious with the hens. Chili sauce bolsters tomato juice for a more substantial result. I cut out the aspic with my chicken cookie cutter and slip a spatula under the jelly to lift it out of the pan in which it has set. The leftover bits of aspic can be remelted and placed in a small container to solidify and then more aspic chickens can be made. The cut-out aspic sits on a plate in the refrigerator and is added to the platter with the hens just before serving.

The cream-puff ring is good at this season filled with blueberries (or peaches, since they are finally edible), particularly if you can find the scarce wild blueberries. These smaller, more tart and more flavorful berries are superior to the fat cultivated kind.

I made five different cream-puff rings before I landed on the recipe here. Recipes that do not say the paste needs at least a few minutes of drying out are wrong, I can, to my sorrow, report, because without the drying the puff doesn't puff. My best results came from incorporating the eggs by hand, which involved a lot of beating with a wooden spoon, or, even better, by using the food processor. For me, incorporating the eggs with an electric mixer was less successful. According to one friend, the fresher the eggs, the better the result. My rather unconventional way of baking the puff works. The dough puffed nicely on the top shelf of the oven and then finished baking on the bottom shelf. The bourbon is a good foil for the blueberries.

Gravad Beef with Green Sauce and Red Caviar

•

FOR CURING THE BEEF		
	1	*pound boneless top round steak*
	2	*tablespoons coarse (kosher) salt*
	1	*tablespoon sugar*
	1/2	*teaspoon coarsely ground black pepper*
	1/2	*teaspoon dried thyme leaves*
	1/2	*teaspoon leaf sage*
FOR THE GREEN SAUCE		
	1/2	*cup sour cream*
	1	*tablespoon minced chives*
	1/4	*cup tightly packed dill leaves, minced*

FOR THE **GARNISH**	*3*	*small pickling cucumbers or ½ hothouse cucumber, unpeeled, or 1 medium cucumber, peeled*
	1	*tablespoon coarse salt*
	2	*ounces red salmon or lumpfish caviar*

Start to cure the steak 5 days before it is to be served. Pat the steak dry with paper towels. Mix the salt, sugar, pepper, thyme and sage and rub into both sides of the meat. Place it in a plastic bag, tie tightly and refrigerate for 5 days, turning the bag every day. ❀   A few hours before serving, remove the meat from the bag, scrape off the herb mixture, and dry with paper towels. Slice the steak into paper-thin slices against the grain and on the diagonal to make slices about 2 to 3 inches in width. ❀

The sauce can be made a day or two in advance. Combine the sour cream with the minced chives and dill. ❀   Refrigerate until needed.

The cucumbers can be prepared in the morning or up to 2 hours before serving. Slice the cucumber thin, mix with the salt, and allow to sit in a bowl at room temperature for 1 hour. Drain and squeeze dry. ❀   Refrigerate until needed.

To serve, divide the slices of cured beef among eight first-course plates. Arrange the drained cucumber slices on the center of the meat on each plate. Place a tablespoon of the green sauce on the cucumbers and a rounded demitasse spoon of the caviar on the sauce. Serve with thinly sliced French bread.

Cold Rock Cornish Hens
Stuffed with Toasted Rice
and Herbs

•

FOR THE HENS	*5*	*Rock Cornish hens, each weighing about ¾ pound, defrosted*

FOR THE
STUFFING

1½	*cups converted rice*
3	*cups canned condensed chicken broth*
4	*tablespoons butter*
6	*scallions, white bulbs plus 3 inches of green parts, minced*
	Livers, gizzards and hearts of the hens, trimmed and minced
10	*fresh thin sage leaves, minced, or ¾ teaspoon dried leaf sage*
	4-inch stem fresh rosemary, leaves removed and minced, or ¼ teaspoon dried rosemary leaves, crumbled
½	*teaspoon fresh thyme leaves or ¼ teaspoon dried*
4	*tablespoons minced parsley*
	Salt and pepper to taste

FOR COOKING
THE HENS

3	*tablespoons melted butter*
	10¾-ounce can condensed chicken broth

Clean the hens, remove wing tips and freeze with necks for later use to make stock. Pull out all loose internal organs and discard. Reserve the livers, gizzards and hearts for the stuffing. Pat the hens dry inside and out and refrigerate until needed.

Place the rice in an even layer in a 9-by-13-inch cake pan and toast in a preheated 375-degree oven for 8 to 10 minutes, shaking the pan every few minutes so the rice browns evenly. Continue until the rice is well toasted but not burned. Turn out into a large strainer and rinse under cold running water until the rice stops sizzling. Drain well. Bring the chicken broth to the boil in a heavy saucepan and add the rice. Cover and cook over low heat for 18 to 20 minutes, or until the rice is just cooked and the chicken broth is absorbed.

While the rice is cooking, melt the butter in a sauté pan or frying pan and cook the minced scallions over low heat until soft and transparent. Add the minced livers, gizzards and hearts and cook, stirring, for 2 minutes. Add the fresh or dried herbs and cook for another minute. Stir the mixture into the cooked rice, and season with salt and pepper.

Stuff the birds with the rice mixture (there may be some left over) and truss so that the cavities are closed. Julia Child et al.'s *Mastering the Art of French Cooking*, Volume I, has excellent trussing directions. Brush the birds all over with the melted butter and roast in a preheated 425-degree oven for 1 hour, basting frequently and turning the birds every 10 or 15 minutes to brown them evenly. Remove to a platter and allow to cool. Refrigerate. Pour off any butter in the roasting pan, and bring to a boil, scraping the brown bits with a wooden spoon. Pour the deglazed juices into a bowl and refrigerate. ❀

Two hours before serving, cut the birds in half and place them, cut side down, on a serving platter. Discard the fat from the pan juices and splash the juices over the hens. ❀ Return to the refrigerator until an hour before serving.

Arrange the tomato aspic shapes around the hens before bringing to the table.

Tomato Aspic Squares or "Chickens"

MAKES 16

•

2 *cups good quality tomato juice*
12-ounce bottle good quality chili sauce
Juice of 1 lime
1 *teaspoon Tabasco*
2½ *envelopes (2 tablespoons plus 1½ teaspoons) plain gelatin*

Combine the tomato juice, chili sauce, lime juice and Tabasco in a saucepan, sprinkle the gelatin over the liquid and bring to the boil over low heat, stirring constantly. Pour into an 8-inch square cake pan, cool and refrigerate until set. Cut into eight 2-inch squares or use a 2-inch chicken-shaped cookie cutter and cut into chicken shapes.

Just before serving, place the aspic shapes around the hens.

NOTE: The aspic also can be poured into a 4-cup mold and allowed to set. Serve sliced.

Blueberry Cream-Puff Ring

•

FOR THE CREAM- PUFF RING	1/2	cup water
	1/2	cup milk
	7	tablespoons unsalted butter
	1	teaspoon salt
	1	teaspoon sugar
	1	cup bread flour or unbleached flour
	4	large eggs
	1	egg yolk and a few drops of water
FOR THE FILLING	1	pint blueberries
	1/4	cup bourbon
	2	cups heavy cream
		Sugar
		Bourbon to taste
		Confectioners' sugar
FOR THE SAUCE	1	pint blueberries
	2	tablespoons water
	1/4	cup sugar, or more to taste
	2	tablespoons bourbon

To make the cream-puff ring, heat the oven to 400 degrees. Put two baking sheets together, one on top of the other (this keeps the bottom of the pastry from burning) and cover the top sheet with foil. (If you wet the sheet, the foil will stick to it.) Now butter the foil and place the rim of an 8-inch cake pan down on it to mark out a circle. Set aside.

Combine the water, milk, butter, salt and sugar in a heavy enamel pan and, stirring with a wooden spoon, bring slowly to a full boil. Remove from heat, add all the flour at once, and beat, off heat, with a wooden spoon until the mixture comes away from the sides and forms a ball. Return to heat, mash the mixture down onto the bottom of the pan, and then with the wooden spoon bring it up and fold it over, much as if you were kneading bread. The point is to dry out the paste. Continue for about 3 to 5 minutes or until a sandy-looking film of paste forms on the bottom of the pan. Remove from heat and let the paste stand for about 10 minutes, beating it occasionally while it cools. Turn the paste into a food processor bowl fitted with the steel blade, start the motor, and quickly add, one after the other, the eggs. Process about 15 seconds more after the last egg is added.

Run the prepared baking sheet under cold water. With a spoon, drop gobs of the paste on the marked circle. Then wet your fingers with cold water and even out the circle. Gently press down any peaks.

Beat the egg yolk with a few drops of cold water and, with a pastry brush, brush some of this on the top of the ring only. Do not let any egg run down the sides. (Leftover glaze can be frozen and used another time.) Place the ring in the top third of the preheated 400-degree oven for 30 minutes, but check after 15 minutes, to see if it looks cooked. Do not open the oven door during the first 15 minutes. When the dough looks cooked, remove to the bottom third for another 15 minutes. When the ring is nicely puffed and browned, take a long thin knife and make several holes around the middle of the outer edge. This lets the steam out and dries it nicely. Return to the oven, turn off the heat, and let the ring sit for another 15 minutes. Remove it and cool it on a cake rack. Split it in half horizontally and remove any doughy stuff that may be left in the shells. ❁

•

To make the filling, steep the blueberries in the bourbon for at least 2 hours, shaking the bowl once in a while to make sure all the berries get their share. Whip the cream, sweeten to taste, and flavor with some more bourbon. ❁

•

To make the sauce, place the blueberries, water and sugar in an enameled or stainless steel saucepan, bring to a boil, cover, and simmer for 5 minutes. Put through a sieve or a food mill. If needed add more sugar and bring the sauce to a simmer once more. Flavor with bourbon, cool, and refrigerate until served. ❁

•

An hour or two before serving, heat the oven to 400 degrees, turn it off, and put the rings in for 15 minutes. ❁ This crisps them. Just before serving, pipe half the whipped cream into the bottom half. Drain the blueberries, reserving the liquid, and lay them over the cream. Cover with the remaining whipped cream, flavored with the remaining liquid. Cover with the top half and dust with confectioners' sugar. Serve with blueberry sauce.

Gazpacho

Cold Roast Beef with Stroganoff Sauce

Mixed Salad à la Grecque

Peaches and Cream in Meringue Shells

•

Dolcetto
or Sonoma Vineyards Zinfandel

*T*his cold, starch-free, festive meal is perfect for an August night. It begins with a refreshing gazpacho that has acquired a bit of underbody through the addition of consommé. Next is cold sliced rare beef served with a fascinating sour-cream sauce spiked with bacon, mushrooms and flavorings. The combination is reminiscent of beef Stroganoff but somehow more refined, more mysterious and definitely summery. Accompanying the meat is a mixed salad *à la grecque*, a nice change from the usual vinaigrette-dressed salad. Carrots, celery, artichoke hearts and mushrooms are cooked in a mildly acidulated bath to produce an aromatic, unoily, subtle but delicious dish. Dessert is at once wonderfully light, healthful and not so benign. Feathery meringue shells are filled with ripe, diced juicy peaches and plenty of vanilla-flavored whipped cream. It's worth every calorie.

Real, local tomatoes are to be had practically everywhere, even in supermarkets. So now is the season to make gazpacho, which, as anyone who has tried this dish with cottony, golf-ball tomatoes knows, is as good or awful as the tomatoes that go into it. The consommé in this gazpacho cancels out the wateriness that detracts from many versions of the dish. The soup is made without the addition of bread, nor are croutons or other garnishes served with it since such embellishments seem unnecessary when freshness of flavor is the point of it all. It is worth the few minutes of bother to drop the tomatoes in boiling water and then skin them before they are chopped — even home-grown varieties have tough, coarse skins that add nothing desirable in the way of texture. The easy way to make gazpacho is with a food processor, but care must be taken not to end up with mush. The ingredients must be finely chopped, not puréed, at least for this version. For my part, I am enjoying a nostalgic return to the chopping board and chef's knife for this soup. Dried basil is not a substitute for fresh. Minced parsley will do if fresh basil is not available.

An eye round roast weighing slightly less than 2½ pounds yields ample slices to feed eight people with generosity. The roast is cooked quickly in a 400-degree oven with chopped carrot, onion and celery. I normally roast beef at 425 degrees, but such high heat would burn the vegetables. These aromatics are important, since the pan juices and their lovely flavor are added to the sauce. The sour-cream sauce is based on a recipe from the *California Heritage Cookbook*. I decreased the amount of bacon and used fresh herbs where dried were called for, among other adjustments. The sauce is interesting because its ingredients meld together so effectively that it is difficult to determine what it's made of, especially since the meat juices take away the stark whiteness of the sour cream.

Vegetables *à la grecque* can be served as a first course or as a salad. Author Madeleine Kamman saves the liquid in which the vegetables are cooked, reduces it to a few tablespoons and spoons the resulting glaze over the vegetables. I would recommend this when the vegetables are intended for the first course, but prefer a milder version for a salad that accompanies a main course. The vegetables can be removed from their cooking liquid as soon as they have cooled or they can sit in the liquid in the refrigerator overnight.

The carrots and celery are cooked whole or in large chunks and cut later. The mushrooms are trimmed at the cap. I freeze the stems for the stockpot. Canned artichoke hearts (not bottoms) are perfectly acceptable but should be put in a colander and washed well under cold running water to get rid of any metallic undertones. Frozen artichoke hearts are very good, if you can find them. Oil-cured black olives can be found in specialty food stores and some supermarkets. Other good additions to vegetables *à la grecque* include cauliflower, small white onions, leeks and fennel.

Making meringues in the damp of summer can be a risky business un-less you like them gummy and chewy. I prefer mine light and crisp. On one of our recent revoltingly muggy days I took courage in hand and tried an experiment: Would storing meringues for a few hours in a turned-off oven with a pilot light make the difference between chewy and crunchy? It did. The shells were light, dry and perfect. How comfortable to know that me-ringues are possible when the summer fruits with which they pair so per-fectly are in season.

If the superfine sugar called for in the recipe is not on hand, as was the case in this house the day I needed it, do not despair. Regular granulated sugar can be ground down to the proper consistency in about five minutes in a processor fitted with the steel blade. The sugar must be incorporated gradually once the whites take shape and the mixture must be beaten long enough so that it becomes stiff and glossy. To shape the shells, nylon pastry bags, which are flexible, easy to handle and a snap to wash, are far superior to the stiff, unwieldy plastic bags that only give cooks inferiority complexes. Using a pastry bag can be a lovely experience, somewhat like making mud pies but with triumphant control. Of course, the meringue can be spooned onto the prepared jelly-roll pan and baked as individual puffs rather than piped into shells. These would be no less good with the peaches and cream, if not as showy. The entire dessert can be made in advance except for the whipping of the cream and the final assemblage, both of which take only minutes.

Gazpacho

•

2   *large tomatoes, blanched in boiling*
     water for 10 seconds, peeled and
     finely chopped
2   *cucumbers, peeled and finely chopped*
5   *scallions, with ⅓ of green part left on,*
     cleaned and finely chopped
1   *green pepper, seeded and finely chopped*
2½   *cups tomato juice*
     10½-ounce can beef consommé

1/4   cup red wine vinegar
1/3   cup olive oil
1   large clove garlic, crushed
3   tablespoons minced fresh basil or, if
     necessary, parsley
1/4   teaspoon red hot pepper sauce
2   teaspoons salt, or to taste
    Pepper to taste

Combine all ingredients in a large bowl, stir well and refrigerate for several hours. ✿

Cold Roast Beef
with Stroganoff Sauce

•

4   tablespoons butter, at room
     temperature
    2½ pound eye round roast
1   carrot, finely chopped
1   stalk celery, finely chopped
    Salt and pepper to taste

FOR THE SAUCE
1   tablespoon vegetable oil
1   large clove garlic, crushed
1/2   pound bacon, cut with scissors into
     1/2-inch strips
1/4   pound mushrooms, cleaned and sliced
1½   cups sour cream
1   tablespoon prepared horseradish,
     squeezed dry
2   tablespoons minced scallion
2   tablespoons minced parsley
1   tablespoon fresh thyme leaves or 1
     teaspoon dried

1   tablespoon minced fresh chervil, or 1
teaspoon dried
Pan juices from the roast beef
Salt and pepper to taste

Rub 2 tablespoons of the butter on beef and set aside. Melt remaining 2 tablespoons butter in a roasting pan just large enough to hold the beef and cook the chopped carrot, onion and celery in it for about 8 minutes, or until soft and transparent. Move the vegetables to the edges of the pan and set the beef in the middle. Roast the beef in a preheated 400-degree oven for 45 minutes in all. After 30 minutes, salt and pepper the beef and return to the oven for the remaining 15 minutes. For rare beef, the internal temperature will read from 120 degrees to 125 degrees. Remove the beef from the oven and allow it to sit in the roasting pan to cool for 1 hour.

•

To make the sauce, combine the oil and crushed garlic in a sauté pan or frying pan, heat, and add the bacon strips. Sauté, stirring constantly, until the bacon is browned and just crisp. Place a sieve over a bowl and turn the bacon into it. Then place the bacon on paper towels and drain well. Return 3 tablespoons of the fat to the pan and sauté the mushrooms in this for 3 minutes, stirring constantly. Combine the bacon and the mushrooms in a bowl and add the sour cream, horseradish, scallion, parsley, thyme and chervil. Remove the beef from the roasting pan, place it in a plastic bag, and refrigerate. ❀   Turn the vegetables and juices from the roasting pan into a sieve set over the bowl of sauce, and press down hard with the back of a spoon to extract all the juices. Discard the vegetables. Stir the sauce well, taste for salt and pepper, cover with plastic wrap, and refrigerate. ❀

•

To assemble the dish, remove the beef and the sauce from the refrigerator an hour before serving time. Slice the beef thin and arrange in rows down the length of a serving platter. Cover with plastic wrap and return to refrigerator until needed. ❀   Add whatever juices the meat has rendered to the sauce, stir, and pour the sauce into a clean serving bowl. Allow the sauce to sit at room temperature until needed. Pass the sauce separately.

Mixed Salad à la Grecque

•

1	*pound thin young carrots, ends removed*
2	*cups water*
¼	*cup red wine vinegar*
¼	*cup lemon juice*
½	*cup white wine*
⅓	*cup olive oil*
1	*teaspoon salt*
	A cheesecloth spice bag containing 1 small bay leaf, 6 bruised black peppercorns, 6 whole coriander seeds and 1 teaspoon dried thyme
6	*tender inner stalks of celery, leaves discarded*
	14-ounce can artichoke hearts, rinsed in a colander under cold running water and drained, or 9-ounce package frozen artichoke hearts, cooked and drained
32	*small mushroom caps, stems removed at the caps*
16	*oil-cured olives, pitted and, if large, cut in half*

Bring a pot of water to a boil, add the carrots, and cook for 5 minutes. Drain, combine the 2 cups water, vinegar, lemon juice, wine, oil, salt and spice bag in a saucepan, bring to a boil, and add the parboiled carrots. Cook over medium heat for 15 minutes and add the celery stalks. Bring back to a boil and cook for another 5 minutes. Then add the artichoke hearts and the mushrooms and cook for a final 10 minutes. Remove the pan from heat and set the vegetables aside to cool in the liquid, at least 2 to 3 hours. The cooled vegetables in their liquid can be refrigerated overnight.

To assemble, turn out the cooled vegetables into a colander, drain well, and discard the liquid and the spice bag. Cut the carrots into 1-inch-thick slices, the celery stalks into 2-inch chunks and the artichoke hearts into quarters. Combine in a serving bowl with the mushrooms. Decorate with the black olives, cover with plastic wrap, and refrigerate. ✿ An hour or two before serving, remove the salad from the refrigerator and bring to room temperature.

Peaches and Cream
in Meringue Shells

•

TO PREPARE THE **JELLY-ROLL PAN**		*Parchment paper* *Softened butter* *Cornstarch*
FOR THE **MERINGUE** **SHELLS**	*4* *¼* *¼* *1* *½*	*egg whites, at room temperature* *teaspoon salt* *teaspoon cream of tartar* *cup superfine (granulated, not* *confectioners') sugar* *teaspoon vanilla extract*
FOR THE **PEACHES AND** **CREAM FILLING**	*6* *½* *1½* *1*	*large ripe peaches, blanched in boiling* *water for 20 seconds, peeled, pitted* *and diced* *cup confectioners' sugar* *cups heavy cream* *teaspoon vanilla extract or 1* *tablespoon Vanilla Cognac (see* *Index)*

To prepare the jelly-roll pan, cut a piece of parchment paper to fit, butter the paper lightly, and sift cornstarch on the paper to coat the butter. Turn the paper upside down over a sink to get rid of the excess cornstarch. Place the paper on the jelly-roll pan. Press a 3-inch cookie cutter on the paper 8 times to make circles about 2 inches apart. These are the patterns for the shells. Set the pan aside.

•

To make the meringue shells, combine the egg whites, salt and cream of tartar in the large bowl of an electric mixer. Beat at high speed until the whites are stiff enough to hold their shape. Then turn the mixer to low and beat in the sugar, 2 tablespoons at a time. Make sure each addition of sugar is incorporated before adding more. Beat in the vanilla. Turn the mixer to high and beat until the whites are stiff and very shiny. This will take at least 5 minutes.

To form the shells, fit a nylon pastry bag with a number 5 plain tube. Twist the bag at the bottom when you tuck it into the tube. This will keep the meringue from leaking out while the bag is being filled. Unless you have a very large bag, not all the meringue will fit into it and the bag will have to be filled twice. Untwist the bottom of the bag and squeeze the meringue down gently to fill the tube. Holding the bag over one of the circles and starting with the rim of the circle, pipe the meringue in coils to fill the base. If any spaces remain between the coils, push them together with a spatula wetted with cold water. After the base is filled, build up the circumference of each circle with 3 stacked coils of meringue. The sides will measure about 1½ inches deep down to the base layer.

Bake the meringues in a preheated 250-degree oven for 1¼ hours. Then turn off the heat and let the meringues sit in the oven for another half hour to dry out. Remove from oven and place the meringues on a rack to finish cooling. When they are cold, store them either in a tightly covered tin or in a turned-off cold oven with a pilot light, ❁ where they can remain for a few hours to overnight.

•

To make the peaches and cream filling, combine the diced peaches and the sugar in a bowl, cover with plastic wrap, and refrigerate until needed. This can be prepared several hours in advance. ❁ Just before serving, whip the cream with the vanilla extract or Vanilla Cognac until stiff.

To assemble, place a dollop of cream inside each meringue shell, add a healthy amount of peaches, cover with more whipped cream, and top off with another spoonful of peaches. Serve on dessert plates.

Iced Tomato Soup with Hot Crostini

Chickens Baked in a Salt Crust

Potatoes Roasted in Chicken Fat and Butter

Herbed Cucumbers in Cream

Peach Melba

•

Parducci Zinfandel
or Chiroubles

$\mathcal{T}$his meal was born of wonderful foods in season plus my relentless search for ways to cook chicken that my husband will find worth eating. The herb-stuffed chickens are liberated at the table from their crusts of salt, flour and water and emerge flavorful, moist, subtle, aromatic. The presentation is both spectacular and funny.

The first course of iced tomato soup is light, italianate and a pleasant relief from too many summer gazpachos. A lovely amalgam of home-grown tomatoes, olive oil, garlic and fresh basil, it is accompanied by hot *crostini*, butter-saturated slices of French bread baked to crispness with a Parmesan topping.

Dessert is that good old standby, peach Melba, made with ripe peaches poached in a vanilla syrup, filled with good vanilla ice cream and topped with a raspberry sauce made tart with red currant jelly and spiked with *framboise*, if you happen to have any around.

The soup, an Elizabeth David invention, is practically uncooked, which accounts for its fresh flavor. The tomatoes are melted in olive oil, cooked for 5 minutes with the herbs and simmered another 5 minutes with chicken broth. Fresh basil is a necessity; dried won't do.

The baked chicken is a recipe adapted from *Roger Vergé's Cuisine of the South of France.* The salt crust that encases the chicken is as primitive as clay, and serves the same purpose by forming a hermetic seal around the chickens. The dough gets mixed and kneaded — a pleasantly messy process — and then is patted or rolled out. Enveloping the chicken in it is reminiscent of kindergarten. The chicken, interestingly enough, does not become saturated with salt, despite the huge amount in the crust. After the chickens are removed from the oven, they remain hot for at least 40 minutes (or until the crust is penetrated), a virtue I find commendable in any dish. The cooking time in the recipe is adjusted to the time the chicken is held, since the crust forms a kind of oven and the chicken continues to cook in it.

The chickens, when they are brought to the table, look like surreal, free-form Claes Oldenburg sculptures. But they're not soft. The crust has the resilience of marble, so the chisel and hammer (or rigid knife and mallet, but that is too simple in our house) are applied. A lid is tapped off, about three-quarters down from the top, and removed. This liberates the aromas of the birds and their rosemary, bay leaf and garlic stuffing. The chickens are then lifted out of the bottom crusts and carved. (The crusts, whose insides have become perfect molds of the chickens, are, sadly, discarded. They are, by the way, extraordinarily heavy.)

The whole heads of garlic, which emerge without a hint of harshness, are scooped out of the cavities and placed on the side of the serving platter. A little pressure from a fork and the tender insides ooze out of the garlic buds' shells, sweet and mild.

Also served with the chicken are tiny "new potatoes" that have been carved from larger potatoes (since the little new ones are probably no longer on the market). After the potatoes are peeled and parboiled, they are roasted in a delicate combination of butter and chicken fat taken earlier from the birds. The potatoes can be cooked while the chickens are resting out of the oven and keeping hot in their crusts. The cucumbers, which are also at their height now, are an inexpensive and refreshing accompaniment as well as delicate and interesting with the cream (in lieu of oil) and lemon dressing.

Peaches will not be around too much longer, so now is the time to cook with them. However, cooking peaches, even in a vanilla-flavored syrup, will not give them any taste they do not inherently have. I urge you once again to pick peaches with perfume and no green so that they will ripen to taste like something. I find it a necessity to strain the pips out of the raspberry sauce, and I think the red currant jelly, a classic addition, gives interest and body to it. The peaches can be poached a day or two in advance, and the sauce can also be made well before serving. However, the elements must be put together at the last minute. The combination of raspberry sauce, ice cream and poached peaches is pretty, simple and satisfying.

Iced Tomato Soup

•

3	*pounds ripe tomatoes*
3	*tablespoons olive oil*
5	*large cloves garlic*
About 25	*large basil leaves, shredded*
5	*cups chicken broth*
	Salt and pepper to taste
	Pinch of sugar
	Crostini *(following recipe)*

Drop the tomatoes into boiling water for 10 seconds and transfer them with a slotted spoon to a bowl of cold water. Skin, seed and dice the tomatoes and cook them over low heat in the olive oil until they lose most of their shape. Press garlic (in a garlic press) into the tomatoes and add the shredded basil. Cook for 5 minutes. Then add the chicken broth, salt, pepper and sugar and cook for another 5 minutes. ❀   Cool and refrigerate. Serve with hot *crostini*.

Crostini

•

Sixteen	*¼-inch slices bread, cut from a long French loaf*
About 1½	*sticks butter, melted*
½	*cup freshly grated Parmesan cheese*

Dip both sides of the bread slices in the melted butter, place on a cookie sheet, and spread them with a thick layer of the Parmesan cheese. ✿ Bake in a preheated 400-degree oven for 10 to 15 minutes or until the bread is fairly crisp and the cheese is just melted.

Chickens Baked in a Salt Crust

•

	2	*whole chickens, about 3¼ pounds each*
	2	*large sprigs fresh rosemary*
	2	*bay leaves*
	2	*whole heads garlic, unpeeled*
FOR EACH CRUST	*6½*	*cups all-purpose flour*
	4	*cups coarse (kosher) salt*
	About 3	*cups ice water*

Clean the insides of the chickens and remove lungs and any other loose organs. Remove as much fat as possible from the chickens and set aside for rendering in the potato recipe. Pat inside and outside dry. Place in each chicken a large sprig of rosemary, a bay leaf and a whole, unpeeled head of garlic. Truss the birds with string only; do not use skewers. Refrigerate while you prepare the crusts. ✿

Make one crust at a time. Combine the flour and salt in a large mixing bowl. Add the ice water, ½ cup at a time, and knead until the dough is well blended and has some spring. Lightly flour a surface, lay the dough on it, and either with your hands or with a rolling pin spread it out into a circle large enough to enclose one chicken. Lay the chicken, breast down, on the center of the dough. Wrap the dough completely around the bird, enveloping it so that it will be hermetically sealed. Then turn the chicken over and lay it, breast up, on a baking sheet. Repeat for the second chicken.

Bake the birds in a preheated 450-degree oven for 1 hour. Remove and let sit, undisturbed, for 30 minutes (even 40 minutes)✿   while you serve and eat the first course.

To serve, place the first chicken with its crust on a large board and bring it to the table. To break the crust, you will need a strong knife and a mallet or a chisel and a hammer. Tap a circle about three-quarters of the way from the top of the crust (which will be very hard), remove the lid, and lift out the chicken to a platter for carving. Remove the garlic from the cavity and serve on the side. Repeat with the second chicken.

Potatoes Roasted in
Chicken Fat and Butter

•

	Chicken fat from the 2 chickens
½	*onion, diced*
About 8	*large new potatoes*
2	*tablespoons butter*

To render chicken fat, cut the reserved fat from the chickens into a ¼-inch dice and place in a small heavy saucepan with about 2 tablespoons of water. Over a very low flame, simmer until the fat is rendered and the cracklings look yellow and have lost their raw smell. Then add half an onion, diced, and continue to cook until the onions and cracklings are brown. Remove immediately and strain off the fat, which should be clear, yellow and fresh-smelling.✿

Peel the potatoes, cut them into 1½-inch chunks, and turn them (holding the paring knife in one hand and turning the potato against the knife) to make 1¼-inch tiny potatoes. Drop them into a bowl of cold water. Bring a large pot of water to a boil and cook the potatoes for 5 minutes. Drain and refresh with cold water. Put the chicken fat and butter in a roasting pan just large enough to hold the potatoes in one layer and add the potatoes. Roll them around to coat them with the chicken fat and butter. ❀ Roast in a preheated 450-degree oven for about 30 to 40 minutes, until they have formed a brown crust, shaking the pan every 10 minutes or so. Salt lightly and serve immediately.

Herbed Cucumbers in Cream

•

4 to 5	*long thin cucumbers*
About 2	*tablespoons coarse (kosher) salt*
6	*tablespoons heavy cream*
4	*tablespoons lemon juice*
1	*tablespoon chopped chives*
1	*tablespoon chopped parsley*

If the cucumbers are waxed, peel them. If they are not, wash them and leave the peel on. Cut off the ends, slice the cucumbers thin and mix in a bowl with about 2 tablespoons salt, weight with a plate, and let sit to draw the moisture out for about 2 hours. Drain off the liquid, wash the cucumber slices if they are very salty, and dry on paper towels. Combine the remaining ingredients and mix the dressing into the cucumbers. ❀

Peach Melba

•

8	*ripe large unblemished peaches, all of the same size*
¼	*lemon*

> 1   cup *sugar*
> 1¼ cups *water*
> ½   teaspoon vanilla extract, or ½ vanilla
>   bean split up the middle
> 1   quart good vanilla ice cream
> 1   recipe Raspberry Sauce (see following
>   recipe)

Drop the peaches, one or two at a time, into a large pot of boiling water, leave for 10 to 15 seconds, and transfer to a large bowl of cold water. Skin the peaches and rub them with the lemon, or drop them into another bowl of cold water to which you have added a tablespoon of lemon juice.

Bring the sugar, water and vanilla to a boil, lower the heat, and poach the peaches in the syrup for about 7 minutes. Remove them with a slotted spoon and set them on a cake rack over a baking sheet to drain for about an hour. Then halve the peaches and discard the pits.❋   Refrigerate until needed.

Place 2 peach halves, cut side up, in each dessert bowl. Place a scoop of ice cream on each half. Cover with raspberry sauce.

Raspberry Sauce

•

> 2   packages frozen raspberries
> ¾   cup red currant jelly
> 1½ teaspoons potato starch or arrowroot
> 1   tablespoon cold water
> 2   tablespoons framboise (optional)

Thaw the berries, place them in a saucepan, add the jelly, and bring to a boil. Mix the potato starch or arrowroot with the water and add this to the berries. Cook, stirring, until the sauce is clear. Add the optional *framboise.* Push the sauce through a strainer and cool.❋   This can be made a day or two in advance and refrigerated.

Hot and Cold Vegetables with Aïoli

Barbecued Spareribs

Corn Pudding

*Clafouti with Fresh Cherries or Italian
Prune-Plums*

•

*Beer
or Pedroncelli Zinfandel Rosé*

*T*his rustic meal, made up of simple French and American country dishes, has important but minimal refinements and plenty of backbone, just the thing to prod desultory late-summer appetites.

The first course combines hot boiled potatoes in their jackets plus barely cooked cauliflower with icy cold tomatoes, scallions, celery and hard-cooked eggs. These are presented with an aïoli, the tough-minded, wonderful garlic mayonnaise of Provence. Next are deliciously sauced American barbecued spareribs, which are cooked over coals or in the oven, depending on the weather and the availability of a person willing to turn them over a hot grill. The ribs are served with a custardy fresh corn pudding, which is delicate but assertive enough to hold its own with the meat. Dessert is another French country dish, a *clafouti*, which, quite simply, is a crêpe batter baked with either fresh cherries now or, in September when they will appear on the market, Italian prune-plums.

Thanks to the food processor, the *aïoli* can be made without anxiety. The garlic is first minced in the processor and then reduced further when the actual mayonnaise is made. It is always important for the oil (and it must be olive oil) to be at room temperature when it is added to the egg yolks. The boiling water that is drizzled in at the end stabilizes the sauce. And while the water appears to thin it, the thickness is regained after the mayonnaise spends a couple of hours in the refrigerator. By then the garlic has been completely amalgamated into the emulsion and the flavors are beautifully homogeneous.

The platter of vegetables and egg wedges is appealing. I stand a bouquet of scallions and tender celery stalks in an earthenware pitcher or narrow crock in the center of the platter with the hot and cold vegetables surrounding it. This dish can be expanded for a fabulous summer lunch by preparing a whole cooked egg per person and adding cooked artichokes, blanched string beans, barely cooked carrots, a poached white fish and salt cod that has been first soaked and then simmered in a little milk.

It is very fine to plan an outdoor barbecue for a summer night, but even nicer if the food can be cooked indoors should it rain or the humidity remains hideous or if the outdoor chef has had a beastly day at the office. This barbecue recipe is equally good cooked in the oven or on a grill and can be prepared in advance up to the time the ribs receive their final cooking. I look for racks of small ribs and marinate them overnight in a lot of lemon juice mixed with other seasonings. The marinade then becomes one of the ingredients for the final sauce, whose base is a good bottled, commercial barbecue sauce. (The one I use is called Bad News All-Purpose Sauce!) The initial cooking of the ribs takes place in the kitchen on a rack in a roasting pan, which must sometimes be expanded to two pans since the ribs are baked in a single layer. Cake racks will do, as they raise the ribs just enough so that they don't soak in the fat rendered during cooking.

The corn pudding is also prepared several hours before it is baked. I follow the advice of the great Virginia cook, Edna Lewis, who says to remove the corn from the cob by cutting through the kernels and then scraping out the meat and juices which form a thick corn milk or cream. The texture that results from following these instructions is lovely. The pudding is baked in a *bain marie;* that is, the dish is placed in a second pan, which is filled with boiling water. It is safer to add the boiling water with the pan in place in the oven. The result is an intensely corn-flavored, custardy, exquisite dish with a lovely overtone of nutmeg. Whole nutmegs can be grated on a nutmeg grater or on the small holes of a regular kitchen grater. Nutmeg that is bought already grated can be substituted but will not be as good.

It became clear during my research that there is no one recipe for *clafouti*. The batter I worked out was declared a great success by French house guests. It puffed and browned nicely, and the flavor was elegant. To keep the fruit from sinking to the bottom, I use Madeleine Kamman's rule and cook part of the batter in a buttered enamel-on-iron pie plate on top of the stove until it sets. The fruit is then placed on the resulting giant crêpe and the remaining batter is poured over all. When the bottom layer of batter has been set first, the fruit does not sink and the *clafouti* slices more neatly into wedges for serving. When I use cherries, I pit these with a heavy-duty cherry (and olive) pitter before I do any other cooking so that by the time all the vegetables are prepared and one's hands have been washed after handling the spareribs, their color fades from cherry-juice-purple to almost normal. Prune-plums, whose late-summer arrival on the market is imminent, do not pose such problems and are delicious in this dish.

Hot and Cold Vegetables
with Aïoli

•

FOR THE AÏOLI	8 to 9	large garlic cloves, peeled
	4	egg yolks
	1½	tablespoons lemon juice
	½	teaspoon salt
		Freshly ground black pepper to taste
	1½	cups olive oil
FOR THE **GARNISH**	8	small to medium new potatoes, unpeeled
	1	small cauliflower, trimmed and separated into florets
	8	scallions, trimmed

8	*inner stalks celery*
16	*cherry tomatoes, or 2 large tomatoes,*
	unpeeled and each cut into 8 wedges
3	*hard-cooked eggs, each cut into 6*
	wedges

To make the *aïoli,* start the motor of a food processor fitted with the steel blade and, one at a time, drop the garlic cloves through the feed tube. Process until the garlic is minced and the pieces are thrown to the sides of the processor bowl. Turn off the motor and add the egg yolks, lemon juice, salt and pepper. Scrape the garlic down from the sides of the bowl. Process for 1 minute, or until the egg yolks are thick. With the motor running, slowly dribble the oil through the tube. Slowly add the boiling water through the tube, also with the motor running. Decant into a serving bowl, cover, and refrigerate for at least 2 hours. ✿

About 15 to 20 minutes before serving, depending on whether the potatoes are more small or medium in size, put the potatoes on to cook in a pot of boiling salted water. About 10 minutes later, add the cauliflower to a second pot of boiling water and blanch the florets for 5 minutes. Drain the hot vegetables.

To serve, place a tall glass or a small earthenware pitcher or other container in the center of a serving platter and stand the scallions and celery stalks in this. Arrange the remaining vegetables and hard-cooked egg wedges on the platter. Serve with the *aïoli.*

Barbecued Spareribs

•

6 to 7	*pounds small spareribs in whole racks*
⅔	*cup lemon juice (about 6 to 7 lemons)*
2	*teaspoons paprika (preferably*
	Hungarian)
1	*tablespoon soy sauce*
¼	*teaspoon ground black pepper*

> *Marinade from the ribs*
> *18-ounce jar quality all-purpose*
>   *barbecue sauce*
> 1   *cup water*
> 1   *large onion, puréed in food processor*
> ¼   *cup dark brown sugar*
> 1   *tablespoon Worcestershire sauce*
> 1   *tablespoon Dijon mustard*

Wash the spareribs, pat them dry with paper towels, and place the whole racks in a large roasting pan. Combine the lemon juice, paprika, soy sauce and pepper and rub this mixture into the ribs. Cover the pan with plastic wrap and refrigerate overnight, turning the ribs when you remember to do so.

The next morning, remove the ribs from the pan and drain the marinade into a saucepan. Arrange a metal rack on the roasting pan, or as many pans as necessary to cook the ribs in a single layer. (Cake cooling racks can be used to construct roasting racks.) Place the ribs fat side up on the racks and bake in a preheated 350-degree oven for 1½ hours. Remove from oven and allow the ribs to cool on the racks.

While the ribs are undergoing their initial baking, make the sauce. Add the jar of barbecue sauce to the reserved marinade in the saucepan along with the water, onion, brown sugar, Worcestershire sauce and mustard. Bring to a simmer and cook, stirring constantly, until the sugar is melted. Set aside. ❁

When the ribs are cool, cut them into single-rib portions. Drain the fat from the roasting pan or pans and place the ribs in the pans. Pour the sauce over the ribs and set aside. ❁

For the final cooking in the oven, cover the pan or pans with foil and bake at 350 degrees for 1 hour. For the final cooking over charcoal, cook on a grill over medium heat, basting with the sauce and turning with tongs, for about 40 minutes.

Corn Pudding

•

2 tablespoons softened butter
2 cups fresh corn, cut from the cob
   (about 6 medium-large ears)
1/3 cup sugar
1 teaspoon salt
3 eggs
1/2 cup heavy cream
1 cup milk
3 tablespoons melted butter
   Freshly grated nutmeg

Smear a 1½-quart baking dish (a soufflé dish is ideal) with the softened butter and set aside.

To cut the corn from the cob, stand each ear vertically, one at a time, in a mixing bowl and cut down through the middle of the kernels, not too close to the cob. Then run the knife down, close to the cob, scraping off the resulting thick corn "milk." Add the sugar and salt and mix well. In another bowl, beat the eggs and then beat in the cream, the milk and the melted butter. Add to the corn mixture and combine well. ❀ The mixture can wait in the refrigerator for several hours until you are ready to bake it. To bake the pudding, stir the mixture once more and pour it into the buttered baking dish. Grate fresh nutmeg over the surface.

Set the baking dish in a square cake pan and place this on the shelf of the preheated 350-degree oven. Pour boiling water in the cake pan to within 1 inch of the top of the cake pan. Close the oven door and bake the pudding for about 1 hour, or until a knife comes out clean when inserted in the center of the pudding. ❀ The pudding can sit for half an hour before serving, if necessary.

Clafouti with Cherries
or Italian Prune-Plums

•

2	tablespoons softened butter
1½	pounds sweet cherries or 1½ pounds Italian prune-plums
⅔	cup flour
¼	teaspoon salt
½	cup sugar
4	eggs
2	tablespoons Kirsch if cherries are used, or 1 tablespoon lemon juice if Italian prune-plums are used
1	teaspoon vanilla extract
2	tablespoons melted butter
2	cups milk
	Confectioners' sugar

Use the softened butter to grease a 10-inch pie plate that can be placed over direct heat. Set aside. Pit the cherries or halve and stone the prune-plums. Place in a bowl and set aside.

Sift the flour, salt and sugar together into a bowl. Beat in the eggs, one at a time, with a wire whisk. Then beat in the Kirsch or lemon juice, the vanilla extract, melted butter and milk. ❀ The batter can wait for several hours, but should be beaten again before it is used.

To cook the *clafouti*, ladle 1½ cups of the batter into the buttered pie plate, place over low to moderate heat, and cook until the batter is set. Remove the plate from heat and arrange the cherries or the plums (cut side down) on the cooked batter in a tight, single layer. Pour the remaining batter over the fruit and bake in a preheated 400-degree oven for 45 minutes. Allow the *clafouti* to cool to lukewarm or room temperature. ❀ Just before serving, sprinkle with confectioners' sugar and cut into wedges.

Fall

September

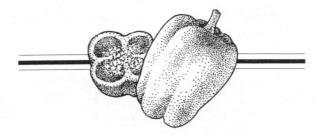

Escoffier's
Red Pepper Conserve
for Cold Meats

MAKES ABOUT 4 CUPS

•

½   cup olive oil
2   medium-large onions, chopped
4   medium-large red bell peppers, seeded
*   and chopped*
1¼ cups red wine vinegar
*   Salt and pepper to taste*
1   clove garlic, crushed
1   pound fresh tomatoes, preferably plum
*   tomatoes, skinned, seeded and*
*   chopped*
¾   cup seedless raisins

Heat the oil in a stainless steel, enamel-on-iron or other nonreactive saucepan, add the onions, and cook over low heat until the onions are soft and golden. Add the chopped red peppers and cook over low heat for 20 minutes, stirring occasionally. Add the vinegar and cook over medium heat for 15 minutes, stirring occasionally. Season with salt and pepper and add the garlic, chopped tomatoes and raisins. Cover and cook very gently for 1½ hours, stirring occasionally. Cool, decant into ½-pint jars, and refrigerate. The conserve will keep for months under refrigeration. Serve with cold meats and pâtés.

Some versions of this conserve call for the addition of sugar and various spices. This is the master's recipe and still the best.

Soupe au Pistou

Broiled Flank Steak

Roasted Red Pepper and Watercress Salad

Fresh Fruit Compote

•

Georges duBoeuf California Gamay Beaujolais
or Côtes du Rhône

This meal, while more light than heavy, has the substance that is wanted at summer's end. The *soupe au pistou* uses many of the fresh, local vegetables that are filling co-ops and truck stands. Beans, a little pasta and a potato add body, and the *pistou*, a potent mélange of garlic, olive oil, fresh tomatoes and fresh basil, makes the soup wildly fragrant. The *pistou* is swirled into the soup just before it is brought to the table, and as the two combine the aroma is pure south of France.

The main course is one of my best standby recipes, a flank steak with a marinade rubbed into it and broiled quickly under high heat. It is delicious hot and perhaps even better cold. I have often made it for picnics. The salad that accompanies it plays the sweetness and softness of roasted red bell peppers against the sharpness and crispiness of watercress. The minced shallots in the dressing make a bridge between the two. Dessert is a compote of fresh fruits whose flavors are brought up by being poached separately in vanilla-flavored syrup.

There is no one recipe for *soupe au pistou*. Beans, vegetables in various combinations, a pasta and the ingredients of the *pistou* itself are universal, although the proportions vary. Some recipes call for grated Parmesan (too minestronelike), saffron (too extravagant when the *pistou* overpowers it) and/or salt pork (unnecessary and complicated). Most classical recipes call for vermicelli as the pasta; but one of my friends, an excellent cook, hit upon *ditalini*, a short, fat macaroni available in some supermarkets and most Italian stores, which does not get mushy. Tiny pasta shells would also do. If, in winter, I could not get zucchini or yellow squash I would substitute any other kind of squash or some frozen peas, or I would increase the amount of those vegetables I could get. But if I have basil or frozen *pistou*, come what may, we will have this soup.

Had a friend not served us this flank steak for dinner, I would never have tried it on my own. I'd be too suspicious of the ingredients in the marinade. Despite the presence of soy sauce, which I tend to worry about, this dish is a sophisticated combination of flavors without a hint of fake Chinesey nothingness. I used to trim and score the flank steak the day before I cooked it and let it sit, with its marinade, wrapped in plastic in the refrigerator. But now I do this only if it suits me to do advance preparations, since it seems to make no difference whatsoever to the flavor if the marinade is put on immediately before the steak is cooked.

While flank steak is no longer the bargain it used to be, it is still a good value, since a little goes a long way, especially if the meat is carved very thin, on the bias and against the grain. Eight can be fed amply on 2½ pounds of meat. The hotter you can get your broiler, the higher the flame and the closer you can get the meat to it, the better it will be. A nice round loaf of French country bread would go well with both the soup and the meat.

Lovely fat red bell peppers are on the market at this time of year. The peppers are best when their skins are scorched off (see Index). Once roasted, peeled and seeded, these peppers freeze well and unmessily if they are placed in a single layer on a cookie sheet on waxed paper. After they are frozen, they can be decanted into heavy plastic bags. They are wonderful for antipasto in the winter, or for peppers and anchovies. Here they are delicious with watercress and as an accompaniment to the flank steak. With all the vegetables in the *soup au pistou*, nothing more is needed for the main course.

The fresh fruit compote is as easygoing as the soup. You can use whatever you have, as long as it poaches well. I find it satisfying to combine late-summer fruits. For green apples, I am cooking these days with Rambos, a nice tart Pennsylvania apple. I use Baldwins or Jonathans for red apples in the fall, and always watch for the Jonathans to come in, since their season is short and their flavor and texture divine. The lovely little Italian prune-plums are also appealing; these are the best cooking plums I know, and they add much in flavor and texture to this compote. I would not be heartbroken if I could not get peaches, since the other fruits are so good. This dessert can, of course, be made a day or two in advance, which is an advantage.

Soupe au Pistou

•

1 cup dried Great Northern beans
   A bouquet garni of 6 sprigs of parsley,
      1 bay leaf and a few sprigs of fresh
      thyme (or ½ teaspoon dried thyme)
   Salt to taste
2 young zucchini, scrubbed but not
      peeled, and cut into 1-inch chunks
2 young yellow squash, scrubbed but not
      peeled, and cut into 1-inch chunks
1 large handful of string beans, ends
      snapped off and cut into 2-inch
      pieces
1 large onion, peeled and diced
2 medium-large carrots, peeled and cut
      into 1-inch chunks
3 small firm turnips (optional), peeled
      and cut into 1-inch chunks
2 tender stalks celery, cut into 1-inch chunks
¼ cup olive oil
¼ cup water
12 cups chicken broth
1 medium potato, peeled and diced
⅓ cup ditalini or tiny pasta shells
   One recipe Pistou (see August,
      Provisioning the Pantry)

Soak the beans overnight in 3 quarts of cold water. The next day, drain them and add 2 quarts of fresh water, the bouquet garni and the salt. Bring to a simmer, skim, and cook until tender, about 1 hour. Leave the beans in their liquid and set aside.

Place the vegetables, except for the potato, in a large pot along with the ¼ cup olive oil and water. I use a 7-quart enamel-on-iron casserole. Cover and cook over medium heat for 15 minutes, stirring frequently until the water has evaporated. Do not brown or scorch the vegetables. Quickly add the chicken broth, salt to taste and diced potato and bring to a boil. Cook, uncovered, for 10 minutes. Add the *ditalini* or tiny pasta shells and cook 10 more minutes. The vegetables should retain some crunch. Remove the bouquet garni from the beans and add the beans and their liquid to the vegetables. ❁

While the soup is cooking, make the *pistou*. Bring the soup with the beans to a simmer. Beat the *pistou* into the soup and heat, but do not let it boil. Serve from the pot at the table.

NOTE: Do not add the *pistou* until just before serving.

Broiled Flank Steak

•

Two	*1¼-pound flank steaks*
3	*cloves garlic, crushed*
¼	*cup soy sauce*
2	*tablespoons tomato paste*
2	*tablespoons peanut oil*
1	*teaspoon cracked black pepper*
1	*teaspoon oregano*

Trim the flank steaks of any fat and score them on both sides in a diamond pattern. Mix the remaining ingredients and rub them into the steaks. ❁ This can be done a day in advance and the steaks refrigerated or just before broiling. Preheat the broiler until it is very hot. Do not scrape off the marinade. Broil the steaks as close to the flame as possible for 3 to 4 minutes on each side. Carve in very thin slices, against the grain and on the diagonal. Serve hot (or cold). ❁

Roasted Red Pepper and
Watercress Salad

•

4 *large red bell peppers*
6 *tablespoons olive oil*
1½ *tablespoons lemon juice*
1 *tablespoon minced shallot*
Salt and pepper to taste
1 *bunch watercress, washed and dried*

Broil the peppers until the skins are blackened and blistered (see Index). Place them in a plastic bag and let them sit for about 10 minutes, or until they are cool enough to handle. Rub off the skins, seed the peppers, and cut into strips. Mix the oil and lemon juice and add to the peppers. Add the minced shallot and salt and pepper. Set aside. ❀ Just before serving, place the watercress in a bowl, add the peppers with the dressing, and toss.

Fresh Fruit Compote

•

2½ *cups water*
1 *cup sugar*
1 *vanilla bean, split*
2 *medium or 3 large red apples, such as*
   Jonathan or Baldwin
1 *lemon*
2 *large or 3 medium pears, ripe but firm*
2 *large or 3 medium green apples, such*
   as Rambo or Granny Smith
4 *ripe peaches*
8 *Italian prune-plums*
32 *black grapes*

Combine the water, sugar and vanilla bean in a saucepan and bring to a simmer over medium heat. Peel the red apples and add their peel to the syrup. Rub the peeled apples with the lemon and set them aside. Simmer the syrup over low heat for 10 minutes. Peel, quarter and core the pears and poach them in the syrup for about 5 minutes, or until they are just cooked. Remove the pears to a serving bowl, using a slotted spoon.

Peel the green apples. Quarter and core them along with the red apples. Simmer these in the syrup until just cooked, about 4 minutes. Transfer them to the bowl. Drop the peaches in boiling water for 10 seconds, remove, and slip off the skins. Halve the peaches and discard the pits. Poach the peaches in the syrup for about 6 minutes, or until just cooked. Transfer to the bowl. Wash the prune-plums and add them whole to the syrup. Simmer for 8 minutes and transfer to the bowl. Finally, simmer the grapes in the syrup for 8 minutes and transfer to the bowl. Strain the syrup over the fruit and chill. ❀ (The vanilla bean can be washed and reused.)

Iced (or Hot) Red Bell Pepper Soup

*Baked Ham with Raisin Sauce and
Mustards*

Grated Zucchini and Spinach in Cream

Onion Rolls

Italian Prune-Plum Tart

•

FIRST COURSE:
San Martin Chenin Blanc
MAIN COURSE:
Juliénas

---

*T*his early fall meal begins with a full-bodied soup that is delicious in its simplicity. The soup uses red bell peppers, which are now at their peak. Then the menu gets serious with baked ham, an all-American raisin sauce and the kind of onion rolls that push nostalgia buttons for anyone who used to gorge on almost identical ones at Ratner's in New York late at night after Dixieland jazz concerts. Grated zucchini becomes substantial enough to stand up to the ham when it is reinforced with chopped spinach and cooked in cream. Dessert is a tart of Italian prune-plum quarters arranged in a pretty pattern on a thin marzipanlike base and glazed with red currant jelly.

The red bell pepper soup is thickish, a bit dense, no sissy. It can be served iced on a muggy September evening or hot if the weather behaves like New England. I made this soup, from Elizabeth David's *Book of Mediterranean Food*, the first time because I constantly look for new ways to use red peppers when they are in season. The recipe sounded all right, if a little simple-minded. What I hadn't anticipated was its intense and wonderful flavor. If roasting fresh peppers is just too much (but it really is so easy; see Index), you can buy roasted peppers in a can or jar for this recipe. I would think, however, that the amount of purée would have to be increased, since peppers you buy roasted are just not as flavorful as those you roast yourself. You don't want the tomato to numb the peppers.

Half a ham will serve eight people amply, with plenty left for sandwiches, to have with eggs or for serious experimentation in more esoteric directions. (And then finally there is the denuded bone, without which split pea soup isn't. I cook the split peas — according to the directions for soup on the package — along with the bone, any remaining scraps of meat and some diced carrots, celery, onion and potato. Salt, pepper and lots of thyme are the seasonings. The soup freezes well, and it is a joy to have a quart or two on hand for a Sunday night when even broiling a hamburger is too much.)

I like Gwaltney's Pagan hams, which are better than most but not as good, I think, as they used to be. I buy the rump or butt end because there is more meat and it is easier to carve. A pair of kitchen scissors is useful for cutting through the rind when it is removed, forty minutes before the ham has finished cooking.

I do not glaze my hams anymore because my husband carves the meat in the kitchen and cuts off the fat and glaze before anyone can see it. The apricot glaze in the recipe here is a pretty presentation and is worth doing if you carve at the table, but I have never found that the glaze made one whit of difference in the taste of the meat.

The raisin sauce, an old Philadelphia recipe given to me by a dear friend, is delicious not only with ham but with any smoked meat. The sauce can be made in advance and reheated just before serving.

The onion rolls, which provide the starch in this meal, are made glorious with the secret ingredients of unflavored malted milk and a fabulously oniony topping. The recipe comes from a wonderful little pamphlet by Sue Anderson Gross called *Bagels, Bagels, Bagels*.

I am addicted to grated zucchini in cream and cook it often now that the food processor has saved my knuckles from the grater. The combination of zucchini and spinach was inspired by a recipe in *Mastering the Art of French*

Cooking, Volume II, by Julia Child and Simone Beck. Theirs is a sauté of the vegetables with a Mediterranean aroma, made with garlic and olive oil. To give the dish the different flavor and body that are needed to go with the very American ham, my version uses shallots, or scallions, and is simmered in heavy cream. It can be made the day before and reheated just before serving.

Ham is a wonderful excuse for serving different mustards. I like to put out Moutarde de Meaux, Dijon and herb-flavored or horseradishy mustards. I have even been known to share a jar of wonderful Creole mustard which a friend gave us.

The Italian prune-plum tart is a good way to use these lovely inexpensive fruits whose season is so short. If you have chosen ripe plums and if you have the wonderful widget that both pits and quarters the plums, this tart takes absolutely no time to put together. The thin layer of ground almonds, almond and vanilla flavoring, lemon peel and egg makes a kind of marzipan base. This and the red currant jelly glaze bring out the flavor of the fruit and add a tartness and freshness. This dessert is elegant with the *crème fraîche*-type concoction of whipped cream into which some sour cream has been beaten (see Index).

Iced (or Hot)
Red Bell Pepper Soup

•

3   *large red bell peppers plus ½ red or*
    green bell pepper
8   *cups tomato juice*
    Pinch of sugar
2   *tablespoons chopped fresh basil, thyme,*
    oregano or parsley, alone or in any
    combination
    Salt and pepper to taste

Roast the 3 whole peppers (see Index) until the skins are black and blistered. Let them sit in a plastic bag for about 10 minutes, or until they are cool enough to handle. Skin and seed them and process the flesh to a purée in a blender or food processor. You should have about ½ cup of purée. Combine the purée with the tomato juice and a pinch of sugar and simmer for 5 minutes. ❁ Cool and refrigerate. If soup is to be served hot, reheat. Whether hot or ice cold, just before serving, garnish with the remaining half raw red or green pepper, cut into a thin julienne, and the fresh chopped herbs. Taste for salt and pepper.

This soup can also be made with roasted peppers bought in a can or jar.

Baked Ham with Raisin Sauce and Mustards

•

½ *whole ham, preferably the butt end,*
    weighing 4 or 5 pounds
1 *cup apricot jam*
1 *teaspoon dry mustard*
    Whole cloves (optional)

Remove the plastic wrap from the ham as well as the paper label that says "water added." Put the ham, fat side up, in a roasting pan, to which you have added about ¼ inch of water. Bake in a preheated 325-degree oven, 18 minutes per pound.

Make the glaze (which is optional) by melting the apricot jam and the dry mustard over a low flame. Sieve it to make a purée and set aside.

About 40 minutes before the ham is completely cooked, remove it from the oven. Cut off the rind and score the fat in a diamond pattern. If desired, stud the points of the diamonds with whole cloves. Spoon the apricot-mustard glaze over the fat. Return to the oven for another 40 minutes, or until the glaze is set. If you don't want to use the glaze, remove rind, score fat, and return ham to the oven for the remaining cooking time. ❁ Allow the ham to rest for 30 minutes to an hour before carving. Serve with assorted mustards and Raisin Sauce (recipe follows).

Raisin Sauce

MAKES ABOUT 2 CUPS

•

½	cup raisins
⅓	cup dried currants
1⅓	cups dry red wine
1	tablespoon flour
1	teaspoon Dijon mustard
1	teaspoon sugar
¼	teaspoon ground cloves
¼	teaspoon ground nutmeg
1	tablespoon minced parsley
1	tablespoon minced green celery leaves
½	teaspoon ground cinnamon soaked in 1 tablespoon cold water

Soak raisins and currants overnight in the wine. Next day, drain off the wine and reserve it. In the top of a double boiler, mix together the flour, mustard, sugar, cloves, nutmeg, parsley and celery leaves. Stir in wine and cook over hot water, stirring constantly, until mixture thickens and boils. Add raisins and currants and stir in soaked cinnamon. Let sauce boil for 1 minute more and taste for seasoning. ❀ Serve warm.

Grated Zucchini
and Spinach in Cream

•

2½	pounds small young zucchini
2½	teaspoons salt
2	packages frozen whole-leaf spinach, partially defrosted
6	tablespoons butter

3   *tablespoons chopped shallots or*
    scallions
1½ *cups heavy cream*
    Salt and pepper to taste

Soak the zucchini for about 20 minutes in cold water. Then wash them under cold running water, and if they still feel gritty scrub them gently with a brush. Trim off the ends. Dry the zucchini and put them through the coarse grating blade of a food processor. Turn out the grated zucchini into a colander set over a bowl, mix in the salt, and let drain while you prepare the spinach.

Partially defrost the spinach and chop it with a knife. Melt 3 table-spoons of the butter in a saucepan and stir in the chopped spinach. Cover and cook over low heat for a couple of minutes. Then uncover, raise the heat, and cook for another few minutes, stirring, until all the moisture has evaporated. Set aside.

Squeeze a handful of zucchini, taste a bit, and if it is too salty, rinse it under cold running water. Squeeze the zucchini dry by handfuls and place on a dish towel to absorb any excess liquid. Melt the butter in a large (11- or 12-inch) stainless steel, enameled or no-stick frying pan. Stir in the shal-lots or scallions and cook for a minute. Then raise heat to moderately high and add the zucchini. Toss and turn for about 4 minutes, then add the spinach. Cook for another few minutes and add the cream. Simmer for several minutes until the cream has been absorbed and thickened. Season to taste. ❁   This can be prepared in advance and reheated before serving.

Onion Rolls

MAKES 32

•

1   *tablespoon (1 envelope) yeast*
2   *cups warm water*
¼   *cup unflavored instant malted milk*
    powder

	2	tablespoons sugar
	1	tablespoon salt
	6	cups unsifted flour
ONION TOPPING	1/2	cup dehydrated minced onions, soaked in water and then squeezed dry
	2	tablespoons vegetable oil
	1/4	teaspoon salt
	1/2	egg white
GLAZE	1	egg
	1	teaspoon water

In a large mixing bowl, dissolve the yeast in the warm water. Add the malted milk powder and sugar and stir until dissolved. Add the salt and flour and stir. You may need more flour to make a fairly stiff dough. Knead, either by hand or in a heavy-duty mixer with a dough hook, for 10 minutes. Place the kneaded dough in an ungreased bowl, cover, and let rise in a warm place until doubled in bulk.

Punch the dough down and divide it into 32 pieces. Shape each piece into a ball and let rise on a greased baking sheet, about an hour, until doubled in bulk.

Combine the onion topping ingredients and set aside. When the rolls have risen, brush the tops with glaze made from the egg beaten with the teaspoon of water. Top the rolls with onion topping. Bake them in a pre-heated 450-degree oven for about 15 minutes, or until brown. ❁

Italian Prune-Plum Tart

•

3/4	cup blanched almonds
1/3	cup sugar
1	large egg
2	tablespoons softened butter

¼	teaspoon almond extract
1	teaspoon vanilla extract
1	teaspoon grated lemon rind
	10-inch Unbaked Tart Shell (see Index)
24	Italian prune-plums, pitted and quartered
1	cup red currant jelly
2	tablespoons port or medium-sweet Madeira
	Mock Crème Fraîche (optional; see Index)

Combine the almonds and sugar in a food processor and blend for 30 seconds, or until smooth. Do not grind to a paste. Add the egg, butter, almond and vanilla extracts and lemon rind and blend for another 20 seconds.

Spread the mixture evenly over the unbaked tart shell. Arrange the plums in a decorative pattern over the mixture. Place the tart on a baking sheet and bake in the center of a preheated oven at 350 degrees for 1 hour. Remove and let cool.

Heat the currant jelly with the port or Madeira until melted. Spoon this mixture over the entire tart and let it cool to room temperature. ❀ Serve alone or with the *crème fraîche*.

Roasted Red Bell Peppers with Anchovies

Grilled or Broiled Butterflied Leg of Lamb

Potatoes with Garlic-Butter Purée

Small White Onions Baked in Foil

Broiled Tomatoes

Sautéed Broccoli

*Sliced Peaches with Mirabelle or Kirsch
and Mock Crème Fraîche*

•

FIRST COURSE·
Verdicchio
MAIN COURSE:
*Sterling Vineyards Cabernet Sauvigon
or Château Haut-Bailly*

*T*his sturdy meal, which celebrates the end of the cookout season, should, if possible, be eaten outdoors, ideally on an evening that is end-of-summer balmy yet crisp with the promise of fall. A supply of sweaters or shawls may be in order for less hardy friends, and should it rain, the party can without too much sacrifice be moved in-doors. Even the meat can be as easily cooked under the kitchen broiler.

Garlic in various treatments produces an extraordinary range of tastes in several of the dishes in this meal. For the first course, red bell peppers are roasted to bring out their depth of flavor. These are combined with anchovies and dressed with a lemony vinaigrette whose several herbs are reinforced with crushed raw garlic. The result may not be subtle but it does, somehow, avoid coarseness.

Next is a butterflied leg of lamb whose flat, boneless succulence is made fragrant with a garlicky wine-lemon marinade, enhanced with sprigs of fresh oregano or whatever fresh herbs are growing in profusion. These flavors merge with the lamb as it is grilled over charcoal and, if the grill has a kettle top, smoked as it is cooked to a brown-encrusted pink delicious-ness.

Brightening the lamb are four vegetables that make an aromatic bou-quet of red, green and white. Small potatoes are boiled and then napped with a most delicate baked garlic purée, whose softness in texture is matched by its sweetness of aroma and flavor. Broccoli is sautéed in olive oil with crushed whole cloves of garlic, which add a pronounced but refined flavor. Small white onions, baked with a little butter in an envelope of foil, have a purity and intensity undiluted by water. The onions give off their own liquid, which combines with the butter to make a natural sauce. For a little tingle and a lot of color, there are chunks of tomatoes, still so good at this season, broiled until they are delicately charred.

The meal ends with the last, alas, peaches of summer. Here they are peeled, sliced and refreshed with Kirsch or *eau de vie de mirabelle*, a delecta-ble, clear and potent liqueur made in either Alsace or Germany from golden plums the size of fat cherries. A bowl of mock *crème fraîche* is passed for those who wish to top the peaches with a little iniquity.

I have indicated three alternative ways to go about the simple business of skinning and roasting red bell peppers. Because these peppers are so plentiful and reasonably priced at this time, I buy lots for the freezer. The peppers should be roasted, skinned, cored and seeded and then laid flat on a jelly-roll pan lined with waxed paper. After they are frozen, they can be popped into heavy plastic bags and stored in the freezer for use in winter when they are either not available or hideously expensive. The sauce in this recipe, which uses anchovy oil, borrows from cookbook author Michael Field. In this way you get the benefit of the flavor from the anchovies' oil while the added olive oil, lemon juice and herbs tone down the saltiness.

Any butcher worthy of the name will happily butterfly a leg of lamb for a customer. My local supermarket was even able to bone a leg for me on a Sunday, when help in the back room is usually sparse. A butterflied leg of lamb has a strange lumpiness that should not be a source of worry. When the meat is broiled it looks quite respectable and has the advantage of yielding well-done slices from the thinner parts and pink slices from the thicker parts. I commend the mild smokiness that a kettle grill gives the lamb.

The garlic-butter purée for the potatoes can be prepared a day or two in advance, especially since the oven must be on for another purpose. Two heads of garlic seem extreme but are not, since the gentle flavor of garlic baked in foil has no relationship whatever to garlic in any other form. (A little lemon juice can be added to the garlic-butter-parsley mixture and used to sauce cauliflower, on which it is particularly splendid.)

The onions can sit in the oven without any attention during their cooking. It is a good idea to open up the foil package and test them for doneness after fifty minutes, since they benefit from a little crunch. The broccoli is sautéed on the stove, and the tomatoes are placed under the broiler while the outdoor cook is busy with the meat. Since the indoor work is accomplished in about ten minutes, the vegetable cook misses little of what is going on outdoors.

Eau de vie de mirabelle, available in most good liquor stores, ranges in price from around $16 to $35. You usually get what you pay for when buying these liqueurs, so I consider each bottle a long-term investment. My liqueurs are used only to enhance the taste of foods and not at all for sipping, so they last. The best (mock or real) *crème fraîche* is made with the best cream. The version here is "cured" for a day ahead.

Roasted Red Bell Peppers
with Anchovies

•

6	large red bell peppers
Two	2-ounce cans flat fillets of anchovies
4	tablespoons olive oil
2	tablespoons lemon juice
2	cloves garlic, crushed

2 tablespoons minced shallot
3 tablespoons minced parsley
1 tablespoon minced fresh chives
½ teaspoon pepper
8 small black Niçoise olives

Roast the peppers until their skins are blistered and charred all over by one of the following methods: Spear the peppers, one at a time, with a long-handled fork and hold over an open gas flame, turning until ready. Or place the peppers under a broiler about 4 inches from the flame and broil, turning with tongs so the flesh isn't pierced. Or place the peppers on a ridged top-of-the-stove steak grill and roast over medium heat, turning the peppers with tongs.

Place the roasted peppers in a plastic bag and let them sit in the bag for about 10 minutes, or until they are cool enough to handle. Then rub the skins off and remove the stems and the seeds. Cut the peppers into 1-inch strips and place in a bowl. Refrigerate until needed. ❀ The peppers can be roasted a day in advance.

To make the marinade, place a small sieve over a bowl and empty the anchovies and their oil into the sieve. Allow the anchovies to drain for 5 minutes and remove them to another dish. Beat the remaining ingredients, except the black olives, into the anchovy oil. Set aside. ❀

Two hours before serving, divide the strips of pepper equally among 8 salad plates. Crisscross the anchovy fillets over the strips, dividing them equally. Spoon equal parts of the marinade over the anchovies and peppers and place a black olive on the top of each portion. Cover the plates lightly with plastic wrap and allow to sit at room temperature until serving. ❀ Serve with thinly sliced French bread.

Grilled or Broiled
Butterflied Leg of Lamb

•

7-pound leg of lamb
Juice of 1 lemon
⅓ *cup dry white wine*
½ *cup olive oil*
3 *cloves garlic, crushed*
½ *teaspoon cracked black pepper*
1 *bay leaf, crumbled*
1 *teaspoon dried oregano*
Several sprigs of fresh oregano or
thyme, if available, for the grill

Have the butcher butterfly the leg of lamb and ask him to remove as much fat as possible. Then, with a sharp knife, remove any fat and fell (the thin skin that covers the leg) that remain. Mix the remaining ingredients (except herb sprigs) in a roasting pan large enough to hold the meat, and place the lamb in the marinade. Turn the lamb over and rub it all over with the marinade. Cover the pan tightly with plastic wrap and refrigerate over-night, turning the lamb whenever you think of it. ❀　Two hours before the lamb is to be cooked, remove it from the refrigerator and allow it to sit at room temperature. Turn it during this time at least once.

To grill the meat outdoors, let the charcoal burn down until the coals have a light coating of gray ash. This will take about 30 minutes. Without wiping off the marinade, place the fresh herb sprigs, if available, on the grill and the lamb over them. Cook the meat for 10 minutes on the one side and then turn it over and cook for 8 minutes on the second side. At this point test for doneness by making a small cut in the thickest part of the meat. If it is bloody red rather than a nice pink, return it to the grill for another 5 minutes. If yours is a kettle grill, sear the meat, with the fresh herbs, for 5 minutes on each side, then cover the grill and continue cooking (and smoking) the meat for 10 minutes, or until the thickest part of the lamb tests done.

To broil indoors, preheat the broiler for at least 20 minutes. Without wiping off the marinade, place the fresh herb sprigs, if available, on the broiler and the lamb over them 4 inches from the heat. Broil for 10 minutes on the first side and 10 minutes on the second side. If at any point the meat looks as though it is charring, turn the heat down. Test for doneness by making a small cut in the thickest part of the meat. If it is bloody red rather than a nice pink, return it to the broiler for another 5 minutes. ❀ Remove the meat, which must rest a few minutes before carving. (Immediately put the tomatoes — see recipe that follows — in the broiler for 8 to 10 minutes.)

Carve the lamb as though it were a flank steak, on the diagonal and against the grain. The thinner parts will be well done and the thicker parts pink.

Potatoes with Garlic-Butter Purée

•

2   large whole, intact heads of garlic
4   tablespoons butter, softened
4   tablespoons minced parsley
    Salt and pepper to taste
24 small new potatoes (about 2 to 2½
       pounds), or enough large Red Bliss
       potatoes which, when peeled and
       trimmed, can be carved into 24
       small potatoes

Place the garlic in a loosely fitting envelope of foil and crimp the edges tightly. Bake in a preheated 350-degree oven for 1½ hours. Remove and allow the garlic to cool. Separate the heads into buds and snip off the end of each bud with a pair of scissors. Holding the garlic over a bowl, squeeze each bud, out of which will spurt a soft garlic purée. Beat the butter into the purée and stir in the parsley, salt and pepper. Set aside for an hour or two. ❀ This mixture can be made at least a day in advance and refrigerated. It should be brought to room temperature before it is placed on the potatoes.

Cook the potatoes for about 15 minutes, or until they test done when pierced with a sharp, pointed knife. Drain, place in a bowl, add the garlic purée, and toss until the potatoes are coated.

Small White Onions
Baked in Foil

•

32   *small white onions (about 1¼ pounds)*
2   *tablespoons butter*
   Salt and pepper to taste

Trim the top and root ends of the onions and skin them. If the skins resist, drop the onions into boiling water for 1 minute, drain them, and zip the skins off. Place the onions in a single layer on a large piece of foil, dot them with the butter, season with salt and pepper, and make a loose-fitting envelope of the foil, crimping the edges tightly. ❀   Place on a jelly-roll pan or gratin dish and bake for 50 to 60 minutes in a preheated 350-degree oven, or until the onions test done when pierced with a sharp, pointed knife.

Broiled Tomatoes
•

4   *large ripe tomatoes*
2   *tablespoons olive oil*
   Salt and pepper to taste
½   *teaspoon sugar*

Core the tomatoes and cut each into quarters. Brush 1 tablespoon of the oil on the bottom of a gratin dish, add the tomatoes, drizzle the remaining oil on them, and sprinkle with salt, pepper and sugar. ✿ Broil under your kitchen-stove broiler about 4 inches from the heat source for 8 to 10 minutes, or until the tomatoes are cooked and the tops are slightly charred.

Sautéed Broccoli

•

2½   pounds broccoli
4   tablespoons olive oil
3   cloves garlic, peeled and smashed with
     the side of a chef's knife
½   cup water
     Salt and pepper to taste

Wash the broccoli, detach the florets, and cut them vertically to make smaller florets. Peel the stems of all thick skin and cut them first into 3-inch pieces and then into a ½-inch julienne. ✿

Over high heat, heat the oil in a large sauté pan, add the florets and julienned stems, and sauté, stirring, still over high heat, until the broccoli is well coated with oil. Add the smashed garlic cloves and continue cooking over high heat for a minute or two more. Add the water, and salt and pepper to taste, place a lid on the pan, and cook, still over high heat and shaking the pan, for another 5 minutes, or until the water has evaporated and the broccoli tests done when pierced with a sharp, pointed knife.

Sliced Peaches with Mirabelle or Kirsch

•

12 *medium to large ripe peaches*
¾ *cup sugar*
1 *drop imported peach essence, if the*
   peaches are not highly fragrant (optional)
¼ *cup* eau de vie de mirabelle *or*
   Kirsch
   Mock Crème Fraîche (following recipe)

Drop peaches one or two at a time into boiling water for 20 seconds, remove with a slotted spoon, and skin them. Cut into slices and discard the
pits. Toss the slices with the sugar and the peach essence, cover tightly with
plastic wrap, and refrigerate for 2 to 4 hours. ❁   One hour before serving,
remove from refrigerator. Stir in the *eau de vie de mirabelle* or the Kirsch.
Serve at room temperature with *crème fraîche.*

Mock Crème Fraîche

MAKES 2 CUPS

•

2 *cups heavy cream, preferably not*
   ultrapasteurized
4 *tablespoons sour cream*

Place the heavy cream in a bowl and whisk the sour cream into it. Cover the
bowl with plastic wrap and let stand at room temperature for 12 to 24
hours, or until the cream has thickened. The *crème fraîche* can now be refrigerated for up to a week. ❁

Artichokes with Fresh Herb-Mustard Sauce

Chicken Sautéed with Red Bell Peppers, Tomatoes, Onions and Sausage

Homemade Linguine or Spaghetti

Italian Prune-Plum Torte on a Short Dough (Mürbeteig)

•

*Pedroncelli Zinfandel
or Corvo Rosso*

This is a perfect early fall meal, using as it does many of the wonderful ingredients that are available at this time of year.

The first course consists of artichokes, which are at a price that probably never will be lower than now. These are served with a quickly made mustardy mayonnaise sauce, highly flavored with the fresh mixed herbs that are flourishing in gardens.

Next is a chicken dish with enough determination to stand up to a cool evening, yet not so heavy that it wouldn't do if the weather were to turn unseasonably warm, as it might. The chicken is combined with the red bell peppers, still a welcome autumnal presence on produce stands and even at supermarkets, along with tomatoes (the end of whose prime time is sadly approaching), onions, a bit of garlic and hot Italian sausages. Accompanying this dish is homemade linguine, for those who love to use their pasta machines, or a decent brand of commercially made spaghetti.

Dessert was inspired by a reader who wrote about an Italian prune-plum-filled, apricot-jam-glazed, cinnamon-flavored torte on a short Viennese dough called *Mürbeteig*. The torte she recalled had come from the now-defunct and still-lamented Window Shop in Cambridge, which used to fill Brattle Street and, it sometimes seemed, all of Harvard Square with the heavenly smells of freshly and expertly made butter-filled cakes and pastries. In my day, clever young men courted their dates with boxes of pastry from the Window Shop, and far more successfully than they would have with long-stemmed roses.

While we are all doubtless grateful that overcooked vegetables are looked upon with the disdain they deserve, I wish to state the case against undercooked vegetables. While they may be high on crunch, they are seriously deficient in flavor. Asparagus and string beans suffer much from new methods of undercooking, but perhaps no vegetable is more shortchanged by being served close to raw than the noble artichoke.

The artichokes in this meal are trimmed of their prickly tips before they are cooked and afterward have their chokes scooped out, both acts of thoughtfulness that the cook can well afford to commit because they take such little time and save guests so much anguish. The sauce, with its thick consistency, is easier to handle at the table than an equally delicious vinaigrette, which can be made following the same recipe, but leaving out the egg yolks and adding, to taste, a bit more vinegar.

The chicken is a terrific company dish because the whole concoction can, if desired, be made a day in advance. It also serves well from a buffet. Combining the chicken with red peppers adds interest that some persons claim chickens lack. The onions, garlic and tomatoes form a lovely sauce, and the hot Italian sausages, because they are sliced rather fine, contribute benign body without burning sensitive palates.

See the Index for the recipe and instructions for making homemade linguine.

The short dough for the torte is more between cake and cookie than a traditional short pastry dough, yet it is less crumbly than a *pâte sablée*. I made this *Mürbeteig*, which came from a recipe in Lilly Joss Reich's excellent *Viennese Pastry Book*, both by hand and in the food processor. The handmade product was so far superior, more tender than the machine-made dough, that it is worth the five minutes it takes to work it by hand. Because of the high butter content (and only unsalted butter should be used), the dough should not spend more than half an hour chilling in the refrigerator, lest it become too hard to roll out.

While the torte also can be made with fresh cherries or apples, use Italian prune-plums during their short but delightful season. The prune-plums are amazing in that they can be boring-to-dull when raw but suc-culent once cooked. The several times I made this torte it leaked some juices, which did not bother the pastry at all. I let the torte cool a bit and then simply spooned the juices over the filling. Because of its size, it was easier to cut the torte on the jelly-roll pan and serve it somewhat surrep-titiously from the sideboard.

Artichokes with Fresh Herb-Mustard Sauce

•

8	artichokes
1	tablespoon minced chives
1	teaspoon fresh thyme leaves or other fresh minced herbs
4	tablespoons minced parsley
4	tablespoons minced shallots
2	egg yolks
1	tablespoon Dijon mustard
3	tablespoons red wine vinegar
	Salt and pepper to taste
1½	cups olive oil

Prepare the artichokes by cutting or breaking off the stems, cutting half an inch off the tops and trimming the leaves with scissors to remove the prickly tips. Place in a large pot, cover with cold water, bring to a boil, and cook for 18 to 20 minutes, or until the heart can be pierced easily with a sharp, pointed knife. Turn the artichokes into a colander to drain, tops down.

When they are cool enough to handle, squeeze the artichokes gently to rid them of excess water and put them on a plate, right side up. Remove the center leaves in a clump and scoop out the hairy chokes with a teaspoon. Discard the chokes and return the clumps of leaves to the centers. The artichokes can be prepared a day in advance,❀ refrigerated and brought to room temperature before serving.

To make the sauce, combine the minced chives, thyme or other herbs, parsley and shallots in a bowl and set aside. Place the egg yolks, mustard, vinegar, salt and pepper in a food processor bowl with the steel blade and process for about 30 seconds. With the motor running, slowly drizzle in the olive oil. Turn the resulting mayonnaiselike sauce into the bowl with the herbs and mix well.❀ Serve the sauce with the artichokes.

Chicken Sautéed with Red Bell Peppers, Tomatoes, Onions and Sausage

•

Two 2½-pound to 3-pound frying chickens, each disjointed into 8 pieces, plus 2 whole chicken breasts, halved
½ cup olive oil
8 hot Italian sausages
3 medium onions, thinly sliced
3 large cloves garlic, minced
5 medium-large red bell peppers, stemmed, seeded and julienned
2 pounds ripe tomatoes (about 6 medium), skinned, seeded and julienned, or a 2-pound, 3-ounce can imported Italian tomatoes, drained
Salt and pepper to taste

Dry the chicken pieces thoroughly with paper towels. Heat the oil in a frying pan or sauté pan large enough to hold all the ingredients. If necessary to use two pans, divide the oil between them and cook half the ingredients in each of the pans.

Brown the chicken pieces quickly over high heat on all sides, a few at a time, and remove them to a bowl as they are browned. Next, brown the sausages, remove, and cut into slices ¼ inch thick. Pour off all but 4 tablespoons of the fat and return the chicken and sausage slices to the pan. Add the onions and garlic, cover, and cook until the onions are soft, about 8 minutes. Remove the cover once or twice and stir. Then add the peppers, stir, and cover the pan. Cook for another 8 minutes.

Finally, add the tomatoes, salt and pepper, and cook, uncovered, stirring frequently, for another 5 minutes. ❁ The chicken can be cooked up to several hours or even a day in advance to this point. If the dish is to be held, remove the pan from heat and cool the contents with the lid askew before refrigerating.

To serve, reheat the dish quickly and spoon, with the sauce, into a large dish. Surround with cooked homemade linguine (see Index) or 1½ pounds cooked packaged spaghetti or linguine.

Italian Prune-Plum Torte
on a Short Dough
(Mürbeteig)

•

FOR THE SHORT DOUGH		
	2	cups all-purpose flour
	⅓	cup sugar
		Pinch of salt
		Grated rind of a lemon
	¼	pound (1 stick) plus 2 tablespoons cold, unsalted butter, cut into 20 pieces
	1	egg
	1	egg yolk
	2¼	teaspoons white vinegar mixed with 2¼ teaspoons water

FOR THE FILLING	2	pounds Italian prune-plums
	½	cup apricot glaze (½ cup apricot jam heated with 2 tablespoons Quetsch, dark rum, Vanilla Cognac [see April, Provisioning the Pantry] or Cognac, and pushed through a sieve)
	¼	cup blanched slivered almonds
	½	cup sugar mixed with 2 teaspoons cinnamon
	3	tablespoons unsalted butter, melted
	1	egg, lightly beaten

To make the dough, combine the flour, sugar, salt and grated lemon rind in a large bowl and with a knife cut the butter in until the mixture resembles coarse cornmeal. Make a well in the center and place the egg and the egg yolk into the flour. Still working with the knife, gradually add the vinegar-water mixture. Then, using only the fingertips, gather the dough together. Finally, knead it a few times until a medium-firm dough is formed. If the dough is sticky, add a sprinkling of flour. Form into a ball, flatten the ball into a thick rectangle, place in a plastic bag, and refrigerate for 20 to 30 minutes — no longer.

While the dough is chilling, prepare the filling by halving and pitting the prune-plums and measuring out the remaining ingredients.

Using a floured rolling pin, roll out the dough on a lightly floured pastry board until it measures 18 inches long by 12 inches wide. Keep turning the dough as it is being rolled and sprinkling the board with flour so that the dough does not stick. Trim the sides evenly and reserve the trimmings for any repairs that might be needed. Transfer the dough to a jelly-roll pan, which will be almost completely covered by the pastry. If the dough should rupture during the transfer, simply press it together with your fingertips and if necessary repair any cracks with the reserved trimmings.

Leaving a 2-inch margin on all four sides, arrange the prune-plums, cut side down, in rows on the dough. Using a pastry brush, paint the prune-plums with the apricot glaze. Next, sprinkle the slivered almonds over the fruit and then the sugar-cinnamon mixture. Starting with the short sides first and ending with the long sides, fold the margins of the dough over twice and form edges for the torte with the fingers. Drizzle the melted butter over the filling and brush the edges of the pastry with the beaten egg.

Bake in a preheated 350-degree oven for 35 to 45 minutes or until the pastry is a deep golden brown. Let the torte cool to room temperature. ❀ To serve, cut the torte lengthwise down the middle and then crosswise into slices about 2½ inches wide.

October

Toasted Almonds

MAKES 4 CUPS

•

3½ tablespoons coarse salt
2 cups tepid water
1 pound (about 4 cups) unblanched
    almonds

Dissolve the salt in the water. Stir the almonds into the brine and let them soak for 40 minutes. Drain well, spread the almonds on a jelly-roll pan, and toast in a preheated 300-degree oven. Stir every 10 minutes and at the end of 30 minutes turn off the oven and leave the almonds in the oven to dry overnight. Decant into jars and cover tightly.

Serve with drinks, or chop and use in bombes or over ice cream.

Prunes in Madeira

•

1   *pound large unpitted prunes*
1   *bottle medium-sweet Madeira*

Wash the prunes, drain, and place in a pretty jar. Cover with Madeira and age for 1 month to 1 year. Use in country pâtés or to garnish pork or veal roasts or chops.

Composed Fall Salad
Fresh Choucroute Garnie Alsacienne
Mustards and Grated Horseradish
Fresh Pears and Gourmandise Cheese

•

*Simi California Gewürztraminer or Trimbach Gewürztraminer
or Kronenbourg Beer*

This meal revolves around my own version of a *choucroute garnie alsacienne*, which will convert even the most dedicated sauerkraut hater. The one I live with finds the smell (stink, he rudely says), texture (soggy) and color (amber) of all commercial sauerkrauts utterly repulsive. But this choucroute, with its lovely variety of smoked meats and boiled potatoes, he says, is different. It is — primarily because the sauerkraut is freshly made at home by an astonishingly simple, fast process. The result is fragrant, slightly crunchy, a fresh white and yellow color, the basis of a dish that embodies the best of home cooking.

The first course is a composed fall salad, an ideal preamble to the *choucroute*, which combines contrasting pale and sharp flavors, textures and colors. Tender lettuces make a bed for fresh and marinated vegetables, a garnish of egg wedges and a mustardy vinaigrette. Dessert is simple and clean, as it should be after the smoked meats and sauerkraut: fresh, ripe pears with Gourmandise cheese, whose creaminess and aroma of Kirsch are wonderful with pears.

The salad can be prepared a few hours ahead and refrigerated. The dressing, naturally, goes on only at the very last. Peeling bell peppers is a bore but I do it (with a swivel-bladed potato peeler) because it makes enough difference to justify the bother. I use red leaf lettuce for lunch and try to remember to stick to green for dinner because candlelight or other dim lights can make the red appear to be rotten brown. A six-wedge egg-wedger makes it simple to cut the eggs neatly. I use imported *herbes de Provence* that come in a lovely unglazed brown pot. This elegant mixture can be found in specialty food stores and also comes in bags at a cheaper price.

Fresh sauerkraut can sometimes be found at delicatessens and even meat markets, but at a cost at least five times that of making your own. The five pounds of wonderful, fresh sauerkraut that I make involve about a dollar's worth of cabbage, a few ounces of coarse salt, a little preplanning and less than half an hour of preparation. Five pounds of wilted cabbage will fill a wide-mouth two-liter preserving jar almost to the top but still leave enough room for the plastic bag of water that goes on top. This keeps the air out without making the seal so airtight that it could explode, which a clamped lid might do. The washed, squeezed sauerkraut will hold without fermenting for a few days if refrigerated.

My *choucroute* recipe has the elements of the traditional but is fresher, more delicate and less pungent, although these are relative terms for a dish that is, as wine makers say, assertive. I use chicken fat because of the flavor it gives the dish and also because I have it available, rendered in a jar in the refrigerator, at all times. Alsatians use goose fat or fresh lard (commercial lard is not good for this). I use chicken broth rather than beef bouillon along with the white wine because to me the color and flavor are cleaner. I also use minced onion instead of whole onion, and I cook the *choucroute* for less than half the time an Alsatian would. I also use a greater variety of meats and sausages, whose different flavors live together amicably.

I find nice pink smoked pork chops at the supermarket. The packages are usually turned upside down since light seems to make the pink turn an unpleasant gray. Polish kielbasa, smoked and plain bratwurst and weiss-wurst can be found at any number of good delicatessen counters. Juniper berries are essential. They can be found among the spices in some super-markets and in specialty food stores.

The order of battle for the *choucroute* is uncomplicated. It is less a matter of work and more one of paying attention to when meats are added or browned and when potatoes are put to the boil and when frankfurters are put in to cook. There is little real preparation. About an hour and three-quarters before it is to be served, the sauerkraut is washed and squeezed dry (about five minutes for this). The spice bag is prepared while the liquids are heating up. The potatoes are peeled and held in cold water when the casserole goes into the oven. And that's it.

The *choucroute*, which is a glory to behold when it is arranged on a large platter, should be accompanied by a variety of mustards and horseradish. I drain bottled horseradish of some of its liquid before I put it into a little bowl. This must be covered tightly with plastic wrap until just before serving, since air dissipates the strength of horseradish very quickly.

For the convenience of packers, pears are shipped unripe, rock-hard and unfit for consumption, so these fruits must be bought a few days in advance and, with luck, ripened at home in a plastic bag. You should buy more pears than you think you need, what with the dangers of the ripening process during which some pears become fragrant and juicy while others simply turn brown to the core and rot. Pears should be carefully examined at the market and those with even a tiny blemish rejected. A hint of perfume implies a more favorable prognosis. While ripened pears will lose some of their hardness, they cannot be held until they become very soft, at least in my recent experience. Forks and fruit knives for each diner are needed for peeling pears and coping with the cheese.

Gourmandise, found in many supermarkets, is an odd, not-very-refined cheese that is too sweet to qualify as a savory. But combined with fresh pears, it takes on a distinction that it otherwise lacks and makes a light ending to what could have been an overwhelming meal.

Composed Fall Salad

•

1	*small head red or green leaf lettuce*
1	*small head Boston lettuce*
6 to 8	*pale yellow leaves of chicory*
1/2	*red bell pepper*
4 to 5	*raw mushrooms*
1/4	*cup thin slivers of red onion*
2	*ounces marinated mushrooms (from the jar)*

3 ounces marinated artichoke hearts
(from the jar), halved lengthwise
3 hard-boiled eggs, each cut into 6
wedges
12 to 16 black Niçoise olives
Pinch of herbes de Provence
2 tablespoons chopped parsley

½ cup olive oil
2 tablespoons red wine vinegar
1 teaspoon Dijon mustard
Salt and freshly ground black pepper
to taste

Wash and dry the greens, tear them into pieces, and discard the coarse ribs of the leaf lettuce. Arrange in a low, flat-bottomed bowl. Using a potato peeler, peel the skin off the red pepper. It's worth the trouble. Cut the pepper into slivers and arrange around the outside edge on the greens. Clean the raw mushrooms, cut off the stems. (Freeze stems for the next stockpot.) Slice the caps thin and arrange in a mound in the center. Arrange the red onions on the fresh mushrooms and place the marinated mushrooms around them. Then add a circle of the marinated artichoke hearts, then the egg wedges and finally the olives. Sprinkle the *herbes de Provence* and chopped parsley over all. ❀ Whisk the remaining ingredients in a bowl and set aside. ❀ Add the dressing at the table just before serving and toss.

Fresh Choucroute Garnie
Alsacienne

•

5 pounds Fresh Sauerkraut (recipe follows)
¼ cup chicken fat, goose fat or fresh lard
1 cup (about 2 medium-large) minced onions
1½ cups dry white wine

2½ cups chicken broth plus another ½ cup
    if needed
1 heaping teaspoon juniper berries
¼ teaspoon black peppercorns, lightly
    crushed
2 large bay leaves
2 whole cloves
3 large cloves of garlic, smashed with the
    side of a knife and peeled
¾ pound thick-sliced bacon, cut into 1-
    inch pieces, blanched for 10 minutes
    in boiling water, refreshed under cold
    water and patted dry
3 smoked pork chops, rind trimmed,
    washed and patted dry
12 small (2-inch) Red Bliss potatoes, peeled
1 pound Polish kielbasa
2 tablespoons vegetable oil
2 smoked bratwurst
2 unsmoked bratwurst
2 weisswurst
8 German frankfurters

About 1¾ to 2 hours before the *choucroute* is to be served, drain the sauerkraut in a colander and wash it thoroughly with cold water. Squeeze out the water by handfuls and set the sauerkraut aside.

Melt the fat or lard in a large, heavy casserole (at least 6 quarts) and cook the onions until soft but not brown, for about 10 minutes. Add the sauerkraut, the wine and the chicken stock and bring to the simmer. Tie the spices and garlic in a piece of cheesecloth and bury the bag in the sauerkraut. Add the bacon and distribute it through the sauerkraut. Then bury the pork chops in it. Put the casserole into a preheated 350-degree oven for 1 hour.

Put a large pot of salted water on to boil for the potatoes.

After the hour is up, remove the casserole from the oven and bury the Polish kielbasa (unsliced) in the sauerkraut. If all the liquid has been absorbed (it shouldn't be), add another ½ cup chicken broth. Return the casserole to the oven for another 25 minutes.

While the kielbasa is cooking, put the potatoes on to boil. Start testing for doneness, using a sharp, pointed knife rather than a fork, after 18 minutes. The potatoes will be done, probably in 20 minutes, when the knife meets no resistance. Do not overcook them.

Meanwhile, put another pot of water on to boil for the frankfurters.

Heat the oil in a large frying pan and brown the two kinds of bratwurst and the weisswurst, cooking these over a low flame for about 20 minutes.

Ten minutes before the *choucroute* is cooked, put the frankfurters in to boil.

Remove the casserole from the oven and place the pork chops and the kielbasa on a cutting board. Slice these so that you have 8 pieces of each meat. Discard the chop bones. Then cut each of the bratwursts and the weisswurst into 4 pieces, to make 8 pieces of each meat. Leave the frankfurters whole. Drain the potatoes.

Remove the sauerkraut with a slotted spoon and arrange it on a large platter, making a bed of it. Reserve some of the liquid to pour over leftovers, should there be any. Drain off any excess liquid. Then place the cut meats and the potatoes around the sauerkraut. Place the frankfurters on top. Serve with various mustards (Dijon, moutarde de Meaux, German) and drained bottled horseradish.

Fresh Sauerkraut

•

5¼   *pounds (approximately) cabbage*
7   *tablespoons coarse (kosher) salt*
      2-liter (approximately 10-cup) wide-
      necked preserving jar

Remove the outer leaves and any blemishes from the cabbage. Quarter and core it and shred it with the thin slicing blade of a food processor. Divide the cabbage between two large bowls and add half the salt to each bowl. With your hands, mix the salt thoroughly into the cabbage and set aside for 25 minutes. At this point the cabbage will be wilted and it will have released some liquid.

Spoon the cabbage into the jar and pack it down tightly. You can use a wooden spoon; I use the back of my hand, which is possible with a wide-mouthed jar. Pour the juices remaining in the bowls over the cabbage. The jar will be quite full.

Place a large plastic food bag on the cabbage and make sure the bag covers its entire surface. Fold the edges of the bag back over the rim of the jar. Place a second bag inside the first bag and pour 2 or 3 cups of water into it. Secure this bag with a tie. Work the bag with water around the surface so that it covers all the cabbage. Then secure the outside bag around the water bag with another tie. The bag will come above the top of the jar. Arrange it so that it flops evenly over the top. Then set the jar on a shallow soup plate or bowl to catch any liquid that seeps out. Set the jar on a kitchen counter for 6 days, when the sauerkraut will be ready for use. ❀ If you like a stronger sauerkraut, let it ferment longer. The room temperature should not exceed 72 degrees during the fermentation period.

Fresh Pears
and Gourmandise Cheese

·

10 to 12 *ripe, well-perfumed pears*
    1 *pound Gourmandise cheese, cut into 16*
        wedges

Place the pears in a basket and the cheese wedges on a wooden board or serving plate. Be sure each person is provided with a dessert fork and a knife sharp enough to peel the pears.

Sautéed Chicken Livers and Red Bell
Peppers in Cassolettes or over Toast Points

Roast Beef with Pan Gravy and
Horseradish Sauce

Mashed Potato Cake

Gratinéed Tomatoes

Buttered String Beans

Caramelized Pears

•

FIRST COURSE:
Savigny-lès-Beaune
MAIN COURSE:
Nuit-St.-Georges "Château Gris"

This is a polished meal for friends
who appreciate restraint and style. It starts with an unusual and sensational
combination of chicken livers sautéed with roasted red bell peppers, whose
continued availability invites invention. This is served, for those with the
ambition, in edible cassolettes (tart-shaped rosette shells) or, more simply,
over toast points.

Next is a quickly cooked, rare roast eye round of beef with a richly flavored pan gravy and a subtle horseradish sauce. Accompanying the meat are three contrasting vegetables: mashed potatoes, but baked as a cake so that a brown crust encases a creamy inside; gratinéed tomatoes, to take advantage of the last good supply until next summer; and string beans, which finally are being sold at a reasonable price. The meal ends with irresistibly inexpensive, plentiful and delicious Bartlett pears, here caramelized and mixed with cream for a wonderful flavor of butterscotch.

The union of chicken livers with red bell peppers is magical, since the livers take on an extraordinary and delicate flavor slightly reminiscent of field mushrooms. Once the peppers are roasted, which can be done a day in advance, and the livers cleaned, the dish can be made literally in 10 minutes. In the interest of avoiding as much last-minute preparation as possible, the livers can be cooked in the morning, refrigerated and then reheated quickly just before serving. The dish, which was inspired by an Elizabeth David recipe in *A Book of Mediterranean Food*, is wonderful over toast but more elegant in cassolettes.

Cassolette or tart-shaped rosette molds are to be found in various shapes in every cookware store I have shopped over the last year. I like the three-inch-wide by one-inch-deep fluted mold that cooks up into a slightly larger shell. One is perfect for a first-course serving. I suspect that many of these molds are sitting, never used, in kitchen drawers because making cassolettes involves deep-fat frying, a process that can seem terrifying.

Deep-fat frying requires no special skill, but certain rules must be followed. First, unwavering attention is demanded of the cook. This means that once the oil is placed over heat, the cook may not leave the kitchen or indulge in a telephone conversation. Children must be banned from the kitchen during the process. Should any distraction occur, the heat must be turned off and the pan of oil moved to the back of the stove. The handle of the pot in which the oil is being heated should be turned toward the back of the stove to prevent accidents.

A deep-fry thermometer is essential. This should be placed in the oil when the heat is turned on and the temperature must be monitored constantly. The oil should be heated slowly. It will take about 20 minutes to bring two quarts of cool oil to 370 degrees over low heat, so time should be budgeted accordingly. Oil can be reused, but only once or twice at most. Let it cool, strain it through a coffee filter into jars and store in the refrigerator.

All other needed equipment should be in place before you start to heat the oil. The cassolette mold should be screwed into its holder and placed into the oil along with the deep-fry thermometer when the heat is turned on. A jelly-roll pan lined with paper towels should be to the left of the pan so that the cooked shells can be placed on it to drain. A knife or fork to push the shells off the mold should be on a plate to the right of the pot along with a pair of tongs to remove the shells from the oil.

A heavy aluminum saucepan is perfect for deep frying. The French make a deep-fry pot with two ears while the American pot has a long handle. Both come with baskets that are not used in making cassolettes but which are invaluable for potato chips and French fried potatoes. After the cassolettes are made, the mold should be left to cool and then detached from its handle and wiped dry with paper towels.

Cassolettes can be filled with any creamed dish for a first course or with various vegetables as an accompaniment to meat or fish.

I set out to buy a standing four-rib roast for this meal but was so appalled by the price that I settled on a lovely long, narrow eye of the round roast, which was nicely barded with a thin layer of beef fat. The flavorful meat was cut into neat, small slices and went so far that I had enough left over for roast beef hash for two. I cook beef at a constant high temperature for a crusty brown outside and a rare inside. The horseradish sauce that accompanies it, along with the gratinéed tomatoes, uses fresh bread crumbs. To keep a supply of bread crumbs at all times, I amass heels of toasting bread in the freezer, which I will reduce in a processor to bread crumbs when I have enough. The crumbs are stored in a jar, again in the freezer, and can be spooned out as needed.

Potatoes, ostensibly the most amenable of vegetables, generally do not take to advance preparation. This dish can be assembled a few hours before it is baked, but care must be taken not to cover the potatoes tightly with plastic wrap, which would give them a stale taste. Rather, drape them with waxed paper.

The pears for this recipe must be firm but ripe enough to have some perfume. Again, the nose is the best guide for buying decent fruit. The fourteen-wedge apple slicer (there is also a twenty-wedge slicer, which is perfect for apple tarts) is lovely for these pears, which must be baked in the hottest oven possible (at 500 degrees). The pears can be placed in the oven immediately after removing the potatoes (and resetting the temperature) and allowed to bake while the main course is being eaten. While it is a nice touch to baste the pears while they bake, it is no tragedy if this step is ignored. By the time the main-course dishes are being cleared, the sugar should have caramelized. The cream can then be poured over the pears, and the cooking finished in minutes.

Sautéed Chicken Livers and Red Bell Peppers

•

8   *medium or 6 large red bell peppers*
2   *pounds chicken livers*
    Flour for dusting the livers
3   *tablespoons butter*
½   *cup dry white wine*
1   *teaspoon lemon juice*
    Salt and pepper to taste
8   *cassolettes (see following recipe) or*
        toast points
2   *tablespoons minced parsley*

Roast the peppers by charring their skins under a broiler or over a flame (see Index). Skin, core, and seed them and cut them lengthwise into ½-inch-wide strips. Set aside.

Cut the livers into quarters and clean them of all fat, green spots and membranes. Pat the livers dry on paper towels and dust them lightly with flour. Heat the butter in a frying pan and sauté the livers quickly over high heat for about 4 minutes, or until they are browned all over. Add the wine and lemon juice, bring to the boil, and add the red pepper strips plus salt and pepper. Lower the heat and simmer the mixture for about 5 minutes, stirring occasionally. ✿ The liver mixture can be made several hours in advance and reheated quickly. Just before serving, spoon the hot mixture into 8 cassolettes or over toast points with crusts removed. Sprinkle with parsley.

Cassolettes

MAKES ABOUT 20

•

2   *eggs*
1   *cup milk*
1   *tablespoon peanut or corn oil*
1   *cup sifted all-purpose flour*
1/2 *teaspoon salt*
   Oil for deep frying

Beat the eggs lightly in a bowl and stir in the milk and the oil. Beat the flour and salt into the liquid and strain the batter into another bowl, preferably one that is deep and narrow. Cover with plastic wrap and let the batter rest for 1 hour before using.

To make the cassolettes, pour about 2 quarts of oil into a heavy sauce-pan or deep-frying pan, or enough oil so that it measures about 4 inches in depth. Fit a 3-inch-wide by 1-inch-deep fluted cassolette (tart-shaped ro-sette) mold onto its holder and place the mold in the oil along with a deep-fry thermometer. Heat the oil slowly until the thermometer reads 360 to 370 degrees. This will take about 20 minutes. Remove the heated cassolette mold from the oil and hold it over the pan for 5 seconds or so, or until the excess oil runs off. Dip the hot mold into the batter to within 1/8 inch of the top of the mold and hold the mold in the batter for 15 seconds.

Lift the mold and hold it over the batter for another 10 seconds and then plunge it into the hot oil. Count another 20 seconds. If the shell has not started to free itself from the mold, loosen it by gently pushing down around the top edge with a knife or a fork. Allow the shell to fall off the mold and into the oil. Continue cooking until the shell is brown all over. Keep the oil at a constant 370-degree temperature, although you can let it reach 375 degrees without problems. I allow the thermometer to remain in the oil during the cooking of the cassolettes and either raise the heat when the temperature drops or remove the pot from the heat when it becomes too high.

Remove the cooked shells with tongs and place upside down on a jelly-roll pan lined with paper towels. Repeat until all the batter is used or until you have the desired number of shells (discard the remaining batter). ❀
Extra shells can be stored in an airtight container or frozen. Place the mold

on a dish and allow it to cool. Unscrew it from its holder and wipe it with a paper towel. Do not wash the mold.

Should the shells need recrisping before serving, place them, before filling them, on a cookie sheet in a preheated 350-degree oven for 5 minutes or, for this menu, in a 425-degree oven for 2 to 3 minutes.

Roast Beef with Pan Gravy
and Horseradish Sauce

•

4-pound long, narrow eye round roast,
with a thin layer of fat tied to the
top
1½ cups beef stock or bouillon
½ bunch watercress, washed
Horseradish Sauce (following recipe)

Place the meat in a roasting pan and roast it for 1 hour and 10 minutes in a preheated 425-degree oven, or until an instant thermometer registers 120 degrees when inserted into the center of the roast. Place the meat on a carving board, remove the strings and the fat, ❀ and let it rest for 15 to 20 minutes before carving into thinnish slices.

To make pan gravy add the beef stock or bouillon to the degreased roasting pan, bring to a boil, and cook over moderately high heat, scraping the bottom of the pan with a wooden spoon to loosen the brown bits, until the juices have reduced a bit.

Arrange the meat in overlapping slices in 2 rows down the length of a serving platter. Arrange a bouquet of watercress at each end of the platter. Serve the pan gravy in a sauceboat and the horseradish sauce in a small bowl.

Horseradish Sauce

MAKES ABOUT 2 CUPS

•

4-ounce bottle prepared horseradish
½   teaspoon dry mustard
2   tablespoons fresh bread crumbs
¼   teaspoon confectioners' sugar
6   drops Worcestershire sauce
Salt and pepper to taste
¾   cup heavy cream

Spoon the horseradish into a fine strainer and press out as much vinegar as possible. Discard the vinegar. Combine the horseradish in a bowl with the mustard, bread crumbs, sugar, Worcestershire sauce, salt and pepper. Whip the cream and combine it with the horseradish mixture. Cover tightly with plastic wrap so the strength of the horseradish is not dissipated, ❀ and refrigerate until needed.

Mashed Potato Cake

•

3   pounds russet potatoes
1½ tablespoons flour
1   teaspoon salt
Pepper to taste
3   tablespoons heavy cream
2   large eggs, beaten
4   tablespoons melted butter

Peel the potatoes, cut them into 2-inch-thick slices, and boil until tender. Drain well, return to saucepan, and shake potatoes over medium heat for a couple of minutes to dry them out. Leave potatoes in pan and, with an electric hand mixer, beat them until they are fluffy. Then beat in the flour, salt, pepper, cream and eggs.

Brush the bottom of a 10-inch pie plate, preferably one attractive enough for serving, with half the melted butter and turn the potato mixture into it. Spread the potatoes evenly in the pan and flatten the top with a spatula. Brush the remaining butter over the top. ❀ The dish can be prepared up to 2 hours in advance to this stage. Drape waxed paper loosely over the potatoes and refrigerate. Bring to room temperature before baking. Bake in a preheated 400-degree oven for 35 minutes, or until a brown crust has formed. Or, place in a 425-degree oven with roasting beef 15 minutes before beef is removed and continue baking for about 18 minutes longer. To serve, cut cake into wedges.

Gratinéed Tomatoes

•

½ cup olive oil
6 medium or 4 large ripe tomatoes
2 small cloves garlic, finely minced
2 tablespoons minced fresh basil, or
    parsley if basil is not available
   Salt and pepper to taste
1½ cups fresh bread crumbs

Pour a little of the olive oil on the bottom of an oval baking dish and reserve the remaining oil. Stem the tomatoes, cut them into ½-inch slices, and arrange them, overlapping slightly, in rows down the length of the baking dish. Distribute the garlic, basil or parsley, salt and pepper over the tomatoes and then sprinkle the bread crumbs over the tomatoes in a layer that covers them. Pour the remaining oil evenly over the bread crumbs ❀ and broil about 4 inches away from a medium flame for 5 to 7 minutes, or until the tomatoes are soft and the bread crumbs are browned.

Buttered String Beans

•

2½   *pounds string beans*
4   *tablespoons butter*
Salt and pepper to taste

Wash the string beans, cut off their ends and, if they are large and you have the will, run a potato peeler down each side of the beans to remove their strings. Bring a large pot of salted water to the boil and add the beans. Cook them for about 5 minutes if they have been strung and about 8 minutes if they have not. Start testing by biting into a bean after 4 minutes. The beans are done when they taste sweet and "cooked" but still have a bit of crunch. Immediately turn them out into a colander and run cold water over them to stop further cooking. Drain them well, wrap in paper towels, and refrigerate. ❋   The beans can be cooked to this point anywhere from several hours to a day in advance. Just before serving, place the beans in a frying pan and, shaking the pan constantly, cook them over medium heat for a minute or two to rid them of excess moisture. Then add the butter to the beans and continue cooking, shaking the pan constantly for another 2 minutes, or until the butter is melted and the beans are heated through. Add salt and pepper to taste and turn out into a warm serving dish.

Caramelized Pears

•

8   *medium Bartlett pears, firm but with*
     a good perfume
1   *cup sugar*
4   *tablespoons unsalted butter*
1   *cup heavy cream*

Peel the pears, core them, and cut each lengthwise into thin wedges, or use a 14-wedge apple slicer, which will core and cut the pears into wedges at the same time. Arrange the wedges in a baking dish and spoon the sugar over them in a thick layer. Dot with butter❀ and bake in a preheated 500-degree oven for about 30 minutes, or until the sugar has turned a nice caramel color. If it is convenient, baste the pears a few times with the syrup that forms. Remove the dish from the oven, pour the cream over the pears, and return to the oven for another 5 to 8 minutes, or until a homogeneous, butterscotchy brown syrup has formed. Serve hot, warm or at room temperature,❀ although warm is best.

Mussels with Fresh Coriander Béarnaise

*Veal Ragout with White Onions,
Mushrooms and Artichoke Hearts*

Cauliflower Purée

*Strawberry or Other Fresh or Canned
Fruit Tart*

•

FIRST COURSE:
Macon Blanc
MAIN COURSE:
Beaujolais-Villages

*T*his fall meal combines familiar flavors with wonderful surprises. It starts with plump steamed mussels on the half shell glazed with a sauce that is not merely delicious but is a masterpiece. A most generous gift from Joseph Alsop, whose tastes are both original and impeccable, the sauce is a pale green béarnaise flavored unexpectedly and most successfully with fresh coriander rather than with tarragon. The result is subtle, fascinating, beautiful to look at and utterly delicious not only with mussels but also, in the words of its creator, "with boiled and grilled fish, with hot and cold boiled or roast chicken and with various families of shrimplike crustaceans, as well as crabmeat."

Next is a veal ragout cooked in a rich brown sauce with small white onions, sliced mushrooms and artichoke hearts. A good stock and some full-bodied dry sherry contribute the depth to make a dish that gives considerable satisfaction. Accompanying the ragout is a cauliflower purée. This looks like chive-strewn mashed potatoes, but the flavor, which has none of the cabbagey undertones associated with cauliflower, is a triumph.

Dessert is a fresh strawberry tart with a pastry for my friends whose eyes glaze over the minute I try to assure them there is no great trick to rolling out a crust. This pastry, from Dolores Casella's *A World of Baking,* is made by working the ingredients together with the fingers and then pressing the resulting dough with the hands into a two-piece tart or quiche pan. When baked, it becomes a nut-brown, buttery, light container for any kind of fruit, fresh or canned.

The béarnaise is made in minutes in an old-fashioned blender (I was tempted to discard it when I acquired a food processor but am grateful I did not, since I have yet to achieve as successful a béarnaise or hollandaise with the processor as with the blender). The processor can be used in this recipe, but only to chop the coriander if the sauce is to be made by hand, as many traditional cooks prefer. Coriander, also sold as cilantro or Chinese parsley, is, after an end-of-summer hiatus, once again available in many supermarkets by mid-October. It can always be found in Spanish and Oriental food stores. This recipe requires a substantial bunch of coriander. The sauce can be made just before the mussels are cleaned and cooked.

Eight mussels make a generous first-course portion, and even six would do, since the sauce is not without a certain richness. In any case, buy a few more mussels than you think you need because inevitably a few must be discarded when they do not pass the aliveness test, which consists of tapping those that are open. If they do not close when tapped, throw them out. Also, after the mussels are cooked, discard any that do not open.

Mussels can be a bother to clean, but many of those being sold now are grown on strings and do not often acquire the barnacles and assorted debris that these shiny black bivalve mollusks used to carry as normal baggage. This is not to say that mussels do not need considerable attention. They must be cleaned, preferably just before they are cooked. Mussels shouldn't be soaked in water. Rather, place them in a colander and run cold water over them. Next, using a paring knife, scrape off any mud or junk that adheres to the shells. Then debeard them by grasping the beard between the knife and the thumb and pulling down from the pointed end of the shell toward the rounded end.

Every once in a while veal is worth the splurge, and it is not such a wild indulgence if stew meat cut from the shoulder is bought on sale and stocked in the freezer. The enamel-on-iron casseroles in which I braise meats are not altogether satisfactory for browning because the intense heat can pock-mark the enamel and ruin the surface. The veal must be thoroughly dried before it is browned, and in order to keep the temperature of the fat high, only a few pieces should be added at a time. Otherwise the meat will render its juices and boil rather than brown. Homemade stock is best and is a less painful prospect if the cook makes it in great batches and freezes the result in various-size jars.

Canned artichoke hearts are perfectly acceptable if they are carefully rinsed under cold running water to rid them of any aftertaste they might have acquired from the liquid in the can.

Cauliflower, which has been disgracefully expensive until this time of year, is now in full season at delightfully low prices. The purée here is a nice departure from the usual ways of eating this vegetable and adds panache to the serving board. The texture is lovely when the cooked cauliflower is whipped with an electric mixer, far better to me than when it is put through the processor.

For the dessert, I double the recipe for the tart shell and make two. One gets used immediately and the other (baked) goes into the freezer. It is a great convenience when dessert is needed for unexpected guests. The extra shell can be defrosted and filled with pastry cream or even whipped cream. If you make a double recipe of the pastry cream, half can be frozen, as unlikely as this seems, and defrosted along with the reserved shell. Whatever fresh or canned fruits are at hand can be used for the topping. The red currant jelly glaze will even take away the stark whiteness of fresh sliced pears while it imparts a pleasant tartness.

Mussels with Fresh Coriander
Béarnaise

•

FOR THE	70	*fresh mussels, cleaned*
MUSSELS	1	*cup dry white wine*
	1/2	*cup water*
	1	*medium onion, peeled and quartered*
	6	*parsley stems*
	1/2	*bay leaf*
	1/4	*teaspoon thyme*
	6	*whole black peppercorns*
FOR THE SAUCE	1/4	*cup red wine vinegar*
(MAKES 1½ CUPS)	1/4	*cup dry white wine*
	1	*tablespoon minced shallots*
	1	*bunch fresh coriander (also called cilantro or Chinese parsley), coarse stems removed*
	1/2	*pound (2 sticks) unsalted butter*
	3	*egg yolks*
		Salt and white pepper to taste

Clean the mussels just before cooking (see text). Combine the wine, water and remaining ingredients for the mussels in a pot large enough to hold the mussels very comfortably. Bring the liquid to boil and cook over moderate heat for 5 minutes. Add the mussels, place the lid on the pot, and turn the heat up to high. Shake the pot every couple of minutes, making sure your hands are holding the lid down tightly and that potholders are firmly between your hands and the pot. After 5 or 6 minutes, when the shells have opened, remove from heat and turn out the mussels immediately into a large colander placed over a bowl. (This broth can be strained through several layers of cheesecloth and frozen as is for a soup or reduced and frozen for a sauce.)

Discard the top shells of the mussels and loosen the meat from the bottom shells with a sharp paring knife. Place the mussels in their shells close together on a jelly-roll pans and spoon a bit of the fresh coriander béarnaise over each one. ❀ The mussels can be set aside for an hour at this point. To serve, place the mussels in a preheated 250-degree oven for 10 minutes. Arrange 8 of the warmed mussels on individual first-course plates and serve with French bread.

•

The sauce can be made an hour or two in advance. ❀ Combine the vinegar, wine and shallots in a small saucepan and cook over moderate heat until the liquid is reduced to 2 tablespoons. Strain the liquid into a second saucepan and add the fresh coriander. Stir over low heat until the coriander is wilted. Set aside and allow to cool.

Cut one stick of the butter into 8 pieces and melt it to foaming in a small saucepan over moderate heat, then lower the heat. Place the egg yolks in the container of an electric blender and blend at highest speed for about 15 seconds, or until the yolks are very thick. Add the vinegar-wine reduction with the wilted coriander and blend at highest speed for another 15 seconds, or until the coriander is macerated. It may be necessary to stop the motor once or twice to push the coriander down the sides of the container with a rubber spatula.

With the motor running still at highest speed, feed the hot butter into the container, preferably through the small opening in the cover, in a very thin but steady stream. Continue blending at high speed until the sauce thickens. Should it remain thin, pour it into a measuring cup and feed it into the blender once more in a thin, steady stream with the motor running at high speed. Pour the sauce into a bowl and heat the second stick of butter until it foams. In a thin steady stream, beat the butter into the sauce with a wire whisk.

Veal Ragout with White Onions, Mushrooms and Artichoke Hearts

•

3½ pounds boneless veal shoulder, cut into
    2-inch pieces
4 tablespoons butter
2 tablespoons oil
2 large cloves garlic, minced
2 tablespoons flour
4 cups beef stock, veal stock or beef
    bouillon
½ teaspoon thyme leaves
    Salt and pepper to taste
1 tablespoon tomato paste
6 tablespoons full-bodied dry sherry,
    such as Dry Sack
    3-inch strip lemon peel
24 small white onions, peeled and
    trimmed
½ pound mushrooms, cleaned and sliced
Two 14-ounce cans artichoke hearts, the
    hearts rinsed in a colander under
    cold water, drained, halved and
    trimmed of any brown spots on the
    leaves

Trim the veal of any sinews and fat and dry the pieces thoroughly between paper towels. Heat the butter and oil in a large aluminum, carbon steel or iron frying pan and brown the veal, a few pieces at a time, on all sides. Use tongs to turn the meat so it is not pierced; otherwise the juices will escape. Remove the browned meat to a 6-quart enamel-on-iron or other heavy casserole. When all the veal is browned, discard all but 2 tablespoons of the fat in the frying pan.

Turn the heat to low, add the minced garlic to the remaining fat, and cook, stirring, for 1 minute. Then add the flour and cook, stirring, still over low heat, for another 2 minutes. Stir the stock, thyme, salt, pepper, tomato paste, sherry and lemon peel into the flour mixture, bring to a boil, and cook, stirring and scraping the bottom of the pan with a wooden spoon to loosen all the brown bits. Add the sauce to the veal in the casserole, bring to a simmer, and cook for 30 minutes. Add the onions, bring back to a simmer, and cook for 20 minutes more. Then add the mushrooms and cook for 5 minutes more. Finally, add the artichoke hearts, return to a simmer, and cook for a final 5 minutes. The veal will cook for 1 hour in all.❀ The ragout can be served immediately or it can be cooled, refrigerated and re-heated over a low flame.

Cauliflower Purée

•

2	*medium-large heads cauliflower*
1	*tablespoon lemon juice*
6	*tablespoons butter*
½	*cup heavy cream*
	Salt and pepper to taste
2	*tablespoons minced chives*

Trim the cauliflower of their leaves, coarse stems and any dark spots, separate into large florets, and wash well. Bring a large pot of salted water to a boil and add the florets. Cook for 10 to 12 minutes, or until the cauliflower is soft but not mushy. Drain well in a colander, then return to the pot. Shake the cauliflower in the pot over high heat for a few minutes to rid it of any excess moisture. Then turn it into the large bowl of a standing electric mixer or any large bowl if you use a hand mixer. Beat the cauliflower with the mixer fitted with beaters until it is light and fluffy. Then, one after the other, beat in the lemon juice, butter, cream and salt and pepper. Adjust seasonings.❀ The purée can be made several hours in advance to this point. To serve, heat the purée over moderate heat, stirring frequently with a wooden spoon. Turn it out onto a serving platter or into a bowl and sprinkle with chives.

Strawberry or Other Fresh or Canned Fruit Tart

•

1 *Sweet Baked Pastry Shell (recipe
    follows)*
    Red Currant Glaze (recipe follows)
    *Pastry Cream (see Index); substitute
    for peach essence 1 teaspoon
    Cointreau, Grand Marnier or other
    liqueur*
2 *pints strawberries, washed and hulled,
    or fresh or canned fruit of your
    choice*

To assemble the tart, paint a thin layer of warm glaze over the bottom and sides of the cooled shell, using a brush. Pour the cooled pastry cream into the shell and, starting in the middle, set the strawberries on the cream in ever-increasing circles. Reheat the glaze if necessary and, with a brush, paint each strawberry, letting the glaze run over to coat any pastry cream that shows ✿ Refrigerate until one hour before serving. The tart is best if assembled no more than 4 hours before serving.

Sweet Baked Pastry Shell

•

2 *cups sifted all-purpose flour*
1/4 *cup sugar*
1/4 *teaspoon salt*
3/8 *pound (1½ sticks) butter at room
    temperature*
2 *egg yolks*

Combine the flour, sugar and salt in a bowl, add the butter and egg yolks, and work the mixture with your fingers until it comes together into a dough. Break off pieces of dough the size of small lemons and press these into a 10-inch, two-piece French tart or quiche pan and pat to make an even bottom layer and sides. Bake in a preheated 300-degree oven for 55 to 60 minutes, or until the shell is a lovely nut brown. Cool on a rack for 10 minutes, then place the tart pan on a can and allow the rim of the pan to drop down. Finish cooling, and if you want to remove the pan bottom before transferring the tart to a platter, slide two long spatulas under the shell so that they cross each other and form an X between the crust and the pan bottom. Lift the tart onto the platter and slide out the spatulas.✿

    This recipe can be doubled and two shells made. The second shell can be frozen when it is cooled. To use, defrost the shell, crisp on a jelly-roll pan in a preheated 300-degree oven for 10 minutes, and fill as desired.

Red Currant Glaze

•

1   *cup red currant jelly*
2   *tablespoons Cointreau, Grand Marnier*
        or other liqueur

Just before using, combine the jelly and the liqueur in a small saucepan and bring to the boil. Remelt the glaze if it cools to the point where it cannot be spread easily.

Chicken Livers en Brochette with Endive

Chicken Waterzöoi

Baked Apples with Currant Jelly in White Wine

•

Meursault "Charmes"
or Meursault "Perrières"
or Freemark Abbey Chardonnay

*E*very year around this time, root parsley makes its annual appearance on the market for a few weeks or so, and I take out a family recipe for the great Belgian dish, *waterzöoi*.

Most recipes for this delicate but aromatic poached chicken in a lemony, creamy sauce call for parsley sprigs as a prime flavoring. The best of them, which comes from my husband's Belgian Aunt Suzanne, uses root parsley, also called parsley root or Hamburg parsley. This ingredient looks like a small parsnip and tastes like a combination of celeriac (celery root) and parsley. It gives the *waterzöoi* a wonderful underbody and freshness. The chicken pieces are cooked with the julienned root parsley, leeks, carrots and celery along with chicken stock, then presented on a large platter with the vegetables and some minced parsley for more color. The dish is then served in flat soup plates with plenty of sauce ladled over it from a separate tureen. The *waterzöoi* is eaten with a fork, knife, soup spoon and good French bread.

The first course provides a contrast in color, texture and flavor to the chicken. Little bamboo skewers of hot, broiled chicken livers are teamed with fans of Belgian endive leaves. A Madeira sauce for the livers also serves as a warm dressing for the salad. The combination is mildly startling but successful and very pretty. The meal ends with the nice clean taste of buttery baked apples in white wine made tart with red currant jelly.

The little bamboo skewers for the chicken livers should soak in a pan of cold water for a good six hours so that they will be thoroughly saturated to prevent them from being burned to a cinder under the broiler. The livers can marinate anywhere from two to six hours. I prepare the brochettes just before our guests arrive. Five liver halves are threaded on each skewer with a single strip of bacon, which snakes between and around the livers in a continuing S shape. The skewers are then placed in a roasting pan large enough not to crowd them but small enough to fit under the broiler. This pan, which can easily be removed from the oven every time the skewers need turning, avoids the problem of food sticking to the broiler. It also saves the cook from having to kneel on the floor or, in my case, stand on tiptoe to get to the broiler, and it catches the juices as well. Once the livers are cooked, a sauce can be made by deglazing the pan with the leftover marinade. Individual plates are then prepared with one brochette and three fanned endive leaves.

I prefer blade (unground) mace for the *waterzöoi* because it is more subtle than ground nutmeg. Blade mace can be found among better spices at supermarkets. Root parsley is sold in bunches during October and into November at specialty markets and even in some supermarkets. I discard the leaves of root parsley, which look like flat Italian parsley but lack its flavor, as well as the stalks. Root parsley, which must be peeled, is also an excellent addition to a chicken stock pot or vegetable soups or stews. Celeriac can be combined with parsley in the *waterzöoi* if root parsley is unavailable.

The only real preparation required for the *waterzöoi* involves cutting the carrots, leeks, root parsley and celery stalks into a matchstick julienne. The most efficient tool for this is not a machine but rather a good chef's knife. Those who are more casual about how food looks can use the processor to produce a passable julienne with root vegetables, although not with leeks and celery. Alternatively, all the vegetables could be chopped coarsely in a processor. However, the hand-cut matchstick julienne gives the dish a finished, festive look.

The sauce for the *waterzöoi* is bound at the last minute with egg yolks, lemon juice and cream. It is important that the sauce not be allowed to boil once the enrichment is added. At this stage, it should be stirred constantly and the pot should be removed from the heat the minute a simmer bubble appears. Should the sauce boil, it might curdle, in which case it will not be smooth and beautiful, but the flavor will still be good.

I have done the baked apples with McIntoshes, Staymans and Jonathans. For flavor, the McIntoshes were far superior. However, since McIntoshes do not hold their shape as well as the others when baked, you should watch carefully the last minutes of baking and should not let them overcook. The apples can be baked a day in advance, if necessary, and heated in a moderate oven for about 20 minutes before serving.

Chicken Livers en Brochette
with Endive

•

1½ to 1¾	*pounds chicken livers (about 20 whole chicken livers)*
½	*cup medium-sweet Madeira*
¼	*cup olive oil*
1	*teaspoon dried tarragon*
¼	*teaspoon coarsely ground black pepper*
8	*red radishes*
24	*leaves (about 3 long heads) Belgian endive*
8	*strips bacon*

About 6 hours before the livers are to be cooked, set 8 bamboo skewers to soak in a pan of cold water.

From 2 to 6 hours before the livers are to be cooked, split them, remove all membranes, fat and greenish spots, drain, and put into a bowl. Add the Madeira, olive oil, tarragon and pepper, cover, and refrigerate. ✸

Wash the radishes and cut off the stem and the root ends. With a small knife (a curved-bladed fluting knife is the easiest to use), make parallel vertical slices through the radish but do not cut through the bottom. Start slicing at the middle and work down to each side. Drop the radishes into a bowl of ice water and refrigerate until needed. ✿

Wash the endives, cut off the root ends, and carefully detach 24 large outside leaves. Dry and refrigerate in a plastic bag until needed. ✿

Remove the livers from the marinade but reserve the marinade. Thread the skewers (this can be done at least an hour in advance) by starting with the end of a slice of bacon, then half a liver, then through the slice of bacon, and continue until the skewer holds five pieces of liver. The bacon ribbons around the liver, forming a continuous S.

Swirl the skewers in the marinade, place them in a roasting pan large enough not to crowd them, and refrigerate until they are to be cooked. ✿ Place the pan under a preheated broiler, about 3 inches from the flame, for 7 to 8 minutes. Remove the pan and turn the skewers every 3 minutes or so, to cook the livers evenly. Make a tiny gash in one liver at the end of the cooking time to test for doneness. The livers should be pink but not bloody. Place a skewer on each serving plate. Add the remaining marinade to the roasting pan and bring to a boil, scraping the brown bits into the sauce with a wooden spoon. Then arrange three leaves of endive on each plate in a fan shape, and place a drained radish flower at the base of the fan. Finally, spoon the juices over the livers. Serve immediately.

Chicken Waterzöoi

•

Two   *2½- to 3-pound frying chickens, each*
      cut into 8 pieces
      Salt and freshly ground white pepper to taste
½   *cup butter*
4   *large ribs celery, cut into a 2-inch-long*
      matchstick julienne
3   *large carrots, trimmed, peeled and cut into a 2-*
      inch-long matchstick julienne
4   *leeks, white part and an inch of green,*
      trimmed, split and washed under
      cold running water, then cut into a
      2-inch-long matchstick julienne

2   bunches root parsley (about 10 small
      roots), trimmed, peeled and cut into
      a 2-inch-long matchstick julienne,
      or 15 sprigs fresh parsley, tied into
      a bundle with string, and 3 to 4
      small knobs of celery root
      (celeriac), peeled and cut into a 2-
      inch-long matchstick julienne
3   blades mace or ¼ teaspoon nutmeg
6   cups chicken broth
      Juice of 1 lemon, or more, to taste
4   egg yolks
¾   cup heavy cream
4   tablespoons chopped parsley

Salt the chicken pieces lightly and pepper them moderately heavily. Melt the butter in a large, heavy, ovenproof casserole and add the chicken. Cover and stew the chicken without browning it for about 10 minutes, turning the chicken occasionally. The skin will have started to firm and take on a yellow color. Add the julienned vegetables, the parsley bouquet if you haven't found root parsley, and the mace or nutmeg. Then add the chicken broth and bring to a simmer. Cover and cook over low heat for about 30 minutes, or until the chicken is tender.✿   The chicken can sit in this broth while you are having your first course.

Just before serving, heat the broth to boiling and remove the chicken to a heated flat serving platter. Discard the parsley bouquet if you have used one. With a slotted spoon remove the julienned vegetables and strew these over the chicken pieces. Add the lemon juice to the broth and heat to a simmer. Beat the yolks lightly with the cream and gradually whisk this into the hot broth. Cook over low heat for a couple of minutes to slightly thicken the sauce. Stir constantly and do not let it boil. Ladle some of the sauce over the chicken and sprinkle with the minced parsley. Then pour the remaining sauce into a heated tureen.

To serve, place chicken pieces in shallow soup plates and ladle some sauce over them. Accompany by warm, crusty French bread.

Baked Apples with
Currant Jelly in White Wine

•

8	*large McIntosh apples*
8	*tablespoons red currant jelly*
4	*teaspoons unsalted butter*
1½	*cups dry white jug wine*
6	*tablespoons sugar*

Core the apples, using either an apple corer or a melon baller. Arrange them in a baking dish and place a tablespoon of the red currant jelly in each. If the cavity isn't large enough, let the jelly spill over. Then place ½ teaspoon butter on each apple. Mix the wine with the sugar and pour around the apples. Bake in a preheated 375-degree oven for 40 minutes, or until the apples are tender but not overcooked. ❀   The more these apples are basted during baking, the better they will be. Serve hot, lukewarm or at room temperature, never cold.

• SUNDAY SUPPER FOR EIGHT OR SIXTEEN •

Antipasto

Lasagne with Tiny Meatballs

Green Salad and Fresh Gorgonzola Cheese

Vanilla Ice Cream with Chestnuts in Cognac Syrup

•

Folonari Valpolicella

$\mathcal{T}$his nostalgic Sunday supper recalls student days and primitive attempts to replicate the real or imagined delights of a favorite local Italian restaurant. The earthiness of the past is retained along with the built-in convenience of an easily prepared meal whose recipes can all easily be doubled for a buffet for sixteen. The difference between then and now is a refinement which satisfies the soul while the palate is unassaulted by clutter.

The meal begins with a loaf of peasant bread, carafes of red jug wine and the purity and beauty of a traditional antipasto made with honest ingredients. Next is a lush lasagne rescued from the graininess that afflicts meat sauces. Layers of wide strips of pasta alternate with scores of tiny meatballs, aromatic tomato sauce and ricotta cheese kept free of lumps by the addition of beaten eggs. The dish is topped with thin slices of mozzarella to dispense with the unpleasantness of internal stringiness, topped with more sauce and baked until bubbly. A crunchy green salad and Gorgonzola cheese, fresh and therefore creamy and mild, follow the lasagne. Dessert consists of scoops of quality vanilla ice cream topped with a homemade sauce of imported shelled chestnuts in a Cognac-permeated syrup.

The antipasto, in this case an Italian *hors d'oeuvre variés*, makes a handsome and appetizing presentation with its contrasts in colors and shapes. Its goodness, however, relies on the quality of its several parts. The meats — Genoa salami and prosciutto — are best when bought from Italian or other specialty stores with a rapid turnover in quality-brand cold cuts. The green peppers and mushrooms are marinated at home a night or two before, although the delicious artichoke hearts come already prepared in jars from the supermarket. The platter also contains tuna fish — the Italian kind packed in olive oil is most compatible here — along with egg wedges, tender celery hearts, ripe cherry tomato halves (or regular tomatoes, but only in season), anchovy fillets, little Italian peppers packed in vinegar, good black and green olives, a sprinkling of capers, and a drizzle of good olive oil and red wine vinegar over all. Fresh fennel, when it is available, is an excellent addition.

Lasagne, a most accommodating dish, takes so little time to prepare that it could comfortably be made the morning of the party, or a day in advance or even a month earlier and frozen. The sauce and little meatballs will hold for a few days in the refrigerator and longer in the freezer. (Leftover lasagne, should you be fortunate enough to have any, freezes extremely well.) Imported Italian plum tomatoes make a worthwhile difference in the sauce. Pasta made with semolina, a flour milled from the hard part of wheat, has good body and flavor and is well worth the few pennies more it costs. The ingredients listed on the package will tell you what you're buying. Ricotta should be the freshest possible, so read the pull date. Some Italian food stores manufacture their own fresh mozzarella, but if you are reduced to the supermarket variety, choose the whole-milk kind for its bit of extra creaminess. Mozzarella, which is a bit gummy, is most easily sliced with a wire. I like my cheese slicer because its wire can be replaced if it is broken. Parmesan cheese when fresh has a smooth, soft bite and is sold by the piece. It can be grated in the processor and held in the freezer. The lasagne cuts more comfortably if it is allowed to settle for 10 minutes after it is removed from the oven.

Any combination of plain greens would be appropriate for the salad. It needs no more embellishment than a vinaigrette to which a bit of mustard has been added. Fresh Gorgonzola is usually available at cheese stores and specialty stores that have an extensive stock of cheeses.

With chestnuts, I take the easy way out and buy them in a jar, already shelled and cooked. Specialty food stores carry the Minerva brand, which I like. The chestnuts in cognac syrup can be served not only over ice cream but also with puddings or any plain cake. The sauce keeps indefinitely in the refrigerator and takes no time to prepare.

Antipasto

8 SERVINGS

•

FOR THE	2	green bell peppers
MARINATED	½	teaspoon lemon juice
PEPPERS	1	clove garlic, crushed
FOR THE	16	small button mushrooms
MARINATED	2	tablespoons olive oil
MUSHROOMS	2	teaspoons dry white wine
	1	teaspoon lemon juice
	4	coriander seeds
FOR THE		The marinated peppers and
ANTIPASTO		mushrooms, drained
	8	slices Genoa salami
	8	slices prosciutto, loosely rolled
	Two	3½-ounce cans Italian tuna fish packed in olive oil
		2-ounce can flat fillets of anchovies, drained and the fillets halved lengthwise
	3	hard-cooked eggs, each cut into 6 wedges
	8	cherry tomatoes, cored and halved
		6-ounce jar marinated artichoke hearts, drained and the hearts quartered

	4	celery hearts, halved lengthwise
	8	pepperoncini *(small green Italian peppers packed in vinegar)*, drained
FOR THE GARNISH	4	teaspoons capers, drained
	8	cracked green Greek olives, drained
	16	small black ripe Niçoise olives, drained
FOR THE DRESSING	6	tablespoons olive oil
	1½	tablespoons red wine vinegar

Prepare the peppers and mushrooms the day before. Broil the peppers until the skins are black, place them in a plastic bag for about 10 minutes, rub off the skins, and core, seed and slice the peppers lengthwise into strips. Combine the lemon juice and crushed garlic and stir into the peppers. ❀ Cover and refrigerate overnight.

Clean the mushrooms and remove the stems at the caps. (Freeze stems for stock.) Combine the mushrooms with the olive oil in a small sauté or frying pan and heat, stirring the mushrooms to coat them with oil. Add the white wine, lemon juice and coriander seeds, and bring just to the boil, stirring. Remove from heat and cool. Turn out the mushrooms and the liquid into a bowl, ❀ cover, and refrigerate overnight.

Arrange the antipasto ingredients in a pretty pattern on a large serving platter. Garnish by sprinkling the capers over all and placing the green and black olives around the edge. ❀ Mix the oil and vinegar and drizzle over the antipasto.

Lasagne with Tiny Meatballs

8 SERVINGS

•

Olive oil to grease an 8-by-14-inch lasagne pan, or a 9-by-13-inch rectangular baking pan, about 2 inches deep

FOR THE SAUCE	½	cup minced onion
	4	tablespoons olive oil
	1	teaspoon dried basil
	½	teaspoon dried oregano
	¼	teaspoon fennel seeds
		2-pound, 3-ounce can imported plum tomatoes
	Two	8-ounce cans tomato sauce
		6-ounce can tomato paste
		Salt and pepper to taste

FOR THE MEATBALLS	1	pound ground beef
	½	cup fresh bread crumbs
	¼	teaspoon dried oregano
	2	tablespoons freshly grated Parmesan cheese
	2	eggs, lightly beaten
	2	tablespoons butter
	1	tablespoon peanut oil

FOR THE PASTA		Salt for the water
	1	pound lasagne, preferably made with semolina

FOR THE ASSEMBLY	1	pound ricotta
	3	eggs, well beaten
	½	cup freshly grated Parmesan cheese
	8	ounces whole-milk mozzarella, sliced thin

Oil the lasagne or baking pan and set aside.

The sauce and meatballs can be made a day in advance, if desired. Sauté the onion in olive oil until transparent and soft, but do not let brown. Add the basil, oregano and fennel seeds and cook, stirring constantly, for 1 minute. Add the canned tomatoes with their liquid plus the tomato sauce, tomato paste, salt and pepper. Simmer, covered, ½ hour, stirring occasionally.

While the tomato sauce is cooking, make the meatballs. Thoroughly mix the ground beef, bread crumbs, oregano, Parmesan cheese and eggs. Form into ½-inch balls. There will be about 100. Heat the butter and peanut oil in a heavy frying pan, such as heavy-duty carbon steel, and brown the meatballs, about 10 at a time, on all sides. Remove to a bowl as they are browned. Add the browned meatballs, all at once, to the sauce and simmer, covered, for 15 minutes. Ladle off 1 cup of the sauce, without meatballs, and reserve to top the lasagne after it is assembled. ❀

•

Bring a large pot of water to the boil, add salt, and slip in the lasagne, one at a time, so that the water doesn't stop boiling. Cook, stirring occasionally, until just tender. (I use the minimum cooking time indicated in the directions on the box.) Turn out the lasagne into a colander, rinse with cold water and drain thoroughly.

Mix the ricotta with the beaten eggs and the Parmesan cheese.

To assemble, place a layer of lasagne, slightly overlapping the strips of pasta, in the oiled pan. Ladle on a layer of sauce with meatballs evenly distributed and dollops of the ricotta mixture, then a layer of lasagne. Repeat until all ingredients are used up, ending with a layer of pasta. Ladle ½ cup of the reserved sauce over the final layer of pasta. Cover the sauce with the slices of mozzarella and cover with the remaining sauce. ❀

Bake in a preheated 375-degree oven for 40 minutes. The lasagne will be bubbling hot and the mozzarella will be melted. Let the lasagne stand for 10 minutes to settle before cutting it.

Vanilla Ice Cream with
Chestnuts in Cognac Syrup

8 SERVINGS

•

2   quarts good-quality vanilla ice cream
2   cups Chestnuts in Cognac Syrup (see
     May, Provisioning the Pantry)

Dish out the ice cream on dessert plates, using a scoop, and serve with the chestnuts.

November

PROVISIONING · THE · PANTRY

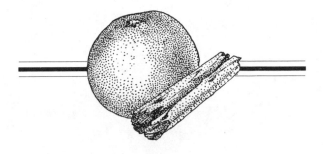

Spiced Oranges

MAKES ABOUT 4 CUPS

•

6	medium-size juice oranges
3	cups sugar
1½	cups rice wine vinegar
12	whole cloves
6	inches stick cinnamon
6	blades mace

Wash the oranges, prick the skins of each in about a dozen places with a fork, and cook the oranges in boiling water for 30 minutes. Drain and cool. Slice off each end of the oranges and discard. Cut the oranges into ¼-inch-thick slices and discard the pips.

Combine the sugar, vinegar and spices in a saucepan and stir over medium heat until the syrup boils. Reduce heat and let the syrup cook for 10 minutes, without stirring. Add the orange slices, cover, and cook over medium-low heat for 30 minutes. Let the slices cool in the syrup and then pack them into pint jars, making sure all the oranges are covered with syrup. Refrigerate for 3 weeks before using.

Serve with turkey, duck, goose and chicken. The syrup can be used to baste any fowl.

Fish Pâté with Pink Herb Sauce

Roast Ducks with Ginger-Lemon Sauce

Spinach Ring
Surrounded by Wild Rice
and Filled with Creamed Sliced Carrots

Mocha Almond Bombe

•

FIRST COURSE:
Sterling Chardonnay
or Pouilly-Fuissé
MAIN COURSE:
Parducci Petite Sirah
or Châteauneuf-du-Pape "Château de Beaucastel"

⁂

With this festive dinner we celebrated the birthday of a dear friend. It started with a creamy white, salmon-ribboned fish pâté, which, thanks to the food processor, was prepared in 15 minutes, not counting cooking. The pâté was sliced and served next to a dollop of pink herb sauce on individual plates, an elegant combination of flavors and colors.

Next came almost fatless, crisp-skinned ducks brought to that happy state by being boiled for five minutes, blow-dried for eight minutes with hot air from a hand-held hair dryer and then roasted in a hot oven without benefit of pronging or basting. The ginger-lemon sauce that accompanied the ducks was tangier than the usual orange sauce and more agreeable, to my taste, than the green peppercorns so fashionable these days. Accompanying the ducks was a spinach ring surrounded by wild rice and filled with creamed sliced carrots. The platter was spectacular enough to be shown off at the table before it met devastation at the sideboard.

Dessert had to be birthday cake. I decided on a light and lovely meringue torte, which I baked the day before and left out to be filled the day of the party. Then, during the night, a greedy raccoon came through an upstairs open window, found the kitchen and the torte and ate it all up. I suppose I could have made the time to bake a proper cake, but this would have been too much after such an involved meal. Instead, I used some of the almonds I had toasted to accompany drinks, along with my stash of ice cream and some ordinary chocolate syrup, for a bombe in the shape of a cake. It wasn't a meringue torte, but it held candles and turned out to be an appropriate ending for this meal.

A successful fish pâté requires absolutely fresh ingredients, which must be refrigerator-cold when they are put together. The fish should be returned to the refrigerator to become thoroughly chilled after it is cut up so that it will absorb the egg whites and cream when puréed. Also, the result seems to be better when I remember to refrigerate the processor bowl and blade. The puréed red peppers add color and mellowness rather than flavor to the herb sauce, so while fresh peppers can be used, canned or jarred red peppers would do as well.

Ducks are so wonderful that it is wicked to waste any part of them. The giblets, necks and wing tips are used for the sauce. The fat is cut up and rendered with bits of neck skin and some chopped onion to be used later for cooking. The fat from the roasting pan is excellent for sautéing or roasting potatoes and turnips.

I cook three ducks for eight, which is a bit generous. Three people to a duck is the general rule. But I like leftovers reheated or for a cold salad. It is harder and harder to find fresh ducks, so most of the time I make do with frozen, overfatted birds. I clean the ducks and make the stock for the sauce the day before.

Until I discovered the blow-drying technique, I had to stab the skin at least every ten minutes to encourage the fat to dissolve. And even then it wasn't perfect. The parboiling-hot-air treatment is much more effective because the pores of the skin are opened and the fat pours out during the cooking, a phenomenon that begins during the blow-drying. The birds go into the oven and can be forgotten until they are done. However, if all the ducks are not cooked on the same shelf of the oven, it is a good idea to switch them halfway through the cooking. My larger roasting pan accepts two ducks but does not come with a rack, so I improvise with overlapping cake racks. The mixture of honey and water gets painted on at the end to produce a more deeply browned skin.

In order to do this meal with one oven, the cooked ducks must come out of the oven an hour before dinner; the hot sauce will reheat them sufficiently. Put them under a loose tent of foil on top of the stove, since nothing else will be cooking by then. The sauce and the carrots are reheated when the ducks are taken away to be carved. The oven temperature should be reduced the minute the ducks come out, and the door opened to cool it off. After about five minutes, the wild rice goes in, and ten minutes later the spinach ring in its hot water bath.

Fresh ginger, essential for the sauce, will keep forever if it is peeled, covered with sherry and refrigerated in a tightly covered jar.

Wild rice is a very grand addition to any meal. An hour sounds like a long time to cook wild rice, but this recipe comes out perfectly every time — fluffy but slightly crunchy, exactly the way it should be. It is a relief to put something in the oven and forget about it: no stirring, no sticking and if it sits for an extra fifteen minutes, no harm. The spinach ring is another no-fail dish. The carrots, which are cooked without water, are intensely flavored and delicious.

The bombe can be made well in advance and with any variety of ingredients. A mold of any shape will do, but I like metal because it unmolds so easily. The mold I used for this bombe has pretty configurations and resulted in a showy dish. The almonds' slight saltiness is imperceptible in the bombe and even intensifies the flavor of the ice creams. Walnuts or any other kind of nut would be almost as good. I used supermarket chocolate syrup in a plastic squirt bottle to make fanciful abstract designs over the top of the unmolded bombe and then felt mildly guilty about achieving a sensational effect just by playing.

Fish Pâté

•

2   tablespoons softened butter
½   pound salmon steak, boned and thinly
       sliced
     Salt and pepper to taste
1   pound fresh flounder or sole fillets,
       skin removed, cut into 2-inch pieces
1   whole egg
3   egg whites
1   cup heavy cream
2   tablespoons Cognac
1   teaspoon salt
½   teaspoon ground white pepper
½   teaspoon dried tarragon
     Pink Herb Sauce (following recipe)

Smear a 4-cup loaf pan with the softened butter and refrigerate. Season the salmon slices with salt and pepper and refrigerate.

All the following ingredients plus the processor bowl and blade should be ice cold. Purée the flounder in a processor fitted with the steel blade. Stop the motor once or twice and scrape the fish down from the sides. With the motor running, add the whole egg and the egg whites. Process for another 2 minutes, stop the motor, scrape down the sides, and process for another minute. With the motor running, add the cream and Cognac in a steady stream. Season with salt, pepper and tarragon, and process for another 20 seconds.

Pack half the mixture into the buttered pan and press down with a spoon to eliminate all air pockets. Arrange the salmon slices to cover. Then spoon the remaining mixture over the salmon. Smooth the top with a spatula and cover with a piece of buttered parchment or waxed paper. Set the loaf pan in a roasting pan, pour boiling water into the roasting pan to come halfway up the sides of the loaf pan, and bake in a preheated 300-degree oven for 1 hour. Remove from oven and let the pâté sit in the water for another 15 minutes. ❁   Cool and refrigerate for several hours or overnight.

To serve, unmold the pâté by running a knife between it and the sides of the pan. A towel moistened with hot water can be applied to the bottom to help release the pâté. Slice into 8 equal portions and serve with pink herb sauce.

Pink Herb Sauce

MAKES ABOUT 2 CUPS

•

3/4	*cup mayonnaise*
3/4	*cup sour cream*
3	*red sweet bell peppers, either freshly roasted, skinned and seeded (see Index) or canned*
4	*tablespoons minced parsley*
2	*tablespoons minced chives*
	Ground white pepper and salt to taste

Mix the mayonnaise and sour cream together in a bowl. Drain the peppers and pat them as dry as you can with paper towels. Purée them in a processor and add to the bowl. Stir in the herbs and taste for pepper and salt.

Roast Ducks with Ginger-Lemon Sauce

•

Three	*4½- to 5-pound ducks, fresh or defrosted*
1	*teaspoon honey thinned with 1 teaspoon hot water*

FOR THE STOCK

2 tablespoons vegetable oil
Wing tips, necks, gizzards and hearts
    of the ducks, chopped into 1-inch
    pieces and patted dry
2 carrots, trimmed and cut into 1-inch
    chunks
2 stalks celery, cut into 1-inch chunks
2 onions, quartered
1 bay leaf
1/2 teaspoon thyme
4 sprigs parsley
Two 13¾-ounce cans chicken broth
Two 10½-ounce cans beef bouillon

FOR THE GINGER-
LEMON SAUCE

1½ tablespoons sugar
1/2 cup red wine vinegar
2 cups stock (above)
1½ tablespoons potato starch or arrowroot
2-inch piece fresh ginger, peeled and
    cut into a fine julienne
Peel of 2 lemons, cut into a fine
    julienne and blanched in boiling
    water for 5 minutes, refreshed with
    cold water, drained and dried
1/4 cup lemon juice, or more to taste
3/4 cup medium-sweet Madeira

To prepare the ducks, first remove globs of fat and reserve, if desired, with the livers for another use. Cut off the wing tips and set aside with the necks, hearts and gizzards for the stock. Pull out loose organs from the cavities and discard. ❀ The ducks can be prepared to this point the day before they are to be cooked.

    Prepare each of the ducks in the following way. Fill a large pot with enough water to cover one duck and bring to a boil. Submerge a duck in the water and after it has come back to a boil, cook for 5 minutes. Remove, drain the cavity, and pat off the excess moisture from the skin with a paper towel. Open the pores of the duck's skin by directing hot air all over it from a hand-held hair dryer. Blow dry the duck for about 8 minutes and wipe off the fat as it is released. Place the duck, breast side up, on the rack of a roasting pan and do the next one.

Roast the ducks in a preheated 450-degree oven for ½ hour. Reduce the heat to 400 degrees and roast for 45 minutes more. Remove the ducks from the oven and return the heat to 450 degrees. Place the ducks on a board and pour off the fat from the pan (or pans) into a bowl. (When the fat is cool, pour it through a strainer lined with wrung-out cheesecloth and refrigerate for other uses.) Return the ducks to the roasting pan(s), paint them with the honey-and-water-mixture, and place in the oven to brown for 15 minutes more. Remove from the oven, transfer to a large platter, and cover loosely with a tent of foil. Set the ducks in a warm place until they are to be carved. ✿

Pour off any fat from the roasting pan (or pans). Deglaze the first pan with a cup of water over high heat, scraping off all the brown bits with a wooden spoon. Pour these deglazed juices into the second pan and repeat. Add the juices to the sauce.

To prepare stock for the sauce (do this well ahead), brown the wing tips, necks, gizzards and hearts of the duck, carrots, celery and onions in the oil, stirring constantly over high heat. Add the bay leaf, thyme, parsley, chicken broth and beef bouillon. Bring to a simmer, skim, and cook, with the lid slightly ajar, for 2 hours. Strain the stock into a bowl. There should be about 4 cups. Skim off the fat (there will probably be ½ cup of this). It is easier to degrease stock after it has been refrigerated for a few hours. ✿ Reserve 2 cups of the degreased stock for the sauce and freeze the remainder.

While the ducks are roasting, make the sauce. Combine the sugar and vinegar in a heavy 6-cup saucepan and cook over high heat for about 5 minutes, stirring until sugar dissolves. Cook until the mixture has caramelized and turned a mahogany color. Remove from heat and immediately pour the 2 cups of stock into the pan. (Stand back; there will be an eruption of steam.) Return to heat and simmer, stirring, until the caramel has dissolved. Ladle out 3 tablespoons of the sauce, blend with the potato starch or arrowroot, and return to the pan. Add the ginger, lemon peel, lemon juice and Madeira and cook for about 5 minutes. Add the deglazed roasting juices and taste for seasoning. ✿ Set aside and reheat just before serving.

Spinach Ring

•

Five	10-ounce packages frozen leaf spinach, partially defrosted
5	tablespoons butter
5	tablespoons flour
1¼	cups milk
½	teaspoon nutmeg
5	eggs
2	tablespoons softened butter
	Salt and pepper to taste

Bring spinach to a boil with a little water, cook for 2 minutes, drain, and squeeze out as much moisture as possible. Chop the spinach in a food processor and set aside.

Melt the butter in a 2-quart saucepan, add the flour, and stir over low heat for 2 minutes. Whisk in the milk and nutmeg and bring to a boil. Off the heat, whisk in the eggs one at a time. Add the spinach and mix thoroughly. Season lightly with salt and pepper. Butter a 6-cup (9½-inch) ring mold with the softened butter. Spoon in the spinach mixture and smooth the top. Cover with a piece of buttered parchment or waxed paper. This can be made several hours in advance to this point and refrigerated.

Bring the ring to room temperature before baking. Put into a pan large enough to hold the mold and pour boiling water to come halfway up the mold. Bake in a preheated 350-degree oven for 45 minutes. To unmold, run a thin, sharp knife around the sides and turn the ring out onto a large platter. Surround with wild rice and fill the center with creamed sliced carrots (following recipes).

Wild Rice

•

1½	cups (9 ounces) wild rice
4	tablespoons butter

3   *shallots, finely minced*
3   *cups chicken stock*
    Salt and pepper to taste

Put the wild rice in a large, fine strainer and run cold water over it to wash it well. Set aside.

Melt the butter in a heavy 3-quart ovenproof pot, such as an enamel-on-iron casserole, add the shallots, and cook over low heat for a few minutes, until the shallots are transparent but not brown. Add the wild rice and cook for 5 minutes, stirring constantly. Add the chicken broth and salt and pepper. ✿   This can be prepared in advance to this point. An hour before serving, bring the broth to the boil, cover, and bake for 1 hour in a preheated 350-degree oven.

Creamed Sliced Carrots

•

2   *pounds carrots, peeled and ends*
       trimmed
4   *tablespoons butter*
½   *teaspoon thyme*
    Salt and pepper to taste
1   *cup heavy cream*

Slice the carrots either crosswise or lengthwise in a processor, using the thin slicing blade. Melt the butter in a heavy saucepan, add the carrots, thyme, salt and pepper, and stir to coat with the butter. Cook, covered, over very low heat for about 15 minutes, stirring occasionally to make sure the carrots don't burn. When the carrots have lost their crispness, add the cream. Cook, uncovered, over medium heat, stirring frequently, until the cream has been absorbed. Adjust seasoning. ✿   The carrots can be made ahead and reheated at the last minute.

Mocha Almond Bombe

•

2   *quarts coffee ice cream*
1   *cup toasted unblanched almonds (see*
     October, Provisioning the Pantry),
     coarsely chopped
2   *quarts butter almond ice cream*
     Chocolate syrup

Line the bottom and sides of a 10-cup mold with all the coffee ice cream and stud with the chopped toasted almonds. Drizzle some chocolate syrup over the entire surface. Pack in enough of the butter almond ice cream to fill the mold. (Some of the ice cream will be left over.) Smooth the top, cover with plastic wrap, and place in freezer for at least 3 hours. ✿ An hour to 1½ hours before serving, remove the mold from the freezer and dip it quickly in a basin of hot water. Dry the mold, run a knife around the rim, and unmold the bombe onto a platter. Place in the refrigerator ✿ (not the freezer) until serving time. To serve, drizzle more chocolate syrup over the bombe and slice at the table with a sharp knife dipped in a tall container of very hot water.

• SUNDAY BRUNCH •

Marinated Olives

Kedgeree Rings with Mango Chutney

Mixed Vegetable Bouquet of Snow Peas, Zucchini, Broccoli, Cauliflower and Carrots

Lemon Pickle

Gingered Poached Pears with Hot Ginger Sauce

•

*Chandon Blanc de Noir
or Lanson Brut N.V.*

This menu is wonderful for a Sunday supper even though it was planned to be perfect for late Sunday breakfast, early lunch, or brunch. Because every dish can be made at least the day before and quickly finished before serving, it is particularly suitable for cooks who like to spend time reading the Sunday paper. Aside from setting the table and perhaps cutting some chrysanthemums for a centerpiece, there is little to do. Best of all, the food is satisfying, comforting and good to eat, separately and in combination.

The meal starts simply with delicious marinated olives (see June, Provisioning the Pantry), which are good with preprandial drinks, especially bloody Marys or mimosas. The real interest lies in the kedgeree, a curried pot of fresh and smoked fish, rice, eggs, parsley and lots of butter. The Victorian British viewed this Indian dish as the perfect waker-upper, and they were quite right. There are many versions of kedgeree, of which this, a family recipe, is, to me, the best. The kedgeree is served with mango chutney, a homemade hot lemon pickle and a lovely bouquet of many-colored and textured vegetables lightly cooked and quickly heated in butter. Cold poached pears, stuffed with gingered whipped cream and served with hot ginger sauce, make a refreshing end to the meal.

The kedgeree is most elegant when packed into ring molds and turned out onto large oval platters. The centers are then filled with chutney and the ends of the platters garnished with the vegetables. This presentation is a nicety, not a necessity, and works best with plain long-grain (not converted) rice, which is a little sticky. (I cook rice the way I cook pasta, in a large amount of salted boiling water. The rice is slowly fed into the water and cooked until it is just done, about 17 minutes, and immediately drained in a colander.) The kedgeree and its accompaniments can also be served on separate platters or in bowls. Eight hungry people can easily polish off this recipe, but if the guests are strong-willed dieters, the hosts may be lucky enough to have some left over. The kedgeree heats and reheats without problems. While fresh fish is always preferable, frozen fish is acceptable for this dish. If frozen fish is used, it is possible to have all the ingredients in the house, ready for a Sunday supper when even the most serious preplanners can find the cupboard is bare.

I prefer my kedgeree with an assertive curry flavor, so I use the maximum amount called for in the recipe, but this is a matter of preference. It is a good idea to taste at the end because some curry powders are weaker than others. Should the dish need more curry, be sure to cook it in extra butter for a full minute. Cooking curry in butter tempers the rawness of the spices while it enhances their flavor. Kipper snacks, with their excellent mild, smoky flavor, are sold in long, narrow cans and are preferable to the larger cans that contain kippered herring. Since the snacks are boned, only the skins need to be discarded.

Cooks who made mango chutney in the summer, when mangoes were in such good supply, should, of course, use the homemade product. Major Grey's chutney, which is sold under several brand names, can be found in specialty aisles of supermarkets. The lemon pickle (see January, Provisioning the Pantry), which is delicious with all curried dishes, is abundantly spiced yet doesn't blast the mouth. It keeps for a very long time, if not forever, under refrigeration. We ate some that I had made over a year before and it was wonderful. This lemon pickle also makes a nice house present when cooks visit cooks or, even better, noncooks.

The vegetable bouquet is a felicitous combination with the kedgeree, with its built-in eye appeal and the full flavors of the broccoli, cauliflower and snow peas, the gentleness of the zucchini and the light sweetness of the carrots. I like to use my lemon stripper to make white striations down the length of the unpeeled zucchini, a pretty effect when the zucchini is cut into slices or chunks.

The poaching syrup can be used to cook additional pears or other fruit, so it should be decanted into a jar and stored in the refrigerator for the next time. Stem ginger in heavy syrup can be found in specialty food sections of supermarkets and in Oriental food stores. The minced ginger with whipped cream is appealing when it fills the cavity of the pear and delicious as it surrounds the pears. The ginger sauce uses the heavy syrup in which the ginger is packed, so nothing is wasted here. Golden syrup, a critical ingredient of the sauce and a mainstay of English kitchens, is similar to corn syrup but lightly caramelized. My experiments with recipes that purported to be suitable for homemade substitutes were disappointing. Happily, golden syrup, imported from England, is available in the specialty food section of many supermarkets and in specialty food stores.

Kedgeree Rings
with Mango Chutney

•

About 4   tablespoons softened butter to grease
         two 6-cup ring molds
     2   pounds fresh cod, haddock or other
         white flaky fish fillets, or two 1-
         pound packages frozen white flaky
         fish fillets of your choice, defrosted
  Four   3½-ounce cans kipper snacks

    2   *cups uncooked rice, preferably not*
        converted if ring molds are to be
        used

    2   *teaspoons salt*

   3/8   *pound (1½ sticks) butter*

6 to 8   *tablespoons curry powder, preferably*
        imported Madras

    8   *hard-cooked eggs*

   ½   *cup minced parsley*
        Salt and freshly ground white pepper
        to taste

    3   *lemons, each cut into 6 wedges*

 Two   *12-ounce jars Major Grey's chutney*
        Lemon Pickle (see January,
        Provisioning the Pantry)

Grease two 6-cup ring molds heavily with the softened butter. If desired, line the molds with waxed paper and grease the paper. Refrigerate the molds until needed.

Place the fish fillets in a large frying pan, add enough water to cover the fish barely, bring to the simmer, and, basting the fillets as they cook, simmer for 5 minutes. Remove the fillets with a slotted spoon, let cool, and flake into bite-size pieces. Drain the kipper snacks, skin them, flake into bite-size pieces and add to the fresh fish. ❊   Refrigerate.

Cook the rice. When it is almost done, melt the butter in a saucepan, add the curry powder, and cook, stirring constantly, for 1 minute. Add the butter-curry mixture to the drained hot rice and toss with a fork, mixing well. Add the fish and toss. Cut the eggs into wedges, using an egg wedger if desired; add them along with the parsley to the mixture and toss again with a fork. Season with salt and pepper.

Pack the warm mixture tightly into the prepared ring molds and cover the molds tightly with foil. Let cool. ❊   They can be refrigerated at this point overnight.

To heat, bring the molds to room temperature and place them in a preheated 350-degree oven for 30 to 40 minutes, or until the kedgeree is heated through. To serve, run a knife around the edges of the molds. Then place a large oval platter on each mold. Using potholders, hold one mold against its platter and flip both mold and platter over together. Center the mold on the platter, unmold the kedgeree, and repeat with the other one. If any of the mixture sticks to the molds, spoon it out and pat it into the ring. Wipe the platters, if necessary, with a damp paper towel and fill the centers of the rings with the chutney. Arrange the mixed vegetables at the ends of the platters and decorate with lemon wedges. Pass the lemon pickle separately.

NOTE: The kedgeree need not be turned into molds. It can be refrigerated, ❀ reheated for 40 minutes in a preheated 350-degree oven and served in a large bowl. The chutney and mixed vegetables are then served in their own bowls.

Mixed Vegetable Bouquet
•

½ *pound snow peas*
4 *thin zucchini*
4 *stalks broccoli (1 large bunch)*
¾ *head cauliflower*
   12-ounce bag tiny carrots or ¾ pound
       long thin carrots
4 *tablespoons butter*
   Salt and pepper to taste

Wash the snow peas, trim the blossom ends, and remove strings from both sides of the pods. Soak the zucchini in cold water for 15 minutes, scrub gently, trim the ends, and run a lemon stripper, if desired, down the length of each zucchini 5 times at even intervals so that the zucchini will appear to be striped. Cut each zucchini into 1½-inch pieces. Wash the broccoli, remove the stems, reserving them for soup or any other use, separate the heads into small florets, and rinse. Core the cauliflower, divide the blossoms into small florets, and rinse. Peel the carrots and trim the ends. If long carrots are used, cut each into 2½-inch pieces and trim the ends with a paring knife so that each piece resembles a whole small carrot.

Next, precook the vegetables one after the other in the same pot of boiling water. Remove each vegetable after its allotted cooking time to the same colander, using a slotted spoon. Cook the snow peas for 2 minutes, the zucchini for 2 minutes, the broccoli for 3 minutes, the cauliflower for 4 minutes and the carrots for 5 minutes. Drain the cooked vegetables well and if they are not to be eaten immediately, ✿ wrap them in paper towels, place in a plastic bag, and refrigerate for as long as overnight.

To serve, heat the butter in a large sauté pan, add the cooked vegetables plus salt and pepper to taste, and cook quickly over a medium-high flame, shaking the pan or stirring the vegetables until they are heated through.

Gingered Poached Pears

•

8 *firm but ripe pears with a good perfume*

1 *tablespoon lemon juice in a large bowl of cold water*

2 *cups water*

1 *cup sugar*

   3-inch piece of vanilla bean or 2 teaspoons vanilla extract

1 *cup heavy cream*

2 *tablespoons confectioners' sugar*

3 *tablespoons stem ginger in syrup, drained and minced very fine*

Core the pears from the blossom (bottom) end, using a melon baller, peel them, but leave the stems intact. Place the fruit in the bowl of lemon juice and water. Set aside.

Combine the 2 cups of water with the sugar and vanilla bean or extract, bring to the boil, lower heat, and simmer for 5 minutes. Add the pears to the syrup and simmer for about 10 minutes, or until the pears test done when pierced with a sharp, pointed knife, basting constantly. Remove the pears to a bowl, pour the syrup over them, cool, and refrigerate until needed. ✿   The pears can be prepared to this point at least a day in advance.

An hour before serving, remove the pears from the syrup and place them on a large plate lined with paper towels. Let them drain well. Decant the poaching syrup (including vanilla bean if it was used) to a jar, label, and refrigerate. It can be used over and over again for poaching pears or any other fruit.

Whip the cream together with the confectioners' sugar until it is stiff, but be careful not to let it turn to butter. Stir in the minced ginger. Fit a pastry bag with a number 3 star tube; twist the bag at the bottom and tuck it into the tube so the filling won't leak out. Place the bag in a bowl, open it at the top, and spoon the whipped cream mixture into it. Pipe cream into the cavities of each pear, filling them well, and set the pears on a serving platter. The bit of excess cream at the base helps to keep the pears upright. With the remaining cream, pipe a border around the pears. ✿ Refrigerate and serve very cold with hot ginger sauce.

Hot Ginger Sauce

MAKES ABOUT 2 CUPS

•

¼ cup ginger syrup, drained from a 10-
 ounce jar of minced stem ginger in
 syrup
¾ cup golden syrup
¾ cup dark rum, preferably Myers's or
 Ron Negrita
⅓ cup minced stem ginger in syrup,
 drained

Combine all ingredients in a small saucepan, mix well, ✿ heat, and serve.

• THANKSGIVING DINNER •

Oysters on the Half Shell with Lemon Halves
and Caraway Rye Bread

Roast Turkey with Chestnut, Prune and Sausage Stuffing

Turnip Gratin

Artichoke Bottoms Filled with Green Pea-Artichoke Purée

Cranberry Sauce

Cold Lemon Soufflé with Raspberry Sauce

(For Leftovers: Turkey Pie)

•

FIRST COURSE:
Muscadet
or Robert Mondavi Fumé Blanc
MAIN COURSE:
Moulin-à-Vent
or Burgess Cellars Zinfandel

*T*urkey is authorized twice a year at our house (although it is sneaked in at other times, but heavily disguised). At Thanksgiving we have it roasted with a wonderful chestnut, prune and sausage stuffing. After the feast, some meat is kept out for those of us who believe the point of turkey is to have turkey, stuffing and cranberry sandwiches the next day. The rest is frozen. Then in February, preferably for lunch with good friends on a snowy Sunday, the leftovers are defrosted and reappear in a turkey pie.

Thanksgiving dinner starts with an enormous glut of oysters on the half shell, which, in this normally egalitarian household, are opened by the men. I get extra oysters because the openers reward themselves handsomely as they get on with their work. The oysters are served with lemon halves clothed in little cheesecloth mittens that are available in kitchenware stores. Later the mittens, which keep the seeds from falling into the oysters, are retrieved, washed and reused. We eat the oysters with thin slices of buttered dense rye bread, which I make because it is so like the *pain de seigle* served with oysters in France.

The turkey, ordered fresh from a neighborhood market, is accompanied by the dressing, unthickened gravy, a turnip gratin that many people mistake for a superior form of potato, and a lovely green-on-green dish of fresh artichoke bottoms filled with green pea and artichoke purée. Cranberry sauce is extraneous with such a menu, but we have it anyhow, and in two versions, because turkey isn't turkey without it. I divide a pound of cranberries and cook half as plain old cranberry sauce, which I like. The other half gets ground, uncooked, with oranges.

In some years, when we have been sixteen and more at our table, I have made five or six different pies; but unless there are little children around who love pie, a most delicious cold lemon soufflé leaves us all feeling better about those second helpings.

I buy the oysters a couple of days before Thanksgiving so that we can scrub the mud off them in advance. The cleaned oysters get packed round-side-down in layers in a plastic dishpan or two, covered with a damp dish towel and refrigerated until they are to be opened. Any unopened oysters will keep for at least a week in the refrigerator.

The bread, an adaptation of a Bernard Clayton recipe, is made the day before. Having a mixer with a dough hook makes breadmaking much more accessible. I use either a *pain de mie* pan, which is a loaf pan with a lid that slides on securely to keep the bread dense and flat on top, or a couple of long, thin cylindrical covered bread pans, which produce small, round slices. But a regular loaf pan weighted with a large cake pan and a brick works equally well. The bread should be cut into super-thin slices, which is much easier to do when it is a day old, and spread lightly with softened unsalted butter.

The turkey gets cleaned the day before. I make the stuffing on Thanksgiving Day, but it could also be made a day in advance. Of course, the stuffing is never put into the bird until just before it is cooked, to discourage bacterial contamination. The first time I encountered prunes soaked in hot tea I was skeptical, but this old French trick does bring out more flavor in the prunes, and of course the soaking plumps them. I do not allow myself many indulgences when it comes to cooking, but not having to peel chestnuts, a time-consuming, finger-breaking job which I detest, is an exception. I buy vacuum-packed chestnuts packed dry in jars. These are imported from France and can be found in specialty food shops and good kitchenware shops.

If you suspect that anyone at your table will turn up a nose at turnips, don't tell. We have converted many turnip-haters with this turnip gratin, which looks exactly like a potato gratin but is lighter and less starchy. Many turnip gratin recipes call for Swiss cheese and some form of ham, but I like the flavor straight, buttery and creamy.

I am sorry to say that canned artichoke bottoms are not a wonderful substitute for fresh. I tried sautéing three brands of canned bottoms in butter and/or sprinkling them with lemon juice, and they all tasted of butter and/or lemon, but not artichoke. I parboil large artichokes until the leaves but not the bottoms are tender. The leaves can then be removed easily and the flesh scraped off to be added to the processor bowl with the peas. The chokes are then discarded and the bottoms trimmed. The cooking of the bottoms is finished in bouillon.

The purée can be spooned into the bottoms, but is much prettier when piped into them with a pastry bag. I use a flexible, easily washable nylon bag, fitted with an open star tube that makes a crinkly design. To fill the bag, insert the tube, twist the bag above the tube and tuck the twisted section inside the tube. Place the bag in a bowl and spoon in the purée. If the bag feels too hot for your hands, wear a pair of washable fabric gloves. Pick the bag up from the top and ease the purée down. This will free the twist from the tube. Use one hand to push the purée out and the other to guide the tube.

The cold lemon soufflé is my slightly modified version of a spectacularly successful recipe given to me years ago and until now shared with very few friends. It can be presented rising majestically over the top of the dish, as though it were a hot soufflé, by pouring the mixture into a too-small soufflé dish fitted with a foil collar. Or more modestly but no less deliciously, it can be served like a pudding, out of a pretty glass bowl. It is lovely with the raspberry sauce, which complements the lemon flavor. Those with a second pastry bag and the forethought to wash out the star tube that was used for the green pea-artichoke purée could pipe some additional whipped cream on the top of the soufflé just before serving, but this really could be viewed as an exaggeration. Should fresh raspberries be available, a tiny box would be worth the splurge for decorating the top of the soufflé.

Caraway Rye Bread

MAKES 1 LOAF

•

Softened butter for greasing the bread pan, its lid and a mixing bowl, plus 1 tablespoon butter, melted and cooled

1   *tablespoon (1 envelope) active dry yeast*
1   *cup lukewarm water*
1   *tablespoon sugar*
1   *teaspoon salt*
1   *tablespoon caraway seeds*
1   *cup medium rye flour*
2¼ to 2½   *cups bread flour, or more if needed*

Grease an 8½-inch-long loaf pan or *pain de mie* pan with some of the softened butter. Add the yeast to the water in the bowl of a mixer with a dough hook, stir, and add the sugar. Let stand for 5 minutes. Add the salt, caraway seeds and melted butter, then stir in the rye flour. Beat in the bread flour a cup at a time until 2 cups have been incorporated. Add up to another

½ cup more flour if the dough is sticky. Knead with a dough hook for 5 minutes and add more flour if the dough is still sticky.

Grease a clean mixing bowl with softened butter. Place the kneaded dough in the bowl and turn it over to coat it with butter. Cover with plastic wrap and let rise in a warm place until doubled in size, about 1 hour. Remove the plastic, punch down the dough, and knead for about a minute to get rid of the air bubbles. Turn the empty bowl over the dough and let it rest for 15 minutes.

Form the dough into a loaf and place in the pan. Cover with plastic wrap and let rise for another 45 minutes, or until the dough has reached the top of the pan. Grease the bottom of a cake pan large enough to cover the entire loaf pan, or grease the inside of the *pain de mie* pan lid. Place the cake pan on the bread pan and put a brick in it, or close the cover of the *pain de mie* pan. Bake in a preheated 400-degree oven for 40 minutes. Remove the lid and turn the bread out of the pan. If it sounds hollow when tapped, it is done. If not, return it to the oven, without the lid, for another 10 minutes. Cool on a rack. ❀   The next day, slice very thin and spread with softened unsalted butter. Serve with oysters.

Roast Turkey with Chestnut, Prune and Sausage Stuffing

8 SERVINGS, PLUS LEFTOVERS

•

16- to 18-pound fresh turkey, cavity cleaned of lungs and other organs, ready for stuffing, wing tips removed

FOR THE STOCK	
	Wing tips and turkey giblets, except liver
3	*tablespoons vegetable oil*
2	*carrots, cleaned and cut into chunks*
2	*stalks celery, cleaned and cut into chunks*

	2 onions, cut into chunks
	½ teaspoon thyme
	1 bay leaf
	Two 13¾-ounce cans chicken broth
	10½-ounce can beef bouillon
FOR THE **STUFFING**	2 pounds prunes, soaked overnight in strong hot tea
	1 cup chopped celery
	1 cup minced onions
	4 tablespoons butter
	2 pounds sausage meat
	½ cup turkey stock
	1 pound mushrooms, cleaned and quartered
	16-ounce jar imported vacuum-packed French chestnuts, halved
	2 cups bread crumbs made in a food processor from French bread
	½ cup minced parsley
	1 teaspoon dried thyme
	Salt and pepper to taste
	¼ cup Cognac
	¼ cup medium-sweet Madeira
FOR ROASTING	2 tablespoons softened butter, plus ½ cup melted butter

Clean the turkey the day before and make a stock by browning the wing tips and giblets in the oil. Then add the chunks of carrots, celery and onion plus the ½ teaspoon of thyme and the bay leaf. Add the chicken broth and beef bouillon, bring to the simmer, and cook, cover slightly askew, for 3 hours. Strain into a bowl and press down on the vegetables. Cool the stock and refrigerate. When cold, degrease it. ❁   Reserve 3 cups for the gravy and ½ cup for the stuffing and freeze the rest.

Do not remove the turkey from the refrigerator until the stuffing is prepared, and stuff only just before cooking.

Drain the prunes, cut them in half, discarding the pits, and place the prune halves in a large bowl. Sauté the celery and onions in the butter for 8 minutes or until they are transparent and add to the bowl. In the same pan, break up the sausage meat with a fork and stir, over medium heat, until all the pink has gone. Drain off the fat and discard it. Add the sausage meat to the bowl. Deglaze the frying pan with the ½ cup of turkey stock and add the juices to the bowl. Add remaining stuffing ingredients, mix lightly, and taste for seasonings. ❀

Stuff the turkey's body and neck cavities, sew up the neck, and truss. Place any excess stuffing in a casserole, cover with foil, and put the lid on. Set aside.

Smear the turkey with the softened butter and roast in a preheated 325-degree oven for 4½ to 5½ hours, depending on the turkey's size. Baste every 20 minutes or so with a brush dipped into the melted butter. Cover with foil if the skin is browning too quickly. The turkey is cooked when the juices run clear or when a meat thermometer inserted in the thickest part of the thigh reads 165 degrees. Remove the turkey from the oven and allow it to rest under a loose tent of foil for 30 to 45 minutes before carving. ❀ Turn the oven up to 350 degrees and bake the casserole with the stuffing for 1 hour. The turnip gratin can go in at the same time. By the time the turkey is carved, both will be cooked.

Degrease the pan juices, add the 3 cups of reserved stock, and bring to a boil, scraping the brown bits off the pan with a wooden spoon. Pour into a gravy boat.

NOTE: Later, remove 3 pounds of leftover meat from the carcass and freeze the meat for Turkey Pie (recipe follows). Freeze any leftover stuffing and serve with the pie.

Turnip Gratin

•

3   pounds white turnips, about 2½ to 3
       inches in diameter
¼   pound (1 stick) butter
1   clove garlic, crushed

1   teaspoon thyme
    Salt and pepper to taste
¾   cup heavy cream
2   tablespoons bread crumbs

Peel the turnips and slice with the thick slicing blade of a food processor. Parboil the slices in a pot of boiling water for 5 minutes and drain. Smear some of the butter on the bottom and sides of a 12-inch ovenproof gratin dish and distribute the crushed garlic over the bottom of the dish. Add the turnips in layers. On each layer dot some more of the butter and sprinkle with a little thyme and salt and pepper. When the pan is filled, pour cream over the turnips, sprinkle with the bread crumbs, and dot with remaining butter. ❀   Bake in a preheated 350-degree oven for 50 to 60 minutes.

Artichoke Bottoms Filled with Green Pea-Artichoke Purée

•

8   large artichokes
1½   cups beef bouillon
6   Boston lettuce leaves
1½   pounds (24 ounces) frozen peas
1   small onion, minced
1   tablespoon minced parsley
¼   teaspoon dried thyme
      Pinch of sugar
      Salt and freshly ground white pepper
2   tablespoons heavy cream
1   tablespoon butter

Wash the artichokes, trim the stems, and boil in salted water for 15 minutes. The flesh on the leaves will be tender and the bottoms not quite cooked. Drain and remove leaves. Scrape the flesh from the insides of the leaves with a teaspoon and reserve. Discard the chokes and trim the bottoms. Heat the bouillon and poach the bottoms, a couple at a time, until tender but not mushy. Drain, but reserve the bouillon. ✿

Make a chiffonade of the lettuce by rolling the leaves and slicing the roll. Add the lettuce, peas and minced onion to a large pot of boiling water and cook for about 8 minutes, or until the peas are soft but not mushy. Drain thoroughly and place in a processor bowl. Add the reserved artichoke flesh plus the parsley, thyme, sugar, salt and pepper. Process in short bursts until smooth and scrape down the sides of the bowl once. Do not overprocess.

Transfer the purée to a heavy saucepan and beat it over low heat to dry it out a bit. Still beating, add the cream a little at a time and then the tablespoon of butter. Taste for seasoning and keep warm. The purée will be soft but stiff enough to hold some shape. ✿   It can be made ahead to this point and reheated before serving.

Heat the artichoke bottoms in the reserved bouillon, drain, and pat dry. Place on a warm serving platter. Spoon the purée into a pastry bag fitted with a number 2 or number 3B open-star tube. Pipe the purée into the artichoke bottoms and serve. Place any leftover purée in a small, heated serving dish.

Cold Lemon Soufflé

•

1	*tablespoon (1 envelope) plain gelatin*
4	*tablespoons cold water*
3	*eggs, separated*
1	*cup sugar*
	Juice and grated rind of 2 lemons
1	*teaspoon vanilla extract*
1³⁄4	*cups heavy cream*
	Raspberry Sauce (see Index)

FOR THE	³⁄4	*cup heavy cream*
GARNISH	2	*teaspoons sugar*
(OPTIONAL)	1	*small box fresh raspberries*

In a metal measuring cup, soften the gelatin in the water. Then dissolve the gelatin by putting the cup in a small frying pan with simmering water. Remove the frying pan from heat but allow the cup to sit in it.

Beat the egg yolks with the sugar until thick and light. Beat in the lemon juice, grated rind, vanilla and finally the gelatin mixture.

In a clean bowl with clean beaters, beat the egg whites until stiff but not dry. Fold the yolk mixture into the whites. Whip the cream, preferably in a cold metal bowl and with cold beaters, and fold it into the mixture. Place in a glass bowl or, if desired, in a 1-quart soufflé dish fitted with a 3-inch-high foil collar that has been oiled lightly on the inside. ❁ Refrigerate for at least 3 hours, but preferably overnight. Remove collar carefully.

Should the optional garnish be used to gild the soufflé, just before serving, whip the cream together with the 2 teaspoons of sugar. Place in a pastry bag fitted with a number 2 star tube. Pipe a border of cream around the top of the soufflé and spokes from the border to the center. Decorate with the fresh raspberries if they are available.

Serve with the raspberry sauce.

Turkey Pie

•

1 *stick (¼ pound) butter, divided in half*
3 *pounds leftover cooked turkey meat,*
   both white and dark, cut into 1-inch
   dice or smaller if necessary
1 *can water chestnuts, rinsed under cold*
   water, drained and sliced thin
2 *large carrots, sliced thin*
½ *pound small mushrooms, cleaned and*
   halved
½ *pound tiny frozen white onions*
2 *teaspoons dried thyme*
   Salt and pepper to taste
6 *tablespoons flour*
3 *cups chicken broth*

½   cup medium-sweet Madeira
½   cup dry white wine
¼   cup dry vermouth
1   pound puff pastry, defrosted if frozen,
        and chilled
1   egg
1   tablespoon milk

Melt half the butter in a large sauté pan, add the turkey meat, water chestnuts, carrots, mushrooms, onions, thyme, salt and pepper, and sauté for 5 minutes.

Melt the remaining butter in a large saucepan, add the flour, and cook, stirring constantly, for 2 minutes. Remove from heat and whisk in the chicken broth and the three wines. Return to heat and stir until the mixture comes to a boil. Add the turkey-vegetable mixture to the sauce, adjust seasoning, and turn out into a deep, 10-inch casserole made of ovenproof glass or a 12-inch oval pie dish.

Roll out the pastry on a lightly floured board into a ¼-inch-thick circle or oval about 1½ inches larger than the pie dish. Cut a 1-inch strip off the pastry, around the circumference, wet the rim of the dish, and press the strip down on it. Then lift the pastry onto the dish. Moisten the strip and the underside edge of the pastry and press the edges together. Knead the scraps once or twice, roll them out, and cut decorations for the top of the pastry. Cut a small circle from the center of the pastry, butter the outside of the nozzle of a pastry-bag tube, and insert it in the hole, wide end up, to act as a funnel. Beat the egg and milk and with a pastry brush paint the top of the pastry. Place the decorations on the pastry and paint these with the glaze. Stretch another piece of excess dough into a string the diameter of a fat spaghetti, twist it, and place it on the pastry around the edge of the hole and the funnel. Paint the twist of dough with the glaze. Bake in a preheated 400-degree oven for about 1¼ hours, or until the crust is brown. Should the crust get dark too quickly, cover it with foil.

Before serving, remove funnel and cut the crust into 8 portions with a sharp pair of kitchen shears. This can be done while the crust sits on the pie. Serve with reheated leftover stuffing.

• BUFFET DINNER FOR SIXTEEN •

Double Mushroom Soup

Roast Fresh Ham Cumberland

Turnip Mousseline

Puréed Spinach with Croutons

Caramel-Glazed Mocha Cream Puffs

•

Georges duBoeuf California Gamay Beaujolais
or Beaujolais-Villages

*N*othing is nicer than having friends for dinner on the Saturday after Thanksgiving, especially if you've been invited out for Thanksgiving Day itself. But guest lists invariably get out of hand at this time of year, what with friends having households full of out-of-town visitors or grown children returned home and suddenly civilized. It is all too easy to ask more people than can possibly fit around the table. The solution, of course, is the buffet dinner.

This meal can go far to restore the buffet dinner's good name, which has been assaulted over the years by tired, cold dishes and main courses with more mush than interest, the better to be consumed without benefit of a knife. Here we start with a soup of fresh mushrooms reinforced with dried

Italian or Polish mushrooms, perfumed with a good dry sherry and served in manageable mugs. The main course is a festive fresh ham or, as some prefer to call it, leg of pork, glazed with the makings of a Cumberland sauce, which then forms the basis of the gravy. The meat, cooked to a succulent tenderness, is carved thin so that while a knife can be put to use by guests who are expert lap jugglers, it is not necessary. Accompanying the fresh ham and embellishing the dinner plates with good color and complementary flavors are an airy turnip mousseline and puréed spinach garnished with fresh, buttery croutons. Dessert is the best of finger foods — little cream puffs glazed with caramel and filled with a mocha cream.

Most of this meal can be made in advance, a boon the menu must have when large numbers are involved. The mushroom soup can be completely assembled the day before and only the sherry added just before the soup is heated and served. The dried wild Italian *porcini* mushrooms, with their heady earthy flavor, are worth searching out. They are sold in 1¾-ounce packets in Italian markets as well as in some specialty food stores. Dried Polish mushrooms are also very good. If finding either of these is too difficult, ordinary dried mushrooms, which many supermarkets sell in plastic containers, can be substituted.

It would be a mistake to count on picking up a fresh ham on the day you want to cook it, but most supermarkets are only too happy to order these for customers. About five days' advance notice is required, so plan accordingly. The meat is basted during its last hour of cooking with Cumberland sauce, a splendid English invention consisting of red currant jelly, ruby port (ordinary red port will do nicely), orange juice, lemon juice and mace. Cumberland sauce is more usually served cold as an accompaniment to ham, pork and meat pies. Using it to baste the fresh ham gives the meat a lovely color and the gravy a rich tartness. The fresh ham needs long, slow cooking — up to five hours, depending on its weight — so count backward carefully to make sure it gets into the oven on time. Plan to have the ham finished a good 40 minutes before it is to be carved. It needs time to settle and will stay warm under a tent of foil. This also lets you raise the oven temperature to bake the turnip mousseline.

I cooked turnips for the mousseline three different ways in the hope that one would result in a drier end product. It made no difference whether the turnips were boiled, steamed or even baked. The purée that was made from them was in each case full of liquid, so I suggest the easiest way, boiling. The turnips must be cooked far enough in advance (the day before the party is fine) for the purée to be put in a strainer to drain off the excess liquid. The cinnamon is almost imperceptible but adds a lovely dimension to the turnips. The dish is very delicate and not at all what non-turnip lovers would expect.

The spinach can also be made the day before, with the final five minutes of cooking occurring just before it is served. While fresh spinach is always preferable, I myself draw the line at hauling, cleaning and cooking the eight or ten pounds I would need for sixteen people. Considering the alternative, compromising with frozen spinach is perfectly acceptable. The spinach should be removed from the freezer two or three hours before you plan to work with it, since it must be partially thawed, a process that always takes longer than one thinks.

The bother about making cream puffs used to be the arm energy involved in beating the eggs into the cooked paste base. The food processor is easy and fast and the results are excellent. The recipe here is double my staple recipe. It fills the smallest processor bowl more than I would like for comfort, but nevertheless it works. When making puffs to serve only eight, I usually persuade myself to make the double recipe, since leftover puff shells keep beautifully in the freezer. Having them in reserve is money in the bank for those times when the prospect of making yet another dessert is unbearable. The shells can be filled with pastry cream as well as with whipped cream. According to Bernard Clayton, the expert on bread and pastrymaking, bread flour makes the puffiest shells. The 14-inch pastry bag holds the entire double batch, which avoids having to refill a bag that wants only to cling to itself after a first batch has been squeezed out of it. Large pastry bags come either in a heavy canvas with a plastic coating inside or in a lightweight nylon. I prefer the latter, which is made in France and carries the "Imper" label. Both types are washable, and having two is better than one, although the thin nylon bag dries very quickly. They can be found at most good kitchenware stores.

All these recipes, with the exception of the fresh ham, can be halved arbitrarily for a terrific dinner for eight. To serve eight, a good substitution is Roast Loin of Pork (see Index).

Double Mushroom Soup

16 SERVINGS

•

1½ *ounces dried wild Italian mushrooms (porcini) or dried Polish mushrooms, or ordinary dried mushrooms sold in plastic containers in supermarkets*

10 *tablespoons (1 stick plus 2 tablespoons) butter*

3 *pounds fresh mushrooms, cleaned and sliced*

4 *large onions, sliced*

Two *10 ¾-ounce cans condensed chicken broth*

6 *cups milk*

2 *cups heavy cream*
Salt and pepper to taste

1 *cup full-bodied dry sherry, such as Dry Sack*

Rinse the dried mushrooms quickly under warm running water, place them in a bowl, and pour boiling water over them to cover. Set aside while you make the soup.

Melt the butter to foaming in a large sauté pan, add the fresh mushrooms, and cook, stirring, until they first give out liquid and then the liquid cooks off. Add the onions and cook over low heat until the onions are soft and transparent. Do not let them color. Turn the mixture out into a processor fitted with the steel blade, and with the motor running add half the chicken broth. Process until the mushrooms are reduced to a purée. Place the purée in a large pan and add the remaining chicken broth along with the milk and cream. Strain the liquid from the dried mushrooms through four layers of damp cheesecloth and add the liquid to the pan. Cut the softened dried mushrooms into slivers and add. Season with salt and pepper. ❁ Just before serving, add the sherry and heat. Serve in mugs or bowls.

Roast Fresh Ham Cumberland

16 SERVINGS

•

10- to 12-pound whole fresh ham, rind
  removed
Salt and pepper
10-ounce jar red currant jelly
1 *cup ruby port*
½ *cup orange juice*
¼ *cup lemon juice*
¼ *teaspoon ground mace*
1 *cup chicken broth*
1 *cup beef bouillon*

Rub the fresh ham with salt and pepper and roast it in a large pan in a preheated 325-degree oven for 25 minutes per pound.

Combine the red currant jelly, port, orange juice, lemon juice and mace and heat until the jelly is melted. Use this to baste the meat frequently during its last hour of cooking. If during this last hour the fresh ham is not browning sufficiently, raise the oven temperature to 400 degrees. If it is browning too quickly, cover the meat with a tent of foil.

The ham is cooked when its internal temperature reads 165 degrees. Let the cooked ham settle under a tent of foil on a carving board while you make the sauce. ❁ Skim off as much fat as possible from the pan juices, add the chicken broth and beef bouillon, and bring to the boil while stirring with a wooden spoon and scraping up any brown bits that stick to the pan. Carve the ham, arrange on a platter, and serve the sauce separately.

Turnip Mousseline

16 SERVINGS

•

6 pounds medium-large white turnips
⅜ pound (1½ sticks) butter
1 cup heavy cream
¼ teaspoon cinnamon
½ teaspoon sugar
   Salt and pepper to taste
8 eggs, separated
⅓ cup melted butter

Cook the turnips either the day before or in the morning, Peel the turnips, cut them into thick slices, and cook in boiling salted water for about 20 minutes, or until the turnips are tender. Drain them well in a colander and purée them in a food processor or put them through a food mill. Turn the purée, which will be very liquid, into a large, fine-meshed strainer and set over a bowl. Pour off the liquid as it accumulates, something it will do rather quickly at first, and then place the strainer with purée plus bowl in the refrigerator. Leave to drain either overnight or for several hours. ❀

Turn the drained purée into a heavy saucepan, place it over high heat, and, stirring constantly, heat the purée for about 5 minutes. Remove from heat and beat in the butter, cream, cinnamon, sugar, salt and pepper. Then beat in the egg yolks, one at a time. The mixture can be prepared several hours in advance up to this point. ❀   About 45 minutes before serving, beat the egg whites until they are stiff but not dry. Fold the whites into the turnip mixture and pile into a 15-inch oval gratin dish that has been brushed with some of the melted butter, or into two 9- or 10-inch round ovenproof dishes suitable for serving. Brush the mixture with the rest of the melted butter. Bake in a preheated 400-degree oven for ½ hour, or until the mousseline is nicely browned and puffed.

Puréed Spinach with Croutons

16 SERVINGS

•

Eight   *10-ounce packages frozen leaf spinach,*
      partially defrosted
½   *pound (2 sticks) butter plus 4*
      tablespoons
3   *tablespoons minced shallots*
      Salt and pepper to taste
6   *slices firm-textured white bread*

Cut the partially thawed spinach into 1-inch cubes, place in a large pan, bring to a boil, and cook, covered, for 5 minutes over moderately high heat, stirring once or twice. Turn out the spinach into a large colander and let it drain while it cools. When it is cool enough to handle, squeeze it, in small handfuls, as dry as possible. In two batches, purée it in a food processor.

Melt the ½ pound butter in a saucepan, add the minced shallots, and cook over low heat for about 5 minutes, or until the shallots are transparent and soft. Add the puréed spinach, season with salt and pepper, ❀ and cook over low heat, stirring constantly, for 5 minutes. Transfer the purée to a serving dish and garnish with the croutons.

The croutons can be made several hours in advance. Remove the crusts from the bread and cut the bread into ½-inch cubes. Melt 4 tablespoons butter in a large frying pan and toss the cubes in it until they are golden brown on all sides. ❀ Reheat briefly if the croutons have not remained crisp.

Caramel-Glazed Mocha Cream Puffs

MAKES ABOUT SIXTY 1½- TO 2-INCH PUFFS

•

FOR THE CREAM-PUFF SHELLS		*Softened butter to grease 2 baking sheets*
	1	*cup water*
	1	*cup milk*
	14	*tablespoons (1 stick plus 6 tablespoons) unsalted butter*
	1½	*teaspoons salt*
	2	*teaspoons sugar (omit for cream puffs with savory fillings)*
	2	*cups bread flour or unbleached flour*
	8	*large eggs*
FOR THE CARAMEL GLAZE	*1½*	*cups sugar*
	6	*tablespoons water*
FOR THE FILLING	*2½*	*cups heavy cream*
	½	*cup confectioners' sugar*
	4	*tablespoons unsweetened cocoa, preferably Dutch*
	2	*tablespoons instant espresso coffee powder*
	2	*tablespoons dark rum, such as Myers's or Ron Negrita*

Line two baking sheets with foil and grease the foil with softened butter. Set aside.

To make the cream-puff shells, combine the water, milk, butter, salt and sugar in a heavy pan and bring slowly to a full boil, stirring constantly with a wooden spoon. Remove from heat, add all the flour at once, and beat, off heat, with a wooden spoon until the mixture comes away from the sides and forms a ball. Return to heat and dry out the paste by mashing the mixture down onto the bottom of the pan with the wooden spoon and bringing it up and folding it over, much as if you were kneading bread. Continue for 3 to 5 minutes, or until a sandy-looking film of paste forms on the bottom of the pan. Remove from heat and let the paste stand for about 10 minutes, beating it occasionally as it cools. Turn the paste out into a food processor fitted with the steel blade and, with the motor running, add, one after the other, the eggs. Process about 15 seconds more after the last egg is added.

Fit a pastry bag, preferably one 14 inches long, with a plain tube with a ½-inch opening. Twist the bottom of the bag into the tube, place the bag in a bowl, and spoon the paste into the bag. Untwist the end and push the paste down from the top. Hold the tube steady about ½ inch above the baking sheet and squeeze out mounds about 1½ inches in diameter, allowing the paste to push up around the tip of the tube. Withdraw the tube and continue to make mounds about 2 inches apart. If any of the mounds have pointy tops, pat these down with a finger moistened with cold water.

Place the filled baking sheets in a preheated 400-degree oven. In no event open the oven door before the shells have baked for at least 15 minutes. It is safer to check after 20 minutes and again 5 minutes later. Bake the shells 25 to 30 minutes, or until they are puffed and browned. Remove from the oven and with a long, thin knife, make a slit near the bottom of each shell to let out any steam.

The shells can be made the day before❀ and stored overnight in tightly closed plastic bags, or they can be made well in advance and frozen while they are still warm.❀ To thaw and recrisp frozen shells, place them, unthawed, in a preheated 375-degree oven for 8 to 10 minutes.

•

Glaze the unfilled shells with caramel the day they are to be eaten. To make the caramel, place the sugar in a heavy saucepan and shake the pan to make an even layer of sugar on the bottom. Then add the water carefully so that none of the sugar splashes onto the sides of the pan. Place over low heat and cook until the sugar melts. Do not stir. When the sugar begins to color, shake the pan gently so that the sugar colors evenly. Remove the pan from heat before the caramel is the rich golden brown it should be, since it will continue to cook off heat. Working quickly and holding the puff shells by the bottom, dip the tops into the caramel and set the shells aside, on their bottoms. When the caramel hardens, and about 4 or 5 hours before the puffs are to be eaten,❀ fill the shells with the mocha cream.

•

Whip the cream together with the confectioners' sugar until it begins to thicken. Add the cocoa and instant espresso coffee and continue to beat until the cream is very stiff. Then quickly beat in the rum. Fill a pastry bag fitted with a plain or star tube with a ⅛-inch opening. Slit the shells in half and pipe the cream into the hollows. Put the puffs back together, arrange on a platter, ❀   and refrigerate until needed.

December

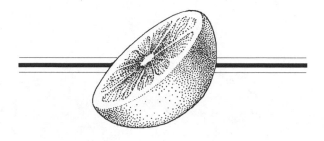

Candied Grapefruit Rind

•

   7   *medium-size thick-skinned, bright-*
       yellow, unblemished grapefruits
   6   *cups sugar*
2½   *cups water*
       Sugar for coating the cooked peels

Cut the grapefruits in half and remove the flesh in segments, leaving the membranes behind. Reserve the flesh for another purpose. Hold the empty rinds under cold running water and pull out the membranes and fibers (but not the white pith) with a spoon or with your fingers. Drain the rinds and cut them into ½-inch-wide strips. Place the strips in a 6-quart pan, cover with cold water, and bring to the boil. Drain and rinse under cold water.

   Repeat the boiling and draining process six more times, but during the last cooking continue to boil the rinds for 10 minutes. Drain well, return the cooked rinds to the pan, and add the sugar and water. Toss to distribute the sugar, cover, and let stand for 30 minutes. Uncover and simmer, stirring occasionally, for about 1 hour or until the rinds are translucent and the temperature of the syrup reaches 238 degrees on a candy thermometer. Turn out the rinds into a colander and drain off any remaining syrup.

When the rinds are lukewarm, roll them in sugar and spread on cake racks to dry until the surfaces are crusty — about 12 hours. Pack in airtight boxes or freeze. The candied rinds keep indefinitely. (Orange, tangerine and lemon rinds can be candied in the same way, but cook them in only four waters.)

Celery Root Rémoulade with Shrimp

Baked Ham and Endives

*Apple Turnovers with Buttered Apples and
Ice Cream*

•

Chiroubles

A woman very dear to us has been unable to come to our house for dinner because she has a back problem that prevents her from sitting in a car. My husband came up with the bright idea of our giving a dinner in her honor, but at her house. There would be eight diners, with a guest list mutually decided upon. It was up to me provide the portable feast. The result was so delicious and worked out so conveniently that others might want to consider giving this dinner as a present at Christmas or any other time.

The plan was for our friend to do absolutely nothing except sit at her own table. The meal had to be simple. We didn't want to descend upon her house with a moving van full of packing cases, nor did we want our friend to be subjected to the anxiety attacks that occur when others cook in one's own kitchen. Further, we didn't want to be faced with a massive cleanup. The aim was: no pots or pans to scrub and only a single dishwasher load for the entire evening.

We arrived with a smallish liquor carton full of food and a gratin dish of Belgian endive wrapped in ham and masked with a nutty Gruyère sauce. Its protective covering of foil would be removed when the dish went into the oven to be heated. The plastic container of celery root rémoulade, the plastic bag of cooked shrimp and the jars with extra rémoulade sauce and minced parsley were put into the refrigerator. The ice cream went into the freezer. The bread was placed on one cookie sheet and the apple turnovers on another. The jar of buttered cinnamony apples and the endive gratin dish remained out, at room temperature, and the oven was turned on to preheat.

Five minutes before we sat down, the bread went into the oven and the celery root, shrimp and extra sauce were divided among individual small plates, sprinkled with parsley and placed on the table. Then the bread was sliced and the gratin dish was put into the oven to bake while we had our first course. Because the ham and endives don't mind cooking longer than their alloted time, it didn't matter if guests dawdled over the first course. This main dish was served without accompaniment or embellishment; since it has everything — meat, vegetable and sauce — it needs nothing else. Each person started with one ham-wrapped endive, lots of sauce and more bread. Those who had seconds of either a half or a whole endive were inspired not by hunger but by gourmandise. It is a substantial dish.

As the main-course plates were being cleared, the apple turnovers were put into the oven to heat. Turnovers never have a sufficiency of fruit, so we served them, on individual dessert plates, with a dollop of cooked buttered apples that had also been warmed. Scoops of vanilla ice cream topped the apples. I used a charming oval scoop to make the ice cream echo the shape of the turnovers.

The celery root rémoulade had been made the day before because when this wonderful winter vegetable is served raw it improves, like stew, with a little time. Celery root, also called celeriac, is in full season in December. While supermarkets do carry it, it is sold more consistently by specialty markets. The price varies in accordance with the fanciness or pretensions of the purveyor, and it is a good idea to check around. I choose medium-size celery roots that weigh about three-quarters of a pound apiece because these are more apt to be solid inside and not mealy. I do not approve of stores that sell celery root with the stalks attached, since when you buy by the pound, you pay for the unusable stalk — or, in other words, garbage.

Celery roots should be peeled with either a potato peeler or a paring knife, but quickly because exposure to air blackens the vegetable. A cut lemon rubbed over the white flesh as it is peeled helps. The peeled roots can then be cut with a julienne blade in a food processor or with the julienne blade of a mandoline. Both result in square-cut strips. The coarse grating blade of a processor, while it does not produce the traditional square shape, will certainly do. I myself would not julienne celery root with a knife, since the vegetable is very hard and the task unrewarding. Some recipes recommend blanching the julienned celery root in boiling water before dressing it, but to me this is a transgression. A bit of lemon juice and salt mixed through the cut root will soften it without diluting its flavor, and the addition of the sauce finishes the job of "cooking" it. I have made celery root rémoulade with a traditional mustard-oil sauce, but I worked out the recipe here because it is more delicate and kinder to the shrimp. The sauce should be made with homemade mayonnaise, but I found it is very good with a decent store-bought variety.

The Belgian endives are cooked the day before, but sauced a few hours or just before the final cooking of the dish. Although endives carry a hefty price tag, they turn out to be not so extravagant. The entire vegetable is edible. To make all the endives the same size, and thus cook uniformly, extra leaves from the fatter heads are peeled off and saved for an elegant salad at another meal, either simply dipped into a fruity green olive oil or dressed with hazelnut oil and sherry vinegar. In any case, since the endives are integral to this dinner, they carry their weight when compared, say, to a roast. Freshly sliced imported boiled ham from a specialty market or the delicatessen counter of a supermarket is waste-free also. The cost of the dish is not unreasonable, and it is good.

The dough for the turnovers can be made a day or two in advance, although the turnovers themselves should be baked the same day they are to be eaten, to keep the fresh taste of the fruit and the crispness of the pastry. The addition of a bit of ordinary lard along with the butter makes these turnovers wonderfully flaky. Turnovers have the advantage of transporting well. I packed them in a mushroom basket between layers of crumpled waxed paper. Apricots only help apples, and the glaze that is brushed onto the pastry is so good that I make it up in large batches. It keeps for months in the refrigerator. I use it also for glazing open-faced fruit tarts and for tortes, preferably as a layer between the cake and a chocolate icing.

Celery Root Rémoulade
with Shrimp

•

	1½	*pounds celery root*
	2	*teaspoons lemon juice*
	1	*teaspoon salt*
FOR THE SAUCE	1½	*cups mayonnaise*
	1	*tablespoon Dijon mustard*
	4	*tablespoons minced parsley plus 2 tablespoons for garnish*
	2	*tablespoons minced celery*
	1	*tablespoon capers, rinsed under cold water and patted dry with a paper towel*
	1½	*teaspoons fresh tarragon or tarragon leaves preserved in vinegar, drained and minced, or ½ teaspoon dried tarragon*
	2 to 3	*tablespoons heavy cream*
FOR THE SHRIMP	1	*pound medium shrimp*
	8	*whole dried allspice berries*
	1	*medium clove garlic, peeled and crushed*
	6	*peppercorns, crushed*

Peel the celery root and put it through a food processor with the julienne blade or the coarse grating blade, or cut it with the julienne blade of a mandoline. Pile it into a bowl and mix the lemon juice and salt through it. Set aside.

Make the sauce by mixing together the mayonnaise, mustard, 4 tablespoons of parsley, the minced celery, capers and tarragon. Thin to the consistency of thick sour cream with the heavy cream. Stir 1¼ cups of the sauce into the celery root and reserve the remaining sauce. Refrigerate both. ❁ This can be made a day in advance.

Wash the shrimp under cold water, put them in a saucepan and add water to cover, then add the allspice, garlic and peppercorns. Bring to a boil, simmer for 1 minute, and remove from heat. Let stand for 3 minutes and drain in a colander. When the shrimp have cooled sufficiently, peel and devein. Refrigerate. ✿

To serve, divide the celery root into 8 portions and mound on individual salad plates. Divide the shrimp into 8 portions and arrange around the celery root. Dribble a little of the extra reserved sauce on the shrimp and garnish each serving with some minced parsley. Serve with French bread.

Baked Ham and Endives

•

½	cup butter
½	cup lemon juice
4	tablespoons hot water
12	heads Belgian endive trimmed to equal size
½	teaspoon salt
12	slices freshly sliced good-quality boiled ham

FOR THE SAUCE	½	cup butter
	½	cup flour
		Cayenne pepper
		Freshly grated nutmeg
	4	cups milk
	1¼	cups grated Gruyère cheese (1 cup for the sauce and ¼ cup to sprinkle on top)

Melt the butter in an enamel-on-iron skillet large enough to hold the endives in one layer or divide ingredients in half and use two skillets. Add the lemon juice and hot water. Arrange the endives in the skillet, sprinkle with the salt, and simmer, covered, over very low heat for 30 minutes. Shake the pan periodically to make sure the endives don't stick or burn. Remove from heat and let cool in the pan. The endives will be almost soft but will still hold their shape. When you can handle them, wrap each head in a slice of ham and place, seam side down, in a 15-inch or 17-inch long gratin pan. Pour the cooled juices over the endives and set aside. ❀ The dish can be prepared to this point the day before, tightly covered with plastic wrap and refrigerated.

For the sauce, melt the butter in a large saucepan, add the flour, and stir over low heat for at least 2 minutes. Do not let this roux brown. Add the cayenne and nutmeg to taste and stir over heat for another 30 seconds. Take off heat, then beat the milk into the roux with a wire whisk. Return to heat and bring to a boil. Add 1 cup of the cheese and stir over low heat until the cheese is melted and the sauce thickened. Pour the sauce over the ham-wrapped endives and sprinkle with the remaining ¼ cup of cheese. ❀ The dish can be prepared to this point several hours before the final reheating. Bake in a preheated 450-degree oven for 15 to 20 minutes, or until the sauce is bubbling and the cheese has browned.

Apple Turnovers with Buttered Apples and Ice Cream

MAKES 10 TURNOVERS

•

FOR THE DOUGH		
	2	cups unbleached flour
	1	teaspoon salt
	¼	pound (1 stick) cold butter, cut into 6 pieces
	¼	cup cold lard
	⅓	cup ice water
	2 to 3	tablespoons flour for the pastry board
	1	egg beaten with 1 tablespoon milk, to glaze the pastry

FOR THE FILLING   *3½*   *pounds Greening or Granny Smith*
AND BUTTERED   *apples*
APPLES   *Juice and grated rind of 1 lemon*
         ½   *teaspoon cinnamon*
         3   *tablespoons sugar*
         ¼   *cup Apricot Glaze (see Index;*
               substitute for flavoring 2
               tablespoons Vanilla Cognac from
               April, Provisioning the Pantry, or 2
               tablespoons Cognac plus ½ teaspoon
               vanilla extract)
         3   *tablespoons butter*
         1   *pint good vanilla ice cream*

Fit a food processor bowl with the steel blade and add to it the flour, salt, butter and lard. Process for 5 seconds, or until the mixture becomes a coarse meal. Run the motor and add the ice water. Process only until the suggestion of a ball is formed. Turn the mass (it will be somewhat shaggy) onto a board and knead about four times with the heel of your hand. Flatten the dough and place it in a plastic bag. ❀ Refrigerate for at least 2 hours or up to 2 days.

Peel and core the apples, slice thin, and cut the slices into thirds. Or, peel the apples, slice and core them with a 20-wedge apple wedger, and cut the slices into thirds. Place in a bowl and add the lemon juice, grated rind, cinnamon and sugar. Mix thoroughly and set aside, covered, for about 1½ hours. ❀

Divide the pastry into 9 equal pieces. Keep the dough you are not working with in the refrigerator. Flour the board lightly and roll out each piece of dough into a circle approximately 7 inches in diameter. The dough should be ⅛ inch thick. Place a 6-inch plate or lid on the dough and, using a sharp knife, cut a circle. Place the circle on a plate and the scraps in a plastic bag and refrigerate both. Continue until 9 circles of dough are cut. Refrigerate each circle as it is made plus the scraps. Then gather all the scraps and make a tenth circle.

•

To fill the turnovers, drain the apple mixture in a colander or a sieve over a bowl and reserve the juices. Use a pastry brush and paint each circle with the apricot glaze, but leave a ¼-inch margin of plain dough. Place about 2 tablespoons of the chopped apples on half of each circle. Use another brush or your fingertip and moisten the margin of the pastry with cold water. Fold the circle over and crimp the edges with a fork. Flip over the pastries and crimp the other side. Place on a cookie sheet lined with parchment paper or brown paper. (A cut-up grocery bag will do very nicely.) Repeat until all the turnovers are made. Brush the tops with the egg-milk glaze and bake in a preheated 425-degree oven for 15 to 20 minutes, or until the turnovers are a rich, golden brown. Remove to a rack to cool. ✿

Melt the butter in a sauté pan and add the remaining apples plus the reserved juices. Cook over high heat for about 5 minutes, stirring. Set aside. ✿

If the turnovers are cold, they can be reheated at 425 degrees for about 10 minutes before serving. If desired, reheat the buttered apples before serving. To serve, place one turnover on each plate, put a dollop of apples beside its straight side, and place a scoop of vanilla ice cream on the buttered apples.

Avocado and Clam Soup

Roast Rolled Loin of Veal Stuffed with Spinach and Sweetbreads

Sautéed Cucumbers

Fennel or Broccoli Timbales

Chocolate-Glazed Chestnut Mousse Cake

•

FIRST COURSE
Clos du Val Cabernet Sauvignon
MAIN COURSE
Château Palmer

$\mathcal{T}$his festive meal is just right for the holidays. Extravagant and immodest, it manages somehow to strike a balance between brazen ostentation and subtle refinement. Guests feel indulged and cosseted while the cook is clearly the marvel of the century. The truth is, no special aptitudes are required, only a bit of courage to take on the initial preparation of the meat.

This spectacular opens with a soup of pale green velvet, a miraculous blend of avocados puréed with minced clams and smoothed with chicken broth and cream, the flavors flowing together into a mellifluous mysterious-

385

ness. The main course, the real production number, consists of that most elegant cut of meat, loin of veal, given its full due. It is boned, stuffed and roasted to a caramel brown on the outside. Sliced, it reveals first a layer of succulent pale meat, then a thin green border of spinach leaves and finally a center of firm, white sweetbreads. This is served with two pale green vegetables whose flavors complement the meat. Most wonderful are sautéed cucumbers, carved into spoon shapes, cooked to the transparency and color of pale jade, but flecked with dark green speckles of minced parsley. Little unmolded timbales round out the course. These are made with fennel — if it is available — or broccoli, in a suspension of bread crumbs, eggs and Parmesan cheese and baked in a *bain marie* until the mixture holds its shape. Dessert is a sumptuous cake consisting of a chestnut mousse in a frame of ladyfingers and glazed with a thin layer of chocolate.

I ask for veal cut from the sirloin or bottom end of the loin. This makes a long, narrow roast that yields smallish slices that look lovely and make the meat go further, a definite advantage considering the price of quality veal. Veal loins usually arrive at supermarkets on specified days of the week and are almost immediately cut up into chops. A roast must be ordered in advance, before such mayhem occurs. Make sure the butcher understands that you want the final weight in boned meat, and if the price includes bones, take them and use them for stock. Supermarket meat attendants can tell you when sweetbreads are expected. They can also cut to order the thin slices of barding fat that must be laid on the veal during its cooking. Specialty butchers are apt to understand exactly what you want and to be able to provide it when you want it, a convenience that does not come cheaply. (I garner a bonus from veal roasts by removing the tenderloin, the thin strip of choice meat that is barely attached to the boned roast. I cut the tenderloin into medallions about three-sixteenths of an inch thick and freeze them. The medallions can be pan fried in butter and a little oil over very high heat and the pan juices deglazed with Madeira, a little veal stock and some cream. Not a bad treat for two people on a dreary winter evening.)

The day before, the sweetbreads are precooked and cleaned and the spinach is blanched. Stuffing and rolling the roast seem to demand the presence of a third hand or a second person to hold the meat closed, but one can solve the problem alone by first sewing the stuffed meat into a rather sloppy roll by holding the meat together with one hand and sewing with the other. Thus both hands are then free to tie the meat tightly and neatly at short intervals, tucking any escaping bits of sweetbreads back into the ends of the meat.

Braised veal can taste boiled and roasted veal can be dry. The road to perfection lies in braising first and then roasting. Braising produces a liquid from the aromatic vegetables, white wine and meat juices that forms the base for a sauce, and the veal is beautifully moist inside. A final hour of roasting seals in this succulence while allowing the outside of the meat to become almost caramelized. The rich pan drippings from the roasting pan are then deglazed with the braising liquid to make the most wonderful of deep brown sauces.

The delicacy and freshness of sautéed cucumbers are perfect for veal. I rid the cucumbers of much of their excess liquid by salting them and of their residual bitterness by blanching them. What remains is pure, undiluted cucumber flavor.

Among the more rewarding objects in my kitchen are a dozen or so little four-ounce porcelain soufflé molds, which can be found most reasonably at close-out shops. These are a nice size for individual timbales that can be prepared well in advance. If you like it, fennel, with its elusive licorice flavor, is a good foil for veal, and this time of year it is available at many specialty markets. Otherwise broccoli is wonderful, available and certainly reasonably enough priced.

That the chestnut mousse cake can be assembled in less than twenty minutes is the least of its virtues. Be sure you buy the chestnut purée that is marked "Chestnut Spread" on one side of the label and *"Crème de Marrons"* on the other. This is imported from France. The ladyfingers, which I buy commercially, should be placed neatly, rounded side out, around the sides of the springform pan, since they will be quite visible when the cake is unmolded. However you fill in the bottom matters not, because the ladyfingers are safely covered with the chestnut mousse.

Avocado and Clam Soup

•

Three	6½-ounce cans minced clams
3	ripe avocados
Three	10¾-ounce cans condensed chicken broth
1¼	cups heavy cream
½	cup milk
	White pepper to taste

In a food processor purée until smooth one can of clams with its liquid with the flesh of one avocado. Empty into a large saucepan and continue with the remaining clams and avocados. Whisk the chicken broth into the mixture, then the cream and the milk. ❊ Heat, season with freshly ground white pepper, and serve.

Roast Rolled Loin of Veal Stuffed with Spinach and Sweetbreads

•

1¼   *pounds veal sweetbreads*
¾   *pound fresh spinach leaves*
3½   *pounds boneless veal loin, cut from*
        sirloin (narrow) end
        Salt, pepper and thyme to season veal
4   *to 5 strips barding fat*
2   *carrots, coarsely chopped*
2   *stalks celery, coarsely chopped*
1   *cup dry white wine*
        10½-ounce can beef bouillon

Soak the sweetbreads for 2 hours under a dripping tap of cold water. Place them in a saucepan, cover with cold water, bring to a simmer, and cook at the simmer for 8 minutes. Place the sweetbreads in a colander, run cold water over them for 10 minutes or until they are cool, and pull off the membranes and gristle surrounding them. Do not be concerned if the lobes are separated in the process. Drain, dry in paper towels, and refrigerate until needed. ❊ The sweetbreads can be prepared to this point a day in advance.

Wash the spinach, trim coarse stems, and blanch the leaves for 1½ minutes in a large pot of boiling water. Immediately drain in a colander and refresh under cold running water. Spread the spinach leaves on about four separate layers of paper towels and place the layers on top of each other. Roll into a package, place in a plastic bag, and refrigerate. ❊ The spinach can be prepared to this point a day in advance.

Spread the veal open, remove the narrow strip of tenderloin, slice thin into medallions, and freeze for another time. Trim the inside of the roast of fat, gristle and membranes and refrigerate until needed.

About 3 hours before the roast is to go into the oven, spread the meat open and cover it with a thick layer of spinach leaves. Arrange the sweetbreads lengthwise down the middle of the meat and season them with salt and pepper. Thread a darning needle with butcher's twine, fold the roast over itself, and sew the roast closed. The roll will be loose. Stuff back into the ends any sweetbreads that may have fallen out. Then tie the roast with twine tightly around its girth at 1-inch intervals to make a compact roll. Also tie twine lengthwise over the ends to hold the stuffing in, again tucking in any rogue sweetbreads as you go along. Rub the roast with salt, pepper and thyme. Place it in a heavy oval casserole, preferably enamel on cast iron, that has a lid and is just large enough to hold the meat. ❀

About 2¼ hours before the veal is to be served, place the casserole, uncovered, in a preheated 500-degree oven for 20 minutes to sear the meat. Remove from the oven, lay the strips of barding fat — overlapping slightly — down the length of the roast, and add the carrots, onions, celery and white wine to the pot. Cover the pot, return it to the oven, and turn the heat down to 350 degrees. Braise the veal in the covered casserole for 40 minutes and remove from oven.

Transfer the meat to a roasting pan with a rack and return to the oven, still at 350 degrees, for 1 hour. Add the beef bouillon to the liquid in the casserole, bring to a boil, stir the brown residue from the sides of the casserole into the liquid, and cook over high heat for 5 minutes. Strain into a saucepan, pressing down on the vegetables to extract all the juices, and set aside. ❀

When the veal has finished roasting, transfer it to a carving board, cover with a tent of foil, and let sit for from 15 to 30 minutes until ready to carve. ❀ Remove the roasting rack and pour the juices from the saucepan into the roasting pan. Bring to a boil and, stirring constantly with a wooden spoon, deglaze the pan, incorporating all the glaze and brown bits into the sauce. Return the sauce to the saucepan and set aside.

To serve, remove all the strings from the veal, including those that were used to sew the meat together. Using a very sharp knife, cut the veal into thin slices and arrange down the center of a serving platter. Use a spatula to serve the veal to keep the sweetbread stuffing in place. Spoon some of the fat off the surface of the sauce, bring the sauce to a boil, and serve with the veal.

Sautéed Cucumbers

•

10 *large cucumbers*
 2 *tablespoons coarse salt*
 6 *tablespoons unsalted butter*
½ *cup minced parsley*
    White pepper to taste

Peel the cucumbers, cut them in half lengthwise, and scoop out all the seeds with a spoon. Cut the cucumbers once more in half lengthwise, to make long quarters, and cut each quarter into thirds. Round the ends of each piece to make a spoon shape and place the pieces in a colander. Coat the cucumbers with the salt and set the colander on a large bowl. Let stand for 2 hours or more while the cucumbers give off excess liquid.

Bring a large pot of water to the boil, add the cucumber pieces, return to the boil, and cook for 3 minutes. Turn out into a colander and refresh under cold running water. Place the cucumbers on a kitchen towel, a handful at a time, pat them as dry as possible, and place in a large sauté pan. Add the butter and cook, stirring frequently, for 5 minutes. Add white pepper to taste and stir in the parsley. ❁ The cucumbers can be completed a few hours in advance and reheated quickly before serving.

Fennel or Broccoli Timbales

MAKES 12 PORTIONS

•

  2 *large fennel bulbs or 1½ pounds broccoli*
 ¼ *cup minced shallots or scallions*
  4 *tablespons butter plus softened butter*
       for twelve 4-ounce soufflé molds
 ¼ *cup minced fennel leaves or parsley*
1¾ *cups fresh homemade bread crumbs*
       plus enough for the soufflé molds
 ½ *cup milk*
 ½ *cup heavy cream*

5   *eggs*
½   *cup grated Parmesan cheese*
    Salt and pepper to taste

Trim the fennel bulbs of coarse outer leaves, quarter, and discard the hard inside cores. Cut the bulbs into eighths and parboil in salted water for 12 minutes. Or, peel the broccoli stems, cut into ¼-inch slices, and parboil for 7 minutes, then add the heads and cook for another 4 minutes. Drain the fennel or the broccoli in a colander, refresh under cold water, and squeeze by the handful to get rid of as much moisture as possible. Chop fine in the processor or by hand.

Sauté the shallots or scallions in butter until soft, but do not let them color. Add the minced fennel or broccoli plus the minced fennel leaves or parsley and cook over low heat for 10 minutes, stirring occasionally.

Combine the bread crumbs, milk and cream in a bowl. Add the eggs and beat with a folk. Stir in the fennel or broccoli mixture, the Parmesan cheese and salt and pepper to taste.

Butter twelve 4-ounce soufflé molds generously, line the bottoms with rounds of waxed paper cut to fit, and butter the waxed paper. Sprinkle the molds with bread crumbs, turning each mold to line it with the crumbs. Fill the molds with the vegetable custard mixture and place them in a shallow roasting pan. ❀   The molds can be covered with a sheet of waxed paper and refrigerated for several hours or overnight.

To cook the timbales, place the roasting pan in a preheated 375-degree oven and pour boiling water into the pan to come a third of the way up the sides of the molds. Bake for 20 to 30 minutes, or until the mixture is firm and has drawn away from the sides. ❀   If the timbales are not to be served immediately, let them sit in the water bath on top of the stove. Run a knife around the insides of the molds, unmold onto a serving platter, and peel off the papers.

Chocolate-Glazed Chestnut
Mousse Cake

•

18 to 20   *ladyfingers (less than 2 packages)*
Two   *17½-ounce cans imported chestnut*

spread (also labeled Crème de
Marrons)

6 tablespoons dark rum, Myers's or Ron
   Negrita
4½ tablespoons cold water
1 tablespoon (1 envelope) plus 2
   teaspoons plain gelatin
1¼ cups heavy cream
1 teaspoon vanilla extract
2 ounces unsweetened chocolate
2 ounces semisweet chocolate
2 tablespoons vegetable oil

Line a 9-inch springform pan 3 inches deep with the ladyfingers, starting with the sides and filling in the bottom of the pan. If necessary, cut up ladyfingers to fill in any spaces on the bottom. Set aside.

Empty the chestnut spread into a mixing bowl and beat with an electric mixer until smooth. Add the rum and beat again until smooth. Place the water in a metal measuring cup and sprinkle the gelatin over it. When the gelatin is soft, place the cup in a small frying pan with an inch of water and heat until the gelatin is dissolved. Remove from heat but allow the cup to remain in the water.

Beat the cream with the vanilla until stiff. Stir the gelatin into the chestnut mixture. Then fold in the whipped cream, being careful to incorporate it well. Pour the mixture into the lined springform pan and refrigerate for a few hours or overnight. ❀

A few hours before serving, remove the sides of the pan. Trim the tops of the ladyfingers flush with the chestnut mousse, using a pair of sharp kitchen shears. Chop the chocolate and combine with the oil in a small, heavy saucepan. Heat, stirring occasionally, over very low heat until the chocolate is just melted. Pour the chocolate over the top of the cake and with a metal spatula guide it across so that some of the chocolate dribbles down the ladyfingers on the sides. Refrigerate until serving. ❀   Slide two long spatulas under the crust so that they cross each other and form an X between the crust and the pan bottom. Lift the cake off onto a serving plate and slide out the spatulas. Slice the cake with a knife that has been dipped into hot water.

Hot (or Iced) Watercress Soup

Rainbow Trout with Wine and Cream Sauce

Tiny Potatoes

Beet, Red Onion and Cherry Tomato Salad

Palm Beach Brownies and Vanilla Ice Cream

•

*Wente Brothers Chardonnay
or Mercurey*

*T*his meal has the polish and grace to mitigate December drears plus the stuff to gratify the soul of an eight-year-old. It begins with an elegant hot watercress soup whose green freshness is enlivened by lovely melting swirls of whipped cream.

Next are small rainbow trout, baked quickly and then masked with a white wine and cream reduction, a delicate sauce worthy of this subtle fish. The trout are accompanied by tiny potatoes and a striking salad made up of three shades of red — beets, baked like potatoes to keep the flavor intense and the texture firm, red onions and whole, skinned cherry tomatoes.

This lovely aura of lightness and sophistication, so painstakingly achieved, is dashed when the ultimate brownie appears for dessert. These are hard-crusted, soft-centered, chewy, fudgy brownies cut into small squares, since a little is a whole lot. To create an illusion of virtue and to defuse accusations that guests are being overfed, vanilla ice cream is scooped into tiny balls piled into a glass bowl and passed with the brownies.

The watercress soup would be appropriate for the most important dinner party, served hot now or cold later on. The watercress, wilted in the flour-butter mixture, retains its bright color, freshness and bite. Despite the addition of flour, the soup has no thickness on the tongue but rather gains the smallest bit of welcome underbody. Because condensed chicken broth is used as the liquid, little (if any) salt is needed, so taste carefully before seasoning. The dollop of whipped cream in each bowl is a visual and gustatory triumph.

It may take some telephoning to find 8- to 10-ounce rainbow trout, but the effort allows you to serve whole fish just right for a single portion. Trout are plentiful in December and make an impressive presentation. They come cleaned with their heads and tails left on. The fins can be snipped off with a pair of kitchen shears.

There is always some last-minute fussing with fish, since it must be cooked just before serving. Check to see whether the fish fit in the baking dish before buttering the pan. Often they take up more space than seems possible, and I occasionally have had to transfer the butter and seasonings to a larger pan. Have the pan with the fish and seasonings prepared in advance. The fish go into the oven before you sit down for the soup — exactly when depends on how cold the fish is, as colder fish take longer to cook. Time this maneuver so that the fish are cooked when the first-course plates are cleared. Then take several minutes in the kitchen to place the fish on a hot serving platter and make the sauce, quickly reducing the pan juices with wine, cream and lemon juice.

The tiny potatoes, carved from larger potatoes, need nothing more than a sprinkling of parsley for color, and are useful for sopping up the delicious sauce. I prefer Red Bliss potatoes for steaming or boiling in winter, since the result is less waterlogged than old white potatoes would be.

The beet, red onion and tomato salad is an excellent accompaniment to the fish, for both the way it looks and the way it tastes. Three people who tried this salad at our house were sure they hated beets, but became converted. Instead of the mushy, watered-down objects they had learned to reject, they found a firm, full-flavored new vegetable.

The secret lies in baking the beets like potatoes. Two hours of baking in a toaster (or conventional) oven and the beets are done to perfection. Once they cool, it's nothing to slip off their skins and slice them.

I prefer beets in the bunch rather than in bulk, since freshness can be gauged by the state of the green tops. However, at this time of year I settle for what I can get. Bunch beets are, of course, easier to come by in late summer or early fall. When you can find them, cut off the stalks well above the beet — it is critical not to cut into the skin of the beets because flavor and color will bleed out — and do not trim the tails until after they are baked. The greens, if in good condition, are delicious cooked according to any simple spinach recipe.

Red onions, with their mildness, are perfect foils for the beets and tomatoes. I use only cherry tomatoes in winter and avoid like the plague large hothouse tomatoes with their spongy texture and plastic nonflavor. Fresh dill, which seems to be on the market most of the year, is ideal with this salad.

The recipe for the brownies comes from *Maida Heatter's Book of Great Chocolate Desserts* with simplified instructions for preparing the pan. Instead of lining the baking pan with foil, I greased it heavily with soft butter and swirled bread crumbs in the pan to coat it thoroughly. Then I turned the pan upside down to get rid of the excess crumbs. I followed her instructions to the letter otherwise, including not letting the chocolate get any hotter than necessary to melt it. The brownies didn't stick and, miracle of miracles, the pan was easy to clean. For the ice cream, a very small oval scoop is an indulgence, but a nice one. These scoops, which are made in Italy, are available in good cookware shops.

Hot (or Iced)
Watercress Soup

•

2	*bunches watercress*
6	*tablespoons butter*
6	*tablespoons flour*
Six	*10¾-ounce cans condensed chicken broth*
2	*egg yolks*
	Salt and pepper

½   cup heavy cream
    Paprika (optional)

Wash the watercress, discard the coarse stalks, and pat or spin dry. Melt the butter in a large saucepan, add the flour, and cook together, stirring constantly, for 1 minute. Add the watercress to the pot and, still stirring, cook until the watercress is wilted. In a food processor fitted with the steel blade purée the mixture until very fine. Stop the motor several times and push the mixture down the sides of the bowl. Return the purée to the saucepan and whisk in the chicken broth, 1 can at a time. Bring the soup to a boil over moderate heat, stirring constantly. Turn off the heat. Beat the egg yolks in a deep bowl. Add 2 large ladlesful of soup, pouring it into the beaten yolks in a thin stream, whisking constantly. Then, in a thin stream, whisk the egg mixture into the saucepan. Stir the soup vigorously for 1 minute. The heat of the soup will cook the eggs. Season carefully with salt (the chicken broth is quite salty) and pepper to taste.✿   The soup can be cooled and held in the refrigerator. If it is to be served hot, reheat it but do not let it come to a boil. Just before serving, whip the cream. Ladle the soup into bowls; top with a healthy dollop of whipped cream and, if desired, a sprinkling of paprika for color.

Rainbow Trout with Wine and Cream Sauce

•

8   small rainbow trout, about 8 to 10
    ounces each, cleaned but with heads
    and tails left on
4   tablespoons softened butter
¼   cup minced shallots or the white part
    of scallions
¼   teaspoon thyme
2   bay leaves
    Salt and pepper

> ¼ pound (1 stick) melted butter
> ½ cup dry white wine
> 1 cup whipping cream
> 1 to 2 teaspoons lemon juice, or more if needed

Wash the trout, snip off the fins with kitchen shears, and pat the fish dry with paper towels. Smear the softened butter over the bottom and sides of a roasting pan or gratin dish large enough to hold the trout in one layer. Measure the pan before buttering to make sure there is room for the fish. Sprinkle the shallots or scallions, thyme and bay leaves over the butter. Place the trout in the pan and season them with salt and pepper. Dribble the melted butter over the fish. ❀ If desired, the fish can be prepared up to this point, covered with plastic wrap and refrigerated for a few hours before cooking.

To cook the fish, place the pan in a preheated 375-degree oven. Bake for 20 minutes if the fish are at room temperature or for 30 minutes if they are cold from the refrigerator. Baste the fish with the butter in the pan at least once during cooking. When the fish are done, remove them to a serving dish. Turn off the oven and place the serving dish in it, leaving the door open. Make the sauce by adding the white wine and cream to the pan and bringing to a boil. Cook, stirring, over moderately high heat, until the wine and cream have reduced and the sauce has thickened somewhat. Add 1 teaspoon lemon juice, taste, and add more if needed. Discard the bay leaves. Remove the serving dish from the oven (use potholders because the platter will be hot), spoon some of the sauce over the fish, and pour the rest of the sauce into a sauceboat.

Tiny Potatoes

•

> 12 medium Red Bliss potatoes
> Salt for the water
> 1 tablespoon minced parsley

Peel the potatoes and cut them into thirds, in chunks. Round off the chunks to make tiny potatoes and drop into a bowl of cold water. When ready to cook, bring a pot of water to a boil, add some salt and the potatoes, and cook for 10 minutes, or until the potatoes are done. Drain and turn out into a serving bowl. Sprinkle with parsley.

Beet, Red Onion and Cherry Tomato Salad

•

4   *medium beets*
1   *large red onion, peeled*
1   *pint ripe cherry tomatoes, blanched in boiling water for 10 seconds and skinned*
4   *tablespoons olive oil*
1   *tablespoon lemon juice*
1   *clove garlic, crushed*
    Salt and pepper to taste
2   *tablespoons minced fresh dill or parsley*

Trim the stalks above the beets, being careful not to cut the skin of the beets. Do not trim the tails. Reserve the greens, if you have these, for another use. Place the beets in a small pan and bake them in a preheated 400-degree oven for 2 hours, or until a sharp, pointed knife pierces the beets easily. Remove and allow to cool at room temperature. Zip the skins off the beets and trim their tops and bottoms. Slice the beets thin and arrange them down one side of a long serving platter.

Slice the red onion thin and arrange down the middle of the platter. Place the tomatoes down the length of the other side of the platter. Combine the oil, lemon juice, garlic, salt and pepper and drizzle over all. ❁ Sprinkle with dill or parsley.

Palm Beach Brownies

MAKES ABOUT 32 SMALL BROWNIES

•

About 2	*tablespoons softened butter*
About ½	*cup fine bread crumbs*
8	*ounces (8 squares) unsweetened chocolate*
½	*pound (2 sticks) unsalted butter*
5	*eggs (graded large or extra large)*
1	*tablespoon vanilla extract*
1	*teaspoon almond extract*
¼	*teaspoon salt*
2½	*tablespoons dry instant powdered coffee, espresso or regular*
3¾	*cups sugar*
1⅔	*cups sifted all-purpose flour*
2	*cups (½ pound) walnuts, chopped very coarsely*

Adjust the rack one-third up from the bottom of the oven and preheat oven to 425 degrees. Heavily butter a 9-by-13-by-2-inch pan and line it with bread crumbs. Make sure every bit of the pan is covered with both butter and bread crumbs.

Melt the chocolate and the butter either in the top of a large double boiler over hot water on moderate heat or in a heavy saucepan over very low heat. Don't let the chocolate get any hotter than necessary to melt it. Stir occasionally until melted. Remove from heat and set aside.

In the large bowl of an electric mixer, beat the eggs with the vanilla, almond extract, salt, dry instant coffee and sugar at high speed for 10 minutes. On low speed add the chocolate mixture and beat only until mixed. Then add the flour and again beat only until mixed. Remove the bowl from the mixer and stir in the nuts. Turn out into the prepared pan and smooth the top with a spatula.

Bake for 35 minutes, reversing the pan front to back as necessary to ensure even baking. At the end of 35 minutes the cake will have a thick, crisp crust on the top, but if you insert a toothpick into the middle it will come out wet and covered with chocolate. Nevertheless it is done. Do not bake it anymore.

Remove the cake from the oven and let it stand on a rack at room temperature until cool. Refrigerate overnight. ❀ To cut the brownies, remove the cake from the refrigerator and let it stand at room temperature for about an hour. Cut the brownies in the pan with a serrated knife into 2- to 2¼-inch squares. Arrange 16 of them on a serving platter and cover with plastic wrap. ❀ Wrap the remaining brownies individually in plastic wrap or waxed paper. Or package them in an airtight container with waxed paper between the layers. Do not let them dry out. These brownies freeze well.

• CHRISTMAS DINNER •

Gravlax with Mustard Dill Sauce or
Walnut Oil Sauce and
Hot Buttered Toast Points

Roast Goose with Apricot-Apple Stuffing

Puréed Celery Root

Watercress Salad

Bûche de Noël and Meringue Mushrooms

•

FIRST COURSE:
Dom Ruinart Champagne
or Hanns Kornell Sehr Trocken
MAIN COURSE:
Sterling Cabernet Sauvignon
or Château Gruaud-Larose

The menu for our Christmas dinner has, over the years, solidified very comfortably.

We start either with a side of smoked Scottish salmon, if somebody has brought one back from London, or with *gravlax*, the glorious Scandinavian cured salmon. My mustard sauce for the *gravlax* is less sweet than most and does not kill the taste of the salmon. It is served from a sauceboat. There is also a walnut oil sauce for those of you who are antimustard. This one is spread thinly on the salmon before serving.

Next comes a crispy roast goose stuffed with dried apricot and apple dressing. The fruit cuts the greasiness of the goose, and the stuffing is both delicious and pretty with its orange flecks of apricot. The only vegetable is a puréed celery root cooked in milk with rice, according to a Michel Guérard suggestion, rather than the more traditional addition of potatoes. The result, an intense, concentrated flavor of celery root, at once smooth and mildly biting, is superb with goose (or with pork).

Those who do not feel a meal is complete without salad may follow the main course with watercress mixed with a light vinaigrette; we save all the room we can for the *bûche de Noël*. This cake, which is traditional among the French at Christmas, is a filled roll decorated to resemble a log. It is usually made with a butter cream, but the recipe here, inspired by the great *pâtissier* Gaston Lenôtre, is filled and iced with a lighter buttery mocha mousse that is still incredibly rich. The log is decorated with charming meringue mushrooms, sprinkled with powdered cocoa to look so real that a friend once volunteered to clean those I had made. I accompany the *bûche* with a mushroom basket — bought for 10 cents from a produce man — filled with additional meringue mushrooms, which can be eaten later before the fire during the present-opening ceremony. The mushrooms look complicated, leading everybody to believe the cook is very clever, although making them is simple.

Gravlax is best made from a fat center piece of very fresh salmon. When this has not been available, I have used frozen, defrosted salmon; while the texture is not quite as firm, the result is not to be sneered at. I bone the salmon myself, which goes quickly when my knife is very sharp. People who work in fish markets exhibit a profligacy that ends up in a loss of much of the salmon along with the bones. It is worth the effort to remove the little bones before the curing process is begun, and much less painful when done with a pair of tweezers or, preferably, pliers, than with the fingers. *Gravlax* must be cured for three days, during which the salmon "cooks" in the salt, sugar and pepper mixture, much as other fish "cook" in lemon or lime juice to become *seviche*. (The mustard dill sauce is also fabulous with herring. I drain the liquid in which the herring bits are packed, rinse the pieces and pat them as dry as I can before I add them to the sauce. This makes a lovely first course by itself or as part of an *hors d'oeuvre variés*.)

I would not buy a goose that weighs more than 11 or 12 pounds, since anything bigger is likely to indicate that the beast is older than the six months of life maximum for it to be edible. Goose, which has a large skeleton and not a whole lot of meat, can be stretched very effectively with a dressing, which adds flavor to the bird as it provides substance to the plate. Most geese are sold frozen, but with a little effort can be found fresh.

All excess fat should be pulled from the cavity, cut into small pieces and rendered slowly with a little water. The fat rendered thus, as well as that rendered during the cooking, will keep for months under refrigeration and is marvelous for cooking. The stock and stuffing can be made the day before, but on no account should the bird be stuffed until just before it goes into the oven.

The *bûche de Noël* offers a marvelous opportunity to use up some of the egg whites that have accumulated in my freezer (see Index). I avoided trying a *bûche* for years because I was certain it would require at least forty days to complete the recipe. Yet once I got to it, it took an hour and a half, not counting the hour the cake sits in the refrigerator before it is iced, and the result is spectacular. The *bûche* will hold for about four days when refrigerated, although it is best the day it is made or the day after. Mushrooms made from cooked meringue hold best and do not sweat. A thermometer that registers instantly, without which no kitchen should be, is useful for checking the temperature of the meringue.

I draw the line at making the marzipan decorations that are traditional with meringue mushrooms on the *bûche*. Marzipan holly leaves and berries and even snowmen can sometimes be found in good kitchenware shops. They can be ordered by mail (see Mail-Order Sources). However, should you not want to go to the bother, the charm of the mushrooms, placed in little groupings as though they are growing out of the log, is charm enough for me.

Gravlax

•

3-pound center piece of salmon
3½ *tablespoons coarse (kosher) salt, or 3*
tablespoons fine salt
1½ *tablespoons sugar*
1½ *teaspoons crushed white peppercorns*
2 *bunches dill, washed and stems lightly crushed*
plus another ½ bunch dill for garnish

Bone salmon by cutting in, along and above the backbone, following as closely as possible the central bone and rib cage. Lift the fillet and set aside. Repeat with other half. Run your fingers down each fillet to locate the remaining little bones. Pull these out either with your fingers or, more easily, with a pair of tweezers or pliers. Trim off the white skin on the inside of each fillet.

Mix the salt, sugar and crushed peppercorns and rub into both sides of each fillet. Line a dish large enough to hold the fish with a generous piece of foil. Using a third of the branches, make a bed of dill on the foil. Lay one fillet, skin side down, on it. Cover the fillet with another third of the dill branches and place the remaining fillet, skin side up, on top. Cover with the remaining dill. Place a second piece of foil on the fish and crimp the edges to the bottom piece of foil to make an envelope. Place a board large enough to cover it on the fish and weight with a brick or two. Refrigerate for 3 days. Once each day, remove the weights and turn the fish over. Weight and refrigerate again. ❀   To serve, unwrap the fish, pat the fillets dry with paper towels, and remove as much of the pepper as possible. Discard the dill. Slice the fillets on the slant into very thin slices, leaving the skin behind. Overlap the slices on a long serving platter or arrange on small individual plates. Garnish with fresh dill. Serve with mustard dill sauce or walnut oil sauce and buttered toast with crusts removed.

Mustard Dill Sauce

MAKES ABOUT 1¼ CUPS

•

4	tablespoons Dijon mustard
1½	teaspoons sugar
2	tablespoons red wine vinegar
1	cup peanut oil
½	bunch dill, minced

Mix mustard, sugar and vinegar in a bowl. Whisking constantly, add the oil slowly. The sauce will be thick and have the consistency of a mayonnaise. Stir in the dill.

Walnut Oil Sauce

•

3   *tablespoons walnut oil*
1   *tablespoon red wine vinegar*
2   *tablespoons capers, drained*

Beat the oil and vinegar together and spoon over the salmon. Rinse the capers in a strainer under cold water, pat dry with a paper towel, and sprinkle over the salmon.

Roast Goose with Apricot-Apple Stuffing

•

11-pound goose, cavity cleaned of lungs and other organs, ready for stuffing, wing tips removed

FOR THE STOCK

Wing tips and neck of the goose, chopped into 1-inch pieces
3   *tablespoons vegetable oil*
2   *onions, cut into small chunks*
2   *carrots, cleaned and cut into small chunks*
1   *bay leaf*
1   *clove garlic, peeled*
Two   *13¾-ounce cans chicken broth*
10½-ounce can beef bouillon

FOR THE STUFFING

Gizzard, liver and heart of the goose
2   *tablespoons butter*
2   *cups minced onions*
1½   *cups minced celery*

1   clove garlic, minced
2   teaspoons chopped leaf sage
1/4   teaspoon thyme
1   cup minced parsley
1/2   cup dry white wine
4   cups peeled and cored Greening or Granny
       Smith apples, chopped coarsely
1 1/2   cups chopped dried apricots
2   cups fresh white bread crumbs, ground
       coarsely in processor
       Salt and pepper
1   egg, beaten

Clean the goose the day before and make a stock by browning the wing tips and pieces of neck in the oil. Then add the onions, carrots, bay leaf and garlic and cook for another few minutes, stirring. Add the chicken broth and beef bouillon, bring to a simmer, and cook, lid slightly askew, for 3 hours. Strain into a bowl, pressing down on the vegetables. Cool the stock and refrigerate. When cold, degrease it.❀   Reserve 3 cups for the gravy and freeze the rest.

·

If desired, the stuffing can be made the day before and refrigerated. Trim the gizzard by removing the skin. Remove the veins and any green parts of the liver. Put the gizzard, liver and heart into the processor and reduce to a fine purée. Melt the butter in a large frying pan, add the onions and celery, and cook for 10 minutes or until transparent. Add the giblet purée and the garlic and cook for another minute or two. Then add the sage, thyme, parsley and wine and cook for another 8 minutes. In a large bowl, combine the apples, apricots and bread crumbs and stir in the cooked mixture. Add salt and pepper to taste and finally stir in the beaten egg. Cool and refrigerate until needed.❀

·

Just before cooking, fill the goose's body and neck cavities with the stuffing, sew up the neck, and truss. Place any excess stuffing in a casserole, cover with foil, and put the lid on. Set aside.

Prick the goose with a sharp-tined fork and place it, breast up, in a roasting pan. Place in a preheated 425-degree oven for 20 minutes, prick the skin again, and reduce heat to 325 degrees. Prick the goose every 20 minutes or so to encourage the fat to drain out. Remove excess fat to a bowl with baster as the goose cooks and save the fat for later use. The goose will probably need to cook for a total of 3 hours, although it should be tested for doneness after 2½ hours. It is done when the legs move easily in the sockets and the juices run yellow, not pink. A meat thermometer inserted in the thickest part of the thigh should read 180 degrees.

Half an hour before the goose is cooked, place the pot of any additional stuffing in the oven. When the goose is removed, raise the heat to 350 degrees and continue cooking while the goose rests and is being carved. Allow the goose to rest for ½ hour before carving. ✹

Drain the fat from the roasting pan and add the 3 cups of reserved stock. Bring to a boil, stirring with a wooden spoon to release any brown baked-on bits, and cook over high heat for about 5 minutes. Pour the juices into a sauceboat.

Puréed Celery Root

•

2 pounds celery root
2 quarts milk
1 cup long-grain rice
   Salt and pepper
½ cup heavy cream

Peel the celery roots and cut them into eighths. Place the milk, rice, salt and pepper in a saucepan and add the pieces of celery root. Bring to a boil, stirring to prevent a scum from forming on the bottom of the pan, lower heat, and simmer, lid slightly askew, for 20 minutes, or until the celery root is tender and the rice cooked. Place a colander in a bowl and drain the celery root-rice mixture in it. Reserve the cooking liquid. In a processor fitted with the steel blade, purée the mixture in several batches for about 4 minutes, adding to each batch a little cream through the funnel. The cream should be thoroughly incorporated. Place the purée in the top of a large double boiler or a pan that can be placed in another pot of hot water. If the purée is very thick, thin it with some of the reserved cooking liquid. Taste for seasoning. ❀   The purée can be made a few hours in advance and reheated over hot water.

Bûche de Noël

•

FOR THE SHEET	*4*	*egg yolks*
CAKE	*⅓*	*cup plus 1 teaspoon granulated sugar*
	½	*cup all-purpose flour*
	3	*egg whites*
	1½	*tablespoons butter, melted and cooled*
	1	*tablespoon Coffee Syrup (recipe follows)*
FOR THE FILLING	*1*	*pound plus 2 tablespoons unsalted butter, softened at room temperature for 1 hour*
AND ICING		
	⅔	*cup Coffee Syrup (recipe follows)*
	3	*egg whites*
	1	*tablespoon granulated sugar*
	1	*scant cup confectioners' sugar sifted together with ½ cup granulated sugar*
	3	*tablespoons unsweetened powdered cocoa*
TO ASSEMBLE		*The sheet cake*
THE *BÛCHE*	*1*	*tablespoon Coffee Syrup (recipe follows)*
		The filling
		The icing
		Meringue Mushrooms (recipe follows)

Line a baking sheet or jelly-roll pan with parchment paper or a rectangle cut from a brown paper bag. Mark a 10-by-12-inch rectangle on the paper.

Combine the yolks and the ⅓ cup sugar in a bowl and beat at medium speed for 3 minutes, or until the mixture is light. Stir in flour. In a clean bowl with clean beaters, beat the egg whites. When they froth, add the remaining teaspoon of sugar and continue beating until stiff but not dry. Stir the melted butter into the egg-yolk mixture and then fold in the egg-white mixture. Using a spatula, spread the batter onto the baking sheet to fit the rectangle. Bake in a preheated 450-degree oven for 7 minutes. Remove from oven and turn the cake out onto the top third of a kitchen towel, paper side up. With a pastry brush dipped in water, wet the paper. After 2 minutes peel off the paper. Cover the cake with the loose part of towel, roll it up tightly within the towel, and set aside to cool.

•

For the filling and icing, beat softened butter at low speed until it is light. Beat in ⅔ cup coffee syrup until mixture is smooth. In a clean bowl with clean beaters, beat the egg whites. When they froth, add the tablespoon of granulated sugar and continue beating until they are stiff but not dry. Fold in the sifted sugar mixture. Then fold this egg-white mixture into the butter-coffee mixture. Set aside three-quarters of the mixture for the filling. Fold the cocoa into the remaining quarter for the icing.

•

Unroll the cake, long end parallel to the edge of the work surface, and brush it with 1 tablespoon of coffee syrup. Spread the filling over the cake, roll it very tightly, and refrigerate for 1 hour. ❀

To decorate, cut a small slice on the diagonal off each end of the cake and place these pieces on the log to simulate cut-off branches. Fit a pastry bag with a ¼-inch open star-shaped nozzle and fill it with icing. Working lengthwise along the log, cover the cake with the icing. The star-shaped nozzle will make the icing look like bark. Pipe icing in circles around the two cut branches and the ends of the log. (Or you can spread the icing on the cake using a spatula and run a fork over it lengthwise to simulate bark.) ❀ The *bûche* can be made at least a day before it is served. Serve on a narrow board or long platter with clusters of meringue mushrooms placed asymmetrically at both ends.

Coffee Syrup

MAKES ABOUT 1 CUP

•

½ *cup sugar*
⅔ *cup water*
3 *tablespoons instant espresso coffee*
    dissolved in 1 tablespoon hot water

Combine the sugar and water, bring to a boil, and stir until the sugar is dissolved. Remove from heat and cool. Stir in the dissolved instant coffee.

Meringue Mushrooms

•

3 *egg whites*
¾ *cup sugar*
1 *teaspoon or more unsweetened powdered*
    cocoa

Line two baking sheets with parchment paper or rectangles cut from a brown paper bag.

Combine egg whites and sugar in a large metal bowl and set over a large pot of boiling water. Do not let the water touch the bowl. Over the heat, beat the mixture constantly with an electric hand mixer until it reaches 120 degrees. Test frequently with an instant thermometer; it will take 8 to 10 minutes. Remove from heat and beat at high speed for 5 minutes more, then at low speed for another 5 minutes. The mixture should be very stiff.

Fit a pastry bag with a ¼-inch plain nozzle and fill with the meringue. Squeeze out fairly flat rounds of the mixture about 2 inches in diameter. With moistened fingers gently flatten the little points on the rounds. These will be the mushroom caps. Make stems by squeezing out the meringue vertically, making each piece 1½ inches tall, ending with pointed tops by pulling up the bag and tube after 1 inch of meringue has been squeezed out. Sprinkle the caps with cocoa. Reserve some uncooked meringue for putting the mushrooms together.

Bake in a preheated 275-degree oven for 40 minutes. Remove and finish constructing the mushrooms by holding a cap in one hand and making a little hole in the flat end with the point of the knife. Then dab a little of the reserved uncooked meringue onto the hole and insert the pointed end of the stem into the cap. Set the mushrooms on their sides on the baking sheets and bake for another 10 minutes at 275 degrees. The mushrooms should be crisp on the outside and soft inside. Meringue mushrooms will hold for a day at least either in an airtight container or in a turned-off oven with a pilot light. ❀

The log should be decorated with the mushrooms no more than an hour or two before serving. ❀ Use 9 or 10 of them to decorate the log and pass the remaining ones separately in a tissue-lined mushroom or other basket.

• COCKTAIL PARTY FOR TWENTY-FOUR •

Herring-Stuffed Tiny Potato Halves

Marinated Brussels Sprouts with Prosciutto

Bratwurst and Apple Phyllo Rolls

Tomato and Anchovy Puff-Pastry Pizzas

Bolivian Cheese Turnovers

Brandade de Morue

•

*C*hristmas week is the time for entertaining with panache, for sharing the groaning board and for gathering friends together, preferably en masse, just for the sheer joy of it. A perfect medium for such largesse is the cocktail party — not the run-of-the-mill celery-sticks-with-curry-dip gathering but one that offers to the ones brought together inventive, imaginative and delicious foods.

The choices for this cocktail party consist of six finger foods, none of which are apt to turn up on the regular social circuit. Two are served at room temperature. First are tiny red potatoes cooked, halved, scooped out, filled with minced herring with sour cream and sprinkled with dill or parsley. Next is a fabulous dish created by William Rice, little Brussels sprouts steamed, marinated and wrapped with strips of prosciutto.

The four hot foods have advantages critical to a cocktail party. They are convenient to heat, are as good warm as hot and, most important, remain eminently edible even in the unlikelihood that they languish on a tray. If you have only one oven, bake the *phyllo* rolls and pizzas first at 350° degrees, then turn up the oven to 450° for the turnovers.

All of these dishes can be made in advance and assembled well before guests descend. Of course, there is no rule against embellishing this spread with more familiar cocktail party foods such as good cheeses, Marinated Olives (see June, Provisioning the Pantry), tiny sugarless cream puff shells filled with chicken or shrimp salad or even a platter of slices of homemade bread spread with good butter.

The *phyllo* rolls and turnovers freeze well and therefore can be made weeks ahead of time. Combining delicately flavored, good-quality bratwurst and apples seasoned with *quatre épices* gives the *phyllo* rolls an unexpected dash that recalls *boudin blanc* (the French white sausage traditional at this time of year) without the work of making your own sausage. Making *quatre épices* is simply a matter of putting together white pepper, ginger, nutmeg, allspice and cloves. The mixture keeps well in a tightly covered jar and is a delicious flavoring for pâtés and terrines, fresh ham and roast pork.

Phyllo is much easier to work with if unused pastry is kept covered with a damp kitchen cloth each time a sheet is removed from the stack. I use a goose feather — available at kitchenware shops — to butter the phyllo strips since anything coarser can wrinkle or even break the pastry. One friend uses fingers to equal advantage. Fresh *phyllo* tends to be less dry than frozen. Either will work, but since the frozen phyllo might crumble, you can count on some waste. Any remaining *phyllo* can be wrapped tightly and refrozen, although I prefer to augment the recipe and keep excess frozen rolls on hand.

The idea for the puff-pastry pizzas, an all-time favorite of my husband's, came from Elaine Kurtz, a painter, friend and cook who consistently produces inventive dishes with a minimum of fuss. The pizzas are easily assembled from premade puff pastry, found in supermarket frozen food cases. The defrosted pastry is rolled out and cut into strips using a knife against a ruler. The sides of the strips are slightly crimped before they are filled. This results in uniformly crisp slices that do not flop, a boon at a cocktail party. The light freshness of the filling comes from thinly sliced cherry tomatoes — the only kind worth buying in winter — dressed with *herbes de Provence,* a little olive oil and a bit of anchovy. Specialty food shops sell the *herbes* in pretty unglazed crocks and in less expensive bags. Experimenting can only lead to still other great toppings, although I would avoid cheese, which can add a leaden quality. The pastry strips can be assembled several hours before they are baked and refrigerated, with the finished product arranged on a large tray and cut into one-inch slices with a pizza cutter for serving

Brandade de morue, the feathery Provençal concoction of soaked salt cod, garlic, oil, cream, lemon juice and mashed potatoes, can be made the day before the party. The cod is put to soak a day or two before that. The food processor can accomplish the bulk of the recipe. But it's necessary to beat in the baked potato pulp with an electric mixer, since the processor turns potatoes into glue. (Any leftover *brandade* can become delicious codfish cakes. For each cup of *brandade*, add half a cup of freshly mashed potatoes, half a minced onion cooked until soft and transparent in a little butter plus a beaten egg. The mixture is chilled and then dropped by tablespoons into a frying pan covered with a thin layer of hot oil. The cakes are flattened with a spatula and fried until browned, about three to four minutes per side.)

The little potatoes can be steamed or boiled and should not be overcooked. The herring for the filling must be well drained and dried before it is minced and mixed with the sour cream. Brussels sprouts are increasingly available in bulk, so it is possible to choose uniformly small ones. The sherry vinegar is a lovely addition to the marinade.

Herring-Stuffed
Tiny Potato Halves

MAKES 48

•

24	*small red potatoes, about 1½ inches in diameter, scrubbed but unpeeled*
Two	*8-ounce jars herring bits in white wine*
½	*cup sour cream*
3	*tablespoons minced dill or parsley*

Cook potatoes in boiling salted water or steam them over salted water for about 15 minutes or until just tender but not mushy. Drain and cool. ✿ The potatoes can be cooked a day in advance.

Turn contents of the herring jars into a strainer and discard the onions and liquid. Pat the herring pieces dry between paper towels and mince the herring into a ⅛-inch dice. Stir in the sour cream.

Cut each potato in half and if necessary cut a thin slice off the bottoms so the potato halves will stand, cut side up. Scoop out some of the flesh with a melon baller and discard the extra flesh. Fill the hollows with the herring mixture and sprinkle the potatoes with minced dill or parsley. Refrigerate, covered with plastic wrap, ✿ but bring to room temperature before serving.

Marinated Brussels Sprouts
with Prosciutto

MAKES 48

•

48 *small Brussels sprouts (about 1¾ to 2 pounds)*
1 *bay leaf*
1 *teaspoon thyme*
Juice of 1 lemon
1 *tablespoon sherry wine vinegar*
5 *drops hot pepper sauce*
Pinch of salt
Pepper to taste
⅓ *cup olive oil*
16 *thin slices prosciutto, each cut into thirds lengthwise.*

Wash the sprouts, trim the bottoms, and cut an X in the exposed base. Steam over boiling water, to which the bay leaf has been added, for about 12 minutes, or until tender but firm when tested with a sharp, pointed knife.

While the sprouts are cooking, mix thyme, lemon juice, sherry vinegar, hot pepper sauce, salt, pepper and oil in a bowl large enough to hold the sprouts. Place the hot sprouts in the bowl, toss with the marinade, and cool. Cover and refrigerate overnight. ✤

To serve, bring the sprouts to room temperature, drain them, wrap a strip of prosciutto around each sprout, and fasten with a toothpick. The sprouts can be assembled several hours in advance, covered with plastic wrap and refrigerated. ✤   They should be brought to room temperature before serving.

Bratwurst and Apple Phyllo Rolls

MAKES 48

•

4   *bratwurst sausages (preferably Usinger's)*
1   *tablespoon butter*
2   *medium Greening or McIntosh or*
       Granny Smith apples
1   *teaspoon lemon juice*
¼   *teaspoon* Quatre Épices *(recipe follows)*
12   *sheets fresh or defrosted* phyllo *dough*
       (about ½ pound)
½   *pound melted butter*

Trim the ends of each bratwurst and cut each sausage into three 2-inch pieces. Cut each of these pieces into quarters, lengthwise. Peel off the casing and discard. Melt the tablespoon of butter in a frying pan and brown the bratwurst pieces quickly on all sides. Set aside and let cool.

Peel, core and finely mince the apples and stir in the lemon juice and the *quatre épices*, making sure the apples are well coated.

Cut the sheets of *phyllo* lengthwise into quarters, to make four strips each about 4 inches wide. Place one strip on a lightly dampened cloth and cover the other pieces with another lightly dampened cloth to keep them from drying out. Brush the strip with melted butter and place a piece of bratwurst across the bottom of the strip, about an inch from the edge, along with a teaspoon of the apple mixture. Roll the strip twice to enclose the filling, then fold the long edges of the dough toward the center to enclose the filling at the sides. Finish rolling the strip and place the roll, seam side down, on a jelly-roll pan lined with waxed paper if the rolls are being made in advance and are to be frozen. Continue with the remaining strips until all the rolls are made. Freeze flat and decant into heavy plastic bags. ❋

   To bake, place the unthawed rolls on a jelly-roll pan, seam side down, and bake in a preheated 350-degree oven for about 30 minutes, or until golden brown. Unfrozen rolls need 15 to 20 minutes in a 350-degree oven. Serve hot.

Quatre Épices

MAKES 5 TEASPOONS

•

1   *tablespoon ground white pepper*
3/4 *teaspoon ground ginger*
3/4 *teaspoon ground nutmeg*
3/4 *teaspoon ground allspice*
     Pinch ground cloves

Mix spices well and store in an airtight jar.

Tomato and Anchovy Puff-Pastry Pizzas

MAKES ABOUT 80 PIECES

•

17¼-ounce package frozen puff pastry, defrosted
About 36 cherry tomatoes (almost 2 pints), thinly sliced crosswise

1   *tablespoon* herbes de Provence *or oregano*

4   *tablespoons olive oil*

Four   *2-ounce cans flat anchovy fillets,*
    drained, with fillets halved lengthwise

Roll out each sheet of puff pastry on a lightly floured board to measure 11 by 16 inches. Cut each sheet into eight 2-by-11-inch strips. Place the strips on jelly-roll pans and with fingers crimp up the edges slightly. Arrange a row of cherry tomato slices down the center of each strip and sprinkle them with the *herbes de Provence* or oregano. Drizzle the oil on the tomatoes. Arrange the anchovy halves on the zigzag down each strip. ❋   The strips can be assembled a few hours before they go into the oven and refrigerated. Bake in a preheated 350-degree oven for 35 to 40 minutes, or until the strips are puffed and brown. Cut each strip into pieces about 1 inch wide. Serve hot.

Bolivian Cheese Turnovers

MAKES ABOUT 44

· •

FOR THE FILLING   12   *ounces small-curd cottage cheese*
    (about 1⅓ cups)

    ½   *teaspoon salt*

    ¼   *cup flour*

    ¼   *teaspoon cayenne pepper*

    5   *scallions, both green and white parts,*
    finely minced

    4   *tablespoons minced cilantro (also*
    called fresh coriander or Chinese
    parsley), or dill or parsley

    1   *egg yolk, beaten*

FOR THE DOUGH   1½   *scant teaspoons (½ envelope) active dry yeast*

    ½   *cup warm water*

    2   *tablespoons butter, at room*
    temperature

½   teaspoon salt
1   teaspoon sugar
1½ cups all-purpose flour
1   egg white, lightly beaten

Prepare the filling by combining all the filling ingredients and beating them until creamy. Set aside.

To make the dough, dissolve the yeast in the water in a large bowl. Stir in the butter, salt, sugar and flour. Knead by hand or with a dough hook about 10 minutes, or until the dough springs back to the touch and loses its stickiness. Pinch off pieces of dough the size of a small egg and stretch into strips ¾-inch in diameter. Cut the strips into ¾-inch pieces and roll into balls. Flatten each ball with the palm of the hand and roll out with a rolling pin into 2½-inch to 3-inch circles. Place about ¾ teaspoon of filling on half of each circle. Moisten the edges with a bit of cold water, fold, and press edges firmly together. Brush the tops with the beaten egg white and place on a buttered jelly-roll pan. Allow to rise until light to the touch, about 1 hour, and brush the tops again with the egg white.

Bake in a preheated 450-degree oven for about 12 to 15 minutes, or until well browned. If the turnovers are to be frozen, prebake them at 450 degrees for 8 minutes and let them cool. Arrange them on a waxed-paper-lined jelly-roll pan, freeze, place in heavy plastic bags. ❁   To finish cooking the frozen turnovers, place them on a jelly-roll pan and allow them to defrost for about 20 minutes. Then bake at 450 degrees for about 10 minutes, or until they are well browned. Serve hot.

Brandade de Morue

MAKES ABOUT 3½ CUPS

•

1   pound salt cod
1   onion, quartered
½   teaspoon thyme
¾   cup full-flavored olive oil

2   *large cloves garlic, peeled and crushed*
     Grated rind of ½ lemon
     Juice of ½ lemon
¾   *cup heavy cream*
     White pepper to taste
¾   *cup warm baked potato pulp (1 large*
     potato)
12 *slices firm-textured white bread, crusts*
     removed, toasted and each slice cut
     into four triangles

Wash the cod, cut it into chunks about 4 or 5 inches long, set into a colander, and place the colander with the fish in a large bowl of cold water. Keep the bowl with the submerged cod in the refrigerator for at least 24 hours and change the water five or more times. Do not let the cod touch the bottom of the bowl.

To poach the soaked cod, bring 6 cups of water to the simmer with the onion and thyme and cook for 5 minutes. Add the cod, return the liquid to a bare simmer, and cook over low heat for 10 minutes. Drain the fish in a colander and let it cool. Discard any dark bits along with the pieces of skin and bones. Pat the fish dry between paper towels and put it in a saucepan with ¼ cup of the olive oil. Place the pan over moderate heat and cook for about 5 minutes, stirring with a wooden spoon to break up the fish. Transfer to a food processor fitted with the steel blade and add the crushed garlic, lemon rind and lemon juice. Run the motor for about 20 seconds and, with the motor still running, slowly add through the feed tube the remaining ½ cup of olive oil, the cream and the white pepper. Process for an additional 10 seconds, or until the mixture is fluffy. Turn out into a mixing bowl, add the warm potato pulp, and beat with a hand electric mixer until the potato is incorporated into the fish and the mixture has the texture of whipped potatoes.❁

The *brandade* can be prepared a day in advance and reheated over hot water in the top of a double boiler. Fluff the hot *brandade* with a fork and turn it out in a mound onto a platter. Surround with crustless toast triangles.

January

PROVISIONING·THE·PANTRY

This savory Indian lemon pickle is delicious with curries and cold meats. The recipe can be doubled and the pickle decanted into ½-pint jars. It keeps under refrigeration indefinitely and makes wonderful gifts.

Lemon Pickle

MAKES ABOUT 2 CUPS

•

2	*large or 3 small lemons (about ½ pound)*
1	*tablespoon coarse salt*
2	*large garlic cloves, crushed*
½	*cup raisins*
1	*teaspoon ground cumin*
1	*teaspoon cayenne pepper*
2	*slices fresh ginger, each the size of a quarter, minced*
1½	*tablespoons mustard seed*
1	*cup distilled white vinegar*
1	*cup sugar*

Cut the lemons lengthwise into quarters but do not sever them at the base. Seed the lemons and sprinkle them with salt. Let them sit in a bowl in the refrigerator for 3 days, turning them as often as you remember. At the end of the third day, add the garlic, raisins, cumin, cayenne, ginger, mustard seed and vinegar and return to the refrigerator for another 24 hours, turning the mixture occasionally.

Strain the liquid into a heavy saucepan. Mince the lemons and raisins in a food processor fitted with the steel blade. Add this to the saucepan along with the sugar and bring to the boil, stirring. Cook over moderate heat, stirring occasionally, for about 35 minutes, or until the liquid reduces and the mixture thickens. Cool and refrigerate.

Beef, Barley and Vegetable Soup

Very Lemony Roast Chicken

Avocado, Artichoke and Mushroom Salad

Bread and Butter Pudding

•

Fetzer "Lake County" Zinfandel
or Beaujolais-Villages

*A*fter the holidays, when everyone is tired of overeating and fancy cooking, it is time to sit down with good friends to a cozy meal of unexotic, nourishing nursery food. Enough of fancy, convoluted combinations, at least for a while.

A perfect, simple meal starts with a substantial but not thick-on-the-tongue beef, barley and vegetable soup that has a rich brown broth studded with carrots, peas and bits of beef marrow adding body but not complicating the taste. Next comes a light course of crispy-skinned, moist, pleasantly tart roast chickens prepared by tucking lemon slices and garlic slivers between the flesh and the skin and basting while they roast with flavored or plain olive oil. The meat inspires enthusiasm even in those who are at best indifferent to this bird. It is accompanied only by a salad, but one of some interest — ripe avocados, artichoke hearts and raw mushrooms served on individual plates in cups of Boston lettuce. The meal ends with the gross satisfaction of a soothing custardy bread and butter pudding, fragrant with vanilla and Mandarine liqueur or rum-soaked golden raisins.

The soup can be made in advance and, in fact, improves with a little age. Soup meat is desirable because it can be cooked long without getting stringy and adds a gelatinous richness that fancier, more expensive cuts cannot. Marrow bones are often available at supermarket meat counters (I hoard them in the freezer until I need them) or from butchers, and are preferable to plain soup bones because they yield the marrow to enrich the final product. While the soup requires three hours of cooking, it demands little attention once the meat is cut up and browned with the bones. I dice the vegetables when the water goes in, but do not add them until later. An envelope or two of powdered concentrated bouillon, which I prefer to cubes because it is less salty, can reinforce the depth of flavor, but this is usually not necessary.

Since the flavor has carefully been bred out of chickens, the constant challenge is to make them taste like something. You are one step ahead if the chicken you buy has never been encased in a plastic bag. The combination of lemon and garlic suggests a solution, yet even great quantities of these stuffed in the cavity only hint at the possibilities. Nor has basting with lemon juice been the answer. This time I loosened the skin (which can be done amazingly easily) and slipped lemon slices and garlic slivers directly onto the flesh throughout the body. This turned out to be a wonderful way to cook chicken. The meat becomes fragrant and moist and permeated with a lemony freshness. The peeled lemon slices disappear with cooking, while the garlic slivers become buttery soft in texture and taste.

The unpeeled garlic cloves that cook in the cavity are used later to flavor the sauce. For this it is worth the little effort to make a stock of the giblets and wing tips. The chicken is basted with olive oil (the best green extra-virgin quality) or with a flavored olive oil. I first made one up for presents for Christmas, with fresh herbs from summer dried on the branch. A nice combination turned out to be wild fennel stalks, thyme, rosemary and savory, along with a few unpeeled garlic cloves (see July, Provisioning the Pantry).

Chickens should be roasted in a hot oven. Cooking them at low temperatures results in soggy, steamed birds.

The frozen artichokes for the salad should be cooked in advance so they have time to cool. Canned artichoke hearts can be used, but they must be rinsed well and drained. The salad itself can be made at least an hour before guests arrive. Avocados, which are plentiful and reasonably priced this time of year, are ripened in a brown paper bag, but their progress must be checked every day; otherwise you can end up with a soggy sack. The mushrooms should be wiped clean with a damp paper towel, never soaked in water, which makes them unpleasantly spongy. Iceberg lettuce is not an acceptable substitute for Boston lettuce or, for that matter, any other kind of lettuce.

Bread and butter pudding is a simple, much-loved dessert, but because it has no pretensions to grandeur it appears infrequently at dinner parties. Too bad. Bread and butter pudding can be brought to blissful heights, especially when it is made with homemade bread. I commend the recipe included here for buttery white bread, which is also delicious with a ripe Brie or a mild liver pâté. This bread is foolproof and easy to make with a heavy-duty mixer and dough hook. However, the pudding need not be sneered at when it is made with a decent-quality thin-sliced commercial bread. The pudding is best made the day before or the morning of the party.

It is possible to avoid the potential mess of buttering bread on both sides. Simply butter one side, place it in the pan buttered side down and then do the other side. If you use an oval gratin dish rather than a rectangular pan, the bread will have to be trimmed and fussed with to cover the surface. You want as tight a fit as possible. The dish should be at least two inches deep to accommodate three layers of bread.

Beef, Barley and Vegetable Soup

•

2	pounds beef marrow bones
1	pound soup meat (boiling beef)
2	tablespoons vegetable oil
2	quarts water
1	tablespoon salt
	Freshly ground pepper to taste
6	tablespoons pearl barley, rinsed in a sieve under cold water
1	cup carrots in 1/4-inch dice
1/2	cup celery in 1/4-inch dice
1/2	cup onion in 1/4-inch dice
1/4	cup minced parsley
1	cup frozen peas
1 to 2	beef bouillon cubes or packets of powdered bouillon (optional)

Wash the marrow bones and pat them dry. Cut the meat into ¼-inch cubes and brown bones and meat in hot oil in a large pot. Add the water, salt and pepper, cover tightly, and simmer for 1 hour. Add the barley and cook for 1 hour more. Remove the bones from the soup with a slotted spoon and remove the marrow. Return the marrow to the pot and discard the bones. Add the carrots, celery, onion and parsley and cook slowly for 45 minutes more. Add the peas and cook an additional 15 minutes. Taste for seasoning. If the soup is too thick, add a little more water and powdered concentrated bouillon or a bouillon cube, if necessary, to strengthen the flavor.✿   The cooled soup can be refrigerated a day in advance and reheated.

Very Lemony Roast Chicken

•

Two   3½-pound chickens

FOR THE STOCK	*1*	*tablespoon vegetable oil*
		Wing tips, necks and giblets of two 3½-pound chickens, hacked into smallish chunks
	1	*carrot, scraped and cut into chunks*
	1	*onion, peeled and cut into chunks*
	1	*stalk celery, washed and cut into chunks*
	1	*bay leaf*
		Pinch of thyme
		Salt and pepper
		10¾-ounce can condensed chicken broth
	4	*cups water*
FOR ASSEMBLY	*2*	*large lemons*
	8	*cloves garlic, peeled and thinly sliced*
	20	*cloves garlic, unpeeled*
		Salt and pepper
	½	*cup or more flavored olive oil (see July,*

Provisioning the Pantry) or plain
olive oil, for basting the chickens
2½ *cups homemade stock (above) or*
chicken broth
2 *sprigs fresh rosemary, or ¼ teaspoon*
dried rosemary

Pull out the lungs and other organs from the cavities of the chicken, along with any pieces of loose fat. Reserve the livers for another use. Cut off the wing tips.

Make stock by heating the oil in a saucepan and adding the necks, giblets, wing tips and vegetables. Brown over high heat, stirring constantly. Add the bay leaf, thyme, pepper, a little salt, the chicken broth and the water. Cover, leaving lid slightly askew, and simmer over a low flame for about 1½ hours.

Remove the yellow part of the peel from the lemons, using a potato peeler or a zester. Blanch the peel for 3 minutes in a quart of boiling water. Turn out into a colander, refresh under cold water, and set aside. Cut away every bit of white pith from the lemons and slice them as thin as possible. Remove the seeds. Turn the first chicken breast side up. Run your fingers between the body and the skin. Separate the skin if it adheres, usually at the breastbone, by cutting with scissors close to the flesh so as not to pierce the skin. Work the skin loose as far down as the drumsticks. Repeat on second chicken. Distribute the lemon slices and the slices of garlic under the skins of both chickens at even intervals. Place some salt and pepper and half the blanched peel plus 10 unpeeled garlic cloves into each cavity. Truss the chickens and brush them all over with the flavored or plain olive oil. ❁

•

Roast the chickens for about 65 minutes in a preheated 425-degree oven. Place them on a roasting rack in a pan on one of their sides and roast for 15 minutes. Baste with oil and turn them breast down. Roast for another 15 minutes, baste again (this time using oil from the bottom of the pan if there is enough), and turn them on their other sides. After 15 more minutes, baste again and turn them on their backs, breast side up. Roast for an additional 20 minutes, basting once again after 10 minutes. The chickens are done when a thermometer inserted in the thickest part of the thigh reads 165 degrees. They may need an additional 5 minutes of roasting. Remove the chickens from the oven when they are done. Remove the trussing strings and scoop out the unpeeled garlic cloves from the cavities. Place the chickens on a platter and cover them loosely with a foil tent.✿   They should sit for 10 to 15 minutes before carving.

Remove the rack from the pan and add the unpeeled garlic cloves and the rosemary. Strain the stock into the pan, or use 2½ cups of any chicken broth. Bring to a boil, scrape the brown bits from the pan and cook over high heat for about 5 minutes. Press down on the garlic cloves and keep stirring. Strain the sauce into another saucepan and degrease. Taste for salt and pepper.✿   When the chicken is carved, reheat the sauce and serve separately.

Avocado, Artichoke and Mushroom Salad

•

1	teaspoon Dijon mustard
	Salt and pepper to taste
2	tablespoons red wine vinegar
½	cup olive oil
	Pinch of herbes de Provence or other herbs (optional)
3	ripe avocados
	9-ounce package frozen artichoke hearts, cooked, drained, cooled and quartered or 14-ounce can artichoke hearts, rinsed under cold running water, drained well, squeezed gently and quartered
½	pound mushrooms, cleaned and thinly sliced
2	stalks celery, cleaned and chopped
3	tablespoons minced parsley
1	head Boston lettuce

Make a vinaigrette in a large mixing bowl by combining the mustard, salt, pepper and vinegar and then slowly whisking in the olive oil. Add, if desired, the *herbes de Provence* or other herbs.

One by one, peel and pit the avocados and cut them, in ¾-inch dice, directly into the vinaigrette. Stir gently to cover the pieces with the dressing to prevent them from discoloring but be careful not to break them. Add the artichoke hearts, sliced mushrooms, chopped celery and parsley and toss carefully.✿ Just before serving, arrange cups of Boston lettuce on individual salad plates and divide the salad among the lettuce cups.

Bread and Butter Pudding

•

2	*tablespoons softened butter for the pan*
⅔	*cup seedless golden raisins*
¼	*cup dark rum or Mandarine liqueur (or substitute Golden Raisins Macerated in Mandarine, drained; see February, Provisioning the Pantry)*
18	*thin slices homemade bread such as Buttery White Bread (recipe follows) or commercial thin-sliced white bread (1 loaf plus 2 or 3 slices more), crusts removed*
½	*pound (2 sticks) unsalted butter, softened for an hour at room temperature*
4	*eggs*
3	*egg yolks*
⅔	*cup sugar*
3	*cups milk*
2	*tablespoons vanilla extract*
	Pinch of salt

Butter a 2-quart baking dish, if possible a rectangular dish 10½ by 7 by 2 inches. Set aside. Combine the raisins with the rum in a small saucepan, heat, stir, and set aside for 15 minutes. If macerated raisins are used, drain and set aside.

Lightly butter each slice of bread on both sides. Fit 6 slices on the bottom of the baking dish, strew half the raisins over this, add a second layer of 6 slices, strew the remaining raisins over this, and top with the last 6 slices of bread. Make a custard by beating together the eggs and egg yolks, sugar, milk, vanilla and pinch of salt. Pour this over the bread and set aside for 30 minutes, or until the bread has absorbed the custard.

Meanwhile bring a kettle of water to a boil and preheat the oven to 350 degrees. Place the baking dish in a large roasting pan and put this in the oven. Pour boiling water into the roasting pan to come halfway up the side of the baking dish. Bake for 60 minutes at 350 degrees, or until the top is golden yellow with small brown areas and slightly crusty. Remove, let cool, and refrigerate.❀   The pudding is best made a day or half a day ahead. Bring to room temperature before serving.

Buttery White Bread

2 LOAVES

•

Softened butter for the bread pans
4   *tablespoons (4 envelopes) active dry*
      yeast
2   *cups warm water*
6   *cups bread flour*
1   *teaspoon salt*
3   *tablespoons sugar*
3   *tablespoons butter, softened*
1   *lightly beaten egg, for glaze*

Butter two 9-by-5-by-3-inch bread pans and set aside.

Place the yeast in mixing bowl and add the warm water. Let sit for 5 minutes until the yeast starts to work. Add the flour, salt and sugar and mix into a dough, using a dough hook on a heavy-duty mixer if possible, or a wooden spoon and then hands. Add the butter and knead for 10 minutes or until the dough is smooth and elastic. Place in a clean bowl, dust lightly with flour, cover with a dish towel, and let rise in a warm place until doubled in bulk, about 1 hour. Punch the dough down, knead it for another minute or so, and let it rise again for about 45 minutes, or until almost doubled.

Cut the dough in half and shape into loaves to fit the pans. Place each loaf in a pan and brush the tops with beaten egg. Bake in a preheated 400-degree oven for 30 to 35 minutes, or until the tops are golden brown and the bread sounds hollow when removed from the pan and tapped. Cool. This bread is excellent for bread and butter pudding, with cheeses and with pâtés.

*Pot-au-Feu Bouillon with Sliced Marrow
and Tiny Cooked Pasta*

*Pot-au-Feu of Brisket, Chicken and
Stuffing, with Leeks, Parsnips, Carrots,
Turnips and Potatoes*

Green Sauce and Horseradish Sauce

Cornichons and Mustards in Variety

Chocolate Pots de Crème

•

*Beaune "Cuvée de l'Enfant Jésus"
or Moulin-à-Vent*

Here is food to place before guests in January, a meal that is soothing, uncomplicated, wholesome and deeply satisfying — as it should be after the holiday assault on the digestive system.

It consists of a *pot-au-feu* — a boiled dinner that provides a whole meal out of one pot. The first course is a clean-tasting soup embellished with sliced beef marrow and tiny cooked pasta. Next are mildly garlicky boiled beef and chicken, a *poule au pot*, which have contributed body to the soup. Surrounding the meats are slices of the chicken's aromatic stuffing and solid, unpretentious winter root vegetables, lightly cooked and deliciously permeated with the stock in which they have simmered. The mercifully bland meats are given a little character by two sauces: a green sauce whose piquancy is smoothed with the addition of a boiled potato, and a delicate horseradish sauce. To help the meats further along are *cornichons,* those lovely little sour French gherkins found in specialty food stores, and mustards, a variety of them if desired. Rather than fruit for dessert, which would introduce an unwanted acidity, there are chocolate *pots de crème,* whipped up in one minute flat in a blender and with a texture and flavor that suggest hours of fussing over a hot stove. The *pots de crème* are made from a recipe of undetermined origin that swept the country a couple of decades ago. It deserves to be resurrected.

The *pot-au-feu* recipe is long-winded, but don't be discouraged; it produces a first course, the main dish and the accompanying vegetables. It is simplicity itself to prepare and demands little attention during its cooking. The only special equipment needed is a *large* stockpot, specifically 16 quarts or more in capacity. Once acquired, the invaluable large stockpot becomes one of the most used utensils in the kitchen.

The *pot-au-feu* is based on a brown stock that is made a day or two in advance, or even weeks earlier if it is stored in the freezer. (It is possible, although less desirable in terms of both quality and economy, to substitute canned chicken broth and beef bouillon in equal quantities for the stock.) The stock gains much of its strength from marrow bones, which also yield the marrow that garnishes the first-course soup. Some cooks tie the browned marrow bones in cheesecloth when they go into the stockpot to keep the marrow from slipping out. I do not bother with this step, since in my experience most of the marrow stays in the bones where it belongs, even after long cooking. Any truant pieces are scooped out when the stock is strained through cheesecloth. Marrow bones can frequently be found in supermarket meat counters. I buy them when I find them and freeze them until they are needed.

The brown stock can also be made on its own for other purposes, in which case an additional 3-pound piece of boiling beef would be browned with the bones and cooked in the stock. The finished stock can then be frozen, ready for use to great advantage in other recipes calling for beef bouillon or stock and far superior to the canned counterpart.

My own preference for soup pasta is the tiny *orzo,* which looks like grains of rice and unexpectedly and delightfully is not. The pasta can be cooked several hours in advance and set aside.

Almost any boneless beef can be used for *pot-au-feu,* but the boiling cuts are more satisfactory, since they dry out least and hold together best. Bottom round, chuck and brisket are all excellent; I prefer brisket for its texture and lack of gristle. The garlic slivers add a delicate flavor to the beef and do not overpower it.

I sneak a chicken into my *pot-au-feu* for the flavor, color and texture it adds. My treatment of the chicken is as for a traditional *poule au pot*, with its parsley-flecked, allspice-perfumed stuffing. The chicken is cooked whole and trussed well. (The directions for trussing a bird in *Mastering the Art of French Cooking*, Volume I, are clear and easy to follow.) The chicken goes into the pot an hour and a half after the beef has been cooking and is carved and placed on the same platter with the meat. The stuffing has enough density so that it can be plucked out whole, but it helps to cut an opening in the carcass with a pair of kitchen shears. The serving platter of meats should be basted liberally with the soup in which they have been cooked. It is amazing how quickly boiled meats can become dry and stringy.

I split the leeks lengthwise down the middle in order to be able to wash out all the sand that hides in this lovely vegetable. All the halves are then put together and tied in a bundle with soft kitchen twine. This keeps them intact and makes it easier to fish them out of the soup. The other vegetables are also cooked in the soup — with the exception of the potatoes, which leave their starchiness behind in a separate pot of cooking water.

Since the oven is not needed for this meal, I use mine at a very low setting to warm the soup plates, dinner plates and serving platters. The hotter this meal, the better it is.

There is no reason why *pot-au-feu* could not be cooked a day in advance, cooled, refrigerated and reheated before serving, except that few refrigerators are large enough to hold the big stockpot in which all the elements should remain together.

While green sauce is more usual with *bollito misto*, the Italian version of *pot-au-feu*, it is elegant and appropriate with the French counterpart and makes a wonderful foil for the meats, as does the Horseradish Sauce (see Index). *Aïoli*, (see Index), the heady Provençal garlic mayonnaise, would also be good with the meats. *Cornichons* and mustards are givens with *pot-au-feu*. So is a dish of coarse salt, which I have eliminated since nobody seems to want to dip into it.

The *pots de crème* can be made a day in advance but should be covered with plastic wrap unless little *pots de crème* pots are used, in which case their lids will keep the dessert from forming a skin on top. The mixture must be blended at low speed for a full minute, and the milk must be very hot, just to the boiling point, before it is added to the blender — that is, hot to the point where a skin will have formed and there is about a quarter of an inch of bubbles on the milk where it meets the sides of the saucepan. The custard will thicken to a medium-firm consistency within a few hours. If the cream should not thicken, it can be salvaged by turning it back into a saucepan and reheating it to warm but not hot and reblending it for a full minute.

Four-ounce containers are ample for each serving, since this dessert is particularly creamy and flavorful. The only problem with the recipe is that it is so easy to make and so good that one tends to make it too often. With this caveat, I know of no other recipe that gives so much for so little investment in ingredients and time. The texture of the *pots de crème* is better when made in a blender than in a food processor. Moreover, it is difficult to pour the liquid from the processor bowl; the mixture really has to be decanted first to a pitcher and then distributed among the serving containers–an extra step and an extra something to wash.

Pot-au-Feu

•

FOR THE BASIC	*4*	*pounds beef marrow bones*
BROWN STOCK	*3*	*pounds veal or beef neck or shin bones,*
(MAKES ABOUT 4		*with some meat attached*
QUARTS)	*4*	*large carrots, peeled and cut into 3-*
		inch chunks
	3	*large onions, quartered*
	8	*parsley sprigs*
	1	*large bay leaf*
	1	*teaspoon thyme*
	½	*teaspoon cracked black pepper*
	1	*tablespoon tablespoon salt*
	7 to 8	*quarts cold water, or enough to cover*
		the bones and vegetables
FOR THE		*4-pound piece beef brisket*
BEEF	*2*	*garlic cloves, peeled and cut into slivers*

FOR THE CHICKEN		4-pound whole chicken, neck and wing tips reserved
	2	cups fresh bread crumbs, made in a food processor or blender
	½	cup milk
	¼	cup minced parsley
		Heart, liver and gizzard of the chicken, trimmed and minced
	1	egg, beaten
	1	large clove garlic, crushed
	½	teaspoon ground allspice
		Salt and pepper to taste

FOR THE FINAL POT-AU-FEU		1	recipe basic brown stock (see above), cold and degreased
	3	large onions, peeled and left whole
	1	whole clove, stuck into one of the onions
	2	large carrots, peeled and cut into 3-inch chunks
	2	stalks celery, trimmed and cut into 3-inch chunks
		Reserved neck and wing tips of the chicken
		Prepared beef
		Canned chicken broth and beef bouillon, in equal quantities, if needed to cover the meat and later the chicken
		Salt to taste
		Stuffed chicken
		Vegetable garnish

FOR THE VEGETABLE GARNISH		8	medium-thin leeks, halved lengthwise, washed of all sand and tied with string into a bundle
	4	large parsnips, peeled, trimmed and halved lengthwise
	16	long thin carrots, peeled and trimmed
	8	small turnips, peeled and trimmed
	8	medium potatoes, peeled

FOR THE SOUP
GARNISH

*1 cup orzo, tubettini or any tiny soup
        pasta, cooked al dente in boiling
        salted water, drained and set aside
    Reserved marrow from the bones in the
        basic stock, sliced*

Make the basic stock a day or two in advance. Fit the bones not too tightly into one or two roasting pans and roast in a preheated 450-degree oven for half an hour. Add the carrots and onions to the bones and roast for an additional half hour or more, until the bones and vegetables are well browned. Turn the bones once during the browning. Remove the bones and vegetables to a large stockpot, about 16-quart capacity or more, and discard the fat from the roasting pan. Add an inch or two of cold water to the roasting pan, bring to a boil, and cook for 5 minutes or so, scraping the brown bits from the bottom of the pan with a wooden spoon. Set aside.

Place the parsley, bay leaf, thyme and cracked pepper on a piece of cheesecloth and tie into a spice bag. Add this and the salt to the pot along with cold water to cover the bones and vegetables. Place over medium heat and bring to a simmer, uncovered. With a large kitchen spoon, skim off the scum as it arises.

When no more scum forms (after about half an hour of skimming), add the contents of the roasting pan to the stockpot, set the lid slightly askew on the pot, and cook over medium-low heat for 6 hours. When the stock is done, remove the bones and push out the marrow into a bowl. Discard the bones, the vegetables and the spice bag and refrigerate the marrow, which will be used, sliced, as a garnish for the soup.

Rinse a piece of cheesecloth several layers thick in cold water, wring it out, and line a large strainer with it. Place the strainer over a large bowl and ladle the stock through the cheesecloth. Transfer the strainer to a second bowl when the first is filled. When the cheesecloth becomes clogged, rinse it out, replace it in the strainer, and continue. When all the stock has been strained, wash out the cheesecloth and save it for the final straining of the soup. Allow the stock to cool, cover with plastic wrap, and refrigerate. ❀ Remove the fat, which will have congealed over the surface of the stock, before using.

The beef can be prepared for cooking several hours in advance. Pat the meat dry, make random gashes in it with a sharp, pointed knife, and insert the garlic slivers into the gashes. ❀ Refrigerate until needed.

The chicken can be cleaned and the stuffing made in advance, but the chicken should not be stuffed until just before it is to go into the pot. Remove the wing tips and reserve. Also reserve the neck. Pull out the lungs and other organs clinging to the cavity. Rinse the chicken and pat dry with paper towels. To make the stuffing, combine the bread crumbs and milk in a bowl and stir until the milk is absorbed. Add the remaining stuffing ingredients and mix well. ❀ When the chicken is stuffed, sew up the cavity and truss the bird.

•

Start to cook the final *pot-au-feu* 5½ hours before it is to be served. Place the cold, degreased basic stock into the stockpot and add the onions, clove, carrots, celery and the neck and wing tips of the chicken. Add the prepared beef. If necessary, add canned chicken broth and beef bouillon in equal quantities to cover the meat. Place the stockpot over medium heat, uncovered, and bring to a simmer, skimming as the stock heats. It will take about 45 minutes for the pot to come to the boil. Taste the soup and add salt if needed. It is better to undersalt and adjust to taste later. Lower heat, cover the pot with the lid slightly askew, and simmer for 1½ hours. Meanwhile, stuff and truss the chicken.

After 1½ hours, add the chicken to the stockpot along with more chicken broth and beef bouillon if needed to cover. Return the soup to the boil, skimming if necessary, lower heat, cover the pot with the lid slightly askew, and cook for 2 more hours.

Remove the meat and the chicken temporarily to a dish and test the meat. If it is tender, do not return it to the stockpot but cover it with foil until the vegetable garnish is cooked. Fit a strainer with the cheesecloth rinsed in cold water and wrung out and pass the soup through the strainer into another pot. Discard the vegetables and chicken wing tips and neck and wash out the stockpot.

•

Return the soup to the clean stockpot along with the meat, if it needs more cooking, and the chicken. Return the soup to the simmer. (At the same time, bring a separate pot of water to boil for the potatoes.) Add the leeks, parsnips, carrots and turnips to the stockpot, bring the soup to the simmer, and cook for 20 minutes or until the vegetables are tender but not falling apart. Return the meat, if it has not continued to cook, with the vegetables, to the stockpot. Taste the soup for salt and make necessary adjustments. Cover the stockpot. Meanwhile, cook the potatoes separately, drain and wrap them into a cloth dish towel to dry and keep warm. ❁

•

To serve the soup as a first course, divide the cooked tiny pasta and slices of marrow among eight warm soup plates and ladle soup into each plate. ❁   There will be enough soup left in the stockpot to keep the meats and vegetables moist and warm.

•

To serve the main course, slice the meat thin against the grain and arrange it on a large warm serving platter. Carve the chicken into at least 8 pieces and arrange on the platter. Cut through the carved chicken carcass with shears, remove the stuffing in one piece, slice, and add to the platter. Discard the string from the leeks. If there is room, arrange the vegetables in bundles on the platter. Otherwise, place them on a separate warm serving dish. Ladle some of the soup over the meats and vegetables. Pass the green sauce, horseradish sauce, a dish of *cornichons*, various mustards and French bread.

The leftover soup will keep in the refrigerator for about 4 days. It can be frozen and used as a rich brown stock or for soup.

Green Sauce

MAKES ABOUT 1¼ CUPS

•

1   *medium potato, peeled, boiled and
        cooled*
5   *tablespoons minced parsley*
6   *anchovy fillets, rinsed under cold water,
        dried on paper towels and chopped*
1   *tablespoon capers, rinsed under cold
        water in a sieve and dried on paper
        towels*

1 cornichon *(small, sour French
     pickle), minced*
1 *garlic clove, mashed*
½ *cup olive oil*
1 *tablespoon red wine vinegar*

Dice the potato and combine it in a bowl with the parsley, anchovies, capers, *cornichon,* garlic and oil. Beat with an electric mixer for 5 minutes. The
potato will become mashed and incorporated into the sauce. Then beat in
the vinegar. Pour into a sauceboat and refrigerate until needed. ❁

Chocolate Pots de Crème

•

2 *cups milk*
2 *eggs*
2 *tablespoons sugar*
4 *teaspoons Cognac, rum or Grand
     Marnier*
2 *teaspoons vanilla extract*
  Pinch of salt
2 *cups (12 ounces) semisweet (real)
     chocolate bits*

Heat the milk just to the boiling point. Place all other ingredients in order
listed in blender. Add the hot milk and blend at low speed for 1 full minute.
Pour into 8 to ten 4-ounce or 6-ounce serving containers — soufflé molds,
custard cups or *pots de crème* pots — and refrigerate. ❁

Assorted Cold Hors d'Oeuvre

Fresh Beef Tongue Braised in Madeira

Browned Potato Cake (Roesti)

Apple Charlotte

•

FIRST COURSE:
Robert Mondavi Gamay
MAIN COURSE:
Juliènas

Soups and stews and the other winter foods are fine, but all that substance eventually needs to be tempered with a bit of grace.

This meal begins with a cheerful French smorgasbord that piques the appetite with its variety. Assorted cold hors d'oeuvre are presented in individual crocks, bowls or serving plates and set around the table before each person, along with a basket of good French bread and a dish of unsalted butter. Guests are instructed to serve themselves and then move the serving dishes to the person on their right. Sometimes they listen.

Next is fresh beef tongue, braised to a buttery taste and served with a rich Madeira sauce. The recipe was adapted from *Michael Field's Cooking School.* If you don't tell, those whose feelings about tongue are delicate can be allowed to believe they are eating the most tender beef, which they are. The sole accompaniment is a Swiss potato cake cut into wedges. Its inside is soft and creamy but with character, its outside crisp and brown, its flavor as pure as grated potato cooked in butter can be. The meal ends with an apple charlotte, a dessert of sophistication despite the simplicity of its ingredients. When the dish is baked, the bread that lines the mold becomes a crispy brown case and the thick apple purée filling ends up slightly caramelized. The dessert is unmolded and bathed with an apricot-rum sauce. Served warm the charlotte is divine; cold it is ambrosial.

You need not serve a lot of any one hors d'oeuvre since variety in color, texture and flavor is the key, not quantity. The point is to have a bit of each. A food processor makes preparation practically effortless. It is very satisfying to include salads using ordinary, available and inexpensive winter vegetables, what with edible lettuce so costly at this time of year. However, these hors d'oeuvre have no season.

The combination of olive oil, rich Italian balsamic vinegar (available in specialty food stores and Italian markets) and a bit of Pernod, *pastis* or any other unsweetened licorice-flavored liquor is wonderful with grated carrots because the blend is delicious and no one flavor is identifiable. To avoid the bother of cooking a tiny quantity of dried beans, I open a can but rinse the beans thoroughly under cold water and drain them before they are dressed. Bunches of fresh red radishes, when you can find them, are immeasurably better than the packaged radishes. Herring in wine sauce and Greek *calamata* olives are available at supermarkets. Black radishes, which are sometimes found at supermarkets, more usually appear at specialty food markets. They have a shape and size similar to beets, with a black skin and snow-white interior, and thus are extraordinary when combined with rendered chicken, duck or goose fat (which I constantly urge be stocked in every refrigerator) and coarse salt.

The choice need not be limited to the recipes given here. Roasted and peeled green or red peppers (see Index) can be cut into strips and served in only the liquid they give out, which is dressing enough. A julienne of celery is excellent with a mustardy mayonnaise and some parsley, and of course celery root rémoulade is fabulous (see Index). Bits of cooked cauliflower, broccoli, string beans or any other leftover vegetable can be transformed with a lemony vinaigrette or good homemade mayonnaise. A couple of slices of leftover roast or boiled beef can be cut into a julienne and mixed with chopped scallions, parsley and a little oil and vinegar. Sliced beets can be mixed with a vinaigrette and sprinkled with chopped hard-cooked egg. Marinated Olives (see June, Provisioning the Pantry) would be a delicious addition. The possibilities are limitless. Prepare hors d'oeuvre ahead, refrigerate and serve cool, not ice cold.

Supermarkets sometimes have fresh tongue, but it is more often available at meat markets. Many will get a tongue for a customer with a few days' notice. Tongue, which is highly regarded by Europeans, suffers from a lack of beauty, particularly before it is peeled and trimmed. Overcoming any aversion to handling tongue can bring great rewards. Tongue must be peeled when it is hot. Holding the tongue steady on a board with a dish towel between it and your hand does wonders to prevent burning. The skin should zip off but I always find stubborn spots that need to be cut off. Once the bones are removed and the roots trimmed, the tongue becomes quite a benign-looking piece of meat.

Some recipes for the heavenly Swiss potato cake called *roesti* require grated raw potatoes, while others ask for grated cooked potatoes. I have had consistent success with parboiled cold potatoes and commend them. They grate easily by hand or can be put through a processor, although this tends to mash them. Raw potatoes become discolored too quickly while fully cooked potatoes disintegrate when grated, and produce a cake lacking in texture. Some recipes say to cook the cake in olive oil; others recommend olive oil and butter or lard. Some add grated onion, cheese or ham to the potatoes. I like my *roesti* straight, with butter, salt and pepper. My recipe makes a thickish cake in a 10-inch pan. To make thinner cakes, the quantity of potatoes could be divided between two 8-inch pans, although I would not cut down on the amount of butter per pan. The grated potatoes are placed in the hot pan and then cooked over low heat. This, of course, takes longer than the quick-cook method over high heat and allows the cook to leave the kitchen to be with guests without worrying that the bottom of the *roesti* will burn. I do realize that the Swiss have been making this dish long before our little miracle surfaces were invented, but there is nothing like a nonstick pan to avoid grief here.

The trick to a successful apple charlotte is to reduce the apple purée so that it will keep its shape on a spoon, make a great plop when it is dropped from a spoon or even hold a spoon upright in the pan. The reduction goes quickly and smoothly when the apples are cooked in a very large sauté pan. The larger the cooking surface, the faster it goes. The purée needs constant stirring toward the end. Of all the apples now available none is better for this dish than Granny Smith. The trimmed bread crusts get turned into fresh bread crumbs via the food processor and are stored in the freezer. A six-cup charlotte mold is an excellent investment, since it is useful for so many other dishes. With some shopping around, decent French tinned molds can be found at a good price. I am leery of leaks in the cheap ones with seams on the side. Thin molds are good only for jellied dishes.

Grated Carrots with Pernod

•

½ pound carrots, scraped and ends cut off
3 tablespoons olive oil
1 teaspoon balsamic vinegar or 2
    teaspoons red wine vinegar
½ teaspoon Pernod or pastis
    Salt and pepper to taste

Put the carrots through the coarse grating disk of a food processor. Combine with remaining ingredients. ✿

White Bean Salad

•

15-ounce can Great Northern beans
1 clove garlic, peeled and minced
2 tablespoons olive oil
1½ teaspoons red wine vinegar
    Salt and pepper to taste
2 tablespoons minced parsley

Drain the beans in a colander and run cold water over them. Drain well and combine with remaining ingredients. ✿

Cucumber Salad

•

1   *large cucumber, peeled*
    Salt and pepper to taste
2   *tablespoons olive oil*
1   *teaspoon red wine vinegar*
1   *tablespoon chopped dill*

Split the cucumber lengthwise and scoop out the seeds with a small spoon. Slice the cucumbers and arrange the slices overlapping on a dish. Refrigerate.❀   Just before serving, drain off any accumulated liquid and sprinkle on remaining ingredients.

Herring Crock

•

Two   *12-ounce jars herring in wine sauce*
  1   *carrot, scraped and ends cut off*
  1   *onion, peeled*
 16   *small black olives*
 ¼   *teaspoon whole peppercorns*

Strain the herring juices into a bowl and reserve. Discard the onions that were packed in the herring. Cut the carrot on the diagonal, using a corrugated-blade decorating knife, if you have one. Slice the onion thin.

    Pack the herring, carrot slices, onion slices, olives and peppercorns in layers in a pretty preserving jar or a glass bowl. Pour the reserved juices over all, cover, and refrigerate❀   overnight or longer.

Genoa Salami and Red Radishes

•

¼ pound sliced Genoa salami
1 bunch (preferably with leaves) red
radishes, washed

Shortly before serving, arrange the salami slices overlapping on a plate. Cut off the root ends of the radishes and all but 2 inches of the leaves. Slice the radishes in half, vertically, and arrange along both sides of the salami.

Grated Black Radish with Chicken, Duck or Goose Fat

•

2 medium black radishes, peeled
2 tablespoons softened rendered chicken,
duck or goose fat, or enough to coat
the grated radish
Coarse (kosher) salt to taste

Shortly before serving, grate the radishes, using the coarse grating disk of a food processor. Combine with the rendered fat and salt.

Fresh Beef Tongue Braised in Madeira

•

	4-pound fresh beef tongue
2	tablespoons butter
1	tablespoon oil
½	cup chopped onions
½	cup chopped carrots
½	cup chopped celery
2	cloves garlic, peeled
6	sprigs parsley
½	teaspoon dried thyme
1	bay leaf
	Freshly ground white pepper to taste
1½	cups medium-sweet Madeira
2½	cups beef bouillon
1	tablespoon potato starch or arrowroot
2	tablespoons heavy cream
1	tablespoon Dijon mustard
½	teaspoon lemon juice, or to taste
	Salt

Place the tongue in a large pot of cold water, bring to a boil, and simmer for 1 hour. Remove the tongue and, while it is hot, peel it, using a sharp knife. Trim and discard the roots and the bones.

Heat the butter and oil in a heavy pot just large enough to hold the tongue. (Use an enamel-on-iron casserole with a lid if you have one.) Add the chopped vegetables and cook them over low heat for about 12 minutes. Place the tongue in the pot along with the seasonings, the Madeira and the bouillon. Bring to a simmer on top of the stove, cover, and place in a pre-heated 325-degree oven for 2 hours. Turn the tongue every half hour. When a fork pierces the tongue easily, remove the meat to a dish and cover it with a tent of foil to keep it warm.

Strain the braising stock into a saucepan, degrease the stock, and boil it down over high heat to 2 cups. Make a paste of the starch and cream and beat this into the stock. Cook for another 5 minutes. Beat in the mustard and stir the sauce, but do not let it boil once the mustard has been added.

Add half the lemon juice and taste. Add more if desired. Add salt to taste. ❀

Slice the tongue and arrange it in overlapping slices on a hot platter. Drizzle some of the sauce down the middle of the slices and serve the remaining sauce separately.

Browned Potato Cake
(Roesti)

•

3   *pounds boiling potatoes (about 8
        medium potatoes)
      Salt and pepper to taste*
¼   *pound (1 stick) plus 2 tablespoons
        butter*

Parboil the potatoes for 8 minutes, drain, and refrigerate for several hours. Peel the potatoes and grate them, using the coarse-grating holes of a hand grater. The potatoes should be firm enough not to disintegrate. Add salt and pepper and mix them through the potatoes. Melt half the butter in a 10-inch nonstick frying pan over high heat and swirl the butter around the sides of the pan. Add the potatoes, press down on them with a wide spatula, lower the heat, and cook for 15 to 20 minutes, or until the bottom and sides are crisp and browned. Place a plate on the pan and, holding both, firmly flip them over. The browned side of the cake will be on top. Raise the heat and melt the remaining butter in the pan. When it is hot slip the cake back into the pan. Lower the heat and cook for another 15 to 20 minutes, or until the bottom is brown. Invert the cake on a serving dish and cut into wedges.

Apple Charlotte

•

½   *pound (2 sticks) unsalted butter,*
       melted and cooled
1   *loaf very thinly sliced good-quality*
       commercial bread, crusts trimmed
5 to 6   *pounds (about 14) Granny Smith*
       apples
¼   *pound (1 stick) unsalted butter*
1   *tablespoon lemon juice*
       Grated rind of ½ lemon
¾   *cup sugar, or more to taste*
½   *teaspoon vanilla extract*
       Pinch of salt

FOR THE SAUCE   1   *cup apricot jam*
                   ½   *cup dark rum, Myers's or Ron*
                       Negrita

Use a pastry brush dipped in the melted butter to coat the sides and bottom of a 6-cup charlotte mold. Cut 3 slices of the bread on the diagonal and trim them so that they will fit together to cover the bottom of the mold. Dip the trimmed pieces in the melted butter and then set them in the mold. If necessary, fill in any holes with bits of bread dipped in butter. Cut another 10 slices of bread in half, into rectangles. Dip these in the butter and stand them upright all around the side of the mold, overlapping them by half an inch. Reserve remaining bread and butter for the top of the charlotte.

Peel and core the apples and slice them thin. Place the apples and the remaining ingredients (except for sauce) in a large sauté pan, frying pan or a wide-bottomed saucepan and bring to a boil. Lower the heat, cover, and cook for 20 minutes, or until the apples are tender. Uncover the pan, turn up heat, and, stirring, cook the apples for about 15 minutes. The liquid must evaporate and the purée must be thick enough to hold its shape in a spoon, plop heavily from the spoon, and almost hold the spoon upright.

Spoon the purée into the mold. Cut enough of the remaining slices of bread in half to cover the purée. Dip the reserved bread in the butter and fill in the top of the charlotte to make a lid. Pour any remaining butter over the bread. Do not be concerned if the bread rises slightly above the mold. It will shrink as it cooks.

Place the mold in a roasting pan or a cake pan to catch the drippings. Bake in a preheated 400-degree oven for 30 to 40 minutes, or until the top and sides are browned. If the top is browning too quickly around the edges, make a "doughnut" of foil and drop it lightly around the inside circumference of the mold. Remove from oven and cool for 30 minutes. Place a platter on top and, holding the plate and mold, turn them over. Allow the mold to remain in place until just before serving. ❁

Make the sauce. Heat the apricot jam, force it through a sieve, and return it to the saucepan. ❁   Add the rum and reheat briefly. Serve the charlotte while it is still warm, with the sauce spooned over it.

Or serve cold. The charlotte can be refrigerated, inverted and with the mold in place. ❁   Bring to room temperature, remove mold, and serve with warm sauce.

Seasoned Shrimp in Scallop Shells

Braised Veal Chops

Sautéed Leeks

Tiny Pasta Shells with Mushrooms

Glazed Oranges with Ginger

•

FIRST COURSE:
St. Véran
MAIN COURSE:
Château Gloria

*I*n midwinter it is good to have a little elegance — what with the piles of inelegant sweaters we are wearing — plus a small reminder that spring will come, not soon, but someday. So this meal begins with a light, cold course that would work as well in May or even July, and has a freshness that is reassuring now. Chunks of fresh shrimp are first seasoned with minced shallots, parsley, lemon juice and a fruity green extra-virgin olive oil from Italy. Just before serving, the shrimp is enrobed with a little mayonnaise and then piled into individual shells that have been lined with shredded lettuce.

Next are loin or rib veal chops, small enough not to break the bank, but large enough to make adequate servings. The meat is braised to a wonderful tenderness with chives and parsley, seasonings that are perfect with it, and served with the sautéed leeks in cream. The sauce, a reduction of the veal juices, dry vermouth, white wine and bouillon, is lovely not only on the meat but also puddling into the tiny pasta shells with sautéed mushrooms. Dessert is a pristine navel orange for each person. The fruit is peeled down to the flesh, drenched with a liqueur-reinforced syrup and topped with candied julienned peel and glazed strips of fresh ginger.

Many of the ingredients seem lavish, but a little is made to go a very long way. Thus, a pound and a half of medium shrimp (whose cost is bearable) is ample for eight, especially when the shrimp are cut into pieces, though left large enough to give the teeth something to bite on. I like to serve seafood in seashells, particularly since I replaced my old large, clunky shells, which were too shallow to hold food safely, with deeper shells that measure about five inches across. Each shell holds an adequate first-course serving and can be used for hot dishes as well. Six-ounce ramekins or individual soufflé dishes would also work, as would portions heaped on beds of shredded lettuce or in lettuce cups on individual plates.

Shrimp should not be overcooked, lest they become unpleasantly mealy. I keep very good green olive oil on hand for dishes such as this, where it makes a difference. The recipe for the whole-egg mayonnaise results in a lighter, not quite authentic sauce that happens to be very nice with the shrimp. It has the added advantage of being made in two minutes flat in a food processor. However, a decent commercial mayonnaise would not be ruinous.

I pick up nice, small veal chops at the supermarket when they look particularly pale, fresh and pretty. These are stashed in the freezer until I want to cook this dish. The braising would make even less-than-superior chops better than they have a right to be. I prefer to use two frying pans to cook the chops because crowding them can mean trouble. When they don't have enough space, they tend to steam rather than braise, which inhibits a nice reduction of the sauce. The meat can conceivably be cooked before guests arrive and quickly reheated just before serving. However, with a little planning, the timing can be worked out so that the chops cook when you sit down. They are then finished off while the first-course plates are being cleared either by a spouse or a helpful guest or both. While the emphasis on food being hot when it is served can be exaggerated, this dish is best placed on a super-hot serving platter and then dished out onto super-hot dinner plates.

Do not panic when the leeks cook down to what seems to be a pathetically small amount. They are as rich as they are delicious and are meant to be eaten with restraint, more as a condiment than as a full-blown side dish. Flavor rather than bulk is important here. This most heavenly, underappreciated vegetable can be found everywhere at this time of year. Leeks accumulate sand and dirt because they are trenched to keep the bottoms white. It is, of course, essential to wash away all the grit, which is possible once the leeks are split down the middle. The leeks can be sautéed the day before and reheated with the cream just before they are served. The green parts can be washed, cut and frozen for use later in making stocks.

The baby sea shells made by Conte Luna or the *orecchiette* (little ears) made by De Cecco are excellent foils for the veal. The tiny shapes have the appeal of the miniature as well as the capacity to hold on to sauce. The mushrooms add depth to the pasta. By now it is probably unnecessary to warn against overcooking pasta.

I buy large, brightly colored California navel oranges, which are shockingly expensive. Nevertheless, only one orange is needed per serving, so after all they are not completely outrageous. I do not use my stripper, to which I am devoted, on the orange peel, since the julienne should be a bit more substantial for this dish. It is admittedly a bother to cut the peels, so it is a good idea to take advantage of the fact that the oranges can be made a day in advance. The process, which requires only rudimentary concentration, seems to go faster when the evening news is on. A good sharp chef's knife is invaluable for cutting the peel and the ginger.

Ginger will keep indefinitely if it is peeled, placed in a jar, covered with sherry and refrigerated. The sherry can later be used to flavor something wonderful. Blanching the orange peels does much to remove any bitterness.

Seasoned Shrimp
in Scallop Shells

•

1½ *pounds medium shrimp*
1 *medium onion, sliced*
1 *bay leaf*
  Salt
½ *teaspoon cracked black pepper*
3 *tablespoons minced shallots*

1   tablespoon lemon juice
1/4 cup olive oil, extra-virgin oil if possible
10   grinds of a peppermill with white
        peppercorns
1/4 cup minced parsley
1/2 cup mayonnaise, homemade if possible
        (see following recipe)
9   leaves romaine lettuce

FOR THE   Chopped hard-cooked egg
GARNISH   Watercress
(OPTIONAL)   Drained black calamata or Niçoise
                        olives

Rinse the shrimp and place them in a saucepan with the onion, bay leaf, 1 teaspoon of salt and cracked pepper. Cover with cold water, bring to a boil, and immediately remove from heat. Let sit for 5 minutes and drain into a colander. When the shrimp are cool enough to handle, shell and devein them and cut each shrimp into 3 pieces. Place in a bowl with the shallots, lemon juice, olive oil, white pepper, salt and parsley. Mix thoroughly, cover tightly with plastic, and refrigerate for at least 2 hours or overnight, if desired. ❁ Just before serving, add the mayonnaise and mix lightly to mask the shrimp.

To serve, stack the romaine leaves, cut them in half lengthwise, and make a thicker, narrower stack. Roll the lettuce leaves and make a chiffonade by slicing crosswise into narrow strips. Divide the lettuce among 8 medium-size (5 inches across) scallop shells or 6-ounce individual soufflé dishes. Divide the shrimp mix among them and serve the shells on individual plates. Garnish, if desired, with chopped egg or watercress leaves or black olives.

Whole-Egg Mayonnaise

MAKES 1 CUP

•

1   egg
¼   teaspoon dry mustard
1   tablespoon lemon juice
½   teaspoon salt
½   cup vegetable oil
½   cup olive oil

Place the egg in a food processor fitted with the metal blade and beat until the egg is thick. Add the mustard, lemon juice and salt and continue processing until well blended. Leave the motor running, and through the feed tube add the vegetable oil, then the olive oil gradually, in a thin, steady stream. ❁

Braised Veal Chops

•

8   loin or rib veal chops, each weighing 4
      to 6 ounces
About ½   cup flour, or enough to dredge the chops
¼   pound butter
2   tablespoons vegetable oil
      Salt and pepper to taste
½   cup dry vermouth
½   cup dry white wine
1   cup beef bouillon plus another ½ cup if
      necessary
¾   cup minced parsley
½   cup minced fresh or frozen chives

Pat the chops dry with a paper towel and lightly coat them with flour. Use two frying pans if one is not large enough to hold all the chops comfortably in one layer. Divide the butter and oil between the two pans and heat. When the foam subsides, add 4 chops to each pan. Brown them on both sides without burning the butter, and lightly salt and pepper them. Add half the vermouth and wine to each pan plus ½ cup of bouillon to each. Divide the parsley and chives in two and add to each pan. Cover and simmer over medium-low heat for 20 minutes. Remove the lid and turn the chops several times to coat them with the herbs. Add more bouillon if the sauce has been reduced so much it is like a heavy syrup; or if it is too liquid, reduce it rapidly over high heat, turning the chops as this is done. Place the chops on a hot serving platter and pour the sauce over them.

Sautéed Leeks

•

3   bunches (about 12 medium) leeks
6   tablespoons butter
    Salt and pepper to taste
6   tablespoons heavy cream

Trim the roots off the leeks and all but ¼ inch of the green leaves. Reserve the green part for stock. Slice the leeks in half vertically, separate the leaves, and wash under running water, making sure all the sand and dirt are removed. Drain the leeks and dry them on a dish towel. Cut them into a 3-by-¼-inch julienne.

Melt the butter in a sauté pan, add the leeks, salt and pepper, and cook for a couple of minutes over medium heat, stirring constantly to prevent them from coloring. Turn the heat down to low and cook for 30 minutes, stirring occasionally. ❀   The leeks can be set aside for serveral hours or refrigerated overnight. Just before serving, add the cream and, stirring, reheat.

Tiny Pasta Shells
with Mushrooms

•

¾   *pound mushrooms*
6   *tablespoons butter*
1   *pound tiny pasta shells or* orecchiete
    (little ears)
    Salt and pepper to taste

Wipe the mushrooms clean and trim the bottoms of the stems. Cut the mushrooms into quarters and sauté them in hot butter over low heat until they give off their liquid. Turn heat up to medium-high and continue to cook, stirring, until the liquid cooks off. Set aside. ❀

Boil the pasta according to package directions until *al dente* (cooked but not mushy). This usually takes 10 minutes, but start to test after 8 minutes. Drain the cooked pasta in a colander, and return to the pot. Add the mushrooms with their butter, and salt and pepper. Toss and heat through.

Glazed Oranges with Ginger

•

8   *large navel oranges*
     2-inch piece fresh ginger
3   *cups sugar*
1½   *cups water*
2   *tablespoons Grand Marnier,*
     Cointreau, Triple Sec or Mandarine
     Napoléon

Carefully remove the peel from the oranges. Use a vegetable peeler and leave all the white pith on the orange. Cut the peel into a 2-inch-long matchstick julienne. Bring 2 quarts of water to a boil and cook the peel in it for 7 minutes. Drain in a strainer, refresh under cold water, pat dry, and set aside.

Peel the ginger and cut it into matchstick julienne. Bring the sugar and water to a boil and cook, stirring slowly, until the syrup is clear. Put a lid on the pan and cook for another 2 minutes. Remove the lid and cook until the syrup reaches a temperature of 244 degrees on a candy thermometer. Add the liqueur along with the orange rind and ginger, and cook, stirring, for a few minutes more.

Use a sharp knife and cut every bit of the white pith from the oranges. Pull out the little white tail from the center and cut a slice from the bottom so that the oranges will stand up straight. Set them in a shallow, flat-bottomed serving dish, spoon some of the rind and ginger onto each of the oranges, and pour the syrup over them.✿   Refrigerate for a few hours or overnight.

February

Golden Raisins
Macerated in Mandarine

•

1½   cups golden raisins
1½   cups Mandarine Napoléon (tangerine-
       flavored liqueur made in Belgium)

Place the raisins in a 1-pint jar and cover with the Mandarine. Let stand in a cool, dark place and use after 2 weeks. The raisins keep indefinitely on the shelf. Use in rice puddings, bread puddings, as a filler for baked apples and over ice cream.

• SUNDAY LUNCH •

Cassoulet

Romaine and Chicory Salad

Cold Orange-Hazelnut Soufflé

•

Côtes-du-Rhône
or Fetzer "Lake County" Zinfandel

This is a Sunday lunch to provide the inner fuel needed for an icy winter day. The centerpiece is a *cassoulet,* an addictive concoction of beans and various meats cooked to an unbelievable richness and fullness of flavor. The *cassoulet* is served in solo splendor, with guests starting cautiously with small portions. Inevitably seduced by the dish, they then go back for more, and sometimes even more. Which is why it is charitable to serve *cassoulet* at lunch, rather than dinner, when its inclination to lie heavily throughout the night can become all too real. Should the *cassoulet* be served in the evening, it could be preceded by Marinated Red Peppers with Anchovies (see Index), an obliging first course with enough assurance to stand up to the *cassoulet.*

After the *cassoulet* is a clean green salad of romaine, fortified with slightly biting, pale green and white leaves from the heart of chicory. The salad is dressed with a simple vinaigrette reinforced with a bit of mustard. Dessert is a marvel of lightness, a cold orange-hazelnut soufflé infused with fresh juice and the flavor of Frangelico, the sublime Italian liqueur that is a

461

sweet essence of hazelnuts. The soufflé, served in either hollowed-out orange shells or a soufflé dish, is garnished with whipped cream, candied orange peel and chopped toasted hazelnuts.

While long cooking times are involved, making a *cassoulet* is not complicated. Certain elements are combined and allowed to simmer. Then another group of ingredients is prepared and cooked separately. Finally the dish is assembled and baked. All steps can be done at various times starting at least two days before the *cassoulet* is to be served. First, the beans — and Great Northern beans are best — must be soaked overnight. The following day, the beans and meats are cooked and the *cassoulet* is put together and refrigerated. On the day of the party, the only thing left is to bring the *cassoulet* to a simmer on top of the stove and then put it in the oven for its final cooking.

As in all good peasant dishes, the ingredients of a *cassoulet* are variable, to a point, depending on what is available at the time. Beans are a given, as are certain meats — salt pork, sausages, lamb and/or pork, along with tomatoes in some form, onions, garlic and other seasonings. The fresh pork or ham rind that was thought to be essential has become next to impossible to find, since the rind is mercilessly trimmed off by packers before they encase their meats in vacuum-plastic wrappers. Those fortunate enough to have access to fresh rind should add a pound of it to the beans along with the salt pork and sausages. The cooked rind is then cut into one-inch squares and combined with the other meats.

Another optional ingredient is goose or duck preserved in fat, also called *confit,* whose presence in a *cassoulet* is viewed as critical in some regions of France and quite unnecessary in others. The lack of preserved goose or duck should never inhibit a cook from making a *cassoulet,* but its presence certainly adds much. Since goose is such a luxury in this country, duck becomes the bird of choice. Some recipes suggest roast or broiled duck as an alternative for the *confit,* but the flavor is undistinguished compared to the real thing. If preserved duck is used, the *cassoulet* will, of course, feed more people or yield more leftovers, which is all to the good because *cassoulet* reheats well, needing only the addition of a little stock. It can also be frozen for at least a month.

Ideally, the fat comes from the duck, but even our fat-laden American ducks do not have enough for *confit.* Chicken fat or fresh pork fat — fatback or fat from pork loins — can be used to make up the required quantity. Fresh pork fat can be difficult to come by, for the same reason that pork rind is. I use chicken fat, which is often available frozen in supermarkets.

The chicken backs I buy for making stock are an even more reliable source of chicken fat, the globules of which can be pulled out and stored in the freezer before the stock is made.

The fat must be rendered before it is used. One pound of fresh fat will yield about two cups or more of rendered fat, and once rendered will keep for at least three months under refrigeration and far longer in the freezer. The cut-up fat is placed in a heavy pot with a little water, which evaporates during the cooking, and simmers slowly over very low heat for about an hour. Halfway through the cooking the fat loses its odd smell and when it is finished is a lovely clear yellow. (When congealed, the fat turns white.) The cracklings are a medium brown but become a rich brown as they continue to cook in the hot fat even when the pot is removed from heat. Some think that the cracklings are the best part of rendered fat, particularly when they are slowly reheated in a frying pan for about fifteen minutes to recrisp them. Bernard Clayton's *The Breads of France* also has an interesting recipe for crackling bread. Cracklings keep for a few days under refrigeration and freeze well.

Temple oranges, in season during the winter, are the choice for the orange-hazelnut soufflé, since the juice is excellent and it is easier to gut them than it is navels. Frangelico can be found in half bottles at most liquor stores.

Cassoulet

8 TO 12 SERVINGS

•

FOR THE BEANS	2	pounds dried Great Northern beans
	1/2	pound piece lean salt pork
	1	large onion, halved
	2	medium carrots, scraped, in 1/2-inch slices
	1	stalk celery with leaves in 1/2-inch slices
	2	large cloves garlic
	4	sprigs parsley
	3	whole cloves

1 bay leaf
½ teaspoon coarsely crushed black pepper
1 teaspoon thyme
Four 13¾-ounce cans chicken broth plus
enough water to cover the beans
1 pound hot Italian sausages

FOR THE OTHER
MEATS

2 tablespoons fat from the preserved
duck, if used, or rendered chicken fat
or lard or shortening
1 pound boned shoulder of lamb, in 2-
inch chunks
1 pound lean pork, in 2-inch chunks
1 large onion, chopped
2 large cloves garlic, minced
1½ pounds ripe tomatoes, or enough to
make 2 cups peeled, seeded and
chopped, or 2 cups drained canned
Italian tomatoes
1 cup dry white wine
1 teaspoon salt
Freshly ground pepper to taste
4½- to 5-pound Preserved Duck
(optional; recipe follows)

TO ASSEMBLE
THE *CASSOULET*

2 cups fresh bread crumbs
½ cup minced parsley
4 tablespoons fat from the confit
(optional) or rendered chicken fat
Additional chicken broth, if needed

Soak the beans overnight in a large pot of cold water. Cook the salt pork in
2 quarts of boiling water for 15 minutes, drain, rinse with cold water, dry,
and set aside. Cut 2 large pieces of cheesecloth to make spice bags and
divide between them the halved onion, the carrot and celery slices, garlic,
parsley, cloves, bay leaf, crushed pepper and thyme. Tie securely into bags
with kitchen twine.

Drain the beans and rinse them under cold running water. Place the beans in an 8-quart pot and add the salt pork, the spice bags, the 4 cans of chicken broth and enough cold water to cover the beans. Bring to a boil slowly, simmering until no scum remains. Reduce heat and simmer for ½ hour. Add the sausages and simmer for 1 hour more, or until the beans are tender but not mushy.

•

While the beans are cooking, heat the duck fat, chicken fat, lard or shortening in a large sauté pan or frying pan. Brown the lamb and the pork, a few pieces at a time, removing them to a bowl as they are done. When all the meat is browned, return the pieces to the pan and add the chopped onion and minced garlic. Sauté, stirring, for 5 minutes. Add the tomatoes, white wine, salt and pepper. Cover and simmer for 1 hour, stirring occasionally.

When the beans are cooked, discard the cheesecloth bags and remove the salt pork and sausages. Cut the salt pork into 1-inch chunks. Slip the casings off the sausages and discard the casings. Then slice the sausages into ½-inch pieces. Add the salt pork and sausage pieces to the lamb and pork mixture and mix well. Lightly brown the preserved duck, if it is used, in a bit of its own fat in a frying pan. Set aside. ❁

•

To assemble the *cassoulet,* drain the beans into a colander set over a bowl and reserve the bean liquid. Place a 1-inch layer of beans on the bottom of an 8-quart casserole, preferably one made of enamel on cast iron. Arrange half the meat mixture and half the duck, if used, on the beans. Then add another layer of beans and a layer of the remaining meats and duck. Finish with a third layer of beans. Ladle on as much of the bean liquid as needed to cover the meats and the beans. Reserve any remaining liquid. Should there not be enough liquid, use more canned chicken broth to cover the mixture.

Mix the bread crumbs with parsley and cover the *cassoulet* evenly. Drizzle the duck or chicken fat, if it is available, over the crumbs. ❁ Bring the casserole to a simmer on top of the stove. Cover and place in a preheated 300-degree oven for ½ hour. Remove the cover, raise the oven temperature to 350 degrees and bake for another hour. Should the *cassoulet* seem dry or the liquid very thick when it is in the oven, add a bit more bean liquid or chicken stock. (Do the same when reheating any leftover *cassoulet.*)

Preserved Duck

•

4½- to 5-pound duck, defrosted frozen,
fat and fatty pieces of skin removed
and reserved for this recipe; wing
tips, liver, gizzard and neck reserved
for another use

5½ *tablespoons coarse (kosher) salt*

¼ *teaspoon thyme*

½ *bay leaf, crumbled*
Pinch of allspice
The unrendered duck fat and fatty
pieces of skin reserved from the
duck, plus 3 pounds unrendered
chicken fat or fresh pork fat
(fatback or fat from pork loins), or
enough unrendered fat in all to
make 7 cups rendered fat

½ *cup cold water*

Cut the duck into serving pieces. Detach the wings and cut each breast in two. Detach the thighs from the legs.

Mix the salt, thyme, bay leaf and allspice and rub all over the duck pieces. Place the duck in a bowl, cover with plastic wrap, and refrigerate for 24 hours, ✿ no longer. Rinse the duck pieces well under cold running water and dry thoroughly.

The fats can be rendered anytime while the duck is marinating. Cut all the unrendered fat plus the duck skin into ¼-inch pieces. A chef's knife should be used on the pork fat. Place all the fats in a 4- or 5-quart heavy pot or enamel-on-iron casserole and add the water. Place over low heat and cook, barely at a simmer, for about an hour, or until the fat is clear and the cracklings have taken on a medium-brown color. Set away from heat for half an hour. The cracklings will continue to brown as the fat cools. Set a large strainer over a bowl and pour the fat through it. Reserve the cracklings, which can be refrigerated for a few days or frozen for longer. Cover the bowl of fat and refrigerate. ✿

To make the *confit*, place the rinsed and dried duck pieces in a clean 5-

quart heavy casserole. Melt the rendered fat if it has congealed and pour it over the duck. The fat should cover the duck completely. Cover the casserole and place in a preheated 225-degree oven for 2 hours, or until the duck is tender and completely cooked. Remove the duck pieces to an earthenware crock or bowl. Place a strainer over a bowl, line the strainer with a few thicknesses of wrung-out cheesecloth and pour the fat through it. Then ladle the strained fat over the duck, which must be completely covered by the fat. As the fat congeals, submerge any parts of the duck that may float to the surface. When the fat is completely cooled, cover the crock or bowl with foil and refrigerate.❋   The preserved duck can be used within a few days and will keep under refrigeration, if it is completely covered with fat, for at least three months.

When the duck is to be used, let it sit at room temperature for 2 or 3 hours to soften the fat. Remove the pieces and brown them lightly in a frying pan in some of the fat. The remaining fat can be frozen and reused when needed to make more preserved duck.

Cold Orange-Hazelnut Soufflé

•

FOR THE PRESENTATION	8	*medium-large temple or navel oranges, or a 1-quart soufflé dish*
FOR THE COLD SOUFFLÉ	³⁄₄	*cup plus 1 tablespoon fresh orange juice*
	1½	*tablespoons (1½ envelopes) unflavored gelatin*
	4	*eggs, separated*
	³⁄₄	*cup sugar*
	1	*tablespoon Frangelico (Italian hazelnut liqueur)*
	1	*cup heavy cream*

<table>
<tr><td>FOR THE
GARNISH</td><td></td><td>Peel of two temple or navel oranges, removed in a fine julienne with a stripper, or removed with a potato peeler and then cut into a fine julienne</td></tr>
</table>

FOR THE
GARNISH
   Peel of two temple or navel oranges,
    removed in a fine julienne with a
    stripper, or removed with a potato
    peeler and then cut into a fine
    julienne

1 *cup sugar*
1/2 *cup water*
1/3 *cup (1 1/2 ounces) hazelnuts*
3/4 *cup heavy cream*
2 *teaspoons sugar*
1 *teaspoon Frangelico*

First prepare the orange shells or the soufflé dish, whichever is to be used for the presentation. For the shells, cut off the top quarter of each orange. Hold the orange over a bowl and with a grapefruit spoon scoop out the flesh and juice into the bowl. Strain the contents of the bowl and measure out the juice needed for the soufflé. Then, with the fingers, carefully pull out the pulp from each shell to make a smooth interior. To prepare the soufflé dish, cut a piece of foil an inch or so longer than the circumference of the dish. Fold the foil in half lengthwise and wrap it around the dish. Fasten the ends with transparent tape and then secure the foil around the dish with a rubber band. Lightly oil the inside of the foil that stands above the dish with peanut oil or any other unflavored cooking oil.

·

To make the soufflé mixture, place 1/4 cup of the orange juice in a metal measuring cup and sprinkle gelatin over it. When the gelatin has softened, place the cup in a small frying pan of water and heat until the gelatin is completely dissolved. Turn off the heat but let the cup sit in the water.

Combine the egg yolks and sugar in a bowl and beat with an electric mixer until very light. Then beat in the remaining orange juice, the table-spoon of Frangelico and the dissolved gelatin. Set aside.

In a clean bowl and with clean beaters, whip the egg whites until they are stiff but not dry. In another bowl, whip the cup of heavy cream until stiff. Fold the orange mixture into the egg whites and next fold in the whipped cream. There will be about 6 cups of the soufflé mixture in all. Spoon the mixture into the orange shells, mounding the tops and smoothing them, or pack into the soufflé dish. ✿ Refrigerate overnight.

·

Prepare the candied peel and the toasted hazelnuts the day before. Cook the peel in a quart of boiling water for 10 minutes. Turn into a strainer and rinse the cooked peel under cold running water. Pat dry on paper towels and set aside.

Place the sugar in a small, heavy saucepan and shake the pan so the sugar makes an even layer. Slowly pour the half cup of water into the pan. Place over medium heat, stirring carefully until the sugar is dissolved. Heat the syrup to 238 degrees on a candy thermometer and immediately add the blanched peel. Cook for another 2 minutes, stirring constantly. Set aside for 5 minutes. Drain the peel in a strainer and discard the syrup. ❀   Refrigerate the peel until needed.

To prepare the hazelnuts, put them in a cake pan in one layer and place in a preheated 425-degree oven (or toaster oven) for 10 minutes. Turn the nuts out onto a cloth towel, gather the towel up around them, and rub the nuts together to remove their skins. A few bits of stubborn skin can be picked off or allowed to remain. Chop the nuts coarsely on a board with a knife. ❀   Set aside.

•

Assemble the dessert an hour before guests arrive. ❀   Whip the cream for the garnish with the sugar and Frangelico, turn into a pastry bag with a number 2 star tube, and pipe a border of cream around the circumference of each orange. Or, if a soufflé dish is being used, carefully remove the collar and pipe a border of cream around the soufflé plus spokes across the top. Place some candied peel in the center of each orange, inside the cream border, or within the spokes on the souffle dish. Sprinkle the chopped hazelnuts over the peel. Refrigerate until served.

Leek and Mushroom Barquettes

Sea Trout Stuffed with Scallop Mousseline

Broccoli Florets with Almonds

Savarin Filled with Fresh Pineapple

•

Chateau Montelena Chardonnay
or Puligny-Montrachet "Les Pucelles"

This mildly exhibitionistic meal, composed entirely of filled or stuffed dishes, enlivens palates oppressed by deep-winter doldrums. It invites admiration, yet is within the capacity of any cook who can read.

The dinner begins with golden brown *barquettes* filled with an earthy leek purée topped with creamy mushroom sauce, then covered modestly with their own puff-pastry lids. The puff-pastry cases are made without struggle from the commercial product found in supermarket freezers. Next are lovely, white-fleshed, unfishy whole sea trout that have been boned and stuffed with a feathery mousseline of fresh sea scallops, the stuffing made possible and painless by the food processor. The fish is served with a satiny sauce based on a reduction of the cooking liquids, some cream and a lovely fillip from basil-flavored cider vinegar, or plain cider vinegar reinforced with a pinch of dried basil. Broccoli florets with golden almond slivers give needed texture and a touch of spring green. Dessert is a ring of light, syrup-soaked *savarin* made from a yeast dough that, in this recipe, is really a paste and requires no kneading. Its center is occupied by the one fruit that is not a bore at this time of year, fresh pineapple, here macerated with deep, dark rum.

The *barquettes* are an example of how good-quality, inexpensive frozen puff-pastry sheets can change a cook's view of life in the kitchen. The pastry is defrosted and cut into rectangles with a large, sharp knife. The cut should be made cleanly and downward rather than pulled so as not to compress the edges, which would prevent the pastry from puffing properly. There is no need even to roll out the dough. The rectangles are refrigerated until baking time — puff pastry likes to be cold — and before they go into the oven an inner rectangle is incised half an inch from the edges to form the lids. My version of these *barquettes* is a simplification and adaptation of a recipe from *The Three-Star Recipes of Alain Senderens*. The dish can be prepared almost in its entirety anywhere from several hours to a day in advance. About ten minutes will be needed to reheat the ingredients, finish the sauce and assemble the *barquettes*.

It is sensible to use boneless fish for company, since whole unboned fish make for messy servings, a pity when the initial presentation is so grand. When you ask at the market to have the fish boned, be sure to say they should be left whole for stuffing. The number you need depends on the sizes available. This varies dizzyingly. Two 2-pound trout or four 1-plus-pound fish, work well, and so would a single 4- to 5-pound fish, in which case cooking times would be extended. Should sea trout not be available, any fresh and firm white-meat fish can be used. Rockfish (striped bass), sea bass or even rainbow trout are possible substitutes.

No trouble should be encountered with the scallop mousseline if all ingredients, the processor blade and the bowl are well chilled. I even chill the Cognac. Purists recommend pushing the final mousseline mixture through a fine-meshed sieve, a refinement I forgo in the interest of time. Since the foil is removed from the fish ten minutes before it is ready, the cook will have to bounce up from the table, but only once and briefly, for this maneuver. It shouldn't take more than six minutes to make the sauce.

Flavoring the sauce with basil vinegar proves that in the kitchen, at least, availability is the mother of invention. Its use here is the brainchild of *Food & Wine* editor William Rice, who one day when we were cooking together decided it would be an interesting addition to a sauce he was inventing. Most herb vinegars are made with wine or rice vinegar, but cider vinegar, with its hint of sweetness, is most successful with basil. It can be made at home when fresh basil is available. Place a loosely packed cup of bruised basil leaves into a jar and cover with cider vinegar that has been brought to a boil. Cap the jar when the vinegar has cooled, and after five days strain the vinegar into a scalded bottle. The vinegar keeps on the shelf indefinitely.

Stalks remaining from the broccoli florets have many uses, but first peel off at least an eighth of the outsides and discard the hard bottoms. For cream of broccoli soup, chop the prepared stalks, sauté with some butter and minced shallots for about fifteen minutes, add chicken broth, and cook for another twenty minutes. Purée in a processor and return to the pan. Then whisk some cream into a bit of Dijon mustard, add this to the soup, and beat. Peeled broccoli stalks can also be grated and stir-fried.

The versatile *savarin*, a yeast dough baked in a ring mold, can be filled with any fresh fruit, with syrup flavorings adjusted to the fruit. This recipe is from the newly reissued *The Great Book of French Cuisine* by Henri-Paul Pelleprat. It is different from most *savarin* doughs, which are dense and bready, and requires practically no effort. The cake is ethereal and so absorbent that it has no difficulty soaking up the warm syrup that is spooned over it. If three tablespoons of currants were added to the paste with the melted butter and if individual conical baking tins were used, the result would be *babas*. Soaked in a rum-flavored syrup, they would become *babas au rhum*.

Leek and Mushroom Barquettes

•

FOR THE BARQUETTES	*1⅓*	*sheets frozen puff pastry, defrosted for 20 to 30 minutes*
FOR THE LEEK FILLING	*2*	*bunches leeks*
	2	*tablespoons butter*
		Salt and pepper to taste
	1½	*cups dry white wine*
	1	*cup heavy cream*

FOR THE	*1*	*tablespoon butter*
MUSHROOM	*2*	*tablespoons minced shallots*
SAUCE	*½*	*pound mushrooms, cleaned and chopped*
		Salt and pepper to taste
	½	*cup heavy cream*
		Strained liquid from the leeks
	3	*egg yolks*

If the puff pastry has been defrosted for more than 30 minutes, refrigerate until the *barquettes* are prepared. On a lightly floured board and using a large, sharp knife and a straight-down movement, cut the full sheet of pastry, which measures about 9 by 10 inches, into three strips along the lines where it has been folded in the package. You will have strips measuring 3 by 10 inches. Then cut a fourth strip from the second sheet. (The remaining pastry can be wrapped tightly and refrozen.) Cut each strip in half to make 8 pieces measuring 3 by 5 inches. Brush off excess flour and place the pieces, flipping them, upside down, on one or two jelly-roll pans. Leave ample room between the pieces because they will swell during baking. Refrigerate the pans for an hour or longer. Before placing the pans in the oven, use the tip of a sharp knife to incise a rectangle on each piece of the cold pastry ½ inch in from the edges, but do not cut through the pastry. When baked, the inside rectangles will puff up to form the lids for the *barquettes.* Bake in a preheated 425-degree oven 12 to 15 minutes, or until puffed and a golden brown.

With the tip of a sharp knife gently cut the lids free from the bottoms and remove them. Pick out any soft dough from inside the lids and the shells and discard.❀   The *barquettes* can be baked several hours in advance and recrisped and warmed before they are filled.

•

To make the filling, discard the green parts of the leeks, split the white parts in half lengthwise and wash well under cold running water to rid them of all grit and sand. Drain the leeks and cut them crosswise into very fine slices. Melt the butter in a large sauté pan, add the sliced leeks, salt and pepper, and cook, covered, on very low heat, stirring often, for about 25 minutes, or until the leeks are soft and transparent. Do not let them color. Add the white wine and cream, cover, and cook over low heat for another

20 minutes, stirring occasionally. If the leeks are to be used within an hour or so, set the cover askew on the pan and set aside.✿   They can be cooked a day in advance and refrigerated.

•

To make the sauce, melt the butter in an 8-inch sauté or frying pan, add the shallots, and cook, stirring, over low heat for 3 or 4 minutes. Add the mushrooms, salt and pepper, and cook, stirring, over medium heat for another 5 minutes. Add the cream, bring to a simmer, cover, and cook over low heat for 10 minutes more. If the sauce is to be used within an hour or so, set the cover askew on the pan and set aside.✿   The mixture can be cooked to this point a day in advance and refrigerated.

•

Allow about 10 minutes to finish sauce and assemble *barquettes*. Place shells and lids in a preheated 425-degree oven for 2 to 3 minutes to recrisp and warm. Reheat leeks in their liquid and strain liquid into mushroom mixture. Return leeks to pan and cover. Heat mushroom mixture to boiling and remove from heat. Whisk egg yolks in a bowl and gradually whisk in about ½ cup of hot mushroom mixture. Then whisk egg mixture into mushroom mixture. Return to medium heat and, whisking constantly, heat for about 30 seconds. Do not let sauce boil.

To assemble, place each *barquette* on an individual plate, spoon leeks into cases, and then spoon mushroom sauce over leeks. Place covers on cases and serve.

Sea Trout Stuffed
with Scallop Mousseline

•

2   *whole sea trout about 2 pounds each,*
or 4 whole sea trout about 1¼
pounds each, boned but left whole
for stuffing and heads left on

FOR THE MOUSSELINE	½	pound very fresh sea scallops, washed, patted dry and refrigerated for at least 1 hour
	1	egg white, chilled
	¼	teaspoon dried basil
		Salt and pepper to taste
	2	tablespoons Cognac, chilled
	1	cup heavy cream, chilled

FOR COOKING THE FISH AND FOR THE SAUCE	1	cup dry white wine
	1	carrot, sliced thin
	2	medium onions, sliced thin
	2	tablespoons butter
	1	tablespoon minced shallots
	½	cup heavy cream
	1	teaspoon basil-flavored cider vinegar or 1 teaspoon cider vinegar and a pinch of dried basil, or more if needed, to taste

Refrigerate the fish until it is to be stuffed. To make the mousseline, all ingredients must be very cold, including the food processor bowl and blade (or blender container), which should be refrigerated for at least an hour before starting. Process the scallops until they become a smooth paste, stopping the motor once or twice to scrape down the sides of the bowl. With the motor running, feed the egg white, basil, salt and pepper through the tube. With the motor still running, pour the Cognac and the cream very slowly through the tube. The final mixture should be the consistency of stiff whipped cream. (If a blender is used, follow the same procedure but in two batches.) Turn the mousseline out into a bowl, cover, and refrigerate for at least an hour. ❀ It can be made a few hours in advance.

•

Before filling the fish, wash and pat them dry. Spoon equal portions of the mousseline into the cavities and sew closed with kitchen string. ❀ The stuffed fish can be refrigerated for an hour before they are cooked. Pour the white wine into a large roasting pan, distribute the carrot and onion slices in the pan, and place the fish on the vegetables. Cover the pan with foil and bake in a preheated 425-degree oven. Two 2-pound trout should bake, covered, for 25 minutes; then remove the foil and continue baking for an additional 10 minutes. Four 1¼-pound fish should bake, covered, for 15 minutes; then remove the foil and continue baking for an additional 10 minutes. They are done when the fish flake and the mousseline is firm.

Remove the fish with a large spatula to a warm serving platter, blot up any liquid with paper towels, and discard the strings.❀   Cover with a tent of foil to keep the fish warm while you prepare the sauce.

•

Melt the butter in a 1-quart saucepan, add the shallots, and cook over low heat for 3 or 4 minutes. Strain the liquid from the fish roasting pan into the saucepan and discard the vegetables. Over high heat and stirring constantly, reduce the liquid by one-third. Add the ½ cup of cream and, stirring constantly, reduce by one-third. Add the basil vinegar or the dried basil plus vinegar and cook for another 2 minutes. Taste and add more vinegar and/or basil, if needed. Pour into a warmed sauceboat and pass separately.

Broccoli Florets
with Almonds

•

4   *pounds broccoli*
2   *tablespoons butter*
¼   *cup slivered blanched almonds*

Cut the broccoli flowers plus an inch or two of their tender stems from the stalks and cut into florets, following the configuration of the stems. (Reserve the coarse stalks for another use.) Bring about 5 quarts of water to a boil and cook the florets for 4 to 5 minutes, or until they are just tender. Drain. While the broccoli is cooking, melt the butter in a small frying pan, add the almond slivers, and sauté over medium heat, stirring, until golden brown.❀   All this can be done 2 hours in advance.

Just before serving, combine the broccoli and almonds in a sauté pan and reheat quickly, stirring constantly, over medium-high heat. Turn out into a warm serving dish.

Savarin Filled
with Fresh Pineapple

•

FOR THE SAVARIN	2 to 3	tablespoons softened butter for the ring mold
	1	tablespoon (1 envelope) active dry yeast
	¼	cup lukewarm (105 degrees to 115 degrees) water
	3	tablespoons sugar
	¼	cup lukewarm milk
	3	eggs
	2	cups sifted all-purpose flour
	½	teaspoon salt
	⅔	cup unsalted butter, melted and cooled
FOR THE SYRUP	½	cup sugar
	¾	cup pineapple juice, apricot nectar, peach nectar or orange juice
	2	teaspoons lemon juice
	6	tablespoons dark rum (Ron Negrita or Myers's)
FOR THE FILLING	1	pineapple, peeled and cored and the flesh cut into ½-inch dice
	1	tablespoon sugar
	1	tablespoon dark rum
	1	teaspoon lemon juice

Grease a 9½-inch (6-cup) ring mold liberally with the softened butter and set aside.

To make the *savarin*, combine the yeast, warm water and sugar in a large mixing bowl and set aside for 10 minutes to dissolve and activate the yeast. Add the milk, beat in the eggs one at a time, and stir in the flour. The mixture will be a smooth paste rather than a dough. Cover tightly with plastic wrap and set aside to rise in a warm place for half an hour, or until the paste has doubled in volume. A turned-off gas oven with a pilot light is an ideal place for the rising. Stir the paste down, add the salt and melted butter, and mix well. Pour the paste into the buttered ring mold, cover with plastic wrap, and let rise in a warm place for half an hour, or until the paste fills the mold. Bake in a preheated 400-degree oven for 15 minutes, or until a toothpick, straw or cake tester inserted in the center comes out clean. Place the mold on a cake rack for 10 minutes. Run a knife around the inside and outside edges of the mold, place a large plate on top, and invert. The *savarin* will be upside down. Remove the mold.

Make the syrup while the *savarin* is baking. Place the sugar in a small, heavy saucepan and add the ¾ cup of whichever juice is preferred along with the lemon juice. Cook over medium heat, stirring, until the mixture comes to a boil. Reduce heat and, without stirring, cook for 5 minutes. Remove from heat and stir in the rum. Set aside while the *savarin* is cooling on the cake rack.

Spoon the warm syrup evenly over the *savarin* on its plate. Then spoon over the *savarin* the syrup that accumulates in the center of the ring. When all the syrup is absorbed, place a serving plate over the *savarin* and, holding it with one hand and the plate on which the *savarin* is sitting with the other, invert both plates. The *savarin* will be right side up on the serving plate. ❁ The *savarin* can be covered with plastic wrap and refrigerated for a day.

To make the pineapple filling, combine the diced pineapple with the sugar, rum and lemon juice, mix well, cover with plastic wrap, and allow to macerate for a few hours. ❁ The filling can also be made a day in advance, in which case it should be refrigerated.

The *savarin* can be filled several hours before serving. ❁ Spoon the pineapple mixture into the center of the *savarin* and spoon the juices over the cake. Refrigerate and bring to room temperature about an hour before serving.

NOTE: The *savarin* can be filled with strawberries macerated in Kirsch, in which case Kirsch can be substituted for the rum in the syrup. Or, for another menu, the rum-flavored *savarin* can be filled with rum-flavored whipped cream and served without fruit.

Cold Baked Stuffed Green Peppers

Sherried Beef Stew

Individual Onion Puddings

*Fresh Pineapple Boats with Coffee Ice
Cream and Caramel-Ginger Sauce*

•

FIRST COURSE:
Frascati
MAIN COURSE:
Côte Rôtie

*T*his midweek-casual meal for good
friends has lots of body and little subtlety, although it is not without its
refinements. It begins with green pepper halves stuffed with highly seasoned cooked rice that has the aroma of Provence and would alone make a
lovely summer salad. The peppers are baked, but not for too long, so they
retain their shape and enough crispiness to make them interesting. They are
served at room temperature with a handsome garnish of anchovy, pimiento
strips and small black olives.

Next is a peppery, spicy, aromatic beef stew, full and rich and brown
and yet with a lightness that probably can be credited to the sherry, an
unusual addition that works. This stew does not overwhelm, as *boeuf bour-
guignon* tends to do. It contains carrots and celery and is accompanied by

little onion puddings, consisting of onions melted in butter and a Yorkshire pudding batter, baked in muffin tins to a brown crispiness. The balance is good.

Dessert is based on fresh pineapple, a fruit that is plentiful at this time of year and — *mirabile* — comparatively affordable. Even more remarkable, it is even possible to find some pineapples, from Hawaii, that were not picked so green they couldn't ever ripen, so their flavor is superb. The combination of fresh pineapple with coffee ice cream and hot caramel-ginger sauce may seem odd, as it did to me when I lit on it, but is wonderful. The flavors marry well, the textures are startling but not bizarre, and the heat of the sauce with the cold of the fruit and the ice cream is agreeable.

Even those who look down their noses at green peppers as coarse, pushy objects approve of the pepper and rice dish because the peppers meet their match. The oil from the anchovies goes into the rice, but is tempered by the olive oil and lemon juice. The shallots and garlic are perfectly at home in such company, and parsley and dill add freshness. Fresh dill, which used to be exotic but is now found almost everywhere, is used in both the rice and the stew. One bunch is ample for the entire meal. I squander some of my treasured Italian green extra-virgin olive oil for this rice because it makes a perceptible difference.

The pieces of meat for the stew must be well dried on paper towels before they are browned, whether or not they are dredged in flour. Moisture is the enemy. High heat is needed, and only a few pieces of meat should be added to the pan at a time. Otherwise the temperature will dip, the meat will exude its juices, and the result will be a gummy mess, with the meat boiling and never browning. Although I cook stews in a heavy enamel-on-iron casserole, I brown the meat separately in a carbon-steel frying pan. Cast iron will do for those willing to wait for it to heat up, as will heavy aluminum. Heavy-gauge carbon steel is the material chefs in commercial kitchens prefer for browning because it heats up quickly, retains heat and can take very high heat. It is also a comparatively inexpensive material and, once seasoned, easy to care for. However, it is heavy, as so many good pots and pans tend to be.

I have become so addicted to a seasoning called "Pepper and Spice" that this mixture of black and white peppercorns and other whole spices now has its very own peppermill. It and a variety of other seasonings, packaged in charming little bottles with cork stoppers, are the product of two Maryland women whose label reads "Vann's Spices." I have found their excellent mixtures at some kitchenware shops and specialty food shops. They are available by mail from La Cuisine (see Mail-Order Sources).

Long, slow cooking is one secret of stews. Another is ripening time; stews are always better the day after they are cooked. Once the bulk of the ingredients are added and the stew begins to simmer, it needs almost no attention, although it is always a good idea to stir occasionally to make sure a burned crust doesn't appear on the bottom. The sherry is added after the stew has cooked for a good bit because the flavor dissipates with prolonged cooking. The mystery is why this happens to sherry and not to other fortified wines such as Madeira and port. The *al dente* carrots and celery make a pleasing contrast with the fork-tender meat.

Potatoes, which could have been added to the stew, were rejected as the starch because they were so predictable and also because I wanted something that would stand separately on the plate. The onions keep the insides of the little puddings smooth and soft, while the outsides have the appeal of a crispy Yorkshire pudding, which in our house is the best kind. The onion puddings can be put together in minutes. The batter benefits from two beatings with a rest in between, much as a crêpe batter does. If you reduce the oven temperature to 300 degrees, the puddings will hold for about 25 minutes. One can be served to each person, and hot seconds can be brought out later.

In choosing a good pineapple, it is not enough to be able to pull a frond from the stalk with ease. A pineapple should feel ripe under its knobby rind, with some give, but not mushy. It should also exude the kind of perfume that makes you taste it by smelling it. If we used our noses more frequently, we would not end up so often with woody, tasteless excuses for fruit. The ginger can, of course, be omitted, although I cannot imagine doing this. The result will be a perfectly delicious, plain caramel sauce which, by the way, keeps well under refrigeration, with or without ginger.

Cold Baked Stuffed Green Peppers

•

4   *green bell peppers*
1   *cup rice*
    2-ounce can flat fillets of anchovies

2	tablespoons minced shallots
3	large garlic cloves, minced
2	tablespoons chopped dill
4	tablespoons minced parsley
2	tablespoons lemon juice
4	tablespoons green olive oil plus extra olive oil for the pan
10 to 15	grinds black pepper, or to taste
8	strips red pimiento, either freshly broiled or from a jar
8	black Niçoise olives

Wash the peppers, split them lengthwise, stem and seed them, and remove membranes. Set aside.

Put the rice on to cook. Open the anchovies and drain them in a strainer set over a bowl. Reserve the anchovies. Add to the anchovy oil the shallots, garlic, dill, parsley, lemon juice, olive oil and pepper. When the rice is cooked and drained and while it is still hot, add the sauce and mix well. Pack the mixture into the pepper halves. Pour a film of oil on the bottom of a roasting pan just large enough to hold the peppers. Place the peppers in the pan and cover with foil. Bake the peppers for 45 minutes in a preheated 350-degree oven. Remove from oven, remove the foil, and allow to cool. ❀

To serve, place pepper halves on individual plates and crisscross on each an anchovy fillet and a strip of red pimiento. Garnish with an olive, placed where the two strips cross.

Sherried Beef Stew

•

3	pounds stewing beef, cut into 2-inch chunks
	Flour for dredging the meat
3	tablespoons peanut oil
2	large onions, chopped
3	cloves garlic, minced

4	whole cloves
12	whole peppercorns
10	grinds Vann's Pepper and Spice mix (optional)
½	cup minced dill
½	cup minced parsley
1	bay leaf
	2-pound 3-ounce can Italian tomatoes, drained and chopped
1½ to 2	cups beef bouillon
1½	cups dry sherry, such as Dry Sack
1	pound carrots, halved lengthwise and cut into 3-inch pieces
4	stalks celery, strung and cut into 1-inch chunks

Dry the meat on paper towels and dredge in the flour. Heat the oil in a large, heavy frying pan (cast iron, aluminum or carbon steel) and brown the meat over high heat, a few pieces at a time. Remove the meat as it is browned to a large casserole (enamel on iron, if possible). Add the chopped onion to the pot and cook over low heat, stirring, until the onions soften, about 8 minutes. Add the spices, herbs, tomatoes and 1½ cups of the bouillon. Bring to a simmer, cover, and cook over low heat for 1½ hours. Then add the sherry and continue cooking for another 2 hours. Stir occasionally and add a little more bouillon if necessary.

While the stew is simmering, parboil the carrots and celery chunks in a little water for 10 to 15 minutes, or until they are cooked but still crunchy. Drain. When the stew has cooked for 3 to 3½ hours, or until tender, add the vegetables and cook for another 15 minutes. The stew can be cooled and refrigerated. ❁   To serve, bring to a simmer on low heat and let simmer for 15 minutes to heat it through.

Individual Onion Puddings

•

½ pound onions (about 3 medium
    onions)
2 tablespoons butter, plus softened buttter
    for greasing the muffin tins
Salt
Pepper to taste
⅞ cup (1 cup less 2 tablespoons) flour
½ cup milk
2 eggs
¾ cup water

Peel the onions, cut in half, and slice very thin, using, if desired, the thin-slice blade of the processor. Melt the 2 tablespoons butter in a heavy sauté pan, add the onions and salt and pepper to taste, stir, cover, and cook over low heat for ½ hour. ✿ The onions can be cooked in advance and set aside.

About 1½ hours before the puddings are to be cooked, combine the flour, ½ teaspoon salt and milk in a mixing bowl. Beat the eggs in another bowl until they are light, and then beat them into the flour and milk mixture. Beat in the water and continue beating for 5 minutes at high speed. Set aside. ✿

Butter 16 muffin tins or custard cups generously. Divide the cooked onions among them. Beat the batter once more for about a minute and divide it among the tins or cups. The batter should come to within ½ to ¼ inch from the top of the tins.

Bake in a preheated 400-degree oven for 45 minutes, or until puffed, browned and crisped. Serve immediately.

Fresh Pineapple Boats
with Coffee Ice Cream
and Caramel-Ginger Sauce

•

      2   *whole ripe pineapples*
About 1   *pint coffee ice cream*

FOR THE SAUCE   2   *cups sugar*
      ¾   *cup plus 2 tablespoons water*
      ½   *teaspoon vanilla extract*
      ½   *cup butter*
      1   *cup whipping cream*
      2   *tablespoons syrup from preserved*
           ginger
      6   *tablespoons chopped preserved ginger*

Cut the pineapples vertically, through the stalks, into quarters. Remove the cores. Cut the flesh from the rind, using a curved grapefruit knife or a paring knife. Then cut into bite-size pieces, but let them remain on the rind. Refrigerate. ✿

Scoop 8 scoops of the ice cream, using an oval scoop if possible, onto a plate and place in the freezer. ✿

Make the sauce. Combine the sugar with ¾ cup of the water in a heavy saucepan. Bring to a boil over low heat and cook until it turns a deep caramel color, shaking the pan to assure even coloring. Remove from heat, quickly add the 2 tablespoons water, and stand back. When it stops spattering, shake the pan. Add the vanilla and the butter and stir until the butter is dissolved. If necessary, return to heat. Add the cream, ginger syrup and chopped ginger and stir well. Pour into the top of a double boiler over hot water and keep warm. ✿

To assemble, arrange the pineapple quarters on a large platter or on individual plates, place a scoop of ice cream on each quarter, and drizzle some sauce over it. Serve remaining sauce separately in a bowl.

Cream of Scallop Soup

Roast Loin of Pork

Roasted Parsnips

Puréed Broccoli

Pear Charlotte with Pear Sauce

•

Ridge "Coast Range" Zinfandel
or Fleurie

When guests sit down to this less than humble meal it's a waste of time to try to convince them that the cook hasn't spent twelve straight days in the kitchen after secretly matriculating from the Cordon Bleu and withdrawing the last of the family fortune from the bank. Even so, this menu requires little time or special skills or money. The ingredients cost not much more than a cheeseburger at a decent pub.

The secret is using "fancy" foods bought at good prices. The most obvious, bay scallops or calico scallops, which are sold as bay scallops, are fresh, succulent and inexpensive in winter. My own version of cream of scallop soup is delicate and refined. It takes ten minutes to prepare and, except for the final enrichment, can be made in advance.

The boneless pork tenderloin roast for the main course can be a sensational buy, even though the price per pound is hardly in the chicken category. I stock the freezer with these long, thin roasts when they are on sale at a good market and buy only pale gray-pink, finely textured pork. A three-pound roast can be cut into enough elegant-looking but substantial slices to serve eight amply and still leave sufficient for lunch for two the following day.

The pork is accompanied by the much-maligned parsnip. It is at its sweetest now that the ground has frozen and thawed enough for it to be dug. When your guests ask you to identify the deliciousness they are eating, perhaps they will discover, as I once did, that I hated parsnips only until I tasted them. The broccoli purée adds color to the plate and just the right intensity of flavor to complement the pork but not overwhelm the parsnips.

Dessert is an ostentatious, shameless thing, a charlotte made with fresh pears that are endowed with the flavor they lack at this season by poaching them in syrup from canned pears. The pear sauce that accompanies the charlotte uses the canned pears, so nothing is wasted.

The small amount of imported Madras curry powder brings out the flavor of the scallops more than it imposes itself on the soup. Curry will lose its raw taste if it is cooked for a minute or so in butter or oil (stir constantly) before other ingredients are added. The soup must not be allowed to boil once the egg yolk enrichment is added (at the last minute). A trick is to begin with hot soup and turn the heat off a minute after the enrichment is whisked in. Jean Anderson's very good *Grass Roots Cookbook* has an interesting note on storing fish soups uncovered, which apparently inhibits a reaction that makes them curdle. I cannot find an explanation of why, but it works.

I buy "heart-of-loin" pork roasts. Whatever these are called, look for neatly tied long, thin pieces of meat and leave the reddish pork behind in the case.

Normally a marinade is discarded before the meat goes into the oven. I found that this lemony, herbed marinade is most agreeable when cooked along with the meat. The pork needs almost no attention once it goes into the oven.

Parsnips are perfectly wonderful when they are peeled, cut into chunks, lightly parboiled and roasted. They can be prepared ahead through the parboiling step, and then roasted in the same pan as the meat or separately, which I prefer. They are very good cooked in chicken, duck or goose fat, although butter is fine. The broccoli purée is best if the moisture has been squeezed and blotted out after the broccoli is cooked and before it is puréed. The broccoli can be puréed in advance and reheated in the top of a double boiler over simmering water.

The pear charlotte is made either in the useful 6-cup charlotte mold or, for those who are made nervous by unmolding, by setting the rim of a 9-inch springform pan on a serving platter, lining it with ladyfingers and then filling it. The latter method is not only foolproof and anxiety-free, but it also makes for a sensational presentation, since the tops of the ladyfingers do not have to be trimmed and form a crown. Everyone wonders why the tips weren't crushed when the charlotte was unmolded, which of course it wasn't.

Pears can be abysmal at this time of year—hard, tasteless, mealy and refusing to ripen, instead turning brown throughout. So I experimented with Anjou pears, which are less mealy now than the Boscs. I chose only those with a hint of perfume, the most you can hope for, and a blush of color. These I poached in the syrup from canned pears and further reinforced the flavor with a few drops of French pear essence and *eau de vie de poire*. The fresh Boscs picked up a lot of flavor from the syrup and were better than the one unperfumed pear I used as a control. The additional flavorings were helpful because the custard and cream dilute flavor.

Custards curdle when they boil, which everyone knows. But I got into trouble when, in an unjustified rush of confidence, I tried to end-gain by hurrying the thickening process. Saving the curdled mess seemed worth a try, although I wasn't hopeful. I brought out the chinois, a conical, very finely meshed sieve (any superfine strainer should work), and forced the curdled custard through. Miraculously the result was a silky, velvety perfection. I offer this to give hope to those who should know better but who do dumb things anyhow.

The charlotte is best made two days in advance, which gives the cook plenty of time to make and rectify mistakes. Purists insist that ladyfingers be homemade, but I buy them unless I am having a fit of ambition.

Cream of Scallop Soup

•

1   *pound fresh scallops*
5   *cups chicken broth*
1   *cup dry white wine*
4   *tablespoons butter*

> 1   *tablespoon curry powder (preferably*
>   *Madras)*
> 2   *cups heavy cream*
> 3   *egg yolks*
>   *Paprika (optional)*

Wash the scallops under cold water and drain them. Combine the chicken broth and white wine in a nonreactive pot and bring to a boil. Add the scallops, simmer for 2 minutes, and remove the scallops with a slotted spoon. Melt the butter with the curry powder in a frying pan and cook the two for a minute. Then add the scallops and sauté for 4 minutes. Place the scallops, with any butter that remains in the pan, into a food processor with the steel blade. Start the motor and slowly feed the cream through the tube. Blend until the mixture is reduced to a smooth purée. Then whisk the purée into the broth. If the soup is to be eaten later, refrigerate it, but do not cover the pot. 🏵

    Before serving, bring the soup to a boil. Beat the egg yolks in a bowl and then whisk about 1½ cups of the boiling hot soup into it in a thin stream. Then whisk the egg-soup mixture into the remaining soup. Stir briskly for a minute and turn off the heat. The soup must not be allowed to boil once the egg enrichment has been added. Serve in hot bowls, garnished, if desired, with a sprinkling of decent Hungarian paprika.

Roast Loin of Pork

•

>   *3-pound boneless pork tenderloin*
> ¼   *cup peanut oil*
>   *Juice of 1 lemon*
> ½   *teaspoon dried thyme*
>   *Pinch of leaf sage*
>   *Pinch of dried oregno*
> 1   *bay leaf*

3   cloves garlic, unpeeled and lightly
        crushed with the side of a knife
1   cup water
1   cup beef bouillon
1   cup chicken broth

Pat the pork dry with paper towels and place it in a roasting pan. Mix the oil, lemon juice, thyme, sage, oregano and bay leaf and pour the mixture over the pork. Turn the pork to moisten it all over with the marinade, cover with plastic wrap, and refrigerate overnight, or for several hours. Turn the pork every once in a while. ✿

An hour before the pork is to be cooked, remove it from the refrigerator. Place the pork, with its marinade, in a preheated 450-degree oven for 20 minutes, turning it once during this time. Then reduce the heat to 350 degrees, add the garlic cloves to the pan, and pour the water into the pan. Roast for 1½ hours longer. Turn the pork halfway through. Remove the meat to a carving board and place a tent of foil over it. The meat should rest for about 15 minutes. Discard the garlic and any fat from the pan. Pour the beef bouillon and chicken broth into the roasting pan and bring to a boil. Stir with a wooden spoon and scrape up the brown bits. Reduce the sauce until it has a good flavor. To serve, remove the strings from the roast, slice the meat thin, and march it down a serving platter. Spoon a little sauce over the meat and serve the remainder separately.

Roasted Parsnips

•

3   pounds parsnips
4   tablespoons rendered chicken, duck or
        goose fat, or butter
    Salt and pepper to taste

Peel the parsnips with a potato peeler and cut them into large chunks. Discard any woody centers. Bring a pot of salted water to a boil, add the parsnips, and cook for 4 minutes. Drain them in a colander. Melt the fat or butter in a roasting pan large enough to hold the parsnips comfortably in one layer, add the parsnips, and roll the chunks around to coat them with fat.✿　Put the parsnips into a preheated 350-degree oven 45 minutes before they are to be served. Shake the pan every 10 minutes or so to brown the parsnips on all sides. For the last 15 minutes of cooking (after the pork has been removed from the oven to rest before carving), increase the oven temperature to 400 degrees. At the last minute, remove the parsnips from the oven and arrange around the sliced meat. Sprinkle lightly with salt and pepper.

Puréed Broccoli

•

3　*pounds broccoli*
6　*tablespoons butter*
4　*tablespoons minced shallots*
4　*tablespoons heavy cream (optional)*
　Pinch of nutmeg
　Salt and pepper to taste

Cut off the florets from the broccoli and set aside. Trim the tough ends off the stalks, peel the stalks, and cut them into 1-inch pieces. Bring a large pot of salted water to a boil, add the pieces of stalk, and cook for 8 minutes. Add the florets and cook for 4 minutes more. The broccoli should be soft but not mushy. Drain the broccoli well, squeeze out as much moisture as possible, then blot the broccoli on paper towels.

Heat half the butter in a small frying pan, add the shallots, and cook over low heat until the shallots are soft and transparent. Do not let them brown. Place the shallots and their butter in a food processor bowl. Add the broccoli in batches and process until it is reduced to a purée. Turn the purée out into a saucepan, heat through, and beat in the remaining butter. Then beat in the cream, if desired. Season to taste with nutmeg, salt and pepper.✿　If you wish to make this in advance, reheat it by placing the purée in the top of a double boiler and setting it over simmering water.

Pear Charlotte

•

	20-ounce can Bartlett pear halves
3	*fresh pears, firm and with some perfume*
1½	*tablespoons (1½ envelopes) unflavored gelatin*
2	*cups milk*
1	*cup sugar, divided in half*
¼	*teaspoon vanilla extract*
5	*egg yolks*
	Softened butter for a 6-cup charlotte mold
24	*ladyfingers*
1	*cup cold heavy cream*
3 to 4	*drops pear essence (optional)*
3 to 4	*teaspoons* eau de vie de poire, *or more to taste*

Place a metal bowl in the freezer to chill it well for whipping the cream.

Drain the canned pears and place all the juices in a saucepan. Set the canned pears aside for the sauce. Peel and core the fresh pears and cut them into ½-inch dice. Poach the pears in the canned pear syrup until they are just tender. Don't let them get mushy. Drain, reserving the syrup, and set aside to cool.

Place ½ cup of the poaching syrup in a bowl, sprinkle the gelatin on it, and set aside to soften. Save any remaining poaching syrup for the sauce. If the gelatin absorbs all the syrup and is not completely moistened, add a tablespoon or two of cold water.

Combine the milk with ½ cup of the sugar and the vanilla. Bring to a boil and set aside. Beat the egg yolks with the remaining ½ cup of sugar for 3 to 4 minutes, or until thick and pale. Beating constantly and vigorously with a wire whisk, slowly add the milk to the eggs. Return the mixture to a saucepan, place over low heat, and stir constantly with a wooden spoon for about 6 minutes or until the custard coats the spoon. Do not let the custard boil. To test whether it is thick enough, run a finger down the middle of the spoon and then hold the spoon vertically. If the custard does not run over the line made by your finger, it is thick enough. Pour the custard into a bowl and add the softened gelatin. Stir until the gelatin is dissolved. Set the bowl aside and stir the custard occasionally as it cools.

If you are using a 6-cup charlotte mold, lightly butter it and line the bottom with a round of parchment paper or waxed paper. Cut about 8 of the ladyfingers in half on the diagonal, lengthwise. Arrange the cut pieces, rounded side down, on the bottom of the mold, with the points meeting at the center, so they form a flower design. Then line the sides of the mold with more ladyfingers, rounded side out. If they do not come to the top of the mold, cut as many short pieces as necessary and press these around the top to make a border. If the ladyfingers come above the top of the mold, trim them with a pair of scissors.

If you do not wish to use a mold, center the clasped rim of a 9-inch springform pan on a serving platter and line the inside edge of the rim with ladyfingers, standing them vertically with the rounded sides against the rim. Break up into coarse crumbs enough additional ladyfingers to cover the plate inside the rim.

Remove the metal bowl from the freezer and pour the cold cream into it. Beat until stiff. Stir the poached diced pears into the cooled custard along with the pear essence, if you have it, and the *eau de vie de poire.* Fold in the whipped cream and spoon the mixture into the lined mold or cake rim. Cover with a piece of waxed paper and refrigerate❀ for at least several hours and preferably a day or two.

To serve, dip the charlotte mold briefly in hot water, run a knife between the side of the mold and the ladyfingers, place a round serving dish on top of the mold, and turn them both over together. Lift off the mold and discard the paper round. Or, unfasten the springform rim and lift it off. Should any filling have dribbled through the sides under the ladyfingers, clean it off with a damp paper towel. To serve, cut into wedges and serve with pear sauce.

Pear Sauce

MAKES ABOUT 3 CUPS

•

> *The reserved canned pears (preceding recipe)*
> 2 *drops pear essence (optional)*
> ½ *cup sugar*
> 1½ *teaspoons lemon juice*
> 2½ *tablespoons cold water, plus 2 more tablespoons cold water*
> 1 *tablespoon* eau de vie de poire
> *Any remaining poaching syrup*

Place the canned pears and the essence, if you have it, in the container of a food processor and blend until they are puréed. Leave the pears in the container.

Combine the sugar, lemon juice and 2½ tablespoons of the cold water in a heavy saucepan, bring to a boil, then reduce the heat. Cook the mixture from 6 to 10 minutes to caramelize the sugar. Shake the pan frequently so the caramel will color evenly, until it has become a nice dark mahogany color. Remove from heat, quickly add the 2 tablespoons of cold water, and stand back. When the hissing subsides, shake the pan to incorporate the water with the caramel. Turn the processor motor on and slowly add the caramel to the puréed pears through the feed tube. Then add the *eau de vie de poire* and any remaining poaching syrup. When thoroughly blended, place in a bowl and refrigerate. ❁

MAIL-ORDER SOURCES

There are, of course, a great many excellent mail-order sources now for specialty foods and quality cookware. This small group of four simply represents the sources that have supplied me with everything I have needed to make the recipes in this book.

COOKWARE AND SPECIALTY FOODS

La Cuisine, 323 Cameron Street, Alexandria, Virginia 22314 (703) 836-4435. Quality copper, aluminum, cast iron, carbon steel and stainless cookware, a wide variety of baking plaques, molds, knives, fine wooden utensils, specialty equipment (including 20-wedge fruit wedger-corers), chocolates, Fortnum and Mason products, French flavoring essences, marzipan decorations, Vann's spices, various oils and flavored vinegars. Informative catalog.

Williams-Sonoma, Mail Order Department, P.O. Box 3792, San Francisco, California 94119 (415) 652-9007. Fine cookware, baking plaques, specialty equipment, Hédiard products, chocolates, various oils, flavored vinegars and other specialty foods. Catalog several times a year.

HERBS AND SEEDS

Earthworks Herb Garden Nursery Co., 923 N. Ivy Street, Arlington, Virginia 22201 (703) 243-2498. Well-grown herbs, perennial vegetables and scented geraniums. Informative catalog includes information on growing herbs indoors and outdoors.

Le Jardin du Gourmet, West Danville, Vermont 05973. Herb plants and seeds, seeds for European vegetables, gray and red shallots. Catalog.

Index

Page numbers in *italics* refer to text discussions of recipes and their ingredients. Entries in **boldface** refer to specific courses.

About the Author

•

JUDITH HUXLEY was a writer and columnist on food and gardening. Her column "Table for Eight," on which this book is based, appeared in *The Washington Post*. She wrote professionally for many different organizations, among them The Federation of Jewish Philanthropies, the Rockefeller Foundation, and the J. Walter Thompson advertising agency. She wrote discriminating cookbook reviews for *The Washington Post* and was a contributor to *Food & Wine* magazine and *The Washingtonian* magazine.